THE COURTS, THE *CHARTER*, AND THE SCHOOLS

The Impact of the *Charter of Rights and Freedoms* on Educational Policy and Practice, 1982–2007

Edited by Michael Manley-Casimir and Kirsten Manley-Casimir

The adoption in 1982 of the *Canadian Constitution Act*, with its embedded *Charter of Rights and Freedoms*, ushered in an era of unprecedented judicial influence on Canada's public policy. *The Courts, the* Charter, *and the Schools* examines how the *Constitution Act* has affected educational policy during the first twenty-five years of the *Charter* by analysing landmark rulings handed down from appellate courts and the Supreme Court.

This collection of essays by prominent legal scholars and educational commentators considers the influence that the *Charter* has had on educational policies and practices by discussing cases involving fundamental freedoms, legal rights, equality rights, and minority language rights. The contributors demonstrate why and how the *Charter* was invoked, interpreted, and applied in each of these cases, and highlight the broader consequences for Canada's schools. Providing comprehensive, original analysis of important issues and landmark decisions, *The Courts, the* Charter, *and the Schools* makes a significant contribution to the study of educational law and policy in Canada.

MICHAEL MANLEY-CASIMIR is a professor in the Faculty of Education and Director of the Tecumseh Centre for Aboriginal Research and Education at Brock University.

KIRSTEN MANLEY-CASIMIR is a PhD candidate at the University of British Columbia and co-director of the Intensive Program in Aboriginal Lands, Resources, and Governments at Osgoode Hall Law School.

EDITED BY MICHAEL MANLEY-CASIMIR
AND KIRSTEN MANLEY-CASIMIR

The Courts, the *Charter*, and the Schools

The Impact of the *Charter of Rights and Freedoms* on Educational Policy and Practice, 1982–2007

UNIVERSITY OF TORONTO PRESS
Toronto Buffalo London

ISNB 978-0-8020-9199-4 (cloth)
ISNB 978-0-8020-9440-7 (paper)

Printed on acid-free paper

Library and Archives Canada Cataloguing in Publication

The courts, the Charter and the schools: the impact of the Charter of Rights
and Freedoms on educational policy and practice, 1982–2007 / edited by
Michael Manley-Casimir and Kirsten Manley-Casimir.

Includes bibliographical references and index.
ISBN 978-0-8020-9199-4 (bound).   ISBN 978-0-8020-9440-7 (pbk.)

1. Educational law and legislation – Canada.   2. Canada. Canadian Charter of
Rights and Freedoms.   3. Education and State – Canada.   I. Manley-Casimir,
Michael E.   II. Manley-Casimir, Kirsten   III. Title.

KE3805.C69 2009   344.71'07   C2009-905476-0   KF4119.C69 2009

University of Toronto Press acknowledges the financial assistance to
its publishing program of the Canada Council for the Arts and Ontario
Arts Council.

 Canada Council   Conseil des Arts   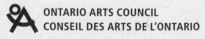 ONTARIO ARTS COUNCIL
for the Arts   du Canada   CONSEIL DES ARTS DE L'ONTARIO

University of Toronto Press acknowledges the financial support for its
publishing activities of the Government of Canada through the Book
Publishing Industry Development Program (BPIDP).

Contents

Acknowledgments

Assembling a collection of chapters from authors – some who are practising lawyers, some academics, and some teachers – but all very busy
people in their own lives is a daunting task. Many of the contributors
are friends and colleagues, and we are proud to recognize their prominence in this collection. In many ways, we have traded on their personal
discipline to write, to tolerate ambiguity when the prospect of a publishing contract was uncertain, and to exhibit extreme patience in dealing with our persistent requests for their chapters, biographical sketches,
or changes to text and notes. Still we have assembled a strong collection
of significant essays on important topics of education policy, and we
would like to thank the various contributors for their cooperation, patience, and collaboration. It is indeed a privilege to count these contributors as friends and colleagues.

We also wish to extend our appreciation to Snezana Ratkovic who
has worked with us assiduously to bring this volume to completion.
Without Snezana's help as an editorial assistant, this volume would
probably not have seen the light of day. We have appreciated Snezana's
unfailing good humour, her demonstrable competence, and her com-
puter skills in preparing the chapters for publication.We also appreciate
the assistance of Rahul Kumar whose computing knowledge remains
invaluable to one of us who is at best still a cybernetic neophyte.

While we owe a debt of gratitude to the anonymous reviewers whose
comments on the unfinished manuscript proved very useful in pointing out errors of law and interpretation as well as infelicities of style,
and while we have attempted to accommodate their concerns, we remain solely responsible for any residual errors or oversights.

January 2009

THE COURTS, THE *CHARTER*, AND THE SCHOOLS

The Impact of the *Charter of Rights and Freedoms* on Educational Policy and Practice, 1982–2007

Introduction
Change and Stability: Assessing the Impact of the *Charter* on Educational Policy and Practice

MICHAEL MANLEY-CASIMIR
AND KIRSTEN MANLEY-CASIMIR

In 1983, while in the Faculty of Education at Simon Fraser University, Michael Manley-Casimir organized the Fourth National Educational Policy Conference on the theme 'The Charter of Rights and Freedoms: Catalyst for Educational Reform?' The conference examined the potential effect of the *Charter of Rights and Freedoms* (hereinafter the *Charter*) on educational policy and practice. Such examination was intended to be primarily from a Canadian perspective but was to be informed by the comparative perspective afforded by the experience of the United States, where constitutional interpretation of educational questions had become almost commonplace since the landmark decision of *Brown* v. *Board of Education* in 1954. Following the conference, Terri Sussel (now Terri Sussel Cohen) and Michael Manley-Casimir edited the papers presented at the conference and wrote a concluding chapter. They published these in the edited volume *Courts in the Classrooms* (Calgary: Detselig, 1986).

Courts in the Classroom set out various perspectives on the possible impact of judicial interpretation of educational issues under the *Charter*. Those papers, written before any judicial decisions interpreting and applying the *Charter* were handed down, nevertheless began to anticipate the possible impact of the *Charter* on educational policy and practice. Authors at that time could only use their knowledge and informed judgment anticipating the direction that judicial decisions in Canada might take. Since that time, the Supreme Court of Canada and provincial Courts of Appeal have adjudicated many cases addressing educational questions. Now – two and a half decades or so after the *Constitution Act, 1982*, after the policy conference mentioned above (1983), and after the publication of *Courts in the Classrooms* (1986) – is therefore an appropriate time to revisit the issues we addressed then. In the intervening years, the role, reach, and impact of the courts in interpreting the *Charter* have grown significantly.

Arguably, the patriation of the Canadian Constitution by the *Constitution Act, 1982*, with its embedded *Charter*, initiated a judicial revolution in governance in Canada. As Michael Ignatieff claims in *The Rights Revolution* (2000), the consequent spate of judicial activity has ushered Canada into a full-blown revolution in human rights, such that 'Canada has become one of the most distinctive rights cultures in the world.'[1] Canadian courts have become much more involved in resolving important matters of social policy than heretofore. Such judicial activism has attracted both affirmation and criticism respecting the new powers of constitutional adjudication accepted by the courts. Those familiar with the impact of constitutional adjudication of educational matters in the United States prior to the *Charter*, surmised that once Canadian courts were 'seized of their purpose,' an array of new constitutionally grounded decisions would occur affecting many aspects of educational policy and practice (Manley-Casimir & Sussel, 1986). This, of course, has happened. The judicial hand has reached into many educational spheres and has altered their contents in significant ways. Clearly, the presupposition is that judicial decisions at these levels are quintessentially authoritative and need to be understood and heeded for future reference.

Over the years, when contemplating the impact of judicial decisions on educational policy and practice, it has been useful to recall the observation of Llewellyn and Hoebel in their work on law and custom among the Cheyenne. They focused on the trouble-case in these terms:

> The case of trouble, again, is the case of doubt, or is that in which discipline has failed or is that in which unruly personality is breaking through into new paths of leadership, or is that in which an ancient institution is being tried against emergent forces. It is the case of trouble which makes, breaks, twists, or flatly establishes a rule, an institution, an authority. Not all such cases do so. There are also petty rows, the routine of law-stuff which exists among primitives as well as among moderns. For all that, if there be a portion of a society's life in which tensions of the culture come to expression, in which the play of variant urges can be felt and seen, in which emergent power-patterns, ancient views of justice tangle in the open, that portion of the life will concentrate in the case of trouble or disturbance. Not only the making of new law and the effect of old, but the

hold and thrust of all other vital aspects of the culture shine clear in the crucible of conflict.[2]

Judicial decisions interpreting and applying the *Charter* represent the making of new law in the Canadian context and in many cases invoke fundamental matters of culture – norms, values, and identity – within a new constitutional framework. So, while the trouble-case is not a perfect analogy, Llewellyn and Hoebel's description does pick up some of the significance that these cases engender for our social arrangements and, in particular, our educational policies and practices.

In the final chapter of *Courts in the Classroom*, Terri Sussel and Michael Manley-Casimir considered the kinds of effects that the application and adjudication of the *Charter* might have on educational policy in Canada. They predicted three possible effects: first, that judicial decisions might extend a 'nationalizing' influence on educational policy; second, that the application of the *Charter* in the arena of educational policy would create the need for legislative rationalization and administrative compliance with an emerging body of judicial interpretation; and third, that judicial decisions addressing *Charter*-based arguments would place limits on administrative discretion in the operation of public school systems. As the chapters in this volume demonstrate, however, the effect of the *Charter* has not been as definitive, coherent, or focused as those putative conclusions implied. Nevertheless, the *Charter* has had and continues to have an important effect on educational policy and practice in Canada.

Perspectives of Contributors

Reading the chapters in this volume reveals the ways – from the perspectives of the various authors – that Canadian appellate courts and the Supreme Court of Canada have adjudicated the variety of educational claims made under the *Charter*. To say that the cumulative effect of such decisions is neither unambiguously clear nor conceptually consistent is an understatement. Although there are some indications of the emergence of a distinctive *Charter*-based jurisprudence, there are also divergent views of the application of the *Charter* to questions of educational policy and practice. Such a state of affairs is not at all surprising. The *Charter* became part of the Canadian Constitution in 1982, with the equality provisions coming into effect in 1985. As a result, the Canadian Supreme Court is often placed in the position of interpreting and applying the *Charter* to instant cases in the absence of established precedents. Since values are themselves often in flux and must adapt to changing societal demands, the Court must be sensitive not just to the way the *Charter* reflects its founding values but also to societal changes that challenge the established and historic interpretations of such constitutionally established values. In addition, the authors of each chapter bring their own unique perspectives to bear on their analysis. Such perspectives add richness and colour to their analyses but also reveal the lack of consensus on the *Charter*'s impact.

The Supreme Court of Canada recognized its role and responsibility in *Hunter* v. *Southam* [1984][3] where the Court affirmed the 'purposive approach' to constitutional interpretation, but it did so mindful of the imagery of the Constitution as a 'living tree capable of growth and expansion.'[4] Such a conception, endorsing a broad and generous approach to constitutional interpretation, placed the Court in the position of interpreting and extending constitutional reasoning to new cases and new circumstances. This approach is explicitly contextual in character. The judiciary attributes meaning and significance not just to the facts and legal issues in the case but also to the social context whence the case arises and the emerging social norms evident in that context. Since then the issues requiring adjudication by the courts have been contested both as educational issues and, subsequently, as facets of constitutional interpretation. The process of judicial interpretation is evident in the chapters comprising this collection of essays.

In Chapter 1, Smith and Foster directly confront the question whether the *Charter* has made a difference. Their examination rests on the normative construct of equality expressed as equal education opportunity and reflected expressly in the language of the equality provisions of the *Charter* in ss.15(1) and (2). Considering the development of judicial reasoning respecting accommodation, reasonable limits, and the limitations of the *Charter* in not establishing a right to education, Smith and Foster nevertheless conclude that the decisions of the Supreme Court have begun to shape our understanding of equality rights. Even so and while such decisions have fallen far short of judicial affirmation of a seamless and coherent evolution of equality jurisprudence, the effect of these decisions has created a climate of change affecting educational practice.

In Chapter 2, MacKay likens equality to a 'lighthouse that can guide educators down the path to inclusive schools.' He argues that the concept of equality can serve to achieve more inclusive, effective, and safer public schools. His perspective rests on the recognition that 'inclusion' implies much more than just disability access and extends to a full and affirmative sense of belonging for all students in all Canadian schools. Conceived this broadly, full inclusion is and should be – in his view – the target of the implementation of the equality provisions of the *Charter*, especially those affirming the equal protection and benefit of the law. Mackay develops this argument by focusing on three aspects of schooling: disability access, the balancing of gay rights and freedoms, and the link between inclusion and safe schools.

In the case of disability access, MacKay identifies the need for individual accommodation as the guiding light from the lighthouse in the realization of equality; here particular attention needs to be assigned to the actual characteristics of the individual whose claim for access rests on the facts and circumstances of his or her disability. In the case of balancing gay rights and freedoms, the dominant conceptual elements should be those of tolerance of difference in schools and the affirmation of diversity as a cardinal value in Canadian society. In the case of school safety, MacKay argues in favour of inclusion as one element that promotes a culture of tolerance and respect among students, hence fostering the promise of reducing violence and harassment.

In Chapter 3, Bowlby and Arbour assess the impact of the *Charter* on special education in Ontario and observe correctly that the provisions of the *Education Amendment Act of 1980* (*Bill 82*) preceded the principles of equality in the *Charter*. Historically, Ontario had been the first province to incorporate explicit provisions affirming special education in provincial legislation through *Bill 82*. This occurred prior to the patriation of the Canadian Constitution and prior to the coming into force of the equality provisions of s.15 in 1985. So, while s.15 of the *Charter* enunciated the principles of equality, once they came into force, they had no direct effect on the provision of special education in Ontario; those provisions derived from the effect of *Bill 82*.

In Chapter 4, Paquette extends the discussion of equality issues by focusing on the connections between the debate regarding freedom of religion and the overarching questions of equity and equality of opportunity. His particular emphasis concerns the freedom of parents to choose their children's schooling and the related issue of public funding for such a choice in private schools. Paquette recognizes clearly that public funding of private schools does not by itself yield the educational benefits often ascribed to such funding. Indeed, he argues that evidence is lacking that private schooling is either more efficient or more effective than public schooling. Paquette then turns his attention to the ethics of allocating public funds to private schools through placement schemes, vouchers, or tax credits, and the advantages and disadvantages of each of these options.

Considering the implications of the *Charter* for the issue of public funding of private schools, Paquette develops an intriguing argument using the judicial reasoning in *Law* and *Falkiner*. He argues that the public funding of private schools through vouchers and tax-credit programs violated s.15 of the *Charter* under the test set out by the Supreme Court of Canada in *Law*. He further argues that the Ontario Court of Appeal in *Falkiner* broadened the concept of immutability in the analysis of s.15 and recognized poverty as an analogous ground of discrimination. In applying the test set out in *Law* and refined in *Falkiner,* Paquette argues that vouchers and tax credits requiring parents to top-up their value to pay private school tuition fees unconstitutionally exclude poor parents and children from access to private schools. Because all taxpayers, including those who are poor, contribute to the consumption taxes used to subsidize private schools, the exclusion of poor families from access to such subsidies is both unfair and ethically unacceptable. Paquette concludes by asserting that the unconstitutionality of voucher and tax-credit schemes is equally applicable to public funding of religious private schools. He suggests that the way to improve access to quality education for poor children is to improve the public education system.

In Chapter 5, Long and Magsino assess the impact of the *Charter* on Canadian schools and conclude that the enactment of the *Charter* and ensuing litigation have contributed to the increasing secularization of both public and denominational schools. Specifically, with respect to public schools, they argue that *Charter* jurisprudence to date indicates a trend towards eliminating religious practices from public schools but makes room for education about religion, providing such education is not indoctrinatory or discriminatory against other religions. With respect to denominational schools, they argue that the *Charter* has played a key role in marginalizing the role of churches in the administration and control of such schools in Newfoundland and Quebec, and has thereby increased the secularization of public education. Further, they assert that *Charter* cases indicate that the Canadian constitutional structure does not provide denominational schools with the requisite protection to maintain and propagate their religious beliefs. They do acknowledge, however, that the right of denominational schools to impose certain requirements on their teachers has generally been protected in courts, providing procedural requirements are met. Long and Magsino's argument rests on the normative assumptions that both freedom of religion and equal protection of the law make it necessary that religious preferences be accommodated within the Canadian education system.

In Chapter 6, Kindred explores the effect of the guarantee of freedom of expression in s.2(b) of the *Charter* on disputes in the educational context. Kindred's perspective rests on the view that the law takes a leading role in resolving important social issues and managing changes to our value systems. He argues that the common perception of *Charter* disputes as the state versus the individual does not accurately reflect the character of the disputes that arise in the educational context. Instead, the resolution of these disputes necessitates the balancing of a number of competing interests – such as those of the school board, teachers, students, and parents – and the *Charter* is a valuable tool in balancing such interests. After analysing the relevant case law, Kindred concludes that teachers have a right to freedom of expression within the school system, including the right to take positions contrary to and critical of their employer and the right to choose the ideas that they teach in the classroom. He views the *Charter* as a valuable tool in carving out a clear and protected role for the interests of teachers in the education system. As such, he argues that it is likely that *Charter* principles will increasingly find their way into cases involving teachers.

In Chapter 7, Dickinson examines the impact of the *Charter* on students' constitutional right to be free from unreasonable search and seizure in the school setting. Underlying his analysis is the view that the way in which students' rights are treated in the school setting constitutes a hidden curriculum, which provides students with important lessons about the fair exercise of authority, about a proper model of justice, and about values central to a democratic society. He argues that the *Charter* cases dealing with school searches have followed the United States jurisprudence in restricting students' constitutional rights in the school setting. Specifically, students have a diminished expectation of privacy in order to promote values that courts have identified as central to education, such as safety, order, and discipline.

Dickinson warns of the danger of failing to consider the difference in regular school detentions and those that involve the possibility of criminal consequences. He argues that the goal of getting students to take responsibility for their wrongful actions should not trump their rights as citizens to be protected against the abuse of state power. In school search cases, he criticizes the focus of courts on the role of the principal rather than on the impact of the search or detention on the student. He concludes that both pre- and post-*Charter* school search cases are consistent in showing judicial deference to school administrators' discretion in conducting school searches, which has resulted in a significantly lower threshold to constitute probable grounds than is required under criminal law. In the context of school searches involving the possibility of criminal sanctions, Dickinson advocates an impact model requiring all investigations involving criminal consequences to be conducted by police rather than school officials. Such a requirement would, he believes, respect a student's *Charter* right to counsel and right to be free from unreasonable search and seizure.

In Chapter 8, Watkinson addresses the issue of corporal punishment in the school context from a distinctively personal perspective. Firmly situated within a children's rights framework, Watkinson outlines the history leading up to and the arguments advanced in the *Canadian Foundation* case – a case that she was instrumental in advancing – and which challenged the constitutionality of the defence for parents, teachers, and others standing in a parent's role in using force to correct children under s.43 of the *Criminal Code*. Specifically, those challenging the constitutionality of s.43 claimed that it violated a child's s.7 rights to security of the person, s.15 equality rights, and s.12 right to be free from cruel and unusual punishment. Watkinson criticizes the Supreme Court of Canada's decision, in which the Court found s.43 constitutional but limited a teacher's defence under that section to cases involving restraining a student rather than cases involving corporal punishment. As the case clearly prohibits corporal punishment being used on a student by a teacher, she recommends that provincial legislation be amended to reflect the changes in the law.

Based on her view of children as vulnerable members of society, Watkinson concludes that the Court's decision affirmed an authoritarian model of discipline for both teachers and parents and positioned children as second-class citizens, without the protections afforded to adults who are assaulted. Because of Canada's international commitments concerning the rights of the child, she argues that provincial curricula need to educate children about their rights to physical and mental integrity, including their rights to be free from forms of physical punishment outside the limits placed on s.43. She concludes that although the Supreme Court of Canada limited the scope of s.43, its decision was disappointing in that the Court failed to recognize children as legal persons endowed with rights, including the fundamental rights to personal integrity and security of the person.

In Chapter 9, Milne argues that the *Charter* has not created a space for the recognition of children's rights to date. Like Watkinson, Milne identifies the difficulty of asserting that children have *Charter* rights where Canadian law does not specifically recognize children as legal persons. In her survey of the case law involving the *Charter* and children's rights, she concludes that most often the child's rights are not the primary target of inquiry; usually the inquiry focuses on parents' or teachers' rights on behalf of the child. Milne concludes that the general tendency of the Supreme Court of Canada has been to either disregard children's rights altogether or reluctantly acknowledge such rights in a diminished form. She concludes that Canadian jurisprudence has far to go in recognizing children's rights as required by Canada's international commitments under the United Nations *Convention on the Rights of the Child*. Milne is, however, cautiously optimistic that the Supreme Court of Canada's mention and general acceptance of that *Convention* in several cases signals a positive movement towards some recognition of children's *Charter* rights in the future.

In Chapter 10, Clarke examines the impact of the *Charter* on minority language educational rights. Clarke starts from the premise that in the face of majoritarian pressures of assimilation, linguistic minorities must constantly struggle to survive. He argues that the guarantee of minority language educational rights set out in s.23 of the *Charter* is unique from other *Charter* rights because s.23 guarantees positive rights, protects both collective and individual rights, and originates from an historical compromise. He argues that the court cases indicate that s.23 rights protect minority language communities within provinces and territories but do not guarantee language rights to the majority language population – for example, British Columbians do not have a constitutionally guaranteed right to French immersion programs since English-speakers are the linguistic majority in that province.

Clarke argues that the principle of equality forms an important part of the minority language educational provisions. The notion of equality raises questions related to eligibility, funding, and the quality of education in minority language schools. In the s.23 cases, Clarke concludes that courts are willing to craft creative, context-specific solutions in order to ensure that constitutional rights to minority language education are respected. In the absence of political solutions to disputes over minority language education, which in Clarke's view are preferable, Canadian courts will play a key role in ensuring that provincial and territorial governments respect the constitutional guarantees set out in s.23.

In the course of making decisions on a particular case, judges focus on the essential elements of the case before them and write their decision with the pertinent facts and circumstances in the forefront of legal consideration. In cases involving the *Charter*, they consider carefully the application and relevance of the *Charter* and its constituent sections. They also, however, in obiter dicta make statements that provide context, without determining the disposition of the case. These statements in educational cases often provide judicial perspectives on the school as a social institution, and provide the focus for the final chapter.

In Chapter 11, Oliverio and Manley-Casimir begin to explore and characterize the meaning and depiction of the school as a social institution as constructed by judges in court decisions. They conclude that provincial statutes, except in Quebec and to some extent in British Columbia, rarely provide any clear expectations as to the social role of the public school, which leaves the interpretation of the role of the school to be defined by the judiciary. The judiciary's task is onerous, especially at the level of the Supreme Court of Canada, in that a single definition of the role of the school is difficult to distill because of the cultural differences between and among various communities across Canada. Many, but not all, of the Education Law cases have arisen in the context of *Charter* challenges. The *Charter* therefore continues to play a central role in bringing the issue of the appropriate role of the school in Canadian society to the attention of the judiciary.

Oliverio and Manley-Casimir examine a wide variety of post-*Charter* cases that have arisen in educational settings in order to arrive at some conclusions about what judges have determined is the appropriate role of the school in the Canadian context. They conclude that the case law reveals that the school plays a vital role in the physical, emotional, social, cultural, and intellectual growth of students. The school is a formative institution in which values are communicated and exchanged so that the essence of society is perpetuated. In order to provide a positive environment within which students can flourish, schools must be free of discrimination, bias, prejudice, and intolerance. Teachers play an important role as role models transmitting values to students intrinsic to Canadian culture and society. School boards play a central role in supervising and teachers and other employees and disciplining them if they act in a manner inconsistent with community standards. School boards are also required to ensure the curriculum reflects social diversity. With the dearth of explication of the role of the school in provincial education statutes, Canadian courts will have to continue to take on the difficult task of defining the role of the school in Canada.

Conclusion

Judicial decisions and the perspectives drawn by the contributors to this volume reflect the variety of interpretations in the years since the *Charter* came into force as part of Canada's constitutional framework. In many respects, judicial decisions have advanced our understanding of the impact of the *Charter* on educational policy and practice. At the same time, there is no clear judicial consensus on what might be seen as the most important provision – the s.15 equality rights as they apply to education. As the contributors here point out, much remains to be done to sort out conflicting claims to educational equality in Canada – claims that are inherently complicated by the provincial prerogative in this policy arena. Nevertheless, it is clear that the judicial decisions of the past twenty-five years have confronted some significant issues and have begun the process of determining constitutionally valid versus invalid claims. As such the 'purposive approach' endorsed by the Supreme Court and set within a distinctively Canadian context is beginning to forge the groundwork of a 'living tree' that will grow and expand over the decades ahead.

1 Equality in the Schoolhouse: Has the *Charter* Made a Difference?

WILLIAM SMITH AND WILLIAM FOSTER

> I see this as genocide. What better way to kill a people than to rob them of their chance for a good education, taking away the opportunity for us to make something of ourselves.[1]

This statement by Lisa Raven, a First Nations student, reflects the ongoing struggle of minority groups and individuals for *equal educational opportunity*, the provision of *real* opportunities *to* and *from* education for *all* students. Equal educational opportunity is an enduring policy theme of public educational policy, not only in Canada but also around the globe.[2] Educational policy and practice provide the framework (or 'scaffolding') for building equal educational opportunity, while the law provides the 'foundation,' ensuring that equal educational opportunity is provided, not on sufferance, but as a matter of right. The *Canadian Charter of Rights and Freedoms*[3] is the keystone of this legal foundation of rights.

As reflected in the prequel of this book, *Courts in the Classroom*,[4] the entrenchment of the *Charter* in 1982 created a high level of expectations for 'profound changes in ... social policy';[5] more specifically, it asserted that the *Charter* would provide a catalyst to significant changes in educational policy and practice in Canada. This chapter focuses on one aspect of these expectations: equality rights for equal educational opportunity. More specifically, our purpose is to demonstrate how the *Charter* has shaped the equality component of the legal foundation of equal educational opportunity since the *Charter* right to equality has been in force.[6]

Although the *Charter* provides the keystone, federal, provincial, and territorial human rights codes provide the primary building blocks of this foundation. Given this book's focus on the *Charter*, however, we limit our comments on the codes to what is strictly necessary for understanding the role of the *Charter* in supporting equal educational opportunity.[7] Although avoiding duplication with other chapters,[8] we deal with both public and independent (private) schools,[9] including 'regular' and 'special purpose' schools,[10] at the elementary and secondary levels.

We begin with: (a) a brief overview of equal educational opportunity; (b) the expectations outlined in *Courts in the Classroom*; and (c) a summary of the normative guidelines for analysing equality rights. The next two sections of the chapter apply these guidelines to illuminate the role of the *Charter* in providing the right to equality in schools and setting the limits to these rights. In the final section, we conclude with reflections on this analysis and its implications for the future of equal educational opportunity in Canadian schools.

Equal Educational Opportunity

Equal educational opportunity can be viewed as a subset of a more general construct of 'equality of opportunity.' The latter ranges from a minimalist expression – free to compete in life's race – to an expansionist expression based on the belief that stingily applied, equality of opportunity will simply mean that disadvantaged individuals may start the race but will finish last, if they finish the race at all. This range of opportunities may be created by a wide assortment of conditions, but they are grounded in the human right of equality – the paradoxical notion that 'human beings are born free and equal in dignity and rights,'[11] and 'equal before and under the law.'[12] The paradox is resolved when we recognize that such statements are normative expressions of how we would like the world *to be*, rather than a description of how it actually *is*: 'From a normative perspective, the idea of equality expresses humanity's vision of how social, moral, and political life ought to be conducted. Equality embodies our most fundamental notions of fairness and justice and is a principle that disregards differences in social status, wealth, gender, and race, *inter alia*, professing instead that all people are equal.'[13] Equality is closely associated with *non-discrimination*, which may be described as 'positive and negative statements of the same principle.'[14] Non-discrimination is often given a more narrow meaning defined by what one cannot do, however, rather than what one must do. In its most expansive form, equality embraces *affirmative action*, considered as any action taken to undo past wrongs against members of historically *disadvantaged* groups, but even this expansive form of equality can be limited by the forms of disadvantage considered.[15] All of these forms of equality provide a platform for other equal educational opportunity rights, beginning with access.

The essence of access is the right to be in school, often expressed as the principle of *zero exclusion*, which signifies that no one is to be excluded from publicly funded schooling. This right has little meaning, however, unless one has a right for something meaningful to happen inside the schoolhouse, hence the notion of *appropriate education*. Ultimately, equal educational opportunity requires results – the student actually benefiting from the education provided – sometimes called *outcomes-based equality*. Accordingly, equal educational opportunity is best viewed as a continuum of policy choices, ranging from a minimalist expression that simply allows a child to attend school to more expansive expressions that 'equalize conditions that engender real educational opportunities.'[16]

In general, the struggle for equal educational opportunity first focused on the right of access, and then shifted to its current emphasis on in-school issues such as appropriate educational services. A concentration on results remains an aspiration for the future. The current preoccupation with in-school issues does not, however, mean that access is no longer a concern or that results are being ignored. Providing equal educational opportunity rights often involves a *balancing act* of competing interests and beliefs. For example, some families advocate public denominational schools, which others see as religious-based discrimination; many parents advocate the inclusion of students with disabilities in a regular classroom, which others see as detrimental to the rights of children without disabilities.

As noted earlier, the importance of the law is to ensure that equal educational opportunity is provided, not on sufferance, but as a matter of right. Education statutes and regulations are the principal means for providing statutory entitlements to equal educational opportunity. It is in the provincial/territorial *Education Act* (or *School Act*) and regulations that the right to education and various services are stipulated. It is the function of the *Charter* and human rights codes to ensure that this legislation respects the normative standards of equality. This legal foundation in turn supports educational policy and practice, which shapes what actually happens in schools and, ultimately, is responsible for transforming equal educational opportunity from a set of values to a reality for students, as illustrated in Figure 1.1.

Figure 1.1 The legal foundation of equal educational opportunity.

Educational Policy and Practice	→	Equal Educational Opportunity				
		Access	→	Appropriate Education	→	Results

Legal Foundation:
Statutory Entitlements
Equality Rights

Expectations from the *Charter*

Courts in the Classroom consisted of a collection of papers that examined the possible implications of the *Charter* for educational policy and practice across Canada: 'The constitutional entrenchment of the new *Canadian Charter of Rights and Freedoms* ... carries within its clauses the seeds of ... dramatic and far-reaching changes for educational policy and practice in Canada.... [W]e, in Canada, could be on the verge of a judicial revolution in educational governance similar in scope to what has occurred in the United States since the *Brown* decision.'[17] This extract from the preface of the volume reflects two characteristics of the state of Canadian scholarship on education law and policy in the early 1980s: a past perspective, preoccupied with U.S. case law, and a future perspective, that looked to the *Charter* to provide a new 'made in Canada' human rights framework for educational policy and practice.

The past perspective reflected the wealth of case law from the United States on equality rights in education and the dearth of such material in Canada. The landmark U.S. case, *Brown* v. *Board of Education*,[18] to which the above quotation refers, set forth the importance of education, both for individuals, and for society as a whole. More importantly, *Brown* overturned the prevailing judicial doctrine in the United States holding that the segregation of the races for purposes of providing public services was constitutionally permissible.[19] In Canada, just prior to the *Brown* decision, the Supreme Court of Canada rendered its own landmark decision, *Bouchard* v. *School Commissioners of Saint-Mathieu-de-Dixville*.[20] Unlike *Brown*, however, *Bouchard* was not heralded as a triumph of equality rights.

In *Bouchard* two students, described as insubordinate and backward, were expelled from school because of their conduct and their inability to follow the course of study. The Supreme Court held that their expulsion was justified, citing, with apparent approval, testimony from a physician called by the school board, who stated that the students were a bad influence on the other children and that it would be better if they were placed in an institution.[21] The landmark quality of *Bouchard* is that it has stood for more than fifty years as an affirmation of a school board's discretion in the exercise of its authority.[22]

The lesson from *Bouchard* was that federal and provincial legislative authority was all but supreme, checked only by the constitutional division of powers between the two levels of government. This meant that the only constitutional impediments to provincial legislative autonomy in education were the denominational guarantees provided by s.93 of the *Constitution Act, 1867*.[23] There was no constitutional bill of rights, as there was in the United States, and human rights legislation was in an early stage of development. This situation did not change appreciably for another thirty years,[24] until the constitutional entrenchment of the *Charter*. It is no wonder that the contributors to *Courts in the Classroom* viewed the *Charter* as the beginning of a new era in Canadian legal history.

Focusing specifically on the *Charter* right to equality, Cruickshank wondered whether evolving *Charter* jurisprudence would follow the U.S. pattern of assessing various types of discrimination according to different 'levels of scrutiny.'[25] While recognizing the likelihood of disability-based litigation, he questioned whether the *Charter* would take students 'beyond the school-house door' and define what happened in the classroom.[26] He was cautious about the extent to which the *Charter* would fulfil the hopes of various advocacy organizations, stating that their optimism might be dashed unless provincial education statutes were reformed.

According to Cruickshank, that the *Charter* contains no right to education other than the right to minority language education is of no small importance in projecting the extent to which it will shape future educational policy and practice. He did assert, however, that the proclamation of s.15 would 'certainly bring education rights into the fold of constitutional rights'[27] even if it did not deliver all the protection that some might want. Finally, he warned that in addition to having recourse to the 'notwithstanding clause,'[28] governments and school boards might attempt to maintain inequalities by revising laws and policies that on their face could be deemed acceptable to *Charter* standards, while in reality maintaining the status quo.

Equality: The Keystone of Equal Educational Opportunity Rights

In Canada, the legal framework for equality and other human rights is found in the *Charter*, complemented by federal, provincial, and territorial human rights codes. According to s.32, the *Charter* applies to legislation and state action but does not apply to private actors except to the extent that they are governed by legislation. The codes, in comparison, apply to both public and private actors. Their scope of application varies but, in general, they provide for human rights in a range of situations that would escape *Charter* scrutiny.[29] The *Charter* provides for a wide range of human rights, including equality rights. The key substantive right for purposes of this chapter, which defines equality in relation to various listed and analogous grounds is s.15 (see Appendix).

Like all rights and freedoms guaranteed under the *Charter*, equality rights are subject to the 'reasonable limits' clause in s.1 (see Appendix). Section 1 can only be used to limit a *Charter* right, not to '*override*' it, something that is only permitted by s.33, the '*notwithstanding*' clause, or by a 'derogation' in the *Charter*.[30]

The *Charter* does not require the adoption of a human rights code by the federal, provincial, or territorial governments but every jurisdiction has done so. All of the codes share a common purpose as well as many characteristics and provisions, but each code is different. While differences in the codes are permissible, no code may provide for equality rights in a way that falls short of *Charter* standards.[31] Jurisprudence arising from the *Charter* also serves as a 'template' for the interpretation of the codes,[32] all of which provide for equality rights.[33]

As a constitutionally entrenched bill of rights, the *Charter* is afforded a 'purposive' interpretation, an approach that best supports and protects the core values that underpin *Charter* rights.[34] Equality rights are always expressed in very general terms in comparison to statutory rights.[35] Consequently, equality rights are more open to interpretation and depend more on the courts to breathe life into them. To understand equal educational opportunity, one must therefore first unpack this wider construct of equality, in keeping with the 'normative guidelines' determined by the courts for each of the four steps shown below in Figure 1.2.

Step 1 deals with the presence of a legally permissible barrier to block the pursuit of the complaint by means of an 'override' (or 'derogation') of equality rights.[36] The override is provided by means of a declaration in a statute in accordance with s.33 of the *Charter*,[37] and, if applicable, the code.[38]

Figure 1.2 The steps in an equality rights complaint.

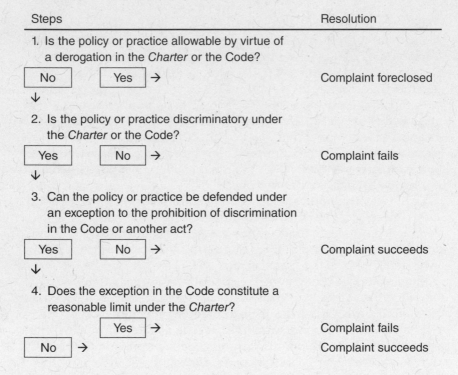

Steps	Resolution
1. Is the policy or practice allowable by virtue of a derogation in the *Charter* or the Code?	
No Yes →	Complaint foreclosed
↓	
2. Is the policy or practice discriminatory under the *Charter* or the Code?	
Yes No →	Complaint fails
↓	
3. Can the policy or practice be defended under an exception to the prohibition of discrimination in the Code or another act?	
Yes No →	Complaint succeeds
↓	
4. Does the exception in the Code constitute a reasonable limit under the *Charter*?	
Yes →	Complaint fails
No →	Complaint succeeds

Step 2 requires the complainant to establish that the action in question has 'crossed the line' that separates discrimination from non-discrimination. This 'boundary' line (Figure 1.3) is determined with reference to the *Charter* and its guiding case law, and to the code as appropriate. In this step, the burden of proof is on the complainant to establish a case to be answered, including any request for affirmative action. This step also takes into account two additional normative standards regarding children's rights.[39]

Step 3 arises when the respondent claims that an action judged to be discriminatory in Step 2 comes under an exception provided for by a human rights code or other legislation. Setting restrictions to equality rights requires the drawing of a second line, this time between discriminatory behaviour that is never allowed and that which is allowed in certain circumstances. This 'limit' line (Figure 1.3) is determined by provisions in the human rights code or other statute. Thus, a respondent may defend a

Figure 1.3 The limits and boundary of equality rights.

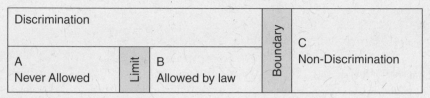

rule or policy considered discriminatory, for example, a school's admission standards, by invoking an exception allowed by the code.

Step 4 requires the respondent to demonstrate that the exception constitutes a reasonable limit under s.1 of the *Charter*. When a provincial government inserts an exception in a code or other statute, it is limiting the prohibition against discrimination (Figure 1.3). The advent of the *Charter* meant that all legislative restrictions on equality rights had a new underlying standard to meet – the reasonable limits standard of s.1, as expressed in the test set forth in *R. v. Oakes*.[40]

Education is an all-but-exclusive provincial/territorial responsibility and human rights codes were enacted to deal with matters coming under their respective jurisdictions. However, the *Charter* provides the constitutional backdrop to these codes, as it does to all legislation and government action. As shown in Figure 1.2, the *Charter* is omnipresent at every step of an inquiry into alleged violations of equality rights, notably in defining what constitutes equality (Step 2) and what is acceptable as a limit to this right (Step 4).

The Right to Equality in School

Except for denominational rights and minority language education cases, in the fifty years since the *Bouchard* decision, *Eaton* v. *Brant (County) Board of Education* [41] is the only equal educational opportunity case to be considered by the Supreme Court of Canada. Accordingly, determining the application of the general construct of equality in a school setting is tentative at best. With this caveat in mind, this section provides an analysis of the 'boundary' of equality rights in school, based on the general normative guidelines summarized in the previous section (Step 2 in Figure 1.2).[42]

Our analysis suggests that the boundary of discrimination (that is, the line that distinguishes discrimination from non-discrimination) is drawn by three elements: (a) the scope of application of the prohibition;

(b) the grounds on which discrimination is prohibited; and, (c) the formulation of what constitutes prohibited discrimination per se.

Scope of Application

With the exception of its specific provisions regarding minority language rights, the *Charter* applies to education by virtue of its general scope of application, which embraces all legislation and government action.[43] Thus, the *Charter* applies to all legislation governing both public and independent schools. The actions of public school boards and schools constitute 'government action' because they are considered to operate as 'state agents.'[44] Independent schools and their officials cannot be regarded as state agents in the same way; accordingly, they are not generally subject to the *Charter*.

Independent schools may, however, attract *Charter* scrutiny by virtue of their role in implementing government education programs, in the same way that hospitals were found to be bound in *Eldridge* v. *British Columbia (Attorney General)*,[45] despite their general exclusion from *Charter* scrutiny.[46] All independent schools must be approved as an alternative to compulsory public schooling and, therefore, are subject at least to minimal government supervision in this regard. It is unlikely that this nexus is sufficient to attract *Charter* scrutiny. However, some provinces require independent schools to follow government-approved programs. In such cases, although they would not be bound by the *Charter* in relation to employment and other general matters, it is likely that they would be bound in relation to their mandate to provide education in accordance with government policy and programs.

By contrast with the *Charter*, the application of human rights codes to education must flow from the specific provisions of each individual code. Most codes do not expressly mention education as an enumerated activity protected from discrimination.[47] Consequently, the application of the codes to public and independent schools must be inferred from a prohibition of discrimination with respect to services provided to the public.

Enumerated or Analogous Grounds

In the *Charter*, discrimination is prohibited on the basis of various listed grounds: race, national or ethnic origin, colour, religion, sex, age, or mental or physical disability. With one exception, socioeconomic conditions, the grounds listed cover most situations that might arise in a school setting.[48] Socioeconomic disadvantage is a major factor in creating inequalities, one that schools have long been called upon to redress.[49] Therefore, any exclusion of such conditions constitutes a serious impediment to the guarantee of rights to equal educational opportunity. The *Charter* includes 'analogous grounds' as a basis for discrimination but it is not yet clear whether social conditions will be considered an analogous ground.[50]

The grounds listed in the *Charter* and the human rights codes typically represent the characteristics of individuals and groups that historically have been the subject of prejudice and stereotyping in society. These prejudices and stereotypes are inherited by schools and are manifested in individual attitudes and behaviours, such as insults, ridicule, provocation, harassment, exclusion from social groupings, and even violence. Although harassment is generally considered a manifestation of discrimination based on gender, it can be based on any listed or analogous ground, and can include students as offenders as well as targets.[51] Students, and others, who are on the receiving end of such discrimination are told in both overt and covert ways that they do not belong.

Discriminatory Purpose and Effect

Discrimination was first defined by the Supreme Court in *Andrews* v. *Law Society of British Columbia*,[52] but is now framed by its decision in *Law* v. *Canada*.[53] *Law* sets forth a three-stage analysis to determine if legislation or state action infringes equality rights, a test that can also be applied to a complaint of discrimination under a human rights code:

1 Does the complaint constitute differential treatment falling within the scope of application of the *Charter* or the code, as the case may be?
2 Is differential treatment based on an enumerated or analogous ground of discrimination as provided for in the *Charter* or the code, as the case may be?
3 Does the complaint constitute discrimination in the meaning of the *Charter* or the code, as the case may be?[54]

According to this test, the complainant must show an adverse effect upon his or her human dignity or freedom;[55] an affront to dignity now seems to be all but equated with discrimination.[56] The parameters for analyzing discriminatory purpose and effect also include the provisions of the codes, which may provide a definition of discrimination, or contain some language that constitutes *interpretative provisions* regarding the meaning of discrimination.

In addition to the *negative* elements defining the prohibition against discrimination – what we must not do, the prohibition may include *positive* elements – what we must do, including accommodation and affirmative action. The obligation to accommodate requires the respondent to take steps to avoid, alleviate, or eliminate a discriminatory situation by taking into account the needs of an individual or a group.[57] Affirmative action is understood as a 'preferential program' that targets *disadvantaged* groups.[58] Since *Law* and *Lovelace* v. *Ontario*,[59] however, affirmative action is now considered part of the right to equality, not an exception to it, as was previously assumed by many commentators.

Many preferential programs are not restricted to disadvantaged groups but contemplate a wide range of participants; therefore, they may be considered affirmative action in some instances but not in others. All of these provisions need to be considered, first, in relation to a charge of discrimination, as discussed above, and second, in relation to a defence to such a charge (as discussed below). Accordingly, one can expect the courts to use the *Law* approach to determine whether discrimination exists in a school setting, relying on contextual analysis in relation to the factors outlined therein. A survey of cases demonstrates this principle with respect to issues ranging from school atmosphere to school policy and practice, all of which require accommodation.

For example, in *Ross* v. *New Brunswick School District No. 15*,[60] the Supreme Court of Canada declared that a school must 'be premised upon principles of tolerance and impartiality so that all persons within the school environment feel equally free to participate.'[61] In *Chamberlain* v. *Surrey School District No. 36*,[62] a school board passed resolutions banning the use of learning resources depicting children with same-sex parents. While recognizing that the school board must balance the interests of different groups, the Court held that when human rights issues were involved, the school board had less discretion than would normally be the case.

Accommodation is a critical means of assuring each student's right to an *appropriate* education. Differences in opinion respecting what is appropriate 'mirror the different levels of equal educational opportunity which one can set for a school system, from a threshold of opportunity to one designed to maximize each student's potential.'[63] For example, in one case, an advocacy group contested the services provided to children with learning disabilities.[64] The government argued that the minister of education and the defendant school boards had statutory discretion as to the specific nature of educational services to be provided to these students. The Court rejected this argument, stating that the decision in *Eldridge* established that discretion 'must conform to constitutional standards and it is therefore reviewable on its merits where a violation of s.15(1) is alleged.'[65]

The reach of the *Eldridge* decision was tested in *Auton (Guardian ad litem of)* v. *British Columbia (Attorney General)*.[66] The complainants in this case sought government funding for a particular intensive behavioural therapy under health services legislation for their autistic children, who were all of pre-school age. Stating that the claimants must show unequal treatment under the law,[67] the Supreme Court distinguished *Eldridge*, in that the sign language sought by the complainants was a means of accessing benefits provided by law.[68] However, it did acknowledge that a broader issue had to be considered, namely, whether the legislative scheme was itself discriminatory.

Finding no such inconsistent exclusion, the Court held that this finding was sufficient to end the inquiry. However, it also chose to address the issue of an appropriate comparator group, deciding that the Court of Appeal had erred in its application of the first stage of the *Law* test. Relying on *Hodge* v. *Canada*,[69] the Supreme Court concluded that in *Auton*: 'The appropriate comparator for the … [complainants] is a non-disabled person or a person suffering a disability other than a mental disability (here autism) seeking or receiving funding for a non-core therapy important for his or her present and future health, which is emergent and only recently becoming recognized as medically required.'[70] In the absence of evidence suggesting that the government's approach to the therapy in question was different from its approach to other 'comparable, novel therapies' for persons with or without a disability, the Supreme Court held that a finding of discrimination could not be sustained.[71]

Several cases in Alberta and Ontario have challenged funding and services for children with autism,[72] and have raised several issues, including entitlement to services under child welfare legislation rather than that governing education. Of these cases, the decision in *Wynberg* v. *Ontario*[73] is of particular interest, because it was a rendered by an appellate court after the Supreme Court of Canada ruling in *Auton*. In

1999, the Ontario Ministry of Community and Social Services inaugurated the Intensive Early Intervention Program (IEIP) for children with autism between the ages of two and five, which was provided at the discretion of the minister under the relevant legislation.[74]

All parties accepted that the appropriate comparator group was children with autism who were under 6 years of age. The Ontario Court of Appeal rejected both the lower court finding that the age cut-off was discriminatory and its view that the IEIP was an under-inclusive ameliorative program, which ceased to be licit when the government removed children over age six from the waiting list despite the lack of alternative services being available from public school boards. Using the contextual analysis provided for in *Law*, and with reference to *Auton*, the Court of Appeal stated that the key issue was 'whether the exclusion of autistic children age six and over from the IEIP deprives or demeans their human dignity. We do not think that the complainants have demonstrated such a denial.'[75]

Wynberg also dealt with the alleged failure to provide the program under the *Education Act*, according to which the minister has an obligation to ensure that 'appropriate special education programs and special education services without fees' are available to all exceptional children.[76] The Court of Appeal rejected the lower court's finding that this failure constituted differential treatment in relation to the relevant comparator group (other children with communication exceptionalities).

In brief, the Court of Appeal found that the IEIP program was not one that could be provided in the public schools system, nor was there credible evidence that it was the only appropriate program for the children involved. Furthermore, it held that the trial judge had erroneously reversed the complainants' onus to establish discriminatory policy or practice. Consequently, it rejected the claim that the failure to provide the program under the *Education Act* was discriminatory. The Court of Appeal clearly appreciated the struggle of the parents on behalf of their children but stated: '[W]here the requirements of s.15(1) are not met, the Charter cannot guarantee success in such a struggle, nor can it require the state to provide whatever assistance is needed to achieve that success, as compelling as that may be on moral or policy grounds. That remains the terrain of legislators.'[77] Taken together, these cases illustrate the meaning of discrimination as framed by *Law*. Once a complainant establishes the existence of a valid case, the burden shifts to the respondent to defend the discriminatory policy or practice.

Exceptions and Reasonable Limits in a School Setting

This section examines permissible exceptions to equality rights in school and the doctrine of 'reasonable limits,' based on the general normative guidelines summarized above (Steps 3 and 4 in Figure 1.2). Statutory exceptions are only relevant in situations where discrimination is proved and the school (or school board) wishes to rebut the charge based on an exceptional provision in the human rights code or some other act. Our analysis of the human rights codes revealed two types of exceptions relevant to schools: a 'bona fide requirement' (BFR)[78] and various types of preferential programs.

The Exceptions

For our purposes, the BFRs of interest are those that apply to the provision of goods and services to the public, found in all codes but two. Except in Quebec and Saskatchewan, a regular or special purpose school, be it public or independent, or a school board, may invoke a BFR to defend an otherwise discriminatory policy or practice. A special purpose school may, however, also be able to avail itself of provisions more specifically tailored to its situation, as discussed below.

The major question for schools in the jurisdictions that provide for relevant BFRs is what requirements will be allowed by the code. Thus, a BFR defence may be partially circumscribed by the language of the provisions in a code. More importantly, the viability of the defence will be determined ultimately by the doctrine of reasonable limits as all such provisions and BFRs adopted under them must satisfy the requirements of s.1 of the *Charter* in accordance with the '*Meiorin* standard' (discussed below).

In Quebec and Saskatchewan, whose codes have no BFR provision , the only possible exceptions on which a school may rely to justify a discriminatory policy or practice are those relating to preferential programs, dealt with below. The inclusion of a BFR in another act will not suffice, unless an override provision is included in the act.[79]

BFRs were originally included in the codes in relation to employment, and it is in that context in which much of the jurisprudence on BFRs has developed. Originally, the employment BFR was viewed as balancing the rights of employees against the legitimate private interests of employers. However, with the advent of the *Charter*, the frame of reference has shifted to individual human rights versus the exigencies of public policy interest. This perspective might seem more normal to a public school, as a state agent, than to an independent school, which is meant to further private interests in addition to any public purpose it may serve. These private interests, like those of private sector employers for example, are legitimate. However, they are viewed through the lens of public policy, and must satisfy the standards set by s.1 of the *Charter*. That independent schools, like employers and other service providers in both the public and private sectors, are provided a BFR defence in a code signals this public policy interest. When a court examines the defence raised by the school it will (or should) be asking: What is the public interest in allowing this defence to limit the equality rights of its students?[80]

'Preferential programs' is the generic expression we have applied to all exceptions found in human rights codes that aim at allowing preferred treatment to groups characterized by one or more of the grounds either listed in the code or found to be analogous to those listed. Two types of such programs were identified that could embrace education: those that target *disadvantaged* groups, therefore meriting, per se, an affirmative action label according to *Charter* standards, and those that deal with programs that either promote the welfare of a group or relate to membership or participation in various organizations, typically nonprofit ones, operated for the benefit of a particular group.

Generally speaking, the reference to groups contemplated by enumerated or analogous grounds in any code could embrace both disadvantaged and advantaged groups, thus qualifying as affirmative action for the former but not for the latter. This distinction may vary, however, with the educational milieu in question. Thus, for example, a special school for Catholic students in some provinces might qualify as affirmative action, if it could be demonstrated that this group had been historically disadvantaged. Such a demonstration could not be made in Quebec, where this group has traditionally been 'privileged.'[81]

Disability is a possible exception, because it is the one ground that is not expressed in *neutral* terms, embracing advantage and disadvantage. However, the exception disappears if the term is understood to encompass ability/disability as the ground. The point is important because, unless the latter view were taken, the exceptions in those codes that refer to disability, either explicitly or implicitly, could not be advanced to allow a special school or program for the gifted or able-bodied (e.g., a sports school).[82] The latter interpretation is also preferable because the former may encourage 'broad-brush, categorical determinations that disability discrimination is entirely different from other forms of discrimination.'[83]

Accordingly, subject to applicable legislative provisions,[84] special schools and programs may be established in any jurisdiction whose code makes provision for preferential programs, subject, of course, to the precise terms of these provisions. As with BFRs discussed above, these provisions only come into play if such a program is found to infringe equality rights. The normative guidelines provided by *Law* and *Lovelace* provide a new lens to examine the longstanding and highly contested debate regarding the provision of educational services to students with disabilities in 'special' (segregated) versus 'regular' (inclusive) settings. However, given the treatment of this debate in another chapter of this book, we omit any further discussion of this important policy issue.

Accommodation and Reasonable Limits

As stated previously, accommodation is first considered in determining whether the contested policy or practice was discriminatory. In the absence of any statutory exceptions, one must accommodate until the discrimination has been eliminated or alleviated to the greatest extent possible. However, in the presence of a valid statutory exception, accommodation can be limited; in these circumstances, consideration shifts to the reasonableness of the accommodation under s.1 of the *Charter* in accordance with the *Meiorin* standard.

This standard is named for the complainant in the first case dealing with exceptions in a human rights code to be decided with reference to the *Charter*.[85] The Supreme Court set forth a new test for assessing a BFR based on a statutory exception to the prohibition against discrimination:

> An employer may justify the impugned standard by establishing on the balance of the probabilities:
> (1) that the employer adopted the standard for a purpose rationally connected to the performance of the job;
> (2) that the employer adopted the standard in an honest and good faith belief that it was necessary to the fulfilment of that legitimate work-related purpose; and

(3) that the standard is reasonably necessary to the accomplishment of that legitimate work-related purpose. To show that the standard is reasonably necessary, it must be demonstrated that it is impossible to accommodate individual employees sharing the characteristics of the claimant without imposing undue hardship upon the employer.[86]

Although this case arose from employment in the public sector, the standard applies equally to the private sector and to non-employment situations in both sectors.[87] This standard applies to exceptions in the codes and, by extension, to BFRs and preferential programs themselves.[88]

Québec (Commission des droits de la personne et des droits de la jeunesse) v. *Collège Notre-Dame du Sacré-coeur (Corp).*[89] illustrates the application of the *Meiorin* standard to a limit contained in a human rights code.[90] In *Notre-Dame*, an otherwise qualified student with a physical disability was denied admission to an independent school based on the school's mission and program. The Quebec Court of Appeal stated that to benefit from s.20 (preferential programs) an institution must first qualify as one envisaged by this provision; then the discrimination must be justified. Its decision concluded that the school could not simply invoke its educational character as justification for its discriminatory behaviour. Rather, it must demonstrate that 'the principal vocation of the institution was such as to place it in conflict with the non-discrimination requirements enunciated in s.10.'[91]

In keeping with the first criterion of the *Meiorin* standard (the underlying legitimacy of the exception), the Court of Appeal looked at the connection of the admission requirement to the school's educational objectives, and found that this criterion was satisfied. It then moved directly to consider the third criterion (the reasonableness of the exception).[92] It held that an individual must be assessed on the basis of his or her personal characteristics, not those imputed to a group. It concluded that the school had not succeeded in proving either that its admission requirements were reasonably necessary to the realization of its principal vocation or that it could not accommodate the complainant without undue hardship.[93] Moreover, as the Court of Appeal observed, at no time did the school undertake an objective assessment of the complainant's physical capacity or give her a chance to demonstrate how she was able to palliate her handicap.[94]

Financial constraints are often raised as a reasonable limit to equality rights. In pre-*Charter* cases an employer would argue that cost should be considered as part of an undue hardship defence under a human rights code.[95] In a post-*Charter* world, the question becomes: To what extent should cost be considered as a reasonable limit to equality rights?

In *Schachter* v. *Canada*,[96] the Supreme Court stated that: 'budgetary considerations cannot be used to justify a violation under s.1.'[97] While affirming this principle in two recent decisions, the Supreme Court added two important caveats. In one case it upheld a complaint against differential benefits for work-related injuries, stating: 'budgetary considerations in and of themselves cannot justify violating a Charter right, although they may be relevant in determining the appropriate degree of deference to governmental choices based on a non-financial objective.'[98] In the other case it found that legislation rolling back pay equity agreements infringed s.15 but was saved under s.1 because of the exigencies of the government's financial crisis.[99]

Government is not required to eliminate discrimination in society, only that which arises from legislation or state action.[100] This view was cited with approval in *Eldridge*, to which La Forest J added that: 'governments must be afforded wide latitude to determine the proper distribution of resources in society.'[101] Support for this latter proposition was found in *Egan* v. *Canada*.[102] However, the minority opinion in *Egan* sounded the following word of caution: 'The very real possibility emerges that the government will always be able to uphold legislation that selectively and discriminatorily allocates resources. This would undercut the values of the *Charter* and belittle its purpose. I also find that many of the concerns raised by Sopinka J – such as according the legislature some time to amend discriminatory legislation – ought to inform the remedy, and should not serve to uphold or legitimize discriminatory conduct.'[103] In *Eldridge*, La Forest J held that the government's 'refusal to expend such a relatively insignificant sum to continue and extend the service cannot possibly constitute a minimum impairment of the appellants' constitutional rights,' as required by the *Oakes'* test.[104] For our purposes, it is important to remember that in *Eldridge* the issue was the provision of sign language interpretation, which was required in order to access health services to which the complainants were entitled. The Supreme Court of Canada decision in *Auton* affirmed this view; however, it left unanswered two key questions for similar cases in an educational setting: First: would the court characterize special education services as those for which there must a statutory entitlement or as services required to access regular educational services?[105] Second: how would the government defence under s.1 have fared, especially in relation to costs?[106]

Wynberg dealt briefly with the s.1 defence offered by the government. The Court of Appeal agreed with the trial judge that the age restriction in the IEIP program could be considered as a limit 'prescribed by law' as per s.1 of the *Charter*.[107] However, it disagreed that the government defence did not meet the criteria established by the *Oakes'* test.[108] In another recent case, government and school board arguments of financial constraint were judged to be insufficient to meet the burden of proof required by the *Meiorin* standard.[109]

The foregoing provides important insights to the evolution of equal educational opportunity rights for students with disabilities, and by extension, to other students as well. Based on *Auton, Notre-Dame,* and other decisions, schools can be expected to accommodate the needs of students on the basis of an equality rights argument. Moreover, although the expense of accommodation will not be ignored, school authorities cannot expect that a defence based on cost will automatically succeed. Assuming that the government has provided an exception in the human rights code or in another statute, the key issue will be whether that exception is deemed to be a reasonable limit as determined by *Charter* case law.

Implications and Conclusion

Equality Rights and Equal Educational Opportunity

As noted above, in *Courts in the Classroom*, Cruickshank argued that Canadian courts would be reluctant to go too far with *Charter*-based regulation of school curricula and programs and questioned whether the *Charter* would in fact take students 'beyond the school house door' to define what happens in the classroom. While observing that legislative change was a key to enhanced rights for students, he noted: '[W]e cannot expect Canadian courts to build upon, or create a right that does not exist – the right to an appropriate education for all children. However, legislative reform by the provinces may be pressed by Charter decisions which highlight the most obvious inequalities for the disabled. The courts will not begin to prescribe special education rights, placements and curricula until a more advanced statutory foundation exists.'[110] He went on to state: '[T]he focus of any potential Charter litigation on education and equality rights should be clear. It cannot be a demand for the right to education – measured in equal test results and equal depth behind the diploma. It can only be a demand for equal *opportunity* to receive an education suited to the child's individual *needs*. Even defined in this way, the courts will only go so far in establishing opportunities and meeting needs. They will concentrate on persons adversely affected by discrimination that is traceable to government law and policy.'[111] Cruickshank's analysis goes to the core of defining the equality component of equal educational opportunity, namely assigning *substance* to the right to equality. First, in terms of the equal educational opportunity continuum: Do equality rights only support equal educational opportunity in relation to access? Do they encompass the right to particular services? Do they include any notion of results? Second, to what extent do they go beyond negative rights (the prohibition of discriminatory acts) to require positive acts to achieve equal educational opportunity.

The lack of case law still makes the answer to these questions speculative. It appears that in the absence of specific legislative provisions, however, the courts are reluctant to venture too far along either continuum. Thus, we have seen that the Supreme Court of Canada distinguished *Auton* from *Eldridge* by stating that the latter concerned access to services provided for by the legislation, whereas the former concerned access to services not provided for by legislation.[112] Applying this reasoning in an educational setting suggests that the substance of the equality component of equal educational opportunity rights is inextricably linked to the substantive rights provided in education legislation. When the latter includes language such as the right to appropriate education, the courts will be more likely to expand the meaning of equal educational opportunity for particular groups such as students with disabilities. When the latter includes no such language, however, the courts will be reluctant to read in too much substance, not wishing to assume the role of policy-maker or arbiter of the allocation of scarce public resources and services.[113] Similarly, one would expect the courts to be even more reluctant to expand the interpretation of equal educational opportunity rights to encompass any form of results. As more and more jurisdictions adopt a results-based management framework, including outcomes-based education, the implication is clear: If students have a right to success from education, then this right should apply to all students.[114] In this same vein, the use of equality rights to require positive actions remains the exception, rather than the rule. For the foreseeable future, such initiatives are likely to be confined to affirmative action responses to clear cases of systemic discrimination.

It is difficult to assess the impact of the absence of education as a constitutionally protected right and its absence as a human right in all codes but two. While its absence does not preclude the application of equality rights in schools, the importance of the nexus between equality rights and statutory entitlement supports the finding that including education in the *Charter* and, to a lesser extent, the codes, could be significant, depending on the language of the guarantee. On one extreme, a strongly worded free-standing right to education coupled with equality rights would, in our view, greatly enhance the legal foundation of equal educational opportunity. On the other extreme, a provision such as the one found in the Quebec *Code* does next to nothing to enhance equal educational opportunity rights.[115]

In the evolving doctrine of equal educational opportunity rights, there is a guiding principle, which has yet to realize its potential: the best interest of children.[116] The reasoning of the Supreme Court of Canada in *Eaton* was firmly grounded in this principle, namely, that the determination of an appropriate placement for a student with a disability should be made 'from a subjective child-centred perspective.'[117] We will not comment on the application of this principle with regard to placement, since another chapter deals with this issue. The Supreme Court's invocation of this principle is, however, important in the evolution of equal educational opportunity rights. It implies a reliance on the results of an evidentiary battle between students (and their parents) and school officials, supported by experts on both sides of the divide, as to which policy or practice is in the best interest of the child. Evidence-based decision-making has considerable currency in the health sector,[118] but it remains to be seen if it will take root in education.[119]

We question the application of the best interest principle to develop equal educational opportunity rights. It appears to replace the standard equality rights analysis by a more paternalistic approach based on what others conclude constitutes the child's best interest, thereby relying on a principle for a purpose that it was never meant to support.[120] It also seems to subtly shift the burden of evidence onto those who are advocating for equal educational opportunity as the normal rules of evidence would suggest that if the evidentiary battle is a draw, then the status quo prevails.[121]

Manley-Casimir and Sussel, the editors of *Courts in the Classroom*, posited that the Supreme Court of Canada would play a key role in advancing *Charter* rights, but the extent of this enhanced role would ebb and flow, reflecting 'periods of modesty and of self-assertion.'[122] We have seen examples of this ebb and flow in several cases. At the level of Canada's highest court, however, there appears to more ebb than flow, when one contrasts its decisions with the lower court rulings in *Eaton* and *Auton*.

Manley-Casimir and Sussel also foresaw the *Charter* as a catalyst for educational change with respect to equality rights, with the Supreme Court acting as a 'national school board.'[123] This image casts the Supreme Court as a super-ordinate policy-making body and can be considered as an education-specific application of the image of the Court as 'a national institution for the development of equality rights jurisprudence.'[124] In this wider sense, the Court is expected to 'harmonize human rights concepts among Canadian jurisdictions.'[125] Thus, for example, when an adjudicator in a human rights dispute considers a given fact-based situation, he or she does so in light of general and more specific principles of human rights law, as shaped by the Supreme Court. Similarly, legislators, policy-makers, and administrators must take account of these principles in the course of their duties. When they fail to do so, they can be called to account on this basis, usually without any recourse to the courts.

We agree with the thrust of the above statements in *Courts in the Classroom*. The Supreme Court has shaped our understanding of equality rights, especially since s.15 of the *Charter* has been in force. This observation should not be taken to imply, however, that this shaping has provided a seamless, coherent evolution of equality rights, either from the courts or the legislatures in response to the decisions of the former. We also realize that a long-term perspective is essential when considering the evolution of constitutional jurisprudence. After all, the mills of the Supreme Court grind slowly, sometimes frustratingly so.

The decision of the Supreme Court in *Eaton* must have had a considerable impact on schools across the country. While many school authorities may have experienced a great feeling of relief when this decision was handed down, disability advocates had every reason to regard it as a 'dramatic setback.' Obviously, only empirical data from local schools and school boards across Canada could allow us to measure the impact of the *Charter* and the Supreme Court, as well as other courts, on ongoing policy and practice.

Despite the need for such data, we can assert that the *Charter* has been and will continue to be a catalyst for educational change. School policy and practice must, as a matter of right, provide equal opportunities to students. While recognizing that this does not mean that schools must eradicate every vestige of inequality, it does mean that schools must take a hard look at the extent to which they are accommodating students of diverse backgrounds, needs, and aspirations.

Conclusion

We began this discussion with a vision of educational change driven by the *Charter* and the Supreme Court of Canada, as foreseen in *Courts in the Classroom*. The starting point of our analysis was the determination of the general construct of equality and then the application of normative guidelines based on this initial analysis.

In brief, we have found that equality rights now emphasize the violation of human dignity, as assessed by the *Law* test, an emphasis that may prove to be detrimental to equality rights in general and equal educational opportunity in particular. The contours of equality rights are shaped by the provisions of the human rights codes that complement the *Charter*'s guarantee of equality. Exceptions to these rights, such as a bona fide requirement defence, must meet the criteria of the *Meiorin* standard, which demands that any such limit provide accommodation for anyone affected by its terms.[126] These general principles apply in a school. While we recognize the limited number of education cases and the snail's pace of court-induced policy development, the *Charter* and the Supreme Court have provided the type of catalyst for change predicted by Manley-Casimir and Sussel.

We reached our conclusions on the basis of available case law, which, in terms of education-specific cases, is rather limited. We have not been able, in the scope of this inquiry, to engage in any empirical research to assess the state of policy and practice at the *chalkface*. Nor have we undertaken an extensive examination of non-education cases seeking analogies for application in schools, let alone of other important aspects related to this inquiry, especially the extent to which equality rights require the expenditure of additional resources or the provision of particular services in order to equalize the opportunities of various groups of students.

We have also underscored the importance of the nexus between equality rights and statutory entitlements in relation to the issue of the 'substance' of equality rights. Thus, for example, if the key provision that underpinned the complaint in *Wynberg* is the right to appropriate education in the *Education Act*, then what role does the *Charter* or the human rights code play in such a case? The answer to this question lies in the future, but we suspect that it reflects a reluctance of the courts to venture too far on either the equal educational opportunity continuum (access to results) or the equality continuum (negative to positive rights), preferring to resolve disputes on the basis of rights and obligations enacted by legislatures. The more the courts look to legislative provisions to provide the substance of equality rights, the more the latter resembles an 'empty shell.'[127] From a normative perspective,[128] the equality provisions ought to shape legislative provisions to ensure that they provide for equality rights. In so doing, the courts will breathe life into the equality provisions themselves, reflecting the substance that early *Charter* watchers predicted many years ago.[129]

The Chief Justice of Canada has described equality as both a *Leviathan* – a great and powerful force – and a *Tantalus* – something that is always just beyond our reach.[130] She concluded her remarks by stating that although we can never achieve complete equality, 'we can work to use the law to combat the evils that flow from inequality. We can remove the barriers, legal and systemic, that hold women, men and children back. We can and must work to promote the fundamental worth and human dignity of each member of society.'[131]

Schools have a special responsibility to fulfil this quest. As MacKay says: 'Education and human rights are intertwined in a *symbiotic* relationship. Each is the foundation for the other.'[132] Schools must not only refrain from discrimination through their own policy or actions but must also not condone discrimination through inaction. School policy and practice, whether adopted or undertaken on a school's own initiative, on the basis of legislation, or on the basis of government or school board policy, must endeavour to prevent discrimination and deal with it when it occurs.

The so-called knowledge society of today expects a great deal of our schools, which are viewed as the gateway to the world of work, as well as to personal and social fulfilment.[133] The conceptual foundation of equal educational opportunity rests on the belief in the transformative power of schools. This belief is neither utopian nor outmoded. In fact, *new public management* thinking – the contemporary paradigm for public policy and administration – stresses the *facilitative* role of government rather than its more traditional *instrumental* role. Reliance on decentralized institutions such as schools and partnerships with community groups is also a key feature of this paradigm, relying as it does on social investment rather than social welfare.[134] Students therefore have a right to expect a great deal from schools and the system that supports them. At the very least, they have the right to be educated in an environment free of discrimination on the basis of race, religion, disability, or other listed or analogous grounds. At best, students can aspire to a school system guided by a more expansionist view of equal educational opportunity, including the provision of positive rights to equality. This continuum of expectations begins with access to the school itself, continues through the medium of school programs and activities, and ends with students achieving the results that schooling is meant to bring about.

The *Charter* and the provincial human rights codes, as well as other legislation, provide normative guidelines for this purpose. The Supreme Court, as well as lower courts and quasi-judicial bodies, interpret these norms, thereby providing further guidance. Taken together, these decisions build a framework for equality rights in general and equal educational opportunity rights in particular. Like any useful policy framework, it must breathe life into abstract principles to guide policy and practice in real-life situations, while avoiding narrow constructs that distort rather than inform: 'Rigid formulas cannot capture the interpretive exercise that is at the heart of a determination as to whether equality rights have been violated.'[135] As foreseen in *Courts in the Classroom*, this framework provides a powerful driving force for the achievement of equality rights for all students.

Among other changes in policy and practice in schools, human rights education as foreseen by the *Convention on the Rights of the Child*,[136] will be a critical component in achieving equal educational opportunity.[137] At the end of the day, however, these rights will be achieved not by legislators or judges,[138] but by school principals, teachers, students and others in thousands of schools across the country. Their efforts will determine whether the United Nations' call for 'education for all'[139] becomes a reality or remains a slogan.

2 The Lighthouse of Equality: A Guide to 'Inclusive' Schooling*

WAYNE MACKAY

Inclusive schooling is now widely regarded as the most effective way to maximize the potential of all the students served by our schools. It has traditionally been associated with bringing disabled students into the regular classrooms but I use the term in a much broader way to embrace taking account of differences of all kinds – age, disability, race, culture, sex, sexual orientation, national origin, and other defining characteristics. An inclusive approach to schooling is a matter of increasing importance in a Canada that is more diverse and multicultural every day. Most educators now support inclusion as a theory but there are still significant debates about how best to implement the policies of inclusion.

I am thus confident of wide support for the policy of inclusion. I am less confident that either educators or the general public will embrace the law, and in particular the concept of equality found in the *Canadian Charter of Rights and Freedoms*[1] and human rights codes, as the lighthouse that can guide educators down the path to inclusive schools. Lawyers and judges are more often regarded as sources of fog shrouding the educational process than as beacons of light to guide educators through the complex fog of public education. Nonetheless, I will argue that the concept of equality, properly understood and applied with adequate resources, can be the lighthouse that guides us to more inclusive, effective, and even safer public schools.

Broadly Defining Inclusive Education

During 2004–05 I conducted an extensive review of Inclusive Education in New Brunswick, and after thirty-five public hearings involving more than 700 individuals and reading 126 written submissions, I produced a 350-page report – *Connecting Care and Challenge: Tapping Our Human Potential*.[2] More recently, in July 2007, I produced a twenty- page book-let on inclusion for the New Brunswick Department of Education. [3] Both are available on the New Brunswick Department of Education web page. I was not far into this interesting and challenging review before concluding that inclusion was about much more than just dis-ability access and I state this conclusion at page 2 of the *Inclusion Booklet*: 'Inclusion is not just about students with disabilities or "exceptional-ities." It is an attitude and an approach that encourages all students to belong. It is an approach that nurtures the self-esteem of all students; it is about taking account of diversity in all its forms, and promoting genuine equality of opportunity for all students in New Brunswick. I cannot overemphasize that effective inclusion is for all students and not just one particular group or category.'[4]

The concept that Canadian schools should be discrimination-free zones and that school boards have a positive duty to promote equality and di-versity in schools is not my original idea but comes from a much higher authority – the Supreme Court of Canada. Mr Justice La Forest, speaking for a majority of the Supreme Court of Canada, makes the following state-ment in *Ross* v. *New Brunswick Board of Education* [1996]:[5] 'The school is an arena for the exchange of ideas and must, therefore, be premised upon principles of tolerance and impartiality so that all persons within the school environment feel equally free to participate. As the Board of Inquiry stated, a school board has a duty to maintain a positive school environ-ment for all persons served by it.'[6] Impressionable young people bring different life experiences to the classroom, and the diversity of those ex-periences increases every day. The above quotation from *Ross* and the re-jection of Malcolm Ross, and his public expression of anti-Semitic views, as an inappropriate teacher role model, emphasize the need for teachers and all concerned with public education to be tolerant and keep open minds. The decision also serves as a signal from the lighthouse of equality about the importance of accommodating diversity in all its rich layers and complexity. To do otherwise will deny an equal opportunity to all stu-dents to achieve their full potential in our schools and the larger society.

One of the early challenges that I faced in my review of education in New Brunswick was defining not only what 'inclusion' means but also the purposes of education itself. The latter was the larger task and one that I only partially completed, but that is a subject for another day. In respect to the concept of inclusion it became clear that it must be a manifestation of equality as enshrined in our *Charter* and is far more than bringing students together in one place. This point is well stated in a 2001 Manitoba education study: 'Inclusion is a way of thinking and acting that permits individuals to feel accepted, valued and secure. An inclusive community evolves constantly to respond to the needs of its members. An inclusive community concerns itself with improving the well being of each member. Inclusion goes further than the idea of physical location; it is a value system based on beliefs that promote participation, belonging and interaction.'[7] Sometimes inclusion, mainstreaming, destreaming, integration, and so on are used interchangeably. Sometimes this language is even utilized as political rhetoric because these words conjure up notions of equality. In reality, however, equality is not an easy political slogan. Equality is often messy, requiring difficult balancing acts. More than anything, though, the language of equality is about belonging, about equal 'concern, respect, and consideration.'[8] Bill Pentney puts it plainly, stating: 'Belonging. Such an achingly simple word. It conjures up some of our deepest yearnings, and for some of us, perhaps our most painful memories. Equality claims begin and end with a desire for belonging, for community. Ideas of equality lie at the heart of the Canadian promise of community.'[9]

The language of equality is also about the equal benefit and protection of the law. When we talk about education, the benefits are enormous. Students who are enabled through a Canadian education receive tremendous benefits in many ways, from life skills, to self-esteem, to employment prospects, and remuneration. There is, however, a stark contrast in the benefits students receive, and there is no question that students whose abilities shine within the existing education structure benefit the most. The language of equality concerns itself with structure as well as outcome. The lighthouse of equality gives us hints and clues in this direction as well.

So, when I talk about an inclusive school system, or inclusion, I am not referring to a specific program, service, or methodology. I am referring to a school system that in both its design and effect continually strives to ensure that each student can participate in the school community, be part of the community in positive and reinforcing ways, and have his or her identity reflected in the operations of the school community. Another fundamental reason for each student to receive an appropriate education is to allow each student to fulfill his or her potential; potential being something that cannot be fully gauged until after the fact. We should therefore be wary of initial assumptions about any particular student's potential and ensure that all potentials are valued and respected.

These are exciting times for those concerned with the promotion of inclusive schooling. Exceptionality, in the form of autism, has even become the topic of a best-selling novel, Mark Haddon's *The Curious Incident of the Dog in the Night-Time*, published in 2004.[10] In this clever book, the author attempts to view the world through the eyes of an autistic child and ponders the limits of definitions and labels in the following insightful passage:

> All the other children at my school are stupid. Except I'm not meant to call them stupid, even though this is what they are. I'm meant to say that they have learning difficulties or that they have special needs. But this is stupid because everyone has learning difficulties because learning to speak French or understanding relativity is difficult and also everyone has special needs, like Father, who has to carry a little packet of artificial sweetening tablets around with him to put in his coffee to stop him from getting fat, or Mrs Peters who wears a beige-coloured hearing aid, or Siobhan, who has glasses so thick that they give you a headache if you borrow them, and none of these people are special needs, even if they have special needs.[11]

This passage is loaded with many weighty questions. How broadly should we define exceptionality or special needs? Do people always pay a price when they are labeled, even if the label is a benign one that is intended to assist the recipients of the label? What is the price of not treating students in an inclusive way, as compared with the price of doing so? What are the comparative roles of parents, school authorities, judicial bodies, and society at large in responding to the diverse needs of the children in our school system today? I do not propose to answer these complex questions here, but rather to explore the legal framework within which some of the answers can be sought. To do this I shall briefly explore three areas – disability access in schools, the balancing of gay rights and freedom of religion, and finally the positive link between inclusive and safe schools.

Disability as an Inclusion Case Study

One of the important areas for considering the inclusiveness of our schools is with respect to the access of physically and mentally disabled students. Both human rights codes and s.15 of the *Charter* prohibit discrimination on the basis of disability and encourage equity programs to promote greater access in a proactive way. Such equity programs are seen as advancing equality and not as reverse discrimination, as has been argued in the United States. It was not that long ago that disabled students did not have access to our schools, but that has changed, and now the challenge for educators is to design programs that accommodate the range of diverse abilities and allow students to reach their varied potentials. There is also the challenge of doing this in a way that does not disrupt the educational experiences for other students. Inclusion is about meeting the needs of all students.

Accommodation of students is not an absolute right. Equality claims under the *Charter* are subject to 'reasonable limits' and under human rights codes reasonable accommodation, but only up to the point of 'undue hardship.' The factors that are relevant to setting the limits of reasonable accommodation are set out in my *Inclusion Booklet*.

- The cost of the accommodation – serious thought about the feasibility of a given accommodation or alternatives must be demonstrated
- The health of any members of the school community or larger community
- The safety of any member of the school community or larger community – both the magnitude of the risk and the identity of those who would bear it are relevant
- Interchangeability of work force and facilities
- The size of the operation (in this case the school district), which may influence the assessment of whether a given financial cost is undue
- The ease with which the workforce or facilities can be adapted to the circumstances
- Significant disruption to a collective agreement
- The reasonable conduct of other parties such as the union and the person seeking accommodation
- The practicality and reasonableness of other less exclusionary options.[12]

Once a denial of equality and the need to be accommodated has been established, there is a high burden on the school authorities to justify limiting the rights of access. Accommodating students with disabilities has both an individual component and a systemic one. In the former, efforts are made to accommodate the individual within the existing system; in the latter, efforts must be directed to changing the system itself to make it more universally inclusive. Both forms of accommodation require a commitment of human and financial resources that move beyond mere positive rhetoric about inclusion.

The meaning of these accommodation rights in practice is a matter of vigorous debate. This debate occurs in court cases, tribunal hearings, and the judicial reviews of both. Courts, and increasingly tribunals, have set out two separate and distinct factors to examine in giving effect to equality in particular contexts. The first, which has received the most attention, is that of individual accommodation. The second factor, which is the least developed and least precise in its implications, is systemic or institutional accommodation.

Individual Accommodation: The Guiding Light

Judicial interpretation, in particular at the level of the Supreme Court of Canada, focuses on the need to view the actual characteristics of the individual in the context of the particular claim when addressing issues of disability. This is so much so that the Supreme Court of Canada in *Eaton* declined to set a legal presumption in favour of 'integration'[13] (where special needs services take place in a 'regular' classroom). Instead, the Court set out a 'best interests of the child test' in which:

> the decision-making body must further ensure that its determination of the appropriate accommodation for an exceptional child be from the subjective, child-centred perspective, one which attempts to make equality meaningful from the child's point of view ... For older children and those who are able to communicate their wishes and needs, their own views will play an important role in the determination of best interests. For younger children, and those like Emily, who are either incapable of making a choice or have a very limited means of communicating their wishes, the decision maker must make this determination on the basis of other evidence before it.[14]

In *Eaton* the Supreme Court of Canada clearly articulated the importance of the best interests of the child test in a way that is reminiscent of family law custody issues. No one can really dispute the need to focus on the best interests of the child, but the real challenges include questions such as how do you measure these best interests and who should be the final judge? What are the comparative roles of parents, education officials, and the courts in defining what is ultimately in the best interests of the child? Compared to the Ontario Court of Appeal decision of Justice Arbour in *Eaton*, the Supreme Court shows greater deference to the expertise of the educational officials and places a higher burden on parents to demonstrate that the educators have got it wrong.[15]

The Court did give legal recognition to the benefits of social inclusion, setting 'integration' as the normal point of departure, as well as setting out the requirement that services for students with disabilities be provided through public funds. It is also clear from *Eaton* that merely plunking a round peg into a square hole will not meet the requirements of equality. With this decision the Court gave a significant burst of light indicating that individual children cannot be sacrificed to the gods of educational efficiency. If the social institutions are not ready for full inclusion, other interim options must be explored. The quality of the inclusion counts.

Specific services and aids for students with disabilities are, generally speaking, individual accommodations to enable the individuals to benefit from education. This area, as educators and government providers are well aware, can be characterized by a seemingly limitless demand for services and the money that goes with them. Rights, though, are not absolute. Rights guaranteed under s.15(1) are subject 'only to such reasonable limits prescribed by law as can be demonstrably justified in a free and democratic society.'[16]

Human rights under human rights acts are similarly circumscribed by the limits set out in the act and by the judicial interpretation of 'accommodation to the point of undue hardship,' a test set out in the landmark cases of *Meiorin*[17] and *Grismer*.[18] This test poses the question whether 'the defendant cannot accommodate persons with the characteristics of the claimant without incurring undue hardship, whether that hardship takes the form of impossibility, serious risk or excessive cost.'[19] In setting out this test, the Supreme Court of Canada highlighted earlier jurisprudence supporting the assertion that 'undue hardship means that more than mere negligible effort is required to accommodate.'[20] The large expenditures required by some successful claims are not irrelevant, particularly if a government's fiscal situation can be characterized as an emergency.[21] In this area the duty to accommodate plays much the same role as the reasonable limits justification under the *Charter*.

While individual accommodation is an important part of equality law in Canada, it is only one facet. It cannot on its own accomplish all of the goals of equality. Take for example Emily Eaton's case, where the Court found that she was in fact more isolated in the 'regular' classroom than in a segregated placement. While Emily was placed in a regular classroom, two components of equality were missing: benefit from the education and belonging within the community, even though she was physically located in the school community. Being physically present in the classroom was a competing value with the benefit of education to Emily: these competing values needed balancing. The Court gave hints and clues as to the direction needed to bring those two competing values together, so that they might be mutually reinforcing.

The Court in Emily Eaton's case chose to emphasize that discrimination on the basis of disability results from 'the failure to make reasonable accommodation to fine-tune society so that its structures and assumptions do not result in the relegation and banishment of disabled persons from participation.'[22] Even though it rejected a legal presumption of inclusion, the Court did suggest a path to equality. The light in this case shone brightly on the need for individual accommodation with some reflection on the issues of systemic barriers to equality.

Systemic Design: Newer Reflections of Light

Through all of the cases dealing with discrimination on the basis of disability, courts have been forced to face the inescapable conclusion that the very construction of societal institutions creates many barriers and gives rise to the need for individual accommodation. The recognition of this monumental problem has been part of a separate line of reasoning running through many recent equality cases.

The Supreme Court of Canada began to address systemic barriers to equality very early on in a case concerning employment standards, requirements, and promotion procedures that had the impact of keeping women out of certain jobs within the Canadian National Railway.[23] Citing the Report of the Royal Commission on Equality and Employment, which came to be known as the Abella Report[24] (for its author Justice Abella – now a Justice of the Supreme Court of Canada), the Supreme Court of Canada affirmed that discrimination often 'results from the simple operation of established procedures,' reinforcing the view that exclusion is the result of 'natural forces.'[25]

The Supreme Court of Canada picked up this line of reasoning in the subsequent case of Eldridge v. British Columbia (Attorney General),[26] where the Court found that in order for all patients to truly benefit from health services, effective communication was essential to the delivery of core medical services in hospitals and emergency rooms. The declaration that the government must provide sign language interpretation in the medical context extended not only to the individual claimants in the case, but generally to all persons who required sign language interpretation for effective communication in the delivery of these medical services. *Eldridge* also affirmed that equality can be violated by omissions as well as actions.

This line of reasoning came to fruition in the later cases of *Meiorin* and *Grismer*, where the Court recognized that its past approach to equality claims was itself a barrier to addressing systemic design issues. In *Meiorin*, the unanimous Supreme Court of Canada abandoned its own traditional approach to equality claims under human rights acts, in favour of an approach that allowed courts and respondents to simultaneously address individual accommodation as well as systemic discrimination, without having one emphasized at the expense of the other. Quoting from equality analysts Shelagh Day and Gwen Brodsky, the Court highlights that:

> Accommodation seems to mean that we do not change procedures or services, we simply 'accommodate' those who do not quite fit. We make some concessions to those who are 'different,' rather than abandoning the idea of 'normal' and working for genuine inclusiveness. In this way, accommodation seems to allow formal equality to be the dominant paradigm, as long as some adjustments can be made ... Accommodation, conceived of in this way does not challenge deep-seated beliefs about the intrinsic superiority of such characteristics as mobility and sightedness. In short, accommodation is assimilationist. Its goal is to try to make 'different' people fit into existing systems.[27]

This significant shift in reasoning creates a dual responsibility on the part of institutional officials. As part of this responsibility, institutional officials must address both individual accommodation needs (particularly in the short term), as well as engage in a process of institutional analysis to uncover the often hidden barriers and make changes to reduce the negative impact of the system or institution. This will have positive impacts in the long term.

As a result, the test outlined to gauge the adequacy of accommodation efforts involves not only an examination of 'to the point of undue hardship' (as outlined above), but also an inquiry into:

1 Whether or not the standard [or procedure] is adopted for a purpose rationally connected to the performance of the function being performed

2 Whether or not the particular standard is adopted in the good faith
belief that it is necessary to the fulfillment of the legitimate purpose
or goal
3 Whether or not the standard is reasonably necessary to accomplish
the legitimate purpose or goal, because the defendant cannot
accommodate persons with the characteristics of the claimant
without incurring undue hardship, whether that hardship takes
the form of impossibility, serious risk or excessive cost.[28]

Courts are unable to make specific pronouncements on precise systemic changes for many reasons. They are limited by the framing of the
issues by the applicants, and by the divergent functions of courts and
legislatures with respect to equality claims. The courts' purpose is to
determine when legislative or governmental actions or inactions run
afoul of the *Constitution* and human rights acts. Courts are much better
at pronouncing upon how governments get it wrong, than upon how
governments can get it right. Nonetheless, courts have given clues and
hints as to what direction the inquiry needs to follow in order to meet
the burden of addressing systemic discrimination.

Courts are wary of their role in these matters and leave scope for legislators to fulfill their function, particularly where remedies will require
significant governmental expenditures. The 2004 Supreme Court of
Canada decision in *Auton v. British Columbia (Attorney General)*[29] is a case
in point. Some were surprised to learn that the Supreme Court of Canada
allowed the appeal and declined to order the Medical Services Commission
to fund the treatment of Applied Behavioral Analysis/Intensive
Behavioral Intervention (ABA/IBI) for autistic children. Nor did the
Court approve compensation to the claimants for funds expended for the
treatment. The Court held, first, that the benefit sought was not a benefit
'provided by law,' in the sense that under the legislative scheme of the
Canada Health Act, these treatments were not 'core services,' such as the
services in *Eldridge*, which the government was required to provide for
all people in British Columbia. The relevant autism treatments were non-
core services subject to permissive language under the statutory scheme.
Second, the Court held that practitioners of this treatment had not yet
been designated as Health Care Practitioners under the provincial statute; therefore the Medical Services Commission did not have the authority to fund this treatment under their authorizing statute.

In *Auton* the Court held that, rather than the appropriate comparator
group being non-disabled or otherwise disabled people receiving non-core

services, the appropriate comparator group was: 'a non-disabled person or a person suffering a disability other than a mental disability ... seeking or receiving funding for a non-core therapy which is emergent and only recently becoming recognized as medically required ... People receiving well-established non-core therapies are not in the same position as people claiming relatively new non-core benefits ... There was no evidence of how the Province had responded to requests for new therapies or treatments by non-disabled or otherwise disabled people.'[30]

The Court certainly sympathized with the petitioners in this case, holding that: 'The government's failing was to delay putting in place what was emerging in the late 1990's as the most, indeed the only known, effective therapy for autism while continuing to fund increasingly discredited treatments ... The issue however, is not whether the government met the gold standard of scientific methodology but whether it denied autistic people benefit it accorded to others in the same situation.'[31]

Three critical questions arise from this case with regard to special needs programming in schools. First, how do schools and ministries of education deal with and implement new research, methodology, and technology both with regard to individual accommodation and systemic barriers? Second, how does this compare with the implementation of new research, methodologies, and technologies in other areas? Finally, who should bear the costs of certain programs to advance inclusion of disabled children?

In coming to its decision in *Auton*, the Supreme Court of Canada specifically supported the findings in *Eldridge* and *Meiorin*, and their focus on systemic issues, by requiring an analysis of existing practices and operations resulting in the exclusion of certain groups. Indeed, systemic elements of discrimination are often lost from sight when parents and advocates focus on specific services to benefit an individual, even making claims to have governments pay large amounts for private delivery of services, in order to give effect to equality.[32] This is understandable, because parents and advocates simply want the best that is available for their child, and governments should be striving to provide the best services that they can afford. The response of education officials to these high-cost claims, by and large, has been to deny them and to argue that courts and tribunals have no role in dictating budgetary or programming priorities for education. The setting of these priorities has traditionally been left to the elected legislative branch and its executive agents. Courts and tribunals have shown a willingness to wade into detailed evidence, while still showing some deference to the elected branches of government.[33]

The first Ontario trial decision in respect to a series of injunctions in relation to ABA/IBI therapy was released on 30 March 2005. In *Wynberg v. Ontario*,[34] the Ontario Superior Court of Justice held that once the government had undertaken to provide the service of ABA/IBI to pre-school children, cutting off the service at the arbitrary age of six, it discriminated on the basis of age. Aiding the Court in coming to this conclusion was the fact that the government was aware that autistic children entering school were not having their needs met by the education system.[35] The Court distinguished this case from *Auton* by finding that once a government decides to provide ABA/IBI service, it cannot then claim that it is a new or emerging therapy. With regard to the responsibility of the minister of education, Justice Kiteley found that the minister had not considered ABA/IBI as a service delivery option. Justice Kiteley found that a myth had been created that ABA/IBI was a therapy or treatment and that the Minister had not considered it as a teaching strategy or educational approach.[36] Based on this assessment, Justice Kiteley found that the government had discriminated on the basis of disability in the provision of special education programs and services. This case was reversed on appeal, and the courts reverted to a more deferential approach to the allocation of scarce educational funds more in line with the judicial approach to health funds in *Auton*.[37]

Courts do recognize the delicacy of allocating finite resources and the comparable expertise of governments in performing this function. Courts prefer to provide guidance as to the nature of the duties to accommodate (both individual and systemic).[38] It is sometimes difficult to keep a clear focus on the comparative roles of courts and legislatures and their respective roles in promoting equality.

The light from the lighthouse is more difficult to make out, especially when the glare of individual accommodation is so bright, once claims to individual accommodation become more numerous and extensive. The importance of addressing systemic discrimination is to reduce the need, cost, and inconvenience of individual accommodation claims. In other words, the promise of an inclusive system is a reduction in the burdens of separate schemes and structures for individual accommodations. Canadian courts are more cautious about directing systemic changes to the education system than requiring individual accommodations. This case by case approach fits more comfortably within the traditional judicial role. It may not be the most cost effective.

That being said, it is not reasonable to anticipate immediately a system that is inclusive of all children. This leaves education officials and teachers with the tough balancing acts required by equality and the difficult decisions about where to concentrate limited resources. Suffice it to say that the dual responsibility to work towards equality in terms of both individual accommodations and systemic changes will require a dual focus. It should also be remembered that in equality, as in many other aspects of life, one size rarely fits all. Not surprisingly, this was also a major conclusion of my report on inclusive schooling in New Brunswick.[39]

Balancing Gay Rights and Freedom of Religion

In the previous case study on including the disabled, the arguments to the contrary are based upon cost and educational effectiveness but not normally on a basis of conflicting rights. It is true that some argue that the focus on students with disabilities comes at the expense of the non-disabled students in the class but that is really more a question of resources and methods than a true conflict of rights. Inclusion properly understood and resourced, is about promoting the rights and interests of all students.

The inclusion of gays and lesbians within the school system and the recognition of their values have produced a more classical example of conflicting rights that need to be balanced. Some parents of particular religious faiths find homosexuality objectionable and argue that the tolerance of homosexuality and related values is an affront to their freedom of religion. How this apparent conflict of rights should be reconciled and whether courts or legislators should perform the delicate balancing act arose to national prominence in the high profile Alberta case of *Vriend v. Alberta*.[40]

In *Vriend*, a laboratory worker was dismissed from his position at King's College in Edmonton, when his employer became aware that he was gay. The college thought it was entitled to dismiss him because the Alberta human rights legislation, the *Individual's Rights Protection Act*,[41] did not include sexual orientation as a prohibited ground of discrimination. There had been numerous attempts to include sexual orientation as a ground, but the government had deliberately chosen to omit it from the *IRPA*. Mr Vriend argued that the college had violated his s.15(1) *Charter* right to equality. The Supreme Court of Canada considered whether the Alberta legislature had the right to omit sexual orientation as a prohibited ground of discrimination, and determined that it did not. The Court then deemed that from that time forward, the *IRPA* should be read to include sexual orientation as a prohibited ground of discrimination. Discrimination on the basis of sexual orientation is now a prohibited ground of discrimination in all provinces, based on both human rights codes and the *Charter*.

The conflict between claims of religious freedom and equality claims for gays and lesbians within schools became even more explicit in *Trinity Western University* v. *British Columbia College of Teachers*.[42] In this case the issue was the certification of teachers with declared anti-homosexual views to teach in the public schools of the province. Trinity Western University (TWU) is a private institution in British Columbia, associated with the Evangelical Free Church of Canada. TWU established a teacher training program offering baccalaureate degrees in education upon completion of a five-year course, four years of which were spent at TWU, the fifth year being under the aegis of Simon Fraser University (SFU). TWU applied to the B.C. College of Teachers (BCCT) for permission to assume full responsibility for the teacher education program. One of the reasons for assuming complete responsibility for the program was TWU's desire to have the full program reflect its Christian world-view.

The BCCT refused to approve the application on the ground that it was contrary to the public interest for the BCCT to approve a teacher education program offered by a private institution that appeared to follow discriminatory practices. The BCCT was concerned that the TWU Community Standards, applicable to all students, faculty, and staff, embodied discrimination against homosexuals. Specifically, the concern stemmed from the list of 'practices that are biblically condemned,' which encompassed 'sexual sins including ... homosexual behaviour.' TWU community members, including the teachers in issue, were asked to sign a document in which they agreed to refrain from such activities.

On application for judicial review, the British Columbia Supreme Court[43] found that it was not within the BCCT's jurisdiction to consider whether the program follows discriminatory practices under the public interest component of the *Teaching Profession Act*[44] and that there was no reasonable foundation to support the BCCT's decision with regard to discrimination. The British Columbia Court of Appeal[45] found that the BCCT had acted within its statutory jurisdiction, but affirmed the trial judge's decision on the basis that there was no reasonable foundation for the BCCT's finding of discrimination.

The majority of the Supreme Court of Canada, like the lower British Columbia courts, reversed the ruling of the BCCT and directed that the Trinity Western University education program be certified, allowing their students to teach in the public schools. The Court drew a clear line between belief and conduct, and ruled that the graduates of the Trinity Western University program were entitled to hold their anti-homosexual beliefs as a matter of freedom of religion so long as they did not act on those beliefs in a way that would be discriminatory against gay or lesbian students. The Court also concluded that the BCCT concerns about such discrimination were only speculative and not based on hard evidence.

As the lone dissenter in this case, Madame Justice L'Heureux Dube would have upheld the decision of the BCCT and not allowed these graduates of Trinity Western University into the public schools. She based her decision on the comparative expertise of the teacher certification board and the desirability of the courts deferring to that expertise. She also argued that the majority decision was inconsistent with the earlier Supreme Court ruling in *Ross*, that a teacher must be an appropriate, non-discriminatory role model.

In *Chamberlain* v. *Surrey School District No. 36* [46] the clash between religious views and gay rights arose in a different context. This case concerned the refusal of an elected school board to approve books about same sex family units as part of the supplementary reading material for the Kindergarten to Grade 1 (K–1) student level. The elected school board has the authority under British Columbia's *School Act* [47] to make such a decision but the question was whether it exercised its discretion in accordance with the principles of its governing statute and in a non-discriminatory fashion.

The school board defended its actions in banning the books on two major bases. First, it argued that including the books, and thereby presenting homosexual family units in a positive light, would offend the religious view of a majority of the parents within the constituency that it was elected to represent. Second, it argued that the books were inappropriate for impressionable young students at the Kindergarten and Grade 1 levels and exposing them to these alternate versions of the family unit would cause cognitive dissonance with family units as they experienced them. The board seemed to ignore the fact that there may have been a number of different family units within its own school district.

Chief Justice McLachlin, speaking for the Supreme Court, rejected the school board's reasons for banning the books and concluded that its exercise of discretion was both discriminatory and not in accordance with the principles articulated in its governing *School Act*. In particular, she ruled that the board was acting on behalf of a particular religious parents' group and not respecting the insistence of the *School Act* on secularism, non-discrimination, and the promotion of diversity. The Chief Justice stated:

> The *School Act*'s emphasis on secularism reflects the fact that Canada is a diverse and multicultural society, bound together by the values of accommodation, tolerance and respect for diversity. These values are reflected in our Constitution's commitment to equality and minority rights, and are explicitly incorporated into the British Columbia public school system by the preamble to the *School Act* and by the curriculum established by regulation under the Act ...
>
> The message of the preamble is clear. The British Columbia public school system is open to all children of all cultures and family backgrounds. All are to be valued and respected. The British Columbia public school system therefore reflects the vision of a public school articulated by La Forest J. in *Ross, supra*, at para. 42: ...[48]

Chief Justice McLachlin is equally firm in rejecting the arguments about cognitive dissonance and the impact of exposing young children to alternate family units.

> The number of different family models in the community means that some children will inevitably come from families of which certain parents disapprove. Giving these children an opportunity to discuss their family models may expose other children to some cognitive dissonance. But such dissonance is neither avoidable nor noxious. Children encounter it every day in the public school system as members of a diverse student body. They see their classmates, and perhaps also their teachers, eating foods at lunch that they themselves are not permitted to eat, whether because of their parent's religious strictures or because of other moral beliefs. They see their classmates wearing clothing with features or brand labels which their parents have forbidden them to wear. And they see their classmates engaging in behaviour on the playground that their parents have told them not to engage in. The cognitive dissonance that results from such encounters is simply a part of living in a diverse society. It is also a part of growing up. Through such experiences, children come to realize that not all of their values are shared by others.[49]

She goes on to assert that a certain degree of cognitive dissonance is a necessary part of learning about tolerance. This does not negate freedom of religion, as those opposed to homosexual family units do not have to change their views or adopt the views of gays and lesbians. Tolerance and diversity involve respecting the views of others not embracing them as correct for all people or adopting them as our own views.[50] On the question of whether the children were too young to be exposed to books about same sex families the Court concludes '[t]olerance is always age-appropriate.'[51]

In this case study, the lighthouse of equality shines on the importance of tolerance and diversity in our schools and the value of exposing students to differing views of life – even if such exposure causes some cognitive dissonance. It reinforces the earlier view that schools should be discrimination-free zones but takes it to the next level, by demonstrating the value of inclusion and the educational growth that comes with exposure to differences. Even when rights and values come into conflict they can be balanced in a respectful way. Promoting this kind of equality causes the fog of intolerance to dissipate.

Inclusive Schools Are Safer

The growing diversity in Canadian schools is often identified as one of the sources of disruption and violence in schools. This is a message that comes from many quarters including the media. It is also frequently suggested that the inclusion of students with a wide array of disabilities and challenges has led to significant class disruptions and in more extreme situations, violence directed at both students and teachers. It would appear that this is a perception that is based on feelings and impressions rather than concrete evidence.

Based upon my review of inclusion in New Brunswick, disabled students were neither the primary targets nor the primary victims of school violence and bullying. The only real exception to this was the fact that students with invisible disabilities were sometimes targeted for bullying and exclusion. Contrary to popular belief, it did not appear that disabled students were major instigators of class disruptions. While the problem of disruptions is a real one, the perpetrators are spread across the spectrum of abilities, economic backgrounds, cultures, and geographic regions. Boys more frequently create problems than girls but there are some signs that girls are catching up.

I did not do any scientific or empirical study of the origins of violence and bullying as part of my review but what I did observe challenges the view that diversity and conflicting values are at the heart of the problem. It would, however, be fair to say that the failure to properly accommodate diversity, in its many manifestations, is a significant cause of student frustration, alienation, and withdrawal. This, in turn, can lead to inappropriately acting out in ways that are disruptive and lead to discipline problems. The failure of most school systems to properly include Aboriginal students and accommodate their perspectives goes a long distance in explaining the high levels of discipline problems and dropouts among this student population. Diversity in itself does not pose a threat to school safety but not responding properly to this diversity can lead to disruption and, at the extremes, violence.

The apparent conflict between the values of diversity and inclusion on the one hand, and school safety on the other, played out in the high profile case of *Multani v. Commission Scolaire Marguerite-Bourgeoys*.[52] Twelve-year old Gurbaj Singh Multani had no idea that when he accidentally dropped his ceremonial dagger in his schoolyard in 2001 that the incident would touch off a dispute that would eventually wind up in the Supreme Court of Canada. The dagger was a kirpan and Gurbaj was wearing one because he is a baptized orthodox Sikh. Orthodox Sikhs say the kirpan is not a weapon but a religious symbol that must be worn at all times. But others said, symbol or not, any kind of knife has no place in a school environment. When the school board's governing body ruled that a kirpan violated its ban on students bringing 'dangerous and forbidden objects' onto school property, the dispute headed to the courts ... and ultimately to the country's top Court.

The first-level school board sent Gurbaj's parents a letter in which, as a reasonable accommodation, it authorized their son to wear his kirpan to school provided that he complied with certain conditions to ensure that it was sealed inside his clothing. Gurbaj and his parents agreed to this arrangement. The governing board of the school refused, however, to ratify the agreement on the basis that wearing a kirpan at the school violated art. 5 of the school's *code de vie* (code of conduct), which prohibited the carrying of weapons. The school board's council of commissioners upheld that decision and notified Gurbaj and his parents that a symbolic kirpan in the form of a pendant or one in another form made of a material rendering it harmless, would be acceptable in the place of a real kirpan. Gurbaj's father then filed a motion in the Superior Court for a declaratory judgment to the effect that the council of commissioners' decision was of no force or effect. The Superior Court granted the motion, declared the decision to be null, and authorized Gurbaj to wear his kirpan under certain conditions.[53] The Court of Appeal set aside the Superior Court's judgment.[54] After deciding that the applicable standard of review was reasonableness, the Court of Appeal restored the council of commissioners' decision. It concluded that the decision in question infringed Gurbaj's freedom of religion under s.2(a) of the *Charter* and s.3 of *Quebec's Charter of Human Rights and Freedoms*[55] ('Quebec Charter'), but that the infringement was justified for the purposes of s.1 of the *Charter* and s.9.1 of the *Quebec Charter*.

At the Supreme Court of Canada level in *Multani* the justices were unanimous in the view that the values of diversity and inclusion clearly trumped the minimal threat to school safety posed by a properly sealed kirpan. While in theory a kirpan (essentially a dagger) could be used as a weapon, so could scissors or pencils or many other items commonly found in schools. In spite of the school board's arguments about school safety it produced no real evidence that the existence of kirpans in schools had in fact led to violence. Indeed the existing evidence was to the contrary. Furthermore, all parties agreed that Gurbaj himself was not a discipline problem and posed no threat to safety. Thus, once the Court concluded that the absolute ban on the kirpan violated his freedom of religion, it rejected the board's justification on this limitation as being a reasonable limit in pursuit of school safety.

The essence of the Supreme Court of Canada's ruling in *Multani* is well articulated in the following passage from the case:

> Religious tolerance is a very important value of Canadian society. If some students consider it unfair that Gurbaj Singh may wear his kirpan to school while they are not allowed to have knives in their possession, it is incumbent on the schools to discharge their obligation to instill in their students this value that is, as I will explain in the next section, at the very foundation of our democracy ...
>
> Since we have found that the council of commissioner's decision is not a reasonable limit on religious freedom, it is not strictly necessary to weigh the deleterious effects of this measure against its salutary effects. I do not believe, however, like the intervener Canadian Civil Liberties Association, that it is important to consider some effects that could result from an absolute prohibition. An absolute prohibition would stifle the promotion of values such as multiculturalism, diversity and the development of an educational culture respectful of the rights of others. This Court has on

numerous occasions reiterated the importance of these values ...

A total prohibition against wearing a kirpan to school undermines the value of this religious symbol and sends students the message that some religious practices do not merit the same protection as others. On the other hand, accommodating Gurbaj Singh and allowing him to wear his kirpan under certain conditions demonstrates the importance that our society attaches to protecting freedom of religion and to showing respect for its minorities. The deleterious effects of a total prohibition thus outweigh its salutary effects.[56]

As discussed earlier the inclusion of Sikhs within the school system and the promotion of respect for diversity and minority rights is not a real threat to school safety. The failure to accommodate this kind of diversity and the frustration and alienation which might result, could pose a threat to a safe school environment. Thus the representation by the board in *Multani* that diversity and school safety are opposing forces can now be stood on its head. Diversity properly accommodated in the schools produces a sense of inclusion and belonging that is conducive to a safe and welcoming environment. This is a further reason to support inclusion.

In *Jubran* v. *North Vancouver School District No. 44*,[57] Azmi Jubran claimed discrimination on the basis of sexual orientation because he suffered from homophobic harassment from other students. It was found that the school board had discriminated against him even though it had taken several preventive measures, because it had failed to implement what were shown through evidence to be more effective ways of responding. The fact that the school had documented each incident of harassment and followed up with an investigation and punishment where a perpetrator could be found, was weighed in the school board's favour on the issue of damages. In the end Azmi Jubran did win an award for the resulting damage to his dignity and self-worth. The Tribunal's decision was also vindicated in the British Columbia Court of Appeal.

The interesting part of this case is that Azmi Jubran claimed that he was not homosexual, but that students harassed and bullied him on the basis of perceived sexual orientation because the harassers called him names like 'faggot' and 'queer.' In fact, this is the very reason the British Columbia Supreme Court quashed the decision of the Tribunal. In a very short decision, it held that people must declare themselves to be gay or lesbian in order to claim discrimination on the basis of sexual orientation. The trial court also questioned whether the other students really perceived Jubran as gay.

Ultimately, however, the reasoning behind the Human Rights Tribunal's decision was reinforced when the case reached the B.C. Court of Appeal. Levine JA, speaking for the majority of the court, stated the following when discussing the issue of the harassers' perception of Jubran's sexuality: 'The effect of (the harassers') conduct was the same whether or not they perceived Mr Jubran as homosexual. The homophobic taunts directed against Mr Jubran attributed to him the negative perceptions, myths and stereotypes attributed to homosexuals. His harassers created an environment in which his dignity and full participation in school life was denied because the negative characteristics his harassers associated with homosexuality were attributed to him.'[58]

Disconcertingly, the British Columbia Supreme Court had ignored the fact found by the Tribunal that Azmi Jubran was identified as having Attention Deficit Disorder/Attention Deficit Hyperactivity Disorder (ADD/ADHD). With ADD/ADHD having been affirmed as a disability recognized under the *New Brunswick Human Rights Act*, this could have had some impact on the case. The recognition of the fact that disability or differences in ability forms the basis for much harassment is a necessary first step. Unfortunately, the Tribunal's finding of fact was also not a factor considered by the British Columbia Court of Appeal, which chose instead to focus on the harassment and taunts that centered on Azmi Jubran's perceived sexuality. Consideration of his disability at the appellate level would have afforded more credence to the important ruling at the Tribunal level.

Discriminatory harassment on the basis of prohibited human rights grounds such as sexual orientation, disability, gender, or race (to name but a few examples) is a major form of bullying and violence in schools. Once again, a school system that is more inclusive and accommodating and comes closer to achieving the ideal of schools as discrimination free zones, as articulated in *Ross*, would not only be a better learning environment but also a safer place. A truly inclusive school setting would be one that encourages positive interactions between students rather than violent and discriminatory conduct.

The paragraph that immediately follows the one quoted in the introduction from Mark Haddon's best-selling novel narrated by an autistic child reads: 'But Siobhan said we have to use those words because people used to call children like the children at school *spaz* and *crip* and *mong*, which were nasty words. But that is stupid too because sometimes the children from the school down the road see us in the street when we're getting off the bus and they shout, 'Special Needs! Special Needs! But I don't take any notice because I don't listen to what other people say and only sticks and stones can break my bones and I have my Swiss Army knife if they hit me and if I kill them it will be self-defence and I won't go to prison.'[59]

We should not underestimate the importance of promoting a culture of tolerance and respect among our students. We should also recognize the relationship between promoting substantive equality and reducing violence and harassment. Truly inclusive schools should also be safer schools. This is an important flash of insight from the lighthouse of equality and one that provides a further incentive to make our schools more inclusive places, where students can participate and contribute in constructive ways. As tragedies such as Columbine, Virginia Tech, and, closer to home, Taber, Alberta indicate, the price of alienation and exclusion can be very high indeed. There are costs to producing truly inclusive schools but the costs of not doing so are greater. It is better to pay now than pay later.

Concluding Thoughts on the Equality Lighthouse

While special needs programming has come through a marathon of court cases and tribunal hearings as well as a barrage of new language and commitments to equality, the path for governments is still mired in uncertainty and what some might call a hazy fog. The same can be said in respect to the inclusion of other forms of diversity. The case study on sexual orientation demonstrates the challenges facing both school officials and tribunals and courts in balancing the conflicting claims to freedom of religion and the inclusion of gay perspectives as a matter of equality. Our courts and tribunals aid in giving effect to our constitutionally protected rights to equality, although they are not always able to do so as specifically as we might like. Indeed, many educators might suggest that the courts and tribunals have been major contributors to the fog, rather than a lighthouse providing guidance.

The judicial role is a difficult one limited by the framing of issues by individual claimants and by the courts and tribunals' deference to the roles of the school boards and legislatures. Primarily these adjudicative bodies function to tell governments when they get things legally wrong, rather than to demonstrate how to get things right. There is usually more than one way to accomplish a goal. The law can help provide the framework and indicate a general path. As such, court and tribunal decisions and the development of the language of equality are like a lighthouse aiding the navigation through these unknown waters.

Light emanating from the lighthouse has taken two distinct forms: the glare and the reflection. The glare is the call for individual accommodations to ameliorate the situation of people with disabilities and other manifestations of diversity in societal institutions that are not designed to include them. Many equality advocates have attempted to push the boundaries of this glare as far is it can reach. But the reflection, which is the call for an analysis of the barriers inherent in the operations of societal institutions, is not so easy to see. This systemic reflection has too frequently escaped notice in its implications as well as in its promises for reducing the efforts needed to accommodate individually. If the rules are changed to be more inclusive, then there is less need to accommodate to the rules.

One of the major challenges facing governments is how to implement new research, methodology, and technology in a timely manner as it becomes available, thereby benefiting more students. A second challenge is how to work more cooperatively with various government departments and other interested parties in fulfilling the whole government's responsibility to promote and ensure equality. How should governments apportion finite resources in the context of judicial messages from the lighthouse of equality? This is a tough question to answer and one that requires participation from all parties. This collaborative approach could bring us closer to a truly inclusive education system. An approach that puts into effect both the glare and the reflection, that is, both individual accommodation and systemic or institutional equality, is necessary to discharge fully the government's responsibilities in promoting equality.

Some may consider cases such as *Auton* and *Cudmore* to be a retreat from equality, but they are a reminder that simply focusing on the brightness of individual accommodation is not enough to reach the ultimate goals of equality. Both claimants and institutional officials alike still need to notice the reflection of the light onto societal institutions and pursue the analysis at this systemic level. Furthermore, the ultimate answers have to come from those on the front lines. The courts and tribunals can only provide a framework.

Support from federal officials might be sought in the form of resources to put into effect Canada's international commitments under the

United Nations *Convention on the Rights of the Child.*[60] Although there are constitutional limitations to assigning a strict legal responsibility to the federal government in arenas of provincial control (education being an important one), educators may find some support for initiatives that further Canada's international commitment to implement the substance of the *Convention on the Rights of the Child*. I believe governments want to do the right thing. Cooperation and setting goals and targets to promote inclusive schooling as a part of the substantive implementation of equality is a definite step in the right direction.

The needs to increase genuine access to community, a sense of belonging, and a sense of confidence and self-worth for students with disabilities and other manifestations of diversity are areas that have received inadequate attention. The positive self-esteem that can come from confidence and a sense of belonging may have a tremendous impact on the level of benefit that students can derive from their education. The stress caused by perceived inferiority following a diagnosis of a disability or from cultural or economic exclusion and their impact on student performance should not be underestimated.

Beyond this sense of belonging to the school community is the quality of the relationships and attitudes among students. As was recently publicized in New Brunswick,[61] the harassment of people with disabilities by students and others in the community is not as rare as one would like to believe. It would also appear that students with invisible disabilities, such as learning problems or Attention Deficit Disorder (ADD), are more likely to be the targets of bullying than students with clearly visible disabilities. The harassment of students on the basis of sexual orientation has already been discussed. Attitudes are an important part of the school community, and the social climate is legitimately the concern of education officials.[62] More efforts are needed to proactively ensure a positive connection among diversity, community, curriculum, pedagogy, and the general operations of the school system, in order to inspire a sense of belonging and self-worth among all members of the school community.

The serious consequences of not addressing systemic barriers to equality and particularly the emotional responses to such barriers for students with disabilities and other manifestations of difference, and the negative impact of this neglect on student to student relationships, are critical. It is vital to recognize the connection between violence and harassment and some of the systemic barriers to equality in our schools. The recognition of the seriousness of these issues for students should also underscore the need to move towards inclusive schooling with greater haste. Inclusive schools offer the best hope for delivering on the promises of equality and producing the safe and non-discriminatory schools that the Supreme Court of Canada calls for in *Ross*.[63] The lessons learned in the efforts to include disabled students can be helpful in making schools more inclusive of the many forms of diversity. It is this broader sense of inclusion that must be the ultimate goal, and the lighthouse of equality can help us get there.

3 Special Education and the *Charter*: The Effect of the Equality Provisions and *Charter* Litigation on Educational Policy and Practice in Ontario

BRENDA BOWLBY AND RACHEL ARBOUR

Special education gained significant momentum during the early 1980s at about the same time that s.15 of the *Canadian Charter of Rights and Freedoms*[1] was being drafted and came into force. More than twenty years have passed since s.15 enshrined the right of all Canadian residents to equal treatment under the law, and the time is now ripe to examine the influence, if any, that s.15 has had on the development of special education laws and on manner in which special education is actually delivered.[2]

In Ontario, the legislative recognition of the right of children with disabilities to a public education appropriate to their needs and the framework for providing that education was first set out in the *Education Amendment Act of 1980* ('*Bill 82*').[3] *Bill 82* was drafted and moved through the Ontario legislature at about the same time that the nation was debating the patriation of the Canadian constitution and the creation of the *Charter of Rights and Freedoms*. Although *Bill 82* became law in 1981, while s.15 came into force in 1985, its provisions reflected the equity principles that were ultimately enshrined in the Constitution by s.15 of the *Charter*.

A review of government reports on education prepared in the decades following the Second World War reveals that the impetus for *Bill 82* was not the impending *Charter of Rights*. The real impetus was a growing social movement that rejected the exclusion of persons with disabilities from the mainstream of society, including in some cases, the exclusion of some students with serious disabilities from regular classrooms or from school entirely. This was enhanced by the growth of special education as a new pedagogical discipline; quite simply, the development of new pedagogical strategies were enabling teachers to address the special needs of students whose disabilities prevented them from benefiting from regular education.

A review of *Charter* litigation involving special education is critical to the determination of the extent to which special education policy and practice (i.e., the manner in which special education is actually provided) has been influenced, if at all, by s.15 of the *Charter*. Subsequent to s.15 coming into force, amendments have been made to those enacted by Bill 82. Although these amendments have been influenced to some degree by s.15, the motivation for them appears to have been largely based on 'policy issues' unrelated to s.15. For the most part, court decisions have dealt with challenges by parents to the implementation of special education laws rather than to the laws themselves. Parents have challenged school board decisions regarding individual special education placements, programs, and/or services provided (or not provided) to their children. Most of these court decisions have upheld the decisions taken by school boards or ministries of education and therefore have served to confirm that special education laws, policies, and practices are in compliance with s.15 principles.

The Introduction of Special Education in Ontario: The Historical Context

Historically, persons with severe disabilities – if they survived infancy – were effectively excluded not only from the provincial education system but also from society in general. Prior to *Bill 82*, in the education sector in Ontario and across Canada, children with severe disabilities were usually barred from their neighbourhood schools. This practice resulted in the formation of parent groups such as the Associations for the Mentally Retarded (now called Associations for Community Living), which provided education for children with severe developmental delays in community settings ranging from church basements to stand alone 'schools for the trainable mentally retarded' (as they were referred to at the time) built with donations from the community. In some cases, school boards did provide education for students with developmental delays, but usually in segregated settings. Blind and deaf students were sent to segregated residential schools.

In the United States, constitutional imperatives drove the reform of the education system to provide special education to children with severe disabilities. In 1972, a U.S. federal court ruled in *Mills* v. *Board of Education of the District of Columbia*,[4] that children with disabilities were entitled, pursuant to the Constitution's equal protection clause, to a basic education. This decision led to the framing and passage in 1975 of the *Individuals with Disabilities Education Act* (IDEA) by Congress.[5]

In the 1970s, Canada had no equivalent to the equal protection clause. The *Charter* did not come into force until 1982, and the equality protection of s.15 was delayed until 1985. Ontario did have human rights legislation in place, but 'handicap' (now 'disability') was not added as a protected ground until 1982.[6] Thus, the impetus for *Bill 82* was not the result of constitutional or human rights legislation or other legal imperative. Rather, the impetus for *Bill 82* came from pedagogical and societal imperatives that advocated that the education system in Ontario must provide education for all students.[7]

Thirty years before *Bill 82* became law, the Royal Commission on Education in Ontario, 1950[8] culminating in the *Hope Report*, provided the first significant step forward for special education in Ontario. In addition to recommending compulsory school attendance for children aged 6 to 16, universal Kindergarten programs, and abolition of Grade 13, this important report[9] called for a significant expansion of special education programs for children with learning disabilities. Although the report had no immediate impact on education, its release raised special education as a matter with which governments would have deal.

In 1962, the Robarts Plan advanced the movement in Ontario towards the recognition of the rights of students with disabilities to publicly funded education. Under this plan, three academic streams were introduced at the secondary school level: in addition to the pre-existing five-year stream for students bound for postsecondary education, secondary schools offered a four-year stream providing vocational training and a two-year program providing job training.[10]

The landmark *Hall-Dennis Report* (*Living and Learning: The Report of the Provincial Committee on Aims and Objectives of Education in the Schools of Ontario*) was released in 1968.[11] One of the key features of this report was its recognition of principles and concepts that later became central to *Bill 82*, such as the right of all individuals to have equal access to the learning environment best suited to their needs, and the responsibility of every school authority to provide child-centred education that promotes learning through individual discovery and inquiry.

When introduced a decade later, *Bill 82* was heralded as bringing, for the first time, 'universal access' to publicly funded education to all children in Ontario.[12] In 1980, *Bill 82* came into force and amended Ontario's *Education Act*[13] to put into place the formal legislative framework under which

Ontario's school boards have been required to provide appropriate special education programs and special education services to Ontario's 'exceptional pupils.' This legislation has remained largely unaltered since then.

Bill 82

Bill 82, for the first time, imposed on the minister of education and on school boards specific responsibilities to provide education for children with disabilities, including responsibilities of the minister that have continued unchanged to the present day:

> s.8(3) The Minister shall ensure that all exceptional children in Ontario have available to them, in accordance with this Act and the regulations, appropriate special education programs and special education services without payment of fees by parents or guardians resident in Ontario, and shall provide for the parents or guardians to appeal the appropriateness of the special education placement, and for these purposes, the Minister shall,
>
> (a) require school boards to implement procedures for early and ongoing identification of the learning abilities and needs of pupils, and shall prescribe standards in accordance with which such procedures be implemented; and
>
> (b) in respect of special education programs and services, define exceptionalities of pupils, and prescribe classes, groups or categories of exceptional pupils, and require boards to employ such definitions or use such prescriptions as established under this clause.

The companion piece to this requirement was, and is, found in s.170(1) (7) of the Act, which imposes on each school board the responsibility to 'provide, or enter into an agreement with another board to provide, in accordance with the regulations, special education programs and special education services for its exceptional pupils.'

Bill 82 denied only one exceptionality, the 'trainable retarded.' It was left to the minister under s.8 (3)(b) to define the other categories of exceptionalities. *Bill 82* also incorporated into the *Education Act* a requirement that each school board maintain classes or schools for 'trainable retarded' pupils or enter into contracts with other school boards to purchase those services for such students.

Bill 82 also established the concept of the 'hard to serve pupil': when a student was determined by the school board to be unable to profit from instruction offered by the school board due to a mental disability or a mental and one or more physical disabilities, the school board could find the student to be 'hard to serve.' When a student was declared to be hard to serve, the school board was obliged to assist the parents to obtain a suitable placement for the student and the province was required to pay for the placement.[14]

The requirement that each school board have a Special Education Advisory Committee (SEAC), and the composition of that committee was also mandated by *Bill 82*. The purpose of the SEAC, to be comprised of trustees and representatives of parent advocacy groups for children with exceptionalities, was to give parents of exceptional pupils, through their representatives, the opportunity to provide input into the special education plans of the school board.[15]

While *Bill 82* set out the broad legislative framework of special education, regulations filled in the administrative details. School boards were required by regulation to phase in special education over a five-year period, concluding in the 1985–86 school year.[16] Following the phase in period, each school board would be required to maintain a special education plan setting out the methods by which the school board would meet its obligations under s.170(1)(7). This plan would be subject to review annually by the school board and would be submitted to the minister for review whenever the school board made an amendment to the plan or at least every second year. The minister was given the power, by regulation, to direct amendments to special education plans. These obligations continue today.[17]

The procedures for implementing special education for exceptional students were set out in a regulation that required every school board to establish at least one Identification Placement and Review Committee (IPRC) to identify exceptional pupils and determine their placements. The regulation set out what was to be considered by the IPRC in its process and outlined a process for parents to appeal the IPRC's decisions to an ad hoc Special Education Appeal Board, which was given the power to make recommendations to the school board on whether or not to accept the IPRC's decision.[18]

Beyond the legislative framework and the accompanying regulations, the government's primary directive to school boards on how to implement special education was provided in the form of a 'Handbook' – initially the *Special Education Handbook, 1982*,[19] which was replaced by the *Special Education Handbook, 1984*.[20] The handbooks directed school boards to provide 'a full spectrum of educational settings' (also referred to as a 'range of placements') 'with a focus of returning the student into the regular classroom as possible or achieve success in a specialized setting.'[21] This was in keeping with pedagogical theory based on the Cascade Model[22] of placement, which provided that exceptional students who required a more intensive educational setting than could be afforded in a regular class would be removed from the regular class setting no more than was necessary to meet the students' needs; further, the goal of the removal was to provide these students with what they needed in order to move them back into the regular class as soon as possible.

The Subsequent Amendments

The legislative and regulatory regime of special education described above continued into the 1990s before any changes were made. *Bill 4* in 1993 introduced the first significant amendment to the special education provisions in the *Education Act*[23] by repealing the 'Hard to Serve' and 'Trainable Mentally Retarded' provisions.

The explanation given by the government to the Legislature's Standing Committee on Education for the removal of the 'Hard to Serve' provision was that it had been included in the legislation as a 'safety net' because it was not known whether school boards would be able to provide education for some students who needed health care treatments. By 1993, however, the Ministry of Education was of the view that special education had become a well developed and integral part of Ontario's education system and that appropriate placements were now available for all students. No suggestion was made to the Special Committee that the removal was driven by any constitutional or human rights imperative.[24]

There is no question, however, that the removal of the 'Trainable Mentally Retarded' provisions was driven, at least in part, by constitutional (i.e., s.15) considerations, as the report of the subcommittee makes clear. By 1993, the term 'trainable retarded' had become unacceptable to both parents and the education community. More importantly, the 'Trainable Mentally Retarded' provisions were perceived as limiting the placements for these students and limiting their integration into regular classes. Although such students were regularly being placed into regular classes at this point, at least in Kindergarten and the early grades, the repeal of these provisions removed any perception that the *Education Act* required 'Trainable Mentally Retarded' students only in segregated placements. At the same time the Ministry of Education, reflecting a shift in direction, changed the name of the exceptionality from 'Trainable Retarded' to 'Developmental Disability' pursuant to s.8(3)(b) of the *Education Act, 1990*.

The next amendments occurred in 1997 as part of the otherwise controversial *Education Quality Improvement Act (Bill 160)*. [25] Amendments to special education had been long anticipated by the education community, but the special education amendments of 1997 did not result in any major changes. *Bill 160* removed the legislative requirement that parents obtain leave from the Special Education Tribunal to be able to appeal to a regional special education tribunal. In fact, this requirement had long before proved to be largely superfluous, because the tribunal had only twice in its history denied leave to appeal, and school boards regularly waived the requirement that parents obtain leave, with the result that most cases proceeded directly to a hearing. *Bill 160* also eliminated regional tribunals and designated the Special Education Tribunal as the final level of appeal by parents. These amendments were not 'driven' by either s.15 of the *Charter* or by the *Code*, but by a desire to speed up an appeal process that was being criticized by parents for being too lengthy. The other amendment made at this time was to remove from the *Education Act* the provision that defined the composition of SEACs and to place this provision into a regulation.[26] This change served the purpose only of permitting the government to change the composition of SEACs without the need to amend the statute; it in no way arose from either s.15 or the *Code*.

The last major amendment to Ontario's special education framework occurred in 1998, with the promulgation of the *Identification and Placement of Exceptional Pupils Regulation*.[27] The new regulation outlined, in clearer terms than its predecessor, the composition and responsibilities of IPRCs and SEACs, but did not substantially change the mandates or procedures to be followed by either body. Section 16 of the *Exceptional Pupils Regulation* clarified that IPRCs could not make 'decisions' on special education programs or special education services to be provided to a student and that parents could not appeal special education programs or special education services. However, at the same time, the new regulation provided that IPRCs could make recommendations on services and programs and would have to do so upon parental request.

The new regulation also extended parental rights in the identification and placement process by giving to parents the right to be present during all IPRC discussions, including decision-making, respecting their child. The regulation empowered pupils aged 16 years or older by giving them the same rights as their parents to be present and participate fully in IPRC meetings. The regulation also included a requirement that each school board create a parent guide on special education to be given to every parent whose child was referred to an IPRC.

With the possible exception of the extension of rights to students aged 16 or older, the changes reviewed above seem unconnected to s.15. Rather, they were more likely a response to parent lobbying for a greater say in the special education process.

One new provision in the *Exceptional Pupils Regulation*[28] made clear that students who had yet to be identified as exceptional were to be provided with programs and services appropriate to their apparent strengths and needs pending a decision of the IPRC. Section 9 makes clear that principals do not have to wait for IPRC decisions to start providing accommodations to students whose disabilities preclude them from benefiting from the regular curriculum. It is likely that this provision was motivated more by a need to fill the gap created by procedural delays in the special education system than because of s.15 imperatives, but the provision did further s.15 goals by ensuring that accommodation would be provided to a student with disabilities while the student was waiting to be identified.

Finally, the *Exceptional Pupils Regulation* introduced a substantive requirement to be considered by IPRCs (and the board) when making placement decisions. Section 17 provides as follows:

17. (1) When making a placement decision on a referral under section 14, the committee shall, before considering the option of placement in a special education class, consider whether placement in a regular class, with appropriate special education services,
    (a) would meet the pupil's needs; and
    (b) is consistent with parental preferences.
   (2) If, after considering all of the information obtained by it or submitted to it under section 15 that it considers relevant, the committee is satisfied that placement in a regular class would meet the pupil's needs and is consistent with parental preferences, the committee shall decide in favour of placement in a regular class.

This provision was drafted during the course of *Eaton* v. *Brant County Board of Education*,[29] which worked its way through the court system following a lengthy Special Education Tribunal (SET) hearing. *Eaton*, which is discussed below, dealt squarely with the issue of parental rights in determining placement. The promulgation of s.17 occurred after a great deal of pressure had been placed on successive governments by parent groups seeking to give parents more say in their child's placement.

The language of s.17 had been drafted by the Ontario Ministry of Education but not yet promulgated when the Supreme Court of Canada heard the *Eaton* case. This language has been interpreted by some parental advocates and educators as giving parents the right to require that their children be placed in a regular class. However, a careful review of the provision reveals that this interpretation is wrong. Section 17 simply requires that decision-makers take parental preferences into consideration; it does not make those preferences in any way determinative. In the end, the IPRC must make a decision on placement that is appropriate to meet the student's needs, whether in a regular class (which must be considered first) or outside the regular class, regardless of parental wishes. Further, the language in s.17 maintains consistency with the Cascade Model of Placement – that is, a student should be placed outside the regular class only so far as is necessary to enable the student's needs to be met and with the goal of moving the child back to the regular class.

While the wording of s.17 is consistent with the earlier directives that school boards provide a 'range of placements' and follow the Cascade Model when making placements, it is likely that s.17 was included in the new regulation to deal with concerns raised by parent advocacy groups. However, s.17 also incorporates into the regulation a substantive requirement that ensures compliance by the IPRC with s.15 of the *Charter* when making placements; that is, the IPRC must consider the mainstream placement and accommodations that can be made in that setting first but must, in the end, make a determination based on the needs of the individual pupil.

No other changes of significance have been made to the legislative or regulatory regime governing the special education system since the *Exceptional Pupils Regulation* was introduced. There have, however, been a number of directives to school boards issued by the Ministry of Education on issues such as the contents of special education plans and the individual education plans required for each exceptional student. These directives are clearly intended to provide more consistency across the province and do not appear in discernable way to motivated by equity laws.

It should be noted that no court action has been commenced to date that suggests that the general framework established under *Bill 82*, which is still in place, contravenes s.15 of the *Charter* or the *Human Rights Code*. *Bill 82* established a system where students whose disabilities preclude them from accessing the regular curriculum in the same way as non-disabled students have their needs identified and assessed and are provided with special education placements, programs, and services designed to provide them with the same opportunities of reaching their maximum potential as are provided to non-disabled students. This is precisely what s.15 of the *Charter* requires.

Special Education Litigation under the *Charter*

To determine whether s.15 has influenced the development of special education litigation, it is important first to understand how s.15 relates to special education laws.

The equality guarantee set out in s.15 was designed to preclude the creation of laws that have the effect of treating certain groups differently based on unsupportable and, from a societal basis, unacceptable distinctions such as those enumerated in s.15(1). Section 15 also prohibits the application of any law in a way that gives rise to unequal treatment based on discriminatory grounds that are unacceptable to our society.

In *Eaton,* the Supreme Court of Canada has determined, under a s.15 analysis, that special education is the necessary modification of the education system required to ensure that students with disabilities are not discriminated against. Without special education, students whose disabilities prevent them from accessing or benefiting from the regular curriculum presented to other students do not have the same opportunity that the curriculum is designed to provide to other students to reach their maximum potential. Accordingly, it is the inclusion of special education provisions in education legislation and the application of these provisions to ensure that students with disabilities have the same opportunity to benefit from education as their non-disabled peers, which saves education legislation from violating s.15 of the *Charter* in respect of students with disabilities.

To the extent that special education provides differential treatment for students with disabilities and sometimes requires that they receive their education outside the regular classroom, the Supreme Court of Canada has also recognized that this may be part of providing equal treatment to those students.[30]

The jurisprudence which has developed around s.15 has made clear that a law[31] will not violate s.15 simply because it makes a distinction between definable groups based on an enumerated or comparable ground. Indeed, legislative classifications or distinctions have been found to be necessary for the governance of modern society. Consequently, the courts have found that s.15 was not intended to eliminate all distinctions in law, but only those that are unjustifiably discriminatory.[32] At the same time, the Supreme Court of Canada has recognized the principle that requiring the same treatment for all may have the effect of discriminating against certain groups, and in particular, those with disabilities; for people with disabilities, differential treatment actually may be necessary in order to provide 'equal protection' under the law.[33]

With this analysis in mind, we will review the jurisprudence that has arisen from legal proceedings commenced by parents who argued that government was violating the s.15 rights to equal access to education of their children with disabilities.

In the twenty years since s.15 came into force, remarkably few special education cases have proceeded to the point of judgement, with the result that there are only handful of court decisions dealing with s.15 and special education. *Charter* litigation involving special education has exclusively been initiated by parents of students with disabilities and has focused more on the manner and content of the delivery of special education – that is, on the steps taken to implement special education laws – than on the legitimacy of law itself under the *Charter*. Early *Charter* and human rights litigation on special education focused on the physical location in which the educational program was delivered,[34] while recent and continuing litigation seeks the courts' intervention in determining what is 'appropriate education.'[35]

A consistent theme throughout the court decisions is the question of what deference, if any, should be afforded to school boards and provincial governments in their decisions regarding special education.

In a related decision from Saskatchewan, *Trofimenkoff et al v. Saskatchewan (Minister of Education)*,[36] the Saskatchewan Court of Appeal examined the government's decision to close a provincial school for the deaf, which had provided segregated education for hearing impaired students. Parents of children who attended the provincial school opposed the government's decision. The parents' claim included a number of arguments, including an assertion that their children were discriminated against, contrary to s.15 of the *Charter*, under the *Education Act* and

The Education Act Regulations, 1986. However, the Court of Appeal held that there was no violation of the students' s.15 rights because the Saskatchewan *Education Act* imposed an obligation on boards of education to provide and maintain school accommodations, equipment, and facilities necessary and adequate to provide for the educational programs and services of their students, including students with disabilities. The court held that the legislation did not discriminate against students with hearing disabilities and, moreover, that it required boards of education to make special provisions for the education of students with hearing disabilities consistent with s.15 of the *Charter*.

Eaton was the first special education case under the *Charter* to reach the Supreme Court of Canada. In this decision, the Supreme Court considered for the first time under the *Charter* the issue of what is an appropriate educational placement for a student with a disability. In addition, the Court examined the rights of parents to participate in or influence the placement decision.

This case is of particular note for the divergence in approach between the Supreme Court of Canada and the Ontario Court of Appeal in addressing these issues.

The litigation arose out of an appeal of an IPRC decision[37] regarding the placement of a student, Emily Eaton. Emily had no established communication system and had severe developmental delays and physical disabilities as a result of cerebral palsy. After placement in a regular classroom in Kindergarten and Grade 1, an IPRC decided that Emily should be placed in a self-contained special education classroom.

Emily's parents sought her continued placement in a regular classroom and based their arguments on the principles of equality under both the Ontario *Human Rights Code* and the *Charter*. They argued that a placement outside the regular classroom discriminated against Emily on the basis of her disability and violated her rights under the *Charter*. By the time the appeal was heard by the Special Education Tribunal,[38] Emily's Grade 2 year in the regular class had concluded. The tribunal heard evidence that Emily frequently fell asleep in class, or screamed in a manner that disrupted the class and resulted in her removal from class to spend time 'walking' up and down the hall way with her educational assistant (EA), which Emily enjoyed. The tribunal also heard that Emily tended to 'mouth' any small items that she could reach, making it was necessary for the EA be very close to her at all times, and that the other students had begun to address the EA instead of Emily. The Special Education Tribunal found that this all had the impact of 'isolating' Emily in her 'inclusive' placement. The tribunal stated that it had considered what would meet Emily's best interests educationally and determined that she should be placed in the self-contained class-room (where there would be opportunities for inclusion provided).

Emily's parents applied for judicial review of the tribunal's decision based on a claim that Emily's s.15 rights had been violated because the tribunal's decision placed Emily in a self-contained class rather than in a regular class, which was the parental preference. The Ontario Divisional Court[39], which heard the application for judicial review in the first instance, dismissed the application and found that Emily's s.15 rights had not been violated.

The parents appealed this decision to the Ontario Court of Appeal.[40] The Court of Appeal stated that the normative placement for a student is in the regular class and that the tribunal's decision excluded Emily from the regular class because of her disability. The Court of Appeal held this to be discriminatory based on its view that a student's right to an education begins with the right to be a regular classroom. The Court of Appeal found, however, that if the student's parents consented to a placement outside the regular classroom that this would not violate the *Charter*.

The Court of Appeal held that because Ontario's *Education Act* did not create a 'presumption' in favour of the regular classroom, the *Act* was contrary to s.15 of the *Charter*, stating as follows: 'In short, the *Charter* requires that, regardless of its perceived pedagogical merit, a non-consensual exclusionary placement be recognized as discriminatory and not be resorted to unless alternatives are proven inadequate.'[41]

The board of education appealed to the Supreme Court of Canada, which strongly disagreed with the Court of Appeal. The Supreme Court held that the *Charter* protected the right of students with disabilities to an education, not to be placed in a particular classroom setting.

In so finding, the Supreme Court distinguished between disability and other enumerated grounds, finding that in the case of disability:

> The principal object of certain of the prohibited grounds is the elimination of discrimination by the attribution of untrue characteristics based on stereotypical attitudes relating to immutable conditions such as race or sex. In the case of disability, this is one of the objectives. The other equally important objective seeks to take into account the true characteristics of this group which acts as headwinds to the enjoyment of society's benefits and to accommodate them. Exclusion from the mainstream of society

results from the construction of society based solely on 'mainstream' attributes to which disabled persons will never be able to gain access.
Whether it is the impossibility of success at a written test for a blind person, or the need for ramp access to a library, the discrimination does not lie
in the attribution of untrue characteristics to the disabled individual. The
blind person cannot see and the person in the wheelchair needs a ramp.
Rather it is the failure to make reasonable accommodation, to fine-tune
society so that its structures and assumptions do not result in the relegation and banishment of disabled persons from participation, which results
in discrimination against them ... It is recognition of the actual characteristics, and reasonable accommodation of these characteristics which is the
central purpose of s.15(1) in relation to disability.[42]

This is a critical point when analyzing special education under s.15 of
the *Charter*, since special education is based on the assessment of individual needs for the purpose of providing programs and service that
will address those needs. The Supreme Court continued:

It follows that disability, as a prohibited ground, differs from other enumerated grounds such as race or sex because there is no individual variation
with respect to these grounds. However, with respect to disability, this
ground means vastly different things depending upon the individual and
the context. This produces, among other things, the 'difference dilemma'
referred to by the interveners whereby segregation can be both protective
of equality and violative of equality depending upon the person and the
state of disability. In some cases, special education is a necessary adapta-
tion of the mainstream world which enables some disabled pupils access
to the learning environment they need in order to have an equal opportunity in education. While integration should be recognized as the norm
of general application because of the benefits it generally provides, a presumption in favour of integrated schooling would work to the disadvantage of pupils who require special education in order to achieve equality.
Schools focused on the needs of the blind or deaf and special education for
students with learning disabilities indicate the positive aspects of segregated education placement. Integration can be either a benefit or a burden
depending on whether the individual can profit from the advantages that
integration provides.[43]

The Supreme Court recognized that the key to equal treatment is that
a student with a disability receives the modifications necessary in order

to be afforded an equal opportunity to benefit from education. The Court of Appeal, by focusing on the location of the educational program, had failed to recognize that the value of education is found in the service provided to the student, not where it is provided.

Eaton also confirmed that the standard to be applied by decision-makers in assessing the placement of a student is the best interests of that child. Further, the Supreme Court made clear that while a parent's wishes must be considered, those wishes are not determinative of the special education placement, programs, or services to be provided to a student. The Supreme Court also addressed the approach that must be followed by those responsible for deciding educational placements:

> [T]he decision-making body must further ensure that its determination of the appropriate accommodation for an exceptional child be from a subjective, child-centered perspective, one which attempts to make equality meaningful from the child's point of view as opposed to that of the adults in his or her life. As a means of achieving this aim, it must also determine that the form of accommodation chosen is in the child's best interests. A decision making body must determine whether the integrated settings can be adapted to meet the special needs of an exceptional child. Where this is not possible, that is, where aspects of the integrated setting which cannot be reasonably changed interfere with meeting the child's special needs, the principle of accommodation will require a special placement outside of this setting. For older children and those who are able to communicate their wishes and needs, their own views will play an important role in determination of best interest. For younger children, and those like Emily, who are either incapable of making a choice or have a very limited means of communicating their wishes, the decision maker must make this determination of the basis of other evidence before it.[44]

Subsequently, in *Eldridge* v. *British Columbia (Attorney General)*,[45] a case involving access to medical treatment, the Supreme Court relied on the s.15 analysis it used in *Eaton*. The Supreme Court stated again that in some circumstances, s.15 requires governments to take special measures to ensure that people who are disadvantaged by disabilities are able to benefit equally from government services – to provide different treatment in order to avoid discrimination under s.15 of the *Charter*. In *Eldridge*, the 'group' under consideration was comprised of persons with severe hearing impairments who effectively could communicate only by sign language. The Court held that if a person with a hearing impairment could not access medical services because of an inability to communicate effectively, then sign language interpreters must be provided in hospitals to ensure equal access to medical services.

The requirement under the *Charter* that the special education system focus on individual student needs was confirmed again in *Neiberg (Litigation guardian of)* v. *Simcoe County District School Board*.[46] This decision was the result of a motion for certification of a proposed class action, under the *Class Proceedings Act, 1992*.[47] A class action may only proceed against a defendant or defendants if the court is satisfied that, amongst other things, 'a class proceeding would be the preferable procedure for the resolution of the common issues.'[48] The action in the *Neiberg* case alleged violations of both s.7 and s.15 of the *Charter* in respect of a potential class of seventeen students who had been placed in a particular special education class in a particular school. It was alleged that the *Charter* rights of these students had been infringed when the school board reduced the number of educational assistants in the class, thereby leaving inadequate teaching assistance to meet the needs of the students as outlined in their Individual Education Plans and creating an unsafe physical environment. The plaintiffs sought to have their action certified as a class based on a common issue of alleged systemic negligence by the school board, relying on the IEP of one student as evidence of a 'common issue.'

In deciding whether to certify the action as a class action, the court was not obliged to consider the merits of the action itself, but instead was required to focus on whether the matter was appropriate for a class proceeding. The court held that because special education addresses the individual needs of each student, a finding that the *Charter* had been breached in the case of one student would not mean that the *Charter* had been breached for the rest of the students in the proposed class. A finding in respect of the other students in the proposed class could be made only after an individualized assessment of each student's IEP in order to determine whether the s.15 rights of that particular student had been infringed. Since a finding of a breach of the *Charter* in the case of one student would not mean that the reduction in the number of educational assistants was a breach of the *Charter* for all students in the proposed class, there was no common issue to be tried. As a result, in declining to certify the matter as a class action, the court confirmed that the application of s.15 of the *Charter* to special education must occur on an individual basis and not a group basis.

The decision of the Saskatchewan Court of Queen's Bench in *Concerned Parents for Children with Learning Disabilities Inc.* v. *Saskatchewan (Minister of Education)*[49] dealt with the question of whether a student with a disability has a constitutional entitlement under s.15 of the *Charter* to specific 'appropriate special education services.' This case was initiated by parents who were seeking the continuation of a segregated special education placement in which a specific program for students with learning disabilities called the 'Carleton Connection' would be delivered. The placement had been provided for a short time on an experimental basis only. When no decision was made to continue the placement or the program, the parents argued that their children were discriminated against contrary to s.15 of the *Charter* by the elimination of this placement, which they believed was necessary in order to provide an appropriate education for their children.

In this case, the defendant (the Ministry of Education) brought a motion to strike the statement of claim for failing to disclose a reasonable cause of action. The ministry asserted that there was an honest difference of opinion between the parties on the most appropriate way to educate the students involved and that, as a result, the court should decline to review the merits of what was discretionary decision on the part of a school board to eliminate the placement and program in question. The court dismissed the defendant's motion and held that the defendant's argument would fail at trial if the plaintiffs could establish, through expert evidence, that the special educational program established by the board of education was ineffective in comparison to the program they were advocating. This case underlined that courts will consider s.15 challenges made by parents to school board decisions on placements, programs and services provided (or not provided) to students with disabilities.

Subsequently, a large group of Ontario parents of children with autism commenced a s.15 action seeking to require the government to continue Applied Behavourial Analysis (ABA) or Intensive Behavourial Intervention (IBI) therapy for their children. This is one of the most controversial issues confronting special educators and school boards today – whether school boards should be responsible for providing ABA/IBI to students with autism.

IBI therapy is an intensive therapy that is delivered under the supervision of a psychologist by a trained therapist. The therapy is generally delivered one on one with the therapist working directly with the child and is delivered by way of discrete trials in groups of ten. The child is rewarded when he or she provides the correct response. The therapy is not effective for all children, and research has shown the therapy to have the best results if started between the ages of 2 and 5 years and to be less effective after 6 years of age. Generally, IBI has not been provided to students in Ontario schools.

Recently, parents have initiated a surge of litigation in an effort to establish the right of students with autism to receive ABA/IBI through the enforcement of *Charter* principles and values. This litigation has taken the form of special education appeals, human rights complaints, and *Charter* litigation. An unprecedented number of cases have gone before the courts in the past five years either seeking access to ABA/IBI or the continuation of ABA/IBI services for autistic children, resulting in several important decisions recently on the issue of whether the *Charter* requires that students with autism must be provided with ABA/IBI therapy by school boards.

Although the Supreme Court of Canada's decision in *Auton (Guardian ad litem of)* v. *British Columbia (Attorney General)*[50] did not deal with education, the principles discussed in it are important. The case arose in British Columbia, where the provincial government's health care ministry had decided to fund programs providing ABA/IBI to some autistic children up until the age of six. Parents sought, through litigation, based on s.15 of the *Charter*, to oblige the province to provide ABA/IBI therapy to all children with autism, with no age limit. Although the parents were successful at trial and at the first level of appeal, the Supreme Court of Canada found that the limited manner in which the province chose to provide the therapy to children with autism did not violate s.15 of the *Charter*. The Supreme Court held that there was no obligation for the province to fund IBI as part of its health care system, because there is no obligation on government to pay for any particular medical service. Within the context of s.15, government is free to choose which, if any, 'special programs' it will provide to persons with disabilities to ameliorate the hardships imposed on them because of their disability.

Although *Auton* makes clear that government may choose what services it will provide to its citizens, cases such as *Eaton* and *Eldridge* establish that once government does decide to provide a service, that service must be delivered in accordance with the principles of s.15 of the *Charter* – that is, the service must be provided without discrimination.

The Ontario Government had similarly decided to establish a program to provide IBI therapy to children aged 2 to 6 years. In *Wynberg and Deskin* v. *Her Majesty the Queen in the Right of Ontario*,[51] the parents of thirty-five children who either had not been able to access the program or who had 'aged out' of the program brought a *Charter* action against the Ontario government. Using similar arguments to those in *Auton*, the parents claimed that the failure to provide ABA/IBI therapy as a medical service to their autistic children violated their children's s.15 rights. However, the Wynberg plaintiffs raised an additional argument under s.15 pertaining to education; they argued that the government, having enacted the *Education Act* to establish a framework for the provision of free public education to all school-aged children, must ensure that the education services provided are accessible to all children. They argued that without ABA/IBI therapy, which they claimed was also a special education program or service, their children could not access education and receive equal treatment in the provision of educational services.

In order for the parent's argument to be upheld, the court had to find not only that IBI was a special education program or service but also that it was appropriate for the children in question and that the failure to provide the therapy to them was discriminatory under s 15 of the *Charter*.

Despite a paucity of evidence from educators or educational psychologists (only clinical psychologists testified during the hearing), and despite the findings of the Ontario Special Education Tribunal that IBI is a medical therapy and not education or a special education program or service,[52] the trial judge in *Wynberg* found that IBI is a special education service. The trial judge found further that without IBI therapy children with autism could not access the opportunity to learn.[53] She found, therefore, that the government's failure to provide IBI as a special education service resulted in the creation of systemic barriers for children with autism in their ability to access learning.[54] The trial judge concluded that the failure of the government, through the minister of education, to ensure the availability of IBI as a 'special education program' or 'special education service,' was a violation of the s.15 *Charter* rights of the children involved in the litigation. She also found that the failure of the Ontario government to fund IBI therapy as a medical service to all children with autism over the age of 6 years contravened s.15 of the *Charter*.

The Ontario government successfully appealed the *Wynberg* decision to the Ontario Court of Appeal. The Court of Appeal applied the Supreme Court of Canada's reasoning in *Auton* in overturning the trial judge's decision that the government had an obligation to provide ABA/IBI therapy as a medical service to all children with autism. On the education argument, the Court of Appeal found that there was insufficient evidence on which the trial judge could conclude that ABA/IBI therapy could be delivered in the public school system; further, there was no evidence about the effectiveness of existing programs in the public school system for autistic students, so that the trial judge should not have concluded that ABA/IBI is the only effective way students with autism can access education. Moreover, there was insufficient evidence about programming provided to other students to permit the trial judge to conclude, as she did, that autistic students were treated differently from other exceptional students. Accordingly, this part of the decision was overturned due to lack of evidence. The parents subsequently applied for leave to appeal this decision to the Supreme Court of Canada, but the application was dismissed.[55]

Following the trial judge's decision in *Wynberg*, but prior to the decision of the Court of Appeal, the Ontario Superior Court delivered a decision[56] in an application for the judicial review of the Ontario Special Education Tribunal's decision in *Clough*. In *Clough*, the tribunal found that IBI is not 'education' or a 'special education service' but is a form of medical therapy delivered by a therapist under the supervision of a clinical psychologist. The tribunal also found that it had no jurisdiction to order a school board to provide medical therapy to students. The Superior Court held that it was not unreasonable for the tribunal to conclude that IBI was a medical treatment and was not education. The Superior Court declined either to follow or take any guidance from the *Wynberg* trial decision in its deliberations and dismissed the application for judicial review.

At the time of writing this chapter, no court has made a conclusive determination that ABA/IBI is either a special education program or service. However, we can expect that at some point the issue will be ruled on by the Supreme Court of Canada, whether in the *Wynberg* case or another case, unless the Court is of the view that the principles set out in the *Auton* decision adequately address the matter.

Conclusion

It is clear that s.15 of the *Charter* has had little influence on the development of the legislative framework for the delivery of special education in jurisdictions like Ontario, where the system was put into place prior to 1985. The pedagogical concepts that underlie the special education system were well accepted by educators long before s.15 came into force. The greater impact of s.15 on special education has been to provide a vehicle through which parents can challenge school board and government decisions on the programs and services to be provided to exceptional students.

As for the future, we can anticipate that parents of children with disabilities will continue to use s.15 actions to obtain new and different programs and services outside the pedagogical norm for their children. Consequently, such s.15 *Charter* litigation may turn courts into a forum for 'debating' the merits of new pedagogical approaches, programs, and services as parents seek to enforce the equality rights of their children.

4 Equity, Equality of Opportunity, Freedom of Religion, Private School Funding, and the *Charter*

JERRY PAQUETTE

If the title of this chapter sounds imposingly – or foolishly – 'omnibus,' I share your misgivings. It is the kind of sweeping, ostensibly unfocused title, or 'problem statement,' that, over my career as professor, I have insisted more than a few graduate students abandon. Still, the time has come to critique some important threads in the growing Canadian literature on public funding of private schools. The principal threads are questions of educational equity and equality of opportunity in light of the *Canadian Charter of Rights and Freedoms*,[1] freedom of religion, and public funding of private schools. I have already dealt with these issues at length in several earlier pieces, in particular, equity problems inherent in the most common forms of public support for private schools,[2] the question of parental choice and its relationship to the fundamental rights and dignity of parenthood,[3] and potential *Charter* impediments to the most common forms of public funding of private schools.[4] What I have not done to date, and what I now propose to do is to integrate the freedom of religion debate into my framework of reasoning on the overarching questions of equity and equality of opportunity. In doing so, I hope to present a nuanced view of the freedom of religion issues taking account of the concerns and fears of those who advocate public funding of private schools including religious schools.

First, a brief review seems appropriate on the current 'state of play' in Canada. British Columbia, Alberta, Saskatchewan, Manitoba, and Quebec currently provide funding for private schools under a variety of voucher-like arrangements.[5] These schemes differ greatly but what they all share is a requirement that parents 'top up' the tuition benefits the schemes provide to take advantage of those benefits. This requirement arises because the annual per pupil amounts available from these schemes are invariably substantially less than the annual tuition and fee costs of attendance in eligible private schools.

Regarding the religion in education issues, Smith and Foster[6] review the current state of practice and jurisprudence in the area and propose a new framework purportedly more respectful of *Charter* (notably s.15) principles in Canada's new multicultural, multireligious reality than current policy and jurisprudence. On the other side of the religion in education debate, the most notable protagonist is Fahmy, who insists that the courts, and in particular the Supreme Court of Canada, 'got it wrong' on the question of provincial obligation to fund private religious schools. Building on a broad spectrum of case law, Fahmy[7] argues the difficult position that, notwithstanding *Adler* v. *Ontario*,[8] provinces ultimately do have a positive obligation under the *Charter* to fund private religious schools.

In the debate on public funding of private schooling, I have argued that provinces violate s.15 equality rights when they use approaches to subsidizing private school costs that require parents to 'top up' benefit amounts to send their children to eligible private schools. I extend that argument here and say that whether or not the schools in question are religious matters little. Nonetheless, I share some of the fundamental concerns that motivate those who continue to work for government funding of religious private schools. I do not, however, have any 'silver bullet' solutions to resolve the conflicting concerns and rights claims at work in this much-contested policy domain.

In this chapter, I first review briefly the broad equity argument against 'typical' approaches to injecting public funds into private schooling. Second, I summarize the principal elements of potential *Charter* arguments against these approaches. Third, I scrutinize critically and in light of the first two considerations, the arguments, both philosophical and *Charter*-based, in favour of public funding of private schools, and, particularly, of private religious schools. Finally, I highlight what I consider the most troubling aspects of a monolithic secular public school system.

Ethical Argument against 'Typical' Approaches to Public Funding of Private Schooling

First, there is nothing *intrinsically* unethical about public funding of private schooling, although I recognize that Chitty[9] is correct that private schools become more like public schools roughly in proportion to their dependence on the public purse. No moral or ethical impediment to public funding of private schooling exists, to my mind, so long as *all* parents have an equal opportunity to benefit from such funding! This ethical axiom, of course, is not a de facto or covert argument in favour of public funding of private schools, but simply an observation that horizontal equity and fundamental fairness requires that some parents not be excluded from eligibility for such funding because of 'morally irrelevant'[10] characteristics such as race, ethnicity, religion, wealth, or income. Why, in any case, might policy-makers want to spend public resources on private education – and why have states, provinces, and nations been particularly eager to do so in recent years?

Rationale for Committing Public Resources to Private Schools

The classic rationale for committing public resources to private schools rests on the proposition that private schooling is superior to public schooling, at least more effective in achieving valued academic and social goals, and often, the argument goes, more efficient as well. In addition, parental choice in education is viewed as both a good in the general philosophical sense and a fundamental parental right. In general, proponents of public funding of private schooling claim that parental choice of schools is the sole means for parents, especially poor parents trapped in the catchment areas of poor schools, to ensure that their children receive a quality education that conforms to their values and wishes.

Such arguments, of course, are premised on the proposition that, in general and on average, private schools are more effective, and probably more efficient, in fulfiling the valued ends of education, in particular, scholastic achievement and social adjustment. The Achilles heel of this reasoning is that, in general and on average, private schools are neither more efficient nor more effective in delivering valued educational goods.[11] Whether intentionally or coincidentally, public school systems, except in rare open-zoning experiments such as those in Seattle and Boston, use school zoning to deny access to their best and best-resourced schools precisely to students most in need of additional resources to 'catch up' with peers who bring to school substantial initial and ever-increasing advantages in cultural and social capital.

Coons pleads poignantly that not according poor parents choice in selecting the nature of their children's schooling is a denial of their fundamental dignity as parents.[12] This argument seems particularly relevant in Canada given the recent attention to denial of basic human dignity as potential discrimination under s.15 of the *Charter* both by the Supreme Court of Canada in *Law* v. *Canada*[13] and by the Ontario Court of Appeal in *Falkiner* v. *Ontario (Ministry of Community and Social Services)*.[14] This position is congruent with the parents' 'right' (juridically unenforceable, of course) to choose their child's education as enunciated in s. 3 of Article 26 the United Nations *Universal Declaration of Human Rights*.

My response to these rationales for public funding of private schools has taken the following shape. First, evidence is lacking that private schooling is, in general and on average, more efficient or effective than public schooling, and second, the most promising remedy to elitism within public education is open zoning coupled with good information to parents about the choices available to them and the probable impacts of those choices on their children.

I have summarized my position as follows:

- In short, I do not see public funding of private schools as a necessary, or even a promising, way to augment the educational and life chances of society's most disadvantaged children. I do, however, believe that choice within the public sector can be an efficacious way of augmenting both for poor children from educationally disadvantaged families – but only if and when state, provincial, and national legislators have the courage to insist on the following:
- Open school zoning with transportation (I think Seattle had it right here!)
- Interdiction of admission criteria that serve as a proxy for socio-economic status (yes, this means that schools of the arts, for instance, would have to admit their fair share of children who haven't had the luxury of music or dance or whatever from the earliest age)
- Extensive and detailed information programs to parents on choices available to them and the consequences of those choices for their children (this is where the Boston model shines, in my view – and, although I agree with those who like Coons, insist that school choice 'savvy' is not 'occult' knowledge, I don't think one can count on osmosis for all parents, or even an overwhelming majority of them, to exercise school choice in the best interests of their children)
- Stringent limitations on the generation and use of private resources by public schools
- A common core curriculum that ensures that each child, regardless of the educational choices of his or her parents, can participate in the broader intellectual and civic life of her or his society – and not just in some narrow enclave within it.[15]

The Ethics of Public Funds to Private Schools

If resources were not scarce and rationed by governments, all parents would be able to access resources to send their children to the school of their choice. Equity concerns related to ability to pay would disappear. Resources are scarce and contested, of course, and governments must therefore ration funding both for private and public schools, or anything else. Ultimately, the public treasury is but one pot – and it is far from bottomless. The ethical problem with public funding for private schools, then, arises from the necessity to ration such support. Two basic methods of rationing exist – limit the amount available per pupil by placing a ceiling or cap on that amount or limit the number of students receiving support, or some combination of the two.

Three generic approaches exist to channelling public funds to private schools, vouchers, tax credits (either refundable or non-refundable), and placement schemes. Possible variations and combinations of these are limitless but these are the three basic available mechanisms. Vouchers and tax credits ration available public funding support by setting a fixed, variable, or multilevel (for different types of school) per pupil limit on support. Placement schemes, by contrast, ration by limiting the number of places or seats in private schools that government will fund. Any of these mechanisms can be combined with means testing to reduce benefits to parents more able to pay. Despite perennial discussion, moreover, no clear winner has emerged in the vouchers versus tax credit debate since both instruments seem to have much the same impact on the participation behaviour of potential beneficiaries (both parents and schools).

Ethically, a major difference exists between placement schemes, and vouchers and tax credits. For parents to access voucher or tax credit benefits, they must be able to contribute to the costs of private school tuition and fees because vouchers and tax credits are invariably set at per pupil amounts considerably less than the actual cost of sending a child to a private school – even a fairly modestly priced one. Parents, therefore, must have the financial resources to 'top up' the voucher or tax credit amount. They will also have to provide transportation to the school out of their own resources.

Not all parents are able to 'top up.' Some do, of course, at very high relative opportunity costs, sacrificing all manner of things they value greatly to do so, but the point is these parents are still 'able' to pay tuition and fee costs (and usually transportation as well). Many parents simply cannot do so, and as a result, the benefits provided by a voucher or tax credit scheme are simply out of their reach. The consequence is that poor parents are unable to access a benefit provided for in law and paid for from taxes that all citizens, even the poorest, must pay (even the poorest parents, after all, must pay consumption taxes such as provincial sales taxes).

Potential *Charter* Objections to Public Funding for Private Schooling

De facto, this inability to benefit from vouchers or tax credits is unequal benefit from the law. Whether it would violate s.15 of the *Charter*, depends on whether courts would be willing to read parental poverty into s.15 as an 'analogous' ground of prohibited discrimination and thus extend the logic of *Andrews* v. *Law Society of British Columbia*,[16] *Egan* v. *Canada*,[17] and *Vriend* v. *Alberta*.[18] At first blush, the prospects of such extension seem remote. Canadian public policy has many examples of infrastructure and services all supported through taxation but that only those considerably the poverty line are likely to enjoy except very infrequently and mostly very indirectly – for example, provincial and national parks, airports, highway systems, inter alia; much in the same way that poor parents might be said to 'enjoy' some 'benefit' from private schools they cannot afford to patronize. Courts, moreover, have been loath to read economic rights into s.15.

Yet, the courts have recently moved substantially in the direction of extending s.15 analogous grounds into an area highly suggestive of the plight of poor parents denied access to voucher or tax credit programs by virtue of their lack of wealth and income. In *Law*,[19] Iacobucci J articulated a new purposive and contextual approach to discrimination analysis. This three-pronged discrimination test asks the following three questions:

1 Does the impugned law (a) draw a formal distinction between the claimant and others on the basis of one or more personal characteristics, or (b) fail to take into account the claimant's already disadvantaged position within Canadian society resulting in substantively differential treatment between the claimant and others on the basis of one or more personal characteristics?
2 Is the claimant subject to differential treatment based on one or more enumerated and analogous grounds?
3 Does the differential treatment discriminate, by imposing a burden upon or withholding a benefit from the claimant in a manner which reflects the stereotypical application of presumed group or personal

characteristics, or which otherwise has the effect of perpetuating or promoting the view that the individual is less capable or worthy of recognition or value as a human being or as a member of Canadian society, equally deserving of concern, respect, and consideration?

For provinces to increase parental choice only for parents who can afford to supplement the amount provided 'draw[s] formal distinctions' between the children of poor parents and those of more financially secure parents. Such distinctions, moreover, are based precisely on income and wealth and 'fail to take into account' the already disadvantaged position within Canadian society of poor children, a disadvantage variously prejudicial to their intellectual and social development. Moreover, denying funding for private schooling to poor children because their parents cannot afford to supplement the available per pupil government subsidy perpetuates the view that poor children (and their parents) are 'less capable or worthy of recognition or value as ... human being[s] or as ... member[s] of Canadian society' than wealthier children and parents who are allowed access to such funding.

The Ontario Court of Appeal's recent ruling in *Falkiner*[20] extends the *Law* logic even further towards recognizing poverty as a potential ground for analogous discrimination in regard to public funding of private schooling. First, *Falkiner* recognized receiving social assistance as an analogous ground of prohibited discrimination under s.15. Second, *Falkiner* consolidated, extended, and broadened analysis of ways in which adverse effect discrimination can injure fundamental human dignity. Even as the court acknowledged the 'controversial' nature of recognizing the respondents' status as welfare recipients as an analogous ground under s.15, 'primarily because of concerns about singling out the economically disadvantaged for *Charter* protection,'[21] its application of the *Law* framework led the court to do precisely that in *Falkiner*. Writing for a unanimous court (Osborne ACJO did not participate), Laskin JA argued that recognizing welfare recipient status as a ground of discrimination 'would further the purpose of s.15, the protection of human dignity,' ultimately the 'main question' to be decided:[22] 'The nature of the group and Canadian society's treatment of that group must be considered. Relevant factors arguing for recognition include the group's historical disadvantage, lack of political power and vulnerability to having its interest disregarded.'[23]

If single mothers on welfare constitute a group whose human dignity is offended by legislation or regulations that discriminate against them in regard to their welfare entitlement, surely poor children from poor families would be entitled to protection against educational vouchers or tax credits that discriminate against them because of their parents' (or parent's) lack of wealth and income. After all, being a child from a poor family means starting school with a serious educational handicap even if the 'handicap' is not sufficient to trigger identification as a special-needs student.

To reach its conclusion in *Falkiner*, the court had to broaden substantially the concept of 'immutability.' Specifically, the court rejected the idea that 'immutable' implied a characteristic that can never be changed (such as race, for instance). Following the lead of the Supreme Court in *Corbiere* v. *Canada (Minister of Indian and Northern Affairs)*,[24] *Granovsky* v. *Canada (Minister of Employment and Immigration)*,[25] and *Andrews*, the court in *Falkiner* concluded that 'a characteristic that is difficult to change, that the government has no legitimate interest in expecting us to change, that can be changed only at great personal cost or that can be changed only after a significant period of time may be recognized as an analogous ground.'[26] The court acknowledged the extreme difficulty, if not impossibility, for a single mother in the circumstances of the plaintiff to extricate herself from welfare. How much more difficult or impossible is it for a poor child to extricate herself from the disadvantages of being born into a poor family!

Futhermore, the court also stipulated that 'homogeneity' 'has never been a requirement for recognizing an analogous ground.'[27] Welfare parents need not be homogeneous either in terms of grounds of discrimination prohibited by s.15 or in any other way to be protected from discrimination based on their status as welfare recipients. Presumably poor children from poor families would be entitled to similar protection against discrimination in regard to public funding for private schooling.

The court used the final step in the *Law* analysis to conclude that the differential treatment in question (reduction of welfare benefits because a change in the definition of 'spouse' contained in a regulation rendered virtually all co-residents 'spouses' for welfare purposes) did indeed 're-flect ... and reinforce ... existing disadvantages, stereotypes and prejudice'[28] and was not saved because it was designed to ameliorate the overall equity of provision of welfare benefits across the province and system. The same logic suggests that government funding of private schooling could not be saved because it makes private school attendance possible for some children if, at the same time, poor children are excluded (in effect if not in intent) from such benefits simply because they are poor.

The court held that the impugned ground of discrimination must correspond to the actual needs, capacity, or circumstances of the claimant, and concluded in *Falkiner* that exclusion from or reduction in welfare benefits struck at the most basic human needs of the respondents,[29] the need for food, clothing, and basic necessities for single welfare mothers capriciously redefined by regulation as 'spouses.' Surely in the realities of contemporary Canada, the need for high-quality education is no less an 'actual need' of all children than is their need for food, lodging, and clothing. On the contrary, the 'circumstances' of poor children are such that, in general, they find themselves in need of compensatory educational programming to 'catch up' to children from more favoured circumstances who bring to school an abundance of the cultural capital reinforced and rewarded by schools.[30]

With respect to the question of dignity, the court asked whether or not 'the nature and scope of the interests affected by the challenged law go to the core of human dignity,' and responded that, indeed, enforcing the new definition of 'spouse' led to an odious series of humiliating and demeaning intrusions into the personal lives of those adversely affected by it.[31] Again citing *Law*, the court found that 'differential treatment' is more likely to be found discriminatory 'where its impact is localized and severe and where it affects interests that go to the core of human dignity.'[32] It found that the impugned definition was localized because it disproportionately impacted women and single mothers and, moreover, 'affected interests that go to the core of human dignity' since it subjected these women to all manner of invasive surveillance and scrutiny and denied or reduced their entitlement to a 'fundamental social institution,' namely, social assistance.[33]

In a striking parallelism, government funding of private school access by vouchers or tax credits requiring parental ability to supplement them, attacks the interests of poor children in a way that goes 'to the core of human dignity.' Whether or not the adverse effect was consciously planned or intended by those who craft the policy, funding mechanisms that require parents to 'top up' government subsidies in order to send their children to a private school communicate to poor children and their parents that, 'unlike children of the better-heeled in society, you are unworthy of government support for this type of educational benefit and education.' Worse still, providing such funding accords private school funding benefits to middle-class children even though making these benefits available inevitably reduces overall funding to publicly supported systems – and hence reduces services and resources available to poor children who have no option to exit publicly funded schools.

Placement schemes generally do not suffer from this fundamental ethical, and in my view, constitutional flaw. Because they generally provide support for the entire cost of enrolment in a medium-cost private school (often subject to a means test, however), very poor parents are not, de facto, excluded or even disadvantaged in terms of their eligibility to avail themselves of such benefits. Rationing is accomplished by limiting the number of available places government will fund. In effect, a lottery mechanism is used to decide which children receive the number of places government decides to fund and which do not.

Placement schemes, of course, do not have a distinguished history of fulfiling Margaret Thatcher's original vision of her own 'Assisted Places Scheme' as a means to give bright, poor children a chance to go to good (much less the best) private schools.[34] Even the Milwaukee experiment, frequently touted as an outstanding example of an assisted places scheme that 'worked' in terms of opening up the putative benefits of private schooling to very disadvantaged children,[35] has generated little evidence of real educational benefit to participants. Despite its structure as a 'natural experiment' where children of parents selected for participation could be directly compared to children of parents who applied but were not selected, the Milwaukee experiment provided no real evidence of superior outcomes for participating children – in large measure because of a very high attrition rate (in itself surely a major cause for doubt about this project as a potential policy prototype).[36]

Of course, various measures intended to make funding mechanisms more 'compensatory,' that is, by targeting disadvantaged students, can help to reduce both ethical and s.15 objections to public funding for private schools. Such measures, however, are inevitably both expensive and controversial. Effective means testing, for example, can require considerable administrative overhead in processing and verification, and setting schedules of eligibility and benefit is certainly a political process. The alternative, of course, preferred frequently by governments, is to forget about targeting altogether, but doing so makes voucher and tax credit schemes in particular eminently assailable in terms of the ethical and constitutional arguments in question here.

At one end of the equity/s.15 spectrum would be fully funded (covering all tuition, fee, and transportation costs) programs specifically targeted on needy students by an effective means test. These would pose few if any ethical or constitutional problems although they are likely to be politically contentious. At the other end of the spectrum

Figure 4.1 Equity and potential s.15 violation consequences of different mechanisms for providing public funding for private schooling.

Fully Funded, Targeted Assisted Places Scheme – Complete Coverage of *All* Costs (including transportation)	No Negative Equity Impacts – Unlikely to Violate S.15 under *Law/Falkiner* Logic

↓

Limited Value Vouchers or Tax-Credits but with Some Compensatory and/or Regulatory Measures	Some Negative Equity Impacts – Very Unclear Constitutional Status under s.15

↓

Limited Value Vouchers and Tax Credits – No Compensatory Provisions	Extreme Negative Equity Impacts – Likely to Violate s.15 under *Law/Falkiner* Logic

would be limited value vouchers and tax credits with no compensatory targeting measures. These are both ethically unacceptable and likely to violate s.15 of the *Charter* following the *Law/Falkiner* logic.

The Debate for and against Public Funding of Private Schooling in Its *Charter* Context

Aside from dubious faith in the superior overall quality of private schooling as compared with public schooling, what are the principal arguments commonly adduced in favour of public funding of private schooling? Coons' recent response[37] to my piece on public funding issues offers a far-reaching and up-to-date (to say nothing of passionate!) template of the main rationales advanced by proponents of state funding of private education. I will summarize and critique as briefly as possible each major point in this response, first, in terms of my view of its strengths and weaknesses as public policy, and then in terms of its relationship, if any, to the s.15 issues I have canvassed in the previous section. Fahmy provides a summary of constitutional arguments in favour of provincial support for religious private schools.[38] These arguments, of course, run squarely contrary to *Adler*, the definitive Supreme Court of Canada decision in the matter, but they are both interesting in their own right and pertinent to the larger debate on state funding for private schools – and the ethics and, in Canada, constitutionality thereof.

Unethical Methods of Providing Government Funding
for Private Schooling Are a Thing of the Past

Coons begins by suggesting that unregulated, untargeted vouchers or tax credits pegged well below the real world cost of private school education are largely 'chimeras,' 'inventions' of my imagination. From his admittedly American perspective he contends, first, that my 'chief bugbear is a largely unregulated form of school vouchers that democratic reformers have consistently damned since choice first surfaced as a hope for have-nots' and then that '[n]o proposal resembling these chimeras has been adopted, and no ballot proposition so conceived has gained approval from more than thirty percent of voters in any state.' Notwithstanding, he subsequently laments two 'universal voucher initiatives' that 'were not properly regulated,' both in California (held by many to be a bellwether of shifts in American educational policy), one in 1993 and one in 2000. More surprisingly still, Coons then goes even further claiming that 'the initiative process has so far been used *exclusively* [emphasis added] to propose unregulated and unpopular market schemes.' He regrets furthermore that 'during critical years in the struggle to get school choice off the ground, libertarian enthusiasm actively and consciously diverted crucial material support from politically promising initiatives that would have included guarantees of access for the poor. These scarce political resources instead became focused upon naked vouchers, producing the result already described; unregulated choice was properly and consistently blitzed at the polls.' On his own evidence, then, 'naked' untargeted, unregulated per-pupil subsidies, at least as a matter of proposed policy, do not seem to be chimerical or passé in the American context.

They are surely not so in the Canadian context. As noted earlier, each of the five provinces that provide funding for private schools does so with some variant of the much maligned but politically much preferred 'naked' voucher.[39] Ontario's short-lived tax credit was, to all intents and purposes, unregulated and untargeted. Quebec offers a particularly trenchant case example in this respect. Historically, Quebec has provided higher per pupil subsidies to elite collèges classiques that have formed generations of Quebec and national leadership than it has to other schools eligible for subsidies. In a masterpiece of regressive funding policy, Quebec provided relatively generous per pupil subsidies for a handful of elite secondary schools – but not, of course, subsidies generous enough to render such schools accessible to all. The official justification for relatively (but, of course, not too) generous funding to such schools was that these schools were 'deemed to be in the public interest,' while those that merited less generous funding, or none at all, were presumably not in the public interest or were less so. A recent provincial commission on education in Quebec, moreover, argued eloquently against all public funding to private schools.[40] Nonetheless, the government of the day elected to continue much as it had done in the past in this regard, even setting funding levels for specific services for each individual school. Naked, indeed regressive, public funding for private schools is no 'chimera' in Canada.

If unregulated, untargeted, even regressive (i.e., tending to benefit differentially financially secure families), non-means-tested, voucher-type subsidies represent the highest level of probability of s.15 violation as argued in the preceding section, then, following the *Law/Falkiner* logic, all five provinces currently funding private schools likely violate s.15 by their method of funding.

Large State-Run Bureaucratized School Systems Are as Discriminatory or More So Than Unregulated, Untargeted Vouchers or Tax Credits

This line of argument seems to translate into the position that 'the devil we know' is as bad as or worse than 'the devil we don't,' so why not give the latter a try at least. A propos, school boards and districts, it has been observed, will often, over time, take from 'have-nots' in order to give more to 'haves.' That tendency arises from the demographic composition of school boards themselves. As elsewhere in the political system, the poor have little voice in the corridors of school board power. On this Coons and I agree. Where we diverge is on an ethical and viable solution!

If school boards (left to themselves) habitually 'conscript' children of the poor to attend second- or third-class schools while providing munificent resources to schools of the best-heeled in society, whether the mechanism is school zoning, magnet schools, countenancing fundraising at levels that greatly advantage the already advantaged, or whatever, could not such actions on the part of school boards be construed as constituting the same kind of insult to the dignity of poor parents and their children, and hence be a species of the same kind of 'analogous discrimination' as state or provincial funding of private schools? Quite possibly, although I doubt that any solution except a political one in this instance is likely. The poor have no resources to fight a long court battle, especially one against school boards with deep pockets for legal defence. The ethical, and constitutionally sound, way out of the dilemma of this 'quality discrimination' is mandatory open zoning with board-provided transportation and interdiction of socioeconomic status (SES) proxies as screening tools for magnet and other particularly 'desirable' schools, not publicly funding private schools, and certainly not publicly funding private schools in the usual limited unregulated, untargeted voucher or tax credit mode. Of course the political conundrum here is, as Coons rightly divines, that those with political power tend to like the situation just as it is – with the 'best schools' in the public sector reserved by zoning restrictions for children of the 'best people.' Open zoning is a tough political sell!

Open School Choice Can End 'Curriculum Bingo' – and Conflict over It

Here I find the argument of Coons and like-minded proponents of state funding for private schools exceptionally incoherent. In Coons' terms, opening up private school access through state funding 'disposes of curriculum bingo,' that is, the 'chronic disuniformity' of 'civic and moral education' which he characterizes as virtually a 'lottery' dependent on a child's 'random' assignment to a particular public school: 'Confronting life's most crucial questions, the answers for the particular child come by the sheer chance of a compulsory assignment to this school instead of the other. It is parental sovereignty alone that can eliminate this randomness by delegating choice of content to a live human decision-maker. Some adult human actually decides that Mary will get the curriculum of this school and not that other one. Here is progress.'[41]

At the same time, however, Coons insists that 'a school that fails in any year to add the quantum of achievement fixed by the state shall become ineligible for further public support, if within three years it does not correct that failure.'[42] Thus schools of choice are to be free from government regulation on the one hand but are to see their funding cut off if they do not conform to state-imposed standards on the other – hardly a consistent policy stance!

The larger claim made here is that parents should be able to choose, and in part at least at public expense, schools that reflect their own moral and civic virtue preferences. This claim is clearly the intersection point with the claims of those who believe, like Fahmy, that the state (read 'province' in Canada), far from having an obligation to refrain from funding religious education, has a positive obligation to do so.

*Government Has an Obligation to Fund Religious Education,
and, in Particular, Religious Private Schools*

Two questions emerge from insistence on a religious element to publicly funded education. First, should public schools be 'colonized' (to use the Dutch term) along religious lines with denominational religious instruction and indoctrination occurring within *nominally* privately operated and governed schools most of which are affiliated with various faith communities?[43] Second, should governments fund private schools with such affiliations through one or the other of the generic funding methods discussed earlier? For my purpose here, each of these questions comes packaged with a constitutional question as well.

For a thoughtful, principled, and detailed review and critical interpretation of the state of Canadian jurisprudence on the first question, should the state provide religious instruction, one can do no better, in my view, than the recent exhaustive examination by Smith and Foster.[44] Not surprisingly, much of their examination of the status quo on the question revolves around the famous s.93 constitutional compromise on religion in education although their proposed framework for a new understanding is centred on *Charter* principles rather than on s.93.

With regard to the s.93 legacy, Smith and Foster observe that '[a]s far as the nature of rights is concerned, s.93 is best described as a 'grandfather clause' maintaining privileges that are 'frozen in time,' as only those rights recognized by law at the time of Union were protected. Contrary to s.93, society cannot be frozen in time.'[45]

Symptomatic, of course, of the fact that society cannot be frozen in time is the nature of s.93, and of parallel provisions in subsequent legislation delineating the terms of adhesion of Manitoba,[46] Alberta,[47] Saskatchewan,[48] and Newfoundland to the Canadian Confederation, as political 'grandfather clauses,' are recent amendments to the Canadian constitution exempting Quebec from the application of s.93 and Newfoundland from provisions of 'Term 17' of the Terms of Union of Newfoundland with Canada[49] regarding educational rights of dissentient religious minorities as they existed respectively at Confederation and at the time of union.

Smith and Foster construct their *Charter*-based framework on the following 'guiding principles' (some parts of each principle not directly relevant to this discussion are omitted as indicated, as are principles 5 and 6, again for the same reason):

1 State regulation of private religious schools does not infringe freedom of religion ...

2 Majoritarian religious exercises in public schools infringe freedom of religion and given that their purpose is religious not secular, are incapable of justification under s.1 [of the *Charter*] ...

3 Legislation that vests in parents the right to 'opt in' to or 'opt out' of religious instruction or religious exercises, as opposed to allowing parents to exercise the child's right on his or her behalf, might be held to infringe the child's human rights as the framework of choice is not based on the child's 'best interest.' Accommodation for those not wishing to participate in religious instruction or exercises where offered may be provided by permitting them to 'opt out' of or, alternatively, to 'opt in' to, such activities; however, Ontario case law suggests that merely allowing persons to opt out is insufficient accommodation.

4 The refusal of the State to provide for denominational schools in the public system, like the non-funding of private religious schools, does not infringe freedom of religion, as this right does not give rise to any positive requirement on the part of public educational authorities ...

7 Public school authorities must provide educational services in an environment that is not polluted by intolerance, in which all students may participate, without discrimination based on religion. Freedom of religion does not provide a shield for hatred; any allegedly *religious* belief that maligns the religious beliefs of others erodes the very basis of this right. The *Canadian Charter* subsumes its own code of values, which includes a *secular* approach to public policy making; however, the scope and nature of this approach remain to be defined.

Smith and Foster's *Charter*-based framework for religion and education, of course, is diametrically opposed to the position Fahmy attempts to stake out. Arguing that the Supreme Court decided incorrectly in *Adler*, Fahmy provides an interpretation of *Charter* principles and judicial precedent intended to prove a positive state obligation to fund religiously based private schools.

Fahmy invokes three major lines of argument to arrive at her conclusion. First, she argues that freedom of religion (guaranteed by s.2 of the *Charter*) is impaired, and in a way that cannot rightly be saved under s.1 of the *Charter*, by failure of the state to support religious private schools financially. Second, she contends that s.27 of the *Charter*, the multicultural interpretation clause, should be used more aggressively as an antidiscrimination mediating (interpretive) principle and that doing so and giving s.27 its proper weight in the balance of judicial decision-making, would have led to a conclusion different from that arrived at in *Adler* on the key question of government obligation to fund religious independent schools. Finally, Fahmy believes that the majority's s.1 analysis in *Adler* was flawed and that the dissenting opinion of Justice L'Heureux-Dubé was much closer to the mark. She specifically cites the following comments of L'Heureux-Dubé in this respect: 'The complete denial of funding is the most excessive impairment possible [of freedom of religion], not one of a range of possible alternatives.' Moreover, in an ironic twist given the central thrust of this chapter, Fahmy notes:

> Based of the evidence, L'Heureux-Dubé J. found that partial funding, as is currently provided outside Ontario, would achieve the objectives of the legislature and infringe equality rights to a lesser degree. In her view, '[p]artial funding would actually further the objective of providing a universally accessible education system and promote the value of religious tolerance in this context where some religious communities cannot be accommodated in the secular system.' Justice L'Heureux-Dubé's dissenting opinion on this issue is both compelling and equally applicable to an alleged violation of s.2(a). That is, the religious freedom of Ontario's religious minorities [*sic*] communities could be impaired to a lesser degree should the government decide to offer partial funding to independent faith-based schools, and, for this reason, the s.2(a) violation cannot be justified in a free and democratic society.'[50]

Funding Arrangements Should Limit Access to Supplementary Funding by Participating Schools

Here Coons equivocates again on an issue with major ethical and, in Canada, potential s.15 implications. It is true that governments can restrict recourse to supplementary private funding (tuition, gifts, and so forth) either by schools participating in a government funding scheme or, as in the Dutch case, by all schools.[51] Reflecting a considerable body of opinion that schools benefiting from public funding should not be free to 'price out' students from families of moderate means, Coons insists that he has in mind a scheme from which 'nobody can be priced out.'

To achieve this end, he suggests that 'the imposition of tuition – "topping up" – beyond the scholarship could be forbidden (as it is in Milwaukee and Cleveland), or the school could be required to means-test any add-on charges.' This solution to 'pricing out,' interdiction of or stringent limitation on tuition above the available state subsidy, is, in fact, precisely the Dutch solution – less one very important additional provision, namely, that no schools in the Netherlands are allowed to exist outside the Dutch state-subsidized system. Coons and many other advocates of government funding of private schools, on the other hand, have no problem with private schools that continue to exist completely outside a state funding scheme and are allowed to do as they please on every crucial 'identity' issue he cites (curriculum, hiring and personnel, discipline, and admissions[52]) as well as on tuition and fees. Oddly though, Coons then proceeds to characterize the possibility that state-subsidized schools might be permitted to raise extra money privately as a 'legitimate question.' In this way the no 'pricing out' policy could easily be circumvented – even as public schools in 'posh' neighbourhoods, as Coons characterizes them, significantly augment their revenues by recourse to fundraising of all sorts, and increasingly even to full-time professional fundraisers.

If, given s.15 of the *Charter*, equality of benefit under the law is the standard by which provincial funding to private schools must be measured in Canada, then government subsidies to private schools, whatever their guise, cannot, in my view, occur, as they manifestly do currently, in the absence of regulation, specifically regulation of supplementary tuition, fees, or 'contributions' required from state-supported students in order to attend subsidized private schools.

School Choice Is Crucial to the Integrity and Responsibility of the Basic Family Unit

Coons and like-minded advocates of state funding of private schools, in a line of reasoning strikingly parallel to *Law* and *Falkiner* in its focus on basic human dignity, insist that in a poor family deprived of meaningful school choice by closed school zoning parents are deprived of their rightful dignity as parents who shape the education of their children. Such parents are, Coons contends in the strongest terms, demeaned in their children's perception of them by being stripped of their rightful role as deciders of their children's education.[53]

School Choice Would Be an Investment in Social Tolerance

This line of argument insists that socially, culturally – and religiously – diverse schools are a better incubator of social tolerance and cohesion than uniform, 'monocultural' public schools. In a cohesively diverse society, knowing deeply our own ethnocultural, philosophical, and religious identity, and our differences from 'the other' can bind us all together, the argument goes: 'There is no greater injury to genuine community than that which results when the poor are conscripted for institutions that the rich are free to abandon. Society best nourishes social trust among all groups when it trusts them with their own children, just as it trusts the well-off. I find Mr Paquette's disdain for "boutique" schools [a term I had used in my original piece] rather odd and surprisingly elitist. The best way to train up children of the poor to think like Nazis is to treat them and their families as unworthy of self-determination while the rich among us are encouraged to repair to Beverly Hills.'[54]

Fahmy runs the same line of argument, albeit in a much more tentative and uncertain way: 'So long as public schools are held out to be neutral, accessible sites which offer all students equal educational opportunity, the government can continue to argue that funding religious schools will jeopardize this crucial role. However, it should not be assumed that because children play together in the schoolyard they will work together respectfully in the workplace. Nor should it be assumed that religious independent schools cannot adopt the role of "multicultural trainer" without fully exploring whether it is possible to require such schools to comply with certain standards of tolerance, and to enforce such compliance.'[55]

On the other side of this issue are those who maintain, with various degrees of stridency and cogency, that schools divided along ethnocultural, philosophical, and religious lines tend, over time, to balkanize society into irreconcilable camps that seek to impose their beliefs, standards, and will on society at large.

Neither, it seems to me, those who believe that schools drawing mainly or exclusively from one ethnocultural or religious social reference group generally promote social cohesion nor those who view all such schools as promoting intolerance and divisiveness have a convincing case here. The truth is likely somewhere in the middle. Some schools serving ethnocultural and religious minorities are likely very good at promoting both respect for 'others' in society and a determination to live in peaceful, positive, and creative cooperation with them. Others are likely not very good at doing so, and some are almost certainly ethnocentric, racist, supremacist, and/or sexist.[56] In any case, public schools can hardly lay claim to an unblemished record in this respect either.

On balance, however, I am inclined to believe that governments ought not to be in the business of actively promoting segmentation of education along ethnocultural and religious lines. That said, the policy of colonizing publicly funded education (and other public services) along religious lines seems to have served the Netherlands well given its own particular circumstances.

The Overarching Principle: Non-Discrimination against the Poor in Allocation of Public Educational Spending Benefits

These debates yield one overarching principle: non-discrimination against the poor in allocation of public educational spending. As I meditated at considerable length on just what it was that separated Coons from me prior to drafting my response to his reply, I came to the conclusion that this was a principle we both fervently believed in, however much we disagreed on promising policy means to that end. It is also, I think, the principle at the root of the s.15 issue once it is passed through the *Law/Falkiner* 'dignity' sieve.

As I have argued in this chapter and at greater length elsewhere,[57] vouchers and tax credits requiring parents to 'top up' their value to pay private school tuition and fees ineluctably exclude parents too poor to spare the money to do so from the benefits they accord to more financially secure parents. All taxpayers, including the poorest of the poor, contribute through consumption taxes to the public coffers from which such subsidies flow. That state of affairs is fundamentally unfair, and given the extraordinary importance of education in shaping the employment, civic participation, aesthetic enjoyment, and just about any other worthwhile aspect of a person's life, ethically unacceptable in a way that using monies from the same public purse to construct and maintain provincial parks or airports simply is not.

Such a state of affairs also invites the same kind of discrimination analysis used by the Supreme Court of Canada in *Law* and by the Ontario Court of Appeal in *Falkiner*. In brief, poor children are an exceptionally vulnerable group within society with few if any means available to escape that membership. Increased access to private schooling is the intended goal and obvious effect of the policy but poor parents cannot access that benefit. Thus the accrued choice benefit is, in effect, accorded only to more financially secure parents, and only through a mechanism that makes access dependent on wealth and income. When these facts are passed through the *Law/Falkiner* logic, a strong case emerges that all existing provincial subsidies to encourage private school choice on the part of parents violate s.15 of the *Charter*.

The fact that some private schools benefiting from such subsidy schemes are religious changes nothing in the essential ethical and *Charter* argument at stake here. Ultimately, in my view, Fahmy fails in her effort to parlay s.2 and s.27 of the *Charter* into a persuasive argument in favour of a positive obligation on the part of the provinces to fund religious schools. Her citation of L'Heureux-Dubé's contention that '[p]artial funding would actually further the objective of providing a universally accessible education system and promote the value of religious tolerance in this context where some religious communities cannot be accommodated in the secular system' is particularly ironic in this respect. It is precisely *partial* funding, after all, that generates differential access to private school funding benefits based on family wealth and income! Fahmy's attempt to justify public funding for private religious schools on the basis of accrued tolerance, moreover, is both surprisingly reserved and unconvincing.

Given the strong probability that five provinces are violating s.15 of the *Charter* by partially funding student attendance in private schools, why has this question not shown up in court? The answer is hardly arcane or surprising. The class of persons discriminated against by such policy is likely the least, or very close to the least, equipped of all groups of persons to mount and sustain a lengthy and costly class action suit, namely, poor children and their parents. Unless some organization with interest, mandate, and resources, takes up the legal cudgel on behalf of poor children and/or parents in this matter (as was the case in *Falkiner*!), provinces will likely continue to provide limited, unregulated, and untargeted vouchers or tax credits for as long as their governments wish to do so.

Solutions and Lingering Concerns

As is obvious now, I do not share Coons' or his allies' enthusiasm for public funding of private schools as a touchstone solution to the problem of public school closed-zoning policies that reserve richly resourced public schools for children from financially secure parents and 'conscript' children of the poor to attend minimalist schools with minimalist educational programs. The surest way out of the worst – read most unjust – impacts of this situation is *not* public funding of private schools unless one is prepared to do one of two things:

- Accept the political consequences of a lottery approach to allocating fully paid student places in private schools (and even then many questions would linger about what would constitute a 'reasonable' tuition and fee scale to subsidize)
- Emulate the Netherlands and go the full mile towards creating a completely 'pseudo-private' school system with every ethnocultural and religious group having access to 'complete' public funding and with no other 'private' schools allowed.

Neither of these options seems politically viable in the Canadian context. A lottery approach would provoke the wrath of parents who lost the lottery and a Dutch-style 'pseudo-private' approach would evoke visions of hyper-expensive duplication of facilities and services (although James showed that the 'premium' in duplicated costs over a monolithic public system that the Dutch paid was surprisingly small!),[58] and charges of unacceptable entanglement of church and state.

The best way to ameliorate inequality of educational opportunity remains within the public sector, beset though it is with all the maladies of goal displacement, crises of purposes, and just plain bureaucratic bloat. The best way forward is choice – but public sector choice, and only subject to the conditions I outlined at the beginning of the chapter, namely:

- Open zoning with transportation provided
- No SES-proxy admission criteria
- Excellent, obligatory parent choice information programs
- Only minimal use of private resources by public schools
- A common core curriculum in all publicly funded schools.

What then is to become of religious education in such a solution? I must confess that I don't have a compelling and personally satisfying answer. To advocate adoption of religiously based schools into the family of options made available by public systems would likely satisfy no one concerned. Religious groups would mistrust the impacts on their interests of public governance while secular society would decry public support of religion.

Still, while I have no answer, I do have a concern. I do not believe the public interest is well served by expunging religion entirely from education. As a minimum, I think tolerance implies balanced and reasonable knowledge about varying faith and philosophical communities, hence 'religious education' in the non-sectarian, non-indoctrinational sense.

But more than that, I believe that faith communities – and, in particular, parents committed to such faith communities – do have an inherent right to access education informed and shaped by their religious and philosophical beliefs. In that sense, I think Article 26 of the United Nations *Universal Declaration of Human Rights* 'has it right' at some basic moral and ethical level. Although I am painfully aware of the abuses and human rights violations that have been historically and continue on a daily basis to be perpetrated on humankind in the name of religion, I am equally conscious of those visited on humanity by non-religion and anti-religion. In any case, although I have never taught in a religiously based school, I am certainly unwilling to accept that religious education cannot be a very good thing and cannot contribute to peace, tolerance, and social cohesion,[59] although I also certainly do not believe that is always the case.

Furthermore, I find that the most problematic of Smith and Foster's 'guiding principles' for a *Charter*-based public education framework is the last, namely, that ' [p]ublic school authorities must provide educational services in an environment that is not polluted by intolerance, in which all students may participate, without discrimination based on religion.' I think that public school systems need to do much better than that. They need, to the best of their ability, to support and affirm the developing ethnocultural, philosophical, and religious identities of their students, no mean task given that specific exemplars of each frequently come with considerable 'negative baggage' towards other cultures, philosophies, and religions.

Moral neutrality in education is an oxymoron. Education is, as the late Thom Greenfield insisted, 'a moral enterprise,' schools, 'a moral order,' and religion and moral philosophy, after all, greatly inform our sense of ethics, morals, and identity. One wonders how many non-Catholic children are in Catholic schools in Alberta, Saskatchewan, and Ontario precisely because their parents want their children in a school system that gives daily witness to a clear and unequivocal set of moral principles.

On the whole, then, I come away from this analysis believing that I have the legal and ethical analysis generally right but sincerely concerned by both direct and collateral damage that this line of argument might visit on all that is good in religious education.

Notwithstanding these concerns on my part, one final observation cries out to be made. How interesting indeed it would be, from ethical, policy, and constitutional points of view, if some organization oriented towards defence of civil liberties took on the public funding of private schools issue in one of the provinces currently subsidizing private school attendance. At last, Canada would be 'treated' to fiscal equity litigation every bit as interesting as anything our American neighbours have seen to date.

5 Religion in Canadian Education: Whither Goest Thou?

JOHN LONG AND ROMULO MAGSINO

In a relatively short interval of recent Canadian history, the *Canadian Charter of Rights and Freedoms*[1] has had a significant impact on Canadian schooling. This impact is perhaps the most significant in the judicial results of litigation at the intersection of religion and schooling. Elsewhere,[2] we have described even the earliest of these judicial rulings as transformative of the role and status of the public school: 'in the era of the *Charter*, the public school will be viewed officially as a secular institution.'[3] Indeed, it is increasingly evident that contemporary public schooling reflects the hegemony of the secularist outlook and a strong attachment to emergent, judicially sponsored values. While the formal secularization of public schooling has occurred to some degree through the instrumentality of *Charter*-based litigation, secularization as a social force, along with a heightened rights consciousness in society, has produced a transformation also of the arrangements for denominational schools in two Canadian provinces in the past decade.

This chapter describes both of these developments; the former an exercise in the judicial construction of the public school, the latter a social and political construction that achieved a substantial constitutional change in the circumstances of denominational schools in Newfoundland/Labrador and Quebec. Though the specific instrumentalities were different in each of these developments, each has reshaped historic configurations of schooling in Canada. Arguably, both developments reflect the recent judicial and political tendency in Canada towards a strict separation of church and state that is largely an imitation of the constitutional order that prevails in the United States. We can say, therefore, that contemporary arrangements for non-sectarian schooling in most provinces now resemble more those of our American neighbour, recognizing the notable exception of state-funded denominational schools in the public sector in Ontario, Alberta, and Saskatchewan and the partial public funding of private religious schools, such as is explicit in the legislative and regulatory regime for schools in British Columbia and Manitoba. Whether such arrangements are a comfortable fit with the ethos of a pluralist democracy and the Canadian policy of multiculturalism is, however, a question that remains unsettled. An exploration of this question and other important implications for educational policy and practice that emerge from our examination, we leave to our concluding remarks.

Schooling and Religion: The Constitutional Framework

Article 93

In the effort to understand the essential background of Canadian schooling arrangements, it is ordinary but important to observe that without the so-called Confederation compromise in Article 93 of the *Constitution Act, 1867*,[4] there would not have been a Canadian confederation of the original four provinces of Ontario, Quebec, New Brunswick, and Nova Scotia.[5] That compromise concerned primarily the place of religion in relation to schooling, especially the role and status of a religiously affiliated denominational school system separate from a state-sponsored common or public (non-sectarian) school system. In simplest form, Article 93 gives the provincial legislature the constitutional right to 'exclusively make Laws in relation to Education' subject to four provisions designed to protect from prejudicial effect 'any Right or Privilege with respect to Denominational Schools which any class of Persons have by Law in the Province at the Union.'[6] Article 93(2) attempts a symmetry of rights for such schools by extending to the dissentient schools of Quebec, for Catholics and Protestants, the rights given to the Catholic separate schools in Ontario.[7] Article 93(3) provides for an appeal by the denominational minority of the province to the federal cabinet 'from any Act or Decision of any Provincial Authority' concerning its denominational rights or privileges. Article 93(4) allows for the Parliament of Canada to 'make remedial Laws' to correct any recognized prejudicial effect, regardless of the date of the establishment of separate or dissentient schools in the province. Effectively, Article 93 'protected the right of Catholics and Protestants to *dissent* … namely, the right: (a) to establish Catholic or Protestant schools, managed by Catholics or Protestants, and teaching only Catholic or Protestant religion; (b) to hire teachers and admit Catholic or Protestant pupils; and (c) ... to a traditional share of the profit of taxation [i.e., a share equivalent to that available to non-sectarian public schools].'[8] Currently, denominational schools with such constitutional rights and protections exist only in Ontario, Alberta, and Saskatchewan,[9] along with non-sectarian public schools.

With regard to constitutional principles, what is important to notice is that the special arrangement made for two denominations of the Christian faith in Article 93 was not undone by the constitutional entrenchment of the *Charter* in 1982. The *Charter* provided for equality rights with a guarantee of non-discrimination in s.15(1) and freedom of conscience and religion as one of the fundamental freedoms in s.2(a). The framers of the *Charter* recognized the potential conflict between these new guarantees and the historic entitlements regarding denominational schools. As a result, they foreclosed the possibility of conflict between two different constitutional documents governing schools with the inclusion of s.29 in the *Charter* itself: 'Nothing in this *Charter* abrogates or derogates from any rights or privileges guaranteed by or under the Constitution of Canada in respect of denominational, separate or dissentient schools.' This clause in the *Charter* can be considered as 'disarming' sections 2 and 15, effectively blocking any potential threat to denominational schools or the plenary power of a province to legislate schooling arrangements.

It is not surprising that constitutional controversies at the intersection of religion and schooling have arisen in Canada almost entirely in the domain of *non-sectarian* public schools, if only because public sector denominational schools embody religion in their very establishment and operation (an approach not provided for in the Constitution of the United States). Also, that despite quite different *original* constitutional frameworks – state entanglement with religion from the beginning in the case of Canada – there is an increasing similarity between the United States and Canada with respect to each country's 'legal culture' and constitutional framework, as a result of Canada's adoption of the *Charter*.[10] Sedler puts this idea very well, in stating: 'There are now constitutional limitations on the exercise of governmental power designed to protect individual rights and, under the constitutional systems of both nations, the courts can provide relief against governmental action that they find to be violative of those constitutional provisions.'[11] Certain constitutional provisions of the 'rights paradigm' of the *Charter*[12] are especially salient in the religious and schooling controversies that have emerged in Canada.

The *Charter* Paradigm

The *Charter* was officially entrenched in the Canadian constitution by virtue of the *Constitution Act, 1982*.[13] It provided for several categories of rights and freedoms but those directly relevant to issues of religion and public schooling are found in s.2 – Fundamental Freedoms, and s.15 – Equality Rights. (See Appendix for the text of these sections.) It is also important to note that the *Charter* applies to both the federal and provincial legislatures and governments and, as is generally agreed, equally 'applies to public school boards and schools, as well as their officials, because they operate as "State agents" – that is, on behalf of the State.'[14] Further, as is inevitable in jurisprudence on civil rights, guaranteeing human rights and freedoms usually involves a balancing exercise since granting rights to someone may affect another's rights. To deal with this likelihood, the *Charter* has within it a 'reasonable limits' provision whereby a government or its agents may impose limitations on rights in the attempt to strike a balance in specific circumstances. Essentially, this means that reasonable limits may not be set arbitrarily by fiat or by the accumulation of custom or practice; they must be accessible to the public such that the limitations intended can be understood. Additionally, the burden of justifying any limitation on rights lies with the sponsor of such limitations. In this sense, s.1 constitutes a defence against an assertion that a law or action by government or its agents violates some human right or freedom. The interpretation of this section was an early judicial development. *R. v. Oakes*[15] originally established that four criteria must be satisfied to secure a s.1 defence of government action: (1) the law must pursue an objective that is of sufficient importance to override a constitutionally protected right or freedom; (2) there must be a rational connection between the law and the objective; (3) there should be minimal impairment of the protected right or freedom in achieving the objective; and (4) there should be proportionality between the objective sought and the effects of the law such that its positive effects outweigh the deleterious effects on those affected by it.[16]

Equally, judicial definition of what constitutes 'religion' was made early in *Charter* litigation: as encompassed by s.2(a), it is 'profoundly personal beliefs that govern one's perception of oneself, humankind, nature, and in some cases, a higher or different order of being. These beliefs, in turn, govern one's conduct and practices.'[17] Therefore, 's.2(a) contains both the positive right to manifest one's belief (or non-belief), and the negative right to abstain from conformity with the beliefs of others.'[18]

Section 2(a) of the *Charter* may be considered the Canadian counter-part of the American First Amendment provision guaranteeing the *free exercise* of religion,[19] insofar as s.2 of the *Charter* similarly guarantees freedom of conscience and religion (recognizing that there is no Canadian equivalent to the establishment clause). Moreover, s.15(1) of the *Charter* echoes the prohibition in the Fourteenth Amendment against any law denying citizens equal protection of the laws; in fact, though, s.15 is more comprehensive in that it speaks of 'equality before and under the law and equal protection and benefit of the law.' Further, Canadians have been willing to avail themselves of the *Charter*'s invitation in s.24 for anyone who believes her or his rights have been infringed to 'apply to a court of competent jurisdiction to obtain such remedy as the court considers appropriate and just in the circumstances.' Unsurprisingly, the relatively short life of the *Charter* has not yet produced a jurispru-dence as substantial or definitive as in the American experience with schooling issues, and not all issues have yet come to the attention of the Supreme Court of Canada, as is clear in the so-called school prayer issue. Whether the court of last resort in Canada will follow the direction of American constitutional jurisprudence is a matter of speculation but ju-dicial signals are already strong in this direction in several cases. It is convenient to review the particular cases at the intersection of religion and education first and then, as a summary, distil the major legal prin-ciples that seem to be emerging in Canada so far.

Charter Cases at the Intersection of Schooling and Religion

Religious Exercises

The First Amendment to the *Constitution* of the United States has been used successfully to prevent religious practices from having any place in American public schools. An early indication that this same judicial road would be travelled in Canada was given by the decision of the Ontario Court of Appeal in *Zylberberg* v. *Sudbury (Board of Education).*[20] The court held that provincial regulations compelling public schools to hold reli-gious exercises, Bible readings, and the Lord's Prayer, even when stu-dents may be exempted, violated constitutional guarantees of freedom of religion and conscience in s.2(a) of the *Charter*. The court rejected the argument by the Sudbury School Board that the exemption, fully in ac-cord with the *Education Act*,[21] was an adequate protection of this right: 'While the majoritarian view may be that s.28 [the impugned regulation] confers freedom of choice on the minority, the reality is that it imposes ... a compulsion to conform to the practices of the majority ... The peer pressure and classroom norms to which children are acutely sensitive, in our opinion, are real and pervasive and operate to compel members of religious minorities to conform with majority religious practices.'[22]

The court cited the judicial reasoning from *School District of Abington Township* v. *Schempp*[23] and partially from *Engel* v. *Vitale*[24] with approval. In both cases, the U.S. Supreme Court struck down state legislation authorizing school prayer as a violation of the establishment clause of the First Amendment. Citing these American cases with particular approval, the Ontario Court of Appeal said: 'Two conclusions can be drawn from the American decisions. The first is the absence of an establishment clause in s.2(a) does not limit the protection it gives to freedom of conscience and religion. The second is that support can be found in *Abington* ... for our conclusion that the compulsion of students to conform and not exercise the right of exemption is a real restraint on the freedom of conscience and religion guaranteed by the *Charter*.'[25]

Additional arguments presented by the respondent School Board were rebuffed. While expert evidence differed on the harmful effect of religious exercise on non-participating students, the court said that 'there is no burden on those objecting ... to prove, in addition, that it causes actual harm to individual pupils.'[26] Also, the board's claim that it was possibly a salutary effect for minority pupils to deal with the facts of their differences from the majority, given a multicultural society, was dismissed as insensitive and 'inconsistent with the multicultural nature of our society as recognized by s.27 of the *Charter*.'[27] The court further ruled that the federal government had not justified the violation of students' freedom of religion and conscience under s.1, as the law was found to have a clear religious rather than secular objective and one which did not impair the rights in question 'as little as possible.' The court concluded that 'there are less intrusive ways of imparting educational and moral values' and seemed to prefer another strategy: 'The experience of the Toronto Board of Education ... shows that it is not necessary to give primacy to the Christian religion in school opening exercises and they can be more appropriately founded on the multicultural traditions of our society.'[28] But, said the court: 'In saying this we are not to be taken as passing constitutional judgment on the opening exercises used in Toronto public schools. They were not in issue before us and we express no opinion as to whether they might give rise to *Charter* scrutiny.'[29]

Given these remarks by the court, Canadian educators might well wonder whether school opening exercises having a multicultural or multifaith character would survive a *Charter* challenge. The Ontario court's evident use of the doctrinal content of *Lemon* v. *Kurtzman*[30] (i.e., the law must serve a primarily secular not religious objective) would suggest that a multi*faith* exercise might not survive *Charter* scrutiny. Is it possible that a conception of culture or the practice of multiculturalism in schools cannot include the element of religion, at least not where pupils might be expected to hear or otherwise share in sentiments of a religious nature, even if they were doing so in order to show their appreciation or acknowledgment of the heritage of others? The Ontario court's remarks on this point yield an uncertain answer to this question.

The ruling of the Ontario court in *Zylberberg* was never heard by the Supreme Court of Canada but it nevertheless had a forceful impact on two similar cases, one in British Columbia, *Russow* v. *British Columbia (Attorney General)*,[31] and one in Manitoba, *Manitoba Association for Rights and Liberties* v. *Manitoba*.[32] In these cases, complainants presented *Charter*-inspired challenges to the provincial legislative regime regarding opening exercises in schools, like those litigated in *Zylberberg*. The judicial result in the B.C. Supreme Court and in the Court of Queen's Bench in Manitoba was virtually the same as in the Ontario court, both rulings relying on the reasoning and conclusions of the *Zylberberg* court. Similarly, neither province appealed the provincial court decision to the Supreme Court. However, the educational policy outcome of the controversy was different in each province. A comparison of the different policy responses shows that provincial legislative and regulatory regimes provide unique constraints and opportunities for policy deliberation and implementation.[33]

The implications of constitutional supremacy over legislative enactment – the doctrinal underpinning of the *Charter* – are clearly evident in the judicial amendment of the British Columbia *School Act*[34] in *Russow*. In this case, s.164 of the *School Act* was at issue, which read: 'All public schools shall be opened by the reading without explanation or comment, of a passage of Scripture to be selected from readings prescribed or approved by the Lieutenant Governor in Council. The reading of the passage ... shall be followed by the recitation of the Lord's Prayer, but otherwise the schools shall be conducted on strictly secular and non-sectarian principles. The highest morality shall be inculcated, but no religious dogma or creed shall be taught.'[35]

Deciding on the basis of the judicial doctrine of severance, namely, that the legislature would have enacted s.164 except for that portion which the Supreme Court of British Columbia found offensive to s.2(a) of the *Charter*, the court ruled that the resulting residual section would read as follows: 'All public schools shall be conducted on strictly secular and non-sectarian principles. The highest morality shall be inculcated, but no religious dogma or creed shall be taught.' Effectively, the judicial emendation of the statute removed the possibility of religious exercises in public schools. The shift in meaning and application of this section to the B.C. public schools is considerable, perhaps even profound, and there is no doubt that the direction is towards a strict separation of church and state, reminiscent of the *Lemon* doctrine which had high currency in the American school controversies regarding religion during the 1970s and 1980s.

Certainly, the shift was in the same direction in *Manitoba*, and, indeed, the Court of Queen's Bench struck down most of the legislative provisions of the Manitoba *Public Schools Act*[36] in s.84, which governs religious exercises. However, a protocol of parental petition for such exercises, where the number of children warrants this, was retained at the level of individual schools. This was a key aspect of the policy established by the provincial Ministry of Education, in consultation with stakeholder groups: 'Assuming the numerical requirements ... are met, it is conceivable that parents of a variety of faith groups could petition for their own religious exercises ... Parents or guardians signatory to a petition would be entitled to have their children access such religious exercises, and the school board will be required to make the necessary arrangements to implement the exercises. However, the parents/guardians making the petition will be responsible for providing whatever Prayer book, literature, etc. are essential to the conducting of religious exercises.'[37]

Other provisions of the policy in Manitoba are certainly consonant with the notion of a separation of church and state; for example, school boards and individual schools were instructed that they could communicate with parents about the law but 'should not, however, take any action that would be seen as initiating or prompting implementation of religious exercises.'[38] Nevertheless, a possibility exists in Manitoba for the retention of religious exercises in public schools, a dilution of strict church-state separation, in contrast to the development in British Columbia.[39]

Religious Instruction

While religious exercises may be regarded as expressions of faith or worship, they usually have a ceremonial, celebratory, inspirational, or even routine aspect, wherein a specific confessional or denominational perspective or orientation may *not* be explicit. In the case of religious instruction, the intention is usually to convey some specific content or text that has a confessional or denominational aspect and prescriptions, by precept and example, for ordering one's life. An important feature may be the presentation of specific beliefs and the promotion of particular values anchored in a religious ethos, with a view to fostering commitment to such beliefs and values on the part of the young. In contrast, religious education might be conceived of as studies *about* religion without any specific intention of encouraging or discouraging a student to become committed to a particular denominational view.

A fundamental issue in an Ontario school board's adoption of a revised curriculum of religious studies for its elementary schools was whether or not that curriculum was religious instruction or religious education. In 1987, The Elgin County School Board adopted a revised version of its curriculum of religious education, a mandatory part of regular schooling under the authority of the Ontario *Education Act* (1980) and regulations. The revision represented substantial adjustments in the direction of teaching about religion since the beliefs and traditions of other major world religions besides Christianity were represented. However, an exemption mechanism of 'opting out' of the program was retained and the exemption was not dependent on the giving of reasons.

In 1988, in *Canadian Civil Liberties Association* v. *Ontario (Minister of Education)*,[40] the Canadian Civil Liberties Association (CCLA) and certain parents in the county public school system sought judicial review of the constitutional validity of the Ontario regulations and the school board's curriculum. The applicants contended before the Ontario Divisional Court that the regulations and curriculum violated sections 2(a) and 15(1) of the *Charter*. The court rejected an application for an order to stop the board's offering of the curriculum, finding no infringement of constitutional rights. The CCLA and the co-applicants appealed the decision to the Ontario Court of Appeal which overruled the lower court and ordered the county board to cease offering the religious studies curriculum in its schools.[41] In giving its decision, the Court of Appeal observed that the curricular treatment of non-Christian religions was 'entirely non-indoctrinal' but there was 'no similar treatment of Christianity.'[42] Noting that s.2(a) of the *Charter* 'prohibits religious indoctrination, but does not prohibit education about religion,'[43] the Court of Appeal found the curriculum as taught unconstitutional. The province of Ontario did not appeal to the Supreme Court; instead it amended its regulations to permit boards to offer courses *about* religion.

Accommodation of Religious Minorities

Several disputes have arisen in Canada when religious groups have sought relief from the burden that they believe secular schooling imposes on their religious expression. The ruling of the Supreme Court in *Adler* v. *Ontario*[44] brought judicial closure to a ten-year dispute in the Ontario courts regarding the funding of *private* religious schools. The claims of the minority religious groups in *Adler* and *Bal* v. *Ontario* *(Attorney General)*[45] were essentially parallel. They claimed a violation of their *Charter* right to freedom of conscience and religion and a denial of their right to equal benefit of the law on account of the fact that they could not conscientiously send their children to schools that taught beliefs and moral values incompatible with the values of the parents and the home. The aggrieved applicants pointed to the advantaged position of Roman Catholics in Ontario who are entitled to fully funded religious schooling and argued for the same treatment and arrangements to ensure 'free exercise' of their religious rights and respect for the principles of equality and non-discrimination in their case. In *Adler*, the Supreme Court of Canada dismissed the applicants' claims finding that Ontario's funding of Catholic separate schools was a constitutionally valid historical compromise of the nineteenth century; however, that historical arrangement 'does not open a constitutional door' for other religious groups. Further, the court held that the applicants' decision to enroll their children in private schools was because of their religious convictions and not a result of government action.

In the wake of *Zylberberg*, *CCLA Appeal*, and the Ontario Court of Appeal's ruling in *Adler* v. *Ontario*,[46] the province of Ontario changed its regulations so as to prevent any funding of alternative religious schools at school board discretion, as some Ontario school boards had done. The *Bal* applicants – Christian Reformed, Hindu, Mennonite, Muslim, and Sikh parents – had their children in such religious alternative schools before the change in the Ontario regulation or desired to place their children in such schools. *Bal*, then, was basically a challenge to the decision of the Ontario government to eliminate the discretion of school boards to accommodate such parents. The challenge failed. In 1997, the Ontario Court of Appeal dismissed the application for leave to appeal from the lower court decision in *Bal*, adopting fully the decision and reasoning of the lower court. The Court of Appeal held: 'To grant the relief sought in this application would require that the court undo what the Ontario Court of Appeal has decided in *Zylberberg, Elgin County* and *Adler*.'[47] In 1998, the Supreme Court of Canada dismissed the application for leave to appeal by the *Bal* applicants, echoing the reasoning of the Ontario courts – the *Charter* does not compel the accommodation of parental ambitions for religious schooling within a public system; indeed, it would be constitutionally inconsistent to do so.

Given the outcome in *Bal*, the ruling in *Islamic Federation of Ontario* v. *Ottawa Board of Education*[48] was perhaps predictable at the outset. In this case, a request for the closure of public schools in recognition of two Muslim holy days was denied by the school board and sustained by the court, essentially because the court agreed that acceding to the request would require like treatment of other religious groups and that such a school calendar would be unworkable.

In *Pandori* v. *Peel Board of Education*,[49] the Ontario Board of Inquiry held a school board's no-weapons policy preventing the wearing by a Sikh boy of a religious ceremonial dagger discriminatory, in contravention of the Ontario *Human Rights Code*.[50] The Ontario Divisional Court affirmed the ruling.[51] On virtually the same issue, that is, whether or not freedom of religion requires that the school must accommodate religious ceremonials, the Supreme Court of Canada in *Multani* v. *Marguerite-Bourgeoys* (*Commission scolaire*)[52] reached the same conclusion as the Ontario Divisional Court in *Pandori*. The Supreme Court ruling set aside the earlier decision in 2004 of the Quebec Court of Appeal[53] which had upheld the decision by a school council (conseil d'établissement) in the district governed by the Commission scolaire Marguerite-Bourgeoys that a Sikh boy, Gurbaj Singh Multani, could not wear his kirpan at school. The Supreme Court held that the prohibition against G. Multani was an infringement of his freedom of religion that was 'neither trivial nor insignificant, as it deprived him of his right to attend a public school':[54] 'The infringement of G's freedom of religion cannot be justified under s.1 of the *Canadian Charter*. Although the council's decision to prohibit the wearing of a kirpan was motivated by a pressing and substantial objective, namely to ensure a reasonable level of safety at the school, and although the decision had a rational connection with the objective, it has not been shown that such a prohibition minimally impairs G's rights.'[55]

Further, said the Court: 'Religious tolerance is a very important value of Canadian society. If some students consider it unfair that G may wear his kirpan to school while they are not allowed to have knives in their possession, it is incumbent on the schools to discharge their obligation to instill in their students this value that is at the very foundation of our democracy ... Accommodating G ... demonstrates the importance that our society attaches to protecting freedom of religion and to showing respect for its minorities.'[56]

A School Environment Free of Discrimination

The accommodation of religious groups may, however, prove perilous for public school authorities, depending on the circumstances and the extant legal regime. In *Chamberlain* v. *Surrey School District No. 36*,[57] a school board's ban on controversial learning materials from gay and lesbian groups was quashed and held to be unreasonable 'in the context of the educational regime mandated by the legislature.'[58] In the specific context of s.76 of the B.C. *School Act*[59] (1996), the Supreme Court said: '[T]he words "secular" and "non-sectarian" in the Act imply that no single conception of morality can be allowed to deny or exclude opposed points of view ... Section 76 ... does not limit in any way the freedom of parents and Board members to adhere to a religious doctrine that condemns homosexuality. It does prohibit the translation of such doctrine into policy decisions by the Board, to the extent that they reflect a denial of the validity of other points of view.'[60]

In this case, the Court concluded that the way the school board dealt with three books 'was inconsistent with the School Act's commitment to secularism and non-sectarianism.'[61] Therefore, the board's claim that its decision was designed, in part, to respect the religious freedom of parents objecting to the materials was rejected by the Court. Here the Court underscores the necessity for public schools to favour a secular objective; a show of deference in its policy to the religious sentiments of one group, even if that group represented the majority of parents in the school board's view, would constitute unwarranted discrimination against parents of an opposing, minority view.

In a similar B.C. case, that is, where the issue of homosexuality was indirectly involved, the Supreme Court of Canada ruled in favour of

that they must control the learning environment; but such arguments are to be raised at the justification stage under s.1. These arguments will not be convincing at the earlier stage, claiming that freedom of expression has not been interfered with at all.

Also, school boards (and other governmental actors in the education field) will have to take seriously their obligation to prove that interference with free speech is necessary to address some pressing and substantial harm. In all three of the cases cited, the decision-maker commented that there was insufficient evidence of the nature and significance of the harm being addressed.[39] In each case, the boards seemed to rely on anecdotal or speculative evidence to describe the harm being addressed. This approach simply will not suffice to establish a justification argument under s.1.

While the jurisprudence still lacks a thorough analysis as to how the principles of s.1 will play out in the classroom context, it can be expected that school boards will rely on the arguments that students comprise a captive and vulnerable audience and that the classroom is not a public forum; that the state has a legitimate and unavoidable role in setting curriculum; and that granting too much autonomy to the teacher gives rise to potential disruptions to the learning environment, which ultimately harm students.

Finally, I note that these cases, directly or indirectly, add some clarification to the nature of teaching itself. The recognition of a teacher's *Charter* rights in the school and in the classroom seems to bolster the idea that teaching is a profession, rather than simply a job. The decision-makers in these cases recognize that teachers are entrusted with a captive and impressionable audience, and yet the cases are still willing to entrust the teacher with some degree of personal control over the subject being taught. This level of trust is consistent with the notion of a professional. As well, the recognition of the degree of independent control exercised by a teacher within the classroom is relevant to other, potentially significant questions in education law, such as the ownership of copyright in materials produced by the teacher.[40]

Conclusion

Law and education are each a means of managing changes and conflicts in social values. The *Charter* is perhaps the most valuable tool by which the law achieves this goal. In the context of the education system, the protection of freedom of expression in s.2(b) has been extended to teachers both inside and outside the classroom. Under the umbrella of s.2(b), teachers have been recognized as having a right to some degree of control over the content of their lessons, a right to bring their political and labour power struggles into the classroom, and a right to partici- pate in the decision-making process in the education system by run- ning for elected positions. Though the freedoms protected by s.2(b) will be subject to certain limits, the cases have made clear that the school board and the province will have to provide a strong argument to jus- tify infringing teachers' free speech.

The education system is better seen as a balance of interests than as a state vs. individual model of power. In these cases, the *Charter* has served to affect the balance of power within the education system, and to carve out a clear and protected role for the interests of teachers in the system. Teachers and teacher organizations have begun to see that the *Charter* has the power not just to protect them from state oppression, but to affirm and defend their interests in the education system. It is likely that *Charter* principles will increasingly find their way into cases involving teachers.

7 School Searches and Student Rights under the *Charter*: Old Wine in New Bottles

GREG DICKINSON

We have *Tinker* v. *Des Moines*[1] to thank (or curse) for imprinting the image of school children traversing the now metaphoric 'schoolhouse gate' with a copy of the U.S. Bill of Rights in hand, in their backpacks or just simply on their minds. When Justice Fortas delivered his famous one-liner, it was clear to all that children did not check their civil rights at the schoolhouse gate like hats in a church vestibule. 'It can hardly be argued,' he stated, 'that either students or teachers shed their constitutional rights to freedom of speech or expression at the schoolhouse gate.'[2] The rub was, and still is, however, judicially navigating the problem 'area where students in the exercise of First Amendment rights collide with the rules of the school authorities.' *Tinker* and subsequent jurisprudence made it clear that the U.S. Supreme Court was prepared to whittle away students' rights in the name of the need for order, discipline, the recognition of the rights of others, and just plain decency. In *Tinker*, the Court circumscribed children's free speech by the need to avoid 'substantial disruption' of the business of the school. Subsequently, in *School District No. 403* v. *Fraser*[3] the Court embraced the school's role in teaching students the boundaries of social decency to justify censuring a student for a lewd speech in the auditorium. On the heels of *Fraser*, the Court ruled in *Hazelwood School District* v. *Kuhlmeier*[4] that the censoring of student speech by a principal who pulled two controversial pages from the school newspaper did not violate First Amendment rights because 'legitimate pedagogical concerns' were involved.[5] In both *Fraser* and *Hazelwood* the Court expressed its readiness to carve out a sphere of student rights 'that were not automatically co-extensive with the rights of adults in other settings.'[6] Most important of all in terms of precedent setting, 'the [*Hazelwood*] ruling showed that the

matter of the education of the students ... is the responsibility of educators, parents, and school officials and "not of federal judges," so the
authority rests with those persons who have knowledge and expertise
in the field of education.'[7]

As in many areas of the law, the U.S. Supreme Court has proven a bellwether for the approach the Supreme Court of Canada would adopt
under the *Canadian Charter of Rights and Freedoms* towards student rights,
especially those seemingly in collision with school rules aimed at maintaining order, discipline, and safety. Student search is likely the clearest
example. This chapter examines the *Charter*'s impact on school searches
by briefly reviewing the legal regime governing school discipline in pre-
Charter Canada and then looking in depth at *Charter* cases arising from
student searches conducted by school authorities. I conclude that the
Charter's impact in this area has been less than revolutionary, Canadian
case law has closely followed American jurisprudence and Canadian
courts – including the Supreme Court – have shown an appetite for a re-
strictive rather than expansive interpretation of student rights in the area
of search. The traditional pre-*Charter* judicial 'deference'[8] shown to school
authorities is alive and well. This judicial latitude makes all the more
crucial the education and employment of judicious school leaders who
will exercise their authority and discretion fairly and impart a proper
model of justice through the hidden curriculum embodied in the way
students are treated by those in authority. Because many students will
inevitably hold positions of responsibility and authority in schools, and
elsewhere in society, the lessons they are 'taught' about the importance of
rights and how one wisely exercises authority conferred by the state will
help to shape the democratic society they will live in and perpetuate.

School Discipline before the *Charter* Era

It is much easier to discuss the legal and policy implications of school
searches in post-*Charter* years for one simple reason: the entrenchment
of constitutional rights and the rights consciousness that arose out of
the arrival of the *Charter* provided both the vehicle and the animus for
challenging school administrators' disciplinary actions. Then again,
late twentieth- and early twenty-first-century schools, while similar in
some ways, were very different in many others from those of the 1950s
and 1960s. I dare say that most who attended school then would be
hard pressed to recall a student's having been searched as part of a
criminal investigation. Inasmuch as they were evident and a legal issue
in Canada in the 1960s and 1970s, drugs were mostly a post-secondary

education phenomenon. And far from scuttling off to court with rights-deprived son or daughter in hand, parents tended to reinforce the actions of teachers and administrators on the assumption, right or wrong, that the school was acting in the best interests of their child's character formation. All of this likely explains why it appears impossible to locate case law or any discussion in the literature concerning student searches in the pre-*Charter* era.

The enforcement of school discipline, in general, was rarely on the legal radar. If it was, the legal issues usually involved the alleged excessive use of force. Challenging the substance of rules of conduct or their implementation meant relying on arcane principles of administrative law, an area rich with judicial opportunity to 'duck the question.' Questions of legality, jurisdiction, and regularity were the touchstones in such challenges. One could invoke issues of fairness or natural justice if it were possible to convince the court that the impugned acts were really 'quasi-judicial' rather than 'administrative.' All of this was suffused in the smothering judicial atmosphere of 'curial deference': the courts were not at all keen to intrude on school business.

A classic pre-*Charter* example of the courts' disposition towards a *Charter*-era type of student complaint is the 1971 case of *Re Ward and Blaine Lake School*.[9] Ward was suspended for refusing to comply with the school board's regulation regarding hair style and length. Though ludicrously trivial by today's standards, a student's hair length and style were matters of considerable concern for 1970s' school authorities who passed regulations thereon as their part in a war on the evils of a 'permissive society.'[10] In his judgment in *Ward* Justice Tucker sympathized with the war effort:

> In these days of the so-called 'permissive society' one does not need to indulge in much in the way of flight of imagination to envisage how difficult it would be to conduct a class of boys and girls where they could wear as little or as unusual clothing as some children or some parents might see fit. This would include not only care, cleanliness, and covering of various parts of the body but preventing the unusual types of dress and hair styling which might be calculated to distract the pupils from their work in the classroom or adversely affect a proper and reasonable air of discipline in the school.[11]

Using pre-*Nicholson*[12] principles of administrative law, the court held that because the school boards' actions were purely 'administrative' as opposed to 'quasi-judicial,' they were 'not subject to certiorari.'[13] *Over and out!* This was code for extending the maximum degree of judicial deference under the common law. Had the board's actions been review-able, the court found no evidence that the school authorities had failed in their legal obligations by acting without authority; by stepping out-side the limits of their authority; by failing to perform their duties; by failing to abide by the principles of natural justice; or, by acting with interest or bias, in bad faith or capriciously. So even had the court's decision rested on such considerations, they were hardly *substantive* questions going to the defensibility of the regulation itself. The issues were ones of legitimacy, jurisdiction, good faith, and fair process. An extensive analysis of the distribution of powers under the *British North America Act, 1867* and the derivative powers given school boards under Saskatchewan legislation led the court to conclude that the board had acted well within its authority. And the rules of natural justice men-tioned by the court embodied predominantly a common law code of fair process; it would have taken 'grave reasons' and 'manifest injus-tice' for the court to substitute its opinion for that of the school board about the merits of the regulation itself.

It is hard not to conclude that this case was all about authority – not cleanliness or other pseudo-health concerns, or even an abiding con-cern about disruption. The rule in question and the court's reasoning were symbolic: they were meant to leave no doubt about who was 'in control.' A decade later this power equation – we make the rules, you follow them – would be up for revision under the *Charter*, requiring the factoring in of rational reasons supporting every rule. Moreover, the *Charter*'s potential for recasting the power relationship between admin-istrative decision-makers and the courts would be enormous: the broad wording of sections 24(1) of the *Charter* and 52 of the *Constitution Act, 1982* threatened a severe body blow to the tradition of curial deference. The devil would be in the details, however; how enthusiastically and actively would courts embrace their new constitutional authority? How critically would they examine the reasons for school boards' actions? To what extent would pre-*Charter* assumptions about the virtues of order and discipline, and symbolic authority and its concomitant – judicial deference to school authorities' decisions – survive? If discipline for discipline's sake were no longer sufficient, what new rationales would arise for setting limits on students' civil liberties and legal rights?

In my view, early *Charter* days' predictions, some heady and others cautious, that a new era had been ushered in that would see lifted the pall of judicial deference to school authorities have not been realized in the area of student discipline.[14] Though optimistic that a new rights consciousness was in the air after the arrival of the *Charter*,[15] MacKay cautioned that judicial traditions die hard and that much uncertainty surrounded the prospect that Canadians would suddenly support affording full adult rights to children. As MacKay put it,

> [V]alues and customs change slowly. Canada still lives under a Constitution which trumpets 'Peace, Order and Good Government,' not 'Life, Liberty and the Pursuit of Happiness.' The tradition has been to resolve educational issues in the political, rather than the judicial, arena and courts, as part of their deference to the general social order, have taken a 'hands-off' approach to the decisions of school boards and school administrators. Furthermore the Canadian Constitution has emphasized collective rather than individual rights and this focus will not quickly shift ...
>
> [T]here has not been a complete change of philosophy ... A complete denial of rights is no longer acceptable but neither is a granting of full adult rights.[16]

Twenty-five years of *Charter* experience have lent the ring of truth to MacKay's prophecy. Courts have generally avoided second-guessing educational policies and practices, except concerning religion, deferring to either the legislature in matters of structure, funding, and governance or to school-based administrators and teachers in matters of school discipline.[17] Moreover, collective interests, especially related to the provision of 'safe schools' in an era of near-hysteria over school violence,[18] have prompted the judicial trumping of individual student rights. Schools have been singled out as places where students should reasonably expect to exercise inferior individual rights in the name of safety, order, and discipline, and the collective welfare of the school community and, indeed, society at large. *Charter* jurisprudence on school-based searches provides some of the strongest evidence of MacKay's perspicacity.[19]

School Searches in the *Charter* Era: The Law of Search and Seizure under the *Charter*

Long before the *Charter*, English common law had provided a form of protection against searches and seizures carried out by agents of the Crown. In a speech to the English Parliament in 1763, William Pitt colourfully described this legal protection: 'The poorest man may in his cottage bid defiance to all the force of the Crown. It may be frail; its roof may shake; the wind may blow through it; the storms may enter, the rain may enter, – but the King of England cannot enter; all his forces dare not cross the threshold of the ruined tenement!'[20] Two years later, *Entick* v. *Carrington*[21] confirmed that entry of another's property, even by the King's messengers, was actionable as trespass unless authorized by a justice on the basis of sworn evidence that there was strong cause to enter and search the property. Although the origins of the common law right to be secure against search lay in property rights, suggesting its restriction to the searching of places, the Supreme Court of Canada determined in the landmark case of *Hunter* v. *Southam*[22] that s.8 *Charter* rights against unreasonable search and seizure involved a much broader guarantee of privacy against state intrusion and included searches of the person. Writing for the Court in *Hunter*, Dickson J noted that there was nothing in s.8 suggesting it should be limited to the protection of property. The rights in s.8 were to be read purposively as a broad and general protection. Justice Dickson drew on the U.S. Supreme Court's holding in *Katz* v. *United States*[23] that the Fourth Amendment of the U.S. Constitution (a somewhat wordier analogue of s.8) 'protects people, not places' and should be viewed as part of a broader right of *privacy* – a right 'to be let alone by other people.' Dickson J concluded, however, that the right to be secure from unreasonable search and seizure protected only 'a reasonable expectation of privacy' and was to be balanced against the state's interest in enforcing the law:

> The guarantee of security from unreasonable search and seizure only protects a reasonable expectation. This limitation on the right guaranteed by s.8, whether it is expressed negatively as freedom from "unreasonable" search and seizure, or positively as an entitlement to a "reasonable" expectation of privacy, indicates that an assessment must be made as to whether in a particular situation the public's interest in being left alone by government must give way to the government's interest in intruding on the individual's privacy in order to advance its goals, notably those of law enforcement.[24]

Hunter, then, set the broad parameters of the interpretation and application of s.8. It was to be given a broad, generous, and purposive meaning that went beyond property interests and comprised a sphere in which there could be said to be a reasonable expectation of individual privacy. In procedural terms the case established a presumption of unreasonableness where a search was carried out without proper judicial pre-authorization (a warrant) based on sworn evidence that there was probable cause – reasonable and probable grounds to believe evidence of a crime would be revealed. Although the Court acknowledged that, in some cases, time and circumstances militated against the reasonableness of requiring a warrant, such cases were very much the exception to the rule.[25] And beyond needing to be based on *reasonable grounds* – that is, a sufficient informational basis – a search was also to be carried out in a *reasonable fashion*, and not be excessively intrusive given all the circumstances.

The concept of reasonable expectation of privacy suggests that there are social contexts in which an individual has no such expectation – or only a diminished expectation – by virtue of the circumstances. Roach notes that no such expectation of privacy has been found (or that a diminished one existed) on behalf of individuals and businesses operating in a regulated field of activity, a person staying temporarily with a friend whose house was searched, passengers in a car that was searched, individuals passing through Customs at the border, inmates of prisons, and, most notably, students at school.[26] It is also fair to conclude that the more remote the context from the enforcement of the criminal law per se, the more the courts will permit encroachment into the sphere of personal privacy and grant the standard of reasonableness greater flexibility.[27]

Search and Seizure in Schools

As noted above, searching out pre-*Charter* school search and seizure cases appears very much a fool's errand. When my own research turned up nothing, and fearing I had missed something, I called upon a handful of Canada's leading Education Law scholars and lawyers. Like me, they were unaware of any such cases. The senior scholar among them, Bill Foster, wisely commented that school officials likely did what they pleased and that the parents were probably mostly glad for it![28] I think there are at least four reasonable hypotheses for the absence of such case law:

- The chance that any 'search' or 'seizure' that did occur related to a serious criminal matter that made its way to the courts was likely quite remote.
- Parental and judicial deference to educators in their day-to-day administrative and disciplinary practices made legal challenges relatively unthinkable; parents were not disposed to bringing them, and courts were not disposed to entertaining them.

- The enforcement of school rules was conceptualized as a matter of legitimate authority rather than a 'students' rights' issue; as MacKay says, the tradition was British-style peace, order, and good government, not American-style constitutional restraint on state power.[29]
- And, of course, there was no convenient legal vehicle for mounting such a challenge until the arrival of s.8 of the *Charter* in 1982.

Casting the Die: *R. v. G.(J.M.)*[30]

When, in 1984, an elementary school principal in Thunder Bay, Ontario, removed a tin-foil package from a student's sock he precipitated Canada's first student search case. In obiter dicta the District Court judge who heard the first appeal in the case stated that he had been unable to find any authority giving a principal the right to conduct a search of a student; the Ontario Court of Appeal likewise pronounced that there was no Canadian case dealing with the subject.[31] So the Court of Appeal's ruling had a powerful influence on subsequent cases, including the 1998 decision of the Supreme Court of Canada in *R v. M.(M.R.)*.[32]

J.M.G. was a 14-year-old student in Grade 7. The principal of J.M.G.'s school was told by a teacher that another student had seen J.M.G. putting drugs in his socks. Unsure how to proceed, the principal sought advice from a high school principal and a police officer. He subsequently escorted J.M.G. to his office where, in the vice-principal's presence, he told the student he suspected that he was carrying drugs and asked him to remove his shoes and socks. After J.M.G. swallowed a rolled cigarette that he removed from his pants cuff, the principal reached into the pants cuff area and retrieved a packet containing three cigarette butts. The police were summoned and J.M.G. was charged under the *Narcotic Control Act* with possession of marijuana.

A Youth Court judge convicted J.M.G. on the evidence provided by the principal's search. The District Court set aside the conviction because it could find no statutory or case law authorizing a school principal to search a student. The search was not just unreasonable; in the court's view, it was unlawful. No one was surprised when this ruling was appealed; the tradition of judicial deference to school disciplinary authority had just been slapped in the face.

Two *Charter* issues were argued at the Court of Appeal: was there a violation of J.M.G.'s s.8 right to be secure against unreasonable search and seizure, and his s.10(b) right, on detention, to retain and instruct counsel without delay? On the threshold issue of the *Charter's* application to the actions of a school principal, Justice Grange (for the court) assumed, without deciding the point, that it did apply. Contrary to what many believe, *J.M.G.* does *not* stand for the proposition that a school principal's actions are subject to *Charter* scrutiny.[33]

In the absence of relevant Canadian judicial authority, Justice Grange turned to the U.S. Supreme Court for guidance, specifically to its then recent ruling in *T.L.O.* In *T.L.O.* the Supreme Court considered whether an assistant vice-principal's search of a student's purse for cigarettes violated the student's Fourth Amendment rights. The Supreme Court dealt first with the threshold constitutional issue by ruling that the Fourth Amendment applied to school searches; its application was not limited to criminal authorities and, even though school authorities acted as surrogate parents, they also acted as agents of the state and could not claim parental immunity from the Constitution's application.

The substantive concern for the Court was summed up by Justice White, who asked, 'How, then, should we strike the balance between the schoolchild's legitimate expectations of privacy and the school's equally legitimate need to maintain an environment in which learning can take place?'[34] The Court achieved the balance by easing the restrictions normally associated with search – first, by removing the requirement for judicial pre-authorization (a warrant) and, second, by modifying the level of knowledge required to justify a search. Obtaining a warrant was considered unsuited to the school environment and would unduly interfere with the exercise of 'swift and informal disciplinary procedures.'[35] Further, a school's special environment and need to maintain order and discipline justified a standard of reasonableness short of probable cause, the usual constitutional touchstone. Justices Powell and O'Connor emphasized that the special characteristics of schools justified not affording students the same constitutional protections guaranteed adults and young people outside school. 'In any realistic sense,' they wrote, 'students within the school environment have a lesser expectation of privacy than members of the population generally.'[36]

Combining the need for order with the (albeit limited) privacy interests of students led the Court to establish that the constitutionality of the search of a student depends 'simply on the reasonableness, under all the circumstances, of the search.'[37] Justice White elaborated by stating a two-prong test for reasonableness:

First, one must consider 'whether the ... action was justified at its inception ... second, one must determine whether the search as actually conducted 'was reasonably related in scope to the circumstances which justified the interference in the first place' ... Under ordinary circumstances, a search of a student by a teacher or other school official will be 'justified at its inception' when there are reasonable grounds for suspecting that the search will turn up evidence that the student has violated or is violating either the law or the rules of the school. Such a search will be permissible in its scope when the measures adopted are reasonably related to the objectives of the search and not excessively intrusive in light of the age and sex of the student and the nature of the infraction.[38]

By striking a compromise – a lesser standard of 'reasonable suspicion' – the Court hoped to 'spare teachers and school administrators the necessity of schooling themselves in the niceties of probable cause and permit them to regulate their conduct according to the dictates of reason and common sense,' and 'ensure that the interests of students [would] be invaded no more than is necessary to achieve the legitimate end of preserving order in the schools.'[39]

Applying the *T.L.O.* test, Justice Grange held that the search of J.M.G. was 'not only justified at its inception but indeed was dictated by the circumstances.'[40] Given the principal's statutory duty under s. 236(a) – now 265(a) – of the *Education Act* 'to maintain proper order and discipline in the school,' and given the information he had received, his actions were not unreasonable. They were related to the proper objectives of order and discipline and the nature of the search was not overly intrusive. Reminiscent of the words of the U.S. Supreme Court in *T.L.O.* and the Supreme Court of Canada in *Hunter*, Justice Grange pointed to society's interest in maintaining an orderly school environment, which necessitated the ability to enforce disciplinary rules efficiently. It was 'neither feasible nor desirable' that a principal obtain prior authorization before searching a student and seizing contraband.

Justice Grange explained that even though the *Charter* applied to school principals (at least he assumed so) and police officers, there was a world of difference between the two. Principals, by necessity, had discretion to decide whether to deal in-house with infractions, involve the students' parents or call the police. To exercise that discretion, they needed to know the nature and extent of the students' misdeeds. Moreover, the relationship between a principal and a student was 'not remotely like that of a policeman and citizen,' particularly because a principal 'has a substantial interest not only in the welfare of the other students but in the accused student as well.'[41]

The court recognized there may be times when the circumstances are so 'obvious and so heinous that police participation [is] inevitable.'[42] Indeed; but when that occurs and the police are already present, or when the search is conducted at their behest, does the principal's persona change? Are the rationales for the relaxed constitutional standard still defensible? Justice Grange raised these questions by implication and the Supreme Court of Canada provided an answer – of sorts – in *M.R.M.* These are not trivial concerns; they harbour considerable potential for abuse of constitutional rights, as I discuss below.

The remaining issue for the Court of Appeal was whether J.M.G.'s s.10(b) right to counsel had been violated. This right is premised on a 'detention' – a simple enough word but one loaded with legal meaning. Despite J.M.G.'s undoubted belief that he was not free to leave the office and that his liberty was constrained by a person in authority, Justice Grange ruled that the meaning of detention in s.10(b) was restricted to the criminal justice system. Furthermore, as he had pointed out, the roles of principals and police officers were 'not remotely' similar. It would be absurd to hold that s.10(b) rights were engaged every time a child was detained in school – a common occurrence. It seems to me, however, that there is a grave danger in failing to consider that there are detentions, and there are *detentions*. Granted there may, in general, be a world of difference between the roles of principals and police officers but so is there between a detention for being late or failing to hand in work, and a detention for the purpose of searching for evidence of a crime that could result in incarceration and a criminal record, especially where the detention, search, and questioning are at the advice or behest of the police, or, even more important, take place in their presence! In fairness, Justice Grange did speculate that because 'significant legal consequences' sometimes become 'inevitable,' the principal could become 'an agent of the police in detecting crime.' But that apparently was not argued in this case and J.M.G.'s s.10 argument was dismissed by the Court of Appeal and his conviction restored.

All was not quiet in the aftermath of *J.M.G.* Some criminal lawyers were incensed by the court's reduced threshold for student search and most certainly by its refusal to afford students a s.10(b) right to counsel on being detained for suspected criminal conduct. In a blunt critique in the *Ontario Criminal Lawyers' Association Newsletter*, Stanley AvRuskin asked, 'Is the possession of a marijuana cigarette in a school of such social significance that a contrived argument is launched and accepted in the Ontario Court of Appeal with the result that the *Charter of Rights and Freedoms* does not apply within school grounds to bona fide students? Do students know this [*sic*] by way of informed consent that, when they register at an Ontario school under *The Education Act*, they give up their fundamental constitutional *Charter* [*sic*] rights?'[43] Describing *J.M.G.* as a 'product of overkill,' the experienced counsel of young offenders ended his polemic by urging that 'we should go back to school to learn why young persons there are being shortchanged on their rights.'[44]

J.M.G. was also the subject of academic comment. Wayne MacKay took Justice Grange to task for conferring second-class citizenship on students.[45] Acknowledging that the presumption of unreasonableness established in *Hunter* for warrantless searches was technically inapplicable to searches by school officials, MacKay suggested that the spirit of this presumption could be preserved by establishing another one: '[i]f a breach of the school rule has criminal consequences, then the starting assumption should be that the police and not a school official should do the search.'[46] Concerned about importing *T.L.O.*'s lower threshold into Canadian law, he warned that the lower standard of reasonableness the court had set for school officials might 'provide a strong incentive for the police to develop a cozy relationship with school officials to the mutual benefit of both state agencies and to the detriment of students' privacy rights [under] s.8 of the *Charter*.'[47]

MacKay was equally critical of the court's treatment of the s.10 issue. Commenting on Justice Grange's observation that students are always in a state of detention because of compulsory attendance laws, MacKay likened their plight to that of the involuntary inmates of another social institution where the values of order and discipline are seen to justify the trumping of rights. Grange JA's analysis meant that '*Charter* rights will be triggered only when the detention is in respect of a serious criminal matter, and not when the detention is in the regular course of a student's life. This sounds more like an educational prison than a training ground for citizens to populate a free and democratic society.'[48] MacKay contended that the court's characterization of the nature of school discipline and, consequently, student rights, overemphasized the archaic *in loco parentis* doctrine that increasingly has given way to state agency as the operative legal model. Much as I argue above, and below, he warned that '[t]he view that school officials are paternalistic figures pursuing the child's welfare at all times is a dangerous fallacy.'[49]

Although, in an article of my own, I proposed that the flexible, pragmatic approach of the Court of Appeal would be met by a 'collective sigh of relief by principals across the country,' I also voiced concern about aspects of the decision, especially the confusion it left regarding the principal's legal persona and the issue of police involvement:

> Whenever students are detained ... under circumstances where significant legal consequences are inevitable, they may then be viewed as being detained within the meaning of s.10(b) of the *Charter*. As such, they would be entitled to the right to retain and instruct counsel without delay and be informed of that right. Under these circumstances, the school authorities are acting as agents of the police. *When* do principals become agents of the police? The linch-pin of that determination is the decision to call the police; without that decision legal consequences can hardly be said to be "inevitable."'[50] The court's approach, it seemed to me, appeared to leave principals with 'considerable control over the legal features of their role and [thus] over the extent of rights due students.[51]

The subsequent erosion of principals' discretion effected by provincial 'zero tolerance' regimes[52] has changed my thinking somewhat, as I indicate below.

Although subsequent student search decisions appear mostly to have fallen in line with *J.M.G.*,[53] some courts have continued to struggle with the competing values at stake in school searches and the prospect that principals might be aiding the administration of the criminal justice system, but with reduced constitutional responsibilities, at the same time they are carrying out their duties as educational agents of the state.[54] The Supreme Court of Canada was expected to clear up the matter on its first opportunity to consider school searches. That opportunity came in 1998 as the result of a drug search conducted by a Nova Scotia vice-principal under circumstances remarkably similar to those in *J.M.G.*, with one notable exception – this time the police were present throughout the search.

The Supreme Court Weighs In: *R.* v. *M.R.M.*[55]

The facts in *M.R.M.* were relatively straightforward and, as indicated, bore a striking resemblance to what happened in *J.M.G.* There are, however, two important divergences: in the Nova Scotia case an RCMP officer was present during the search and, unlike in *J.M.G.*, the Supreme Court of Canada granted leave to appeal from the Court of Appeal decision, presumably because of the police's presence and the issue of whether the vice-principal had acted as their agent.

A few weeks before a school dance at a Halifax high school, the vice-principal, Cadue, had been informed by two students that another student, 13-year-old M.R.M., had been selling drugs at the school. Cadue believed the reports because the informants were acquaintances of M.R.M. and information supplied previously by one of them had proven accurate. On the day of the dance, Cadue was advised by one of the informants that M.R.M. would be carrying drugs at the dance. Upon M.R.M.'s arrival at the dance, Cadue telephoned the RCMP and requested that an officer be sent to the school. Subsequently, the vice-principal approached M.R.M. and asked the boy to accompany him to his office, where he inquired whether he was carrying drugs. He also told M.R.M. that he intended to search him.

Before the search began, Constable Siepierski arrived at the office in plainclothes and identified himself as a police officer. He sat silently on a desk and took no active role while Cadue searched M.R.M. Upon request, M.R.M. turned his pockets inside out but nothing was found. After M.R.M. rolled up his pant legs, again at Cadue's request, a bulge was revealed in one of his socks. The sock contained a cellophane bag, which Cadue seized and turned over to Siepierski, who concluded that it contained marijuana. The police officer advised M.R.M. that he was under arrest for possession of a narcotic and read him his rights, including his right to counsel under s.10(b) of the *Charter*.

The Youth Court acquitted M.R.M. after ruling that the fruits of the search conducted by Cadue were inadmissible. Having found evidence of an 'agreed strategy,' whereby Cadue would conduct the search and the police would lay a charge if the search were productive, the court concluded that Cadue had acted as an agent of the police. According to the judge, '[b]y this stage a criminal investigation was in full flight.'[56] As a police agent, Cadue was subject to constitutional obligations that had not been discharged. Consequently, the evidence he gathered was excluded.

As in *J.M.G.* the Court of Appeal assumed the *Charter*'s application on the basis that Cadue was exercising a governmental function as an 'educational state agent,' especially given the Crown's reliance on the vice-principal's statutory powers under the *Education Act* to justify the search. Writing for the court, Pugsley JA acknowledged that s.8 of the *Charter* conferred a reasonable expectation of privacy but noted that the Supreme Court of Canada had ruled that it was subject to limitation in certain contexts, especially regulatory, as opposed to purely criminal, contexts. Like judicial 'Muzak,' the familiar strains of the 'order and discipline' anthem supplied the underlying policy mood for Justice Pugsley's analysis. The critical social imperatives of a 'strong, orderly educational system' and a safe educational environment necessitated granting teachers and principals the powers they required to ensure these objectives were realized, especially with all the drug trafficking that was occurring in schools. The rights of young people in schools, therefore, needed to be interpreted within this context.

Now there is nothing wrong per se with a good, old-fashioned social-utilitarian argument – assuming it is supported by evidence of the evils to be addressed (or conversely the social good to be realized). The problem with the familiar rationale adopted by the Court of Appeal, and taken up subsequently by the Supreme Court of Canada, is that it is rarely – and it apparently was not here – supported by any valid and reliable data for the court's generalization that a sufficiently egregious and pressing social problem exists in the schools to justify the erosion of *all* students' legal rights. If the utility of detecting and preventing crime were the only concern, then why not abridge *all citizens'* rights? Why not give the police authority to randomly search any house? Sooner or later they would be bound to find evidence of serious crimes and to thwart a lot of criminal activity. There is a simple answer: utilitarian rationales alone are insufficient where the power of the criminal law is involved because of its sheer force and the serious threat of state oppression of human liberty and privacy rights.[57] Apparently for the court, however, what is going on in schools when educators search pupils is different: it is not *real* criminal law, despite the fact that in most of the cases the searcher invariably expects to turn over the fruits of the search – and its subject – to the police. So here is where the real issue lies: this is not *real* criminal law in action, at least not while the process is in the hands of the principal (unless, of course, he or she is acting in concert with or as an agent of the police!).

The Nova Scotia Court of Appeal rejected the Youth Court's finding of police agency, concluding that there was insufficient evidence of such a relationship. Mere presence of the police was not enough: there was no evidence that the officer and the vice-principal had acted in concert. And the hapless accused student had offered in testimony that, yes, he thought Mr Cadue had been in charge because he was 'the boss of the school.'

Applying the two-part *T.L.O.* test adopted in *J.M.G.*, Pugsley JA had little difficulty finding, first, that the information conveyed to Cadue – coming as it did from known-to-be-reliable sources – had supplied the necessary grounds for the search based on the lower threshold of reasonable suspicion required for school authorities. And, second, the search had not been excessively intrusive and had been conducted in the relative privacy of the vice-principal's office. As for M.R.M.'s s.10 rights, the Court of Appeal accepted Justice Grange's reasoning that a school detention was beyond the pale of s.10(b) rights and nothing more than an extension of normal school discipline and the execution of the principal's statutory duties under the *Education Act*.

MacKay's condemnation of the Court of Appeal decision in *M.R.M.*[58] was perhaps even more stinging than his critique of *J.M.G.*[59] I, too, commented[60] on problems with the court's reasoning and its implications. Inasmuch as there was considerable agreement between the Court of Appeal and the Supreme Court of Canada, it seems sensible to reserve critical comment until after a summary of the Supreme Court's decision.

The *Charter's* overall application to the vice-principal's actions was not in serious issue at the Supreme Court. The Crown had conceded as much and it was really only a question of which rationale for its application was the correct one. The Court found it unnecessary to answer that question, however, and simply assumed that government agency was a sufficient reason.

The Court's treatment of the derivative issue of just what part of the state the vice-principal was an agent of – the education system or the police – was much lengthier. As I pointed out in my comment on the Supreme Court decision in this case, this issue 'was central to the ultimate determination of the case in at least two ways. First, a principal acting as a police agent would be disqualified from availing himself of relaxed search standards, should the Court agree that such lower standards indeed exist in schools; and, second, detentions by the police and their agents would trigger a s.10(b) *Charter* right to counsel.'[61]

The majority applied the Court's own test from *R* v. *Broyles*[62] to determine the issue of police agency. *Broyles* established that such agency occurred only where the exchange between the accused and an alleged police agent would not have taken place in the same form and manner except for the intervention of the police.[63] Like the Court of Appeal, the Supreme Court found no evidence to satisfy this test and, in fact, pointed to parts of the accused's own testimony that appeared to belie any direction of the affair by the police officer. There was nothing new in the Court's observation that '[a]lthough Mr Cadue knew that criminal charges might result, the primary motive for the search was the enforcement of school discipline, for which he was responsible.'[64] Again, the Court's words at least imply that the legal persona of the principal is defined by intention, requiring a probing of his or her state of mind. This approach presumes a degree of administrative flexibility or discretion that may no longer be realistic in an era of zero tolerance, and mandatory sanctions and reporting to police.

The vice-principal, then, was operating as an educational state agent. Did that mean, following the reasoning in *T.L.O.*, *J.M.G.*, and the Court of Appeal in *M.R.M.*, that a lower standard for reasonable search applied? The answer depended, first, on whether s.8 rights were even engaged at school and, if so, whether the Supreme Court agreed that schools were a special context justifying a lower (in quality and magnitude) reasonable expectation of privacy by students. The Court had no difficulty concluding that a student had a *subjective* (personal) expectation that school authorities would respect the privacy of his or her person and items carried on the person. And, given the historical importance in English law of a privacy interest in one's person, this expectation was also reasonable in an *objective* sense, thus engaging s.8 rights. Citing itself in *Hunter*, and its recognition therein that some contexts justify lesser expectations of privacy, the majority concluded that

> the reasonable expectation of privacy of a student in attendance at a school is certainly less than it would be in other circumstances. Students know that their teachers and other school authorities are responsible for providing a safe environment and maintaining order and discipline in the school. They must know that this may sometimes require searches of students and their personal effects and the seizure of prohibited items. It would not be reasonable for a student to expect to be free from such searches. A student's reasonable expectation of privacy in the school environment is therefore significantly diminished.[65]

In stating the 'evidence' for its rationale for an inferior expectation of privacy and, hence, diminished constitutional responsibilities for educators searching students, the Court revealed its oneness with the public perception that schools *in general* were drug- and weapon-infested dens of social disorder. A blanket rule, therefore, was justified by an undifferentiated assumption about the nature of schools and the prolificacy of problems therein that were thwarting educators' ability to teach and threatening everyone's safety. The Court stated that 'illicit drugs and dangerous weapons' have 'increased to the extent that they challenge the ability of school officials to fulfill their responsibility to maintain a safe and orderly environment. Current conditions make it necessary to provide teachers and school administrators with the flexibility required to deal with discipline problems in schools.'[66]

When courts express policy that erodes civil liberties and rights, especially with penal consequences, the reasons they adopt for that policy should be of the utmost importance, and the nature of the evidence upon which such reasons rest should be capable of withstanding the most careful scrutiny. In *M.R.M.* it is doubtful that the Court had such evidence of the 'current conditions' they felt necessitated their policy stance. As I wondered in my comment on the case: 'Did the justices then take "judicial notice" of an increase in drug and weapon possession in schools sufficient to warrant eroding the constitutional rights of students' right across the country? If so, this is a highly questionable exercise of this judicial prerogative, given the work of Dolmage and others who warn about the danger of inaccurate public perceptions of youth crime crafting false "realties" which, in turn, drive bad public policy.'[67]

Regardless of the quality of the evidence supporting it, the Supreme Court's assumption that there was an escalating drug and weapons problem in schools was the basis of its ruling that a lower standard should apply to searches conducted at school by school authorities. The Court summarized the reduced standard and its application as follows:

(1) A warrant is not essential in order to conduct a search of a student by a school authority.
(2) The school authority must have reasonable grounds to believe that there has been a breach of school regulations or discipline and that a search of a student would reveal evidence of that breach.
(3) School authorities will be in the best position to assess information given to them and relate it to the situation existing in their school. Courts should recognize the preferred position of school authorities to determine if reasonable grounds existed for the search.
(4) The following may constitute reasonable grounds in this context: information received from one student considered to be credible, information received from more than one student, a teacher's or principal's own observations, or any combination of these pieces of information which the relevant authority considers to be credible. The compelling nature of the information and the credibility of these or other sources must be assessed by the school authority in the context of the circumstances existing at the particular school.[68]

In broad terms, the Court did not tell us anything we had not heard before in *T.L.O.* and *J.M.G.* This was essentially the two-prong test from *T.L.O.* – reasonableness at inception and in scope. To be reasonable at inception the search had to be based on information giving the person conducting it a reasonable belief (as opposed to reasonable and probable grounds) that the search would turn up evidence of a breach of school rules or criminal activity (the latter undoubtedly being subsumed in the former). Careful readers will note, however, that the Supreme Court of Canada's test for sufficient grounds – reasonable *belief* – is not exactly the same as that struck in *T.L.O.* by the U.S. Supreme Court, who used the phrase reasonable *suspicion*. One might argue, then, that the test created by the Supreme Court of Canada is more stringent than the *T.L.O.* test, if words mean anything at all. In 'Still Searching for Reason,' I explained the inconsistency in the tests: 'Viewed as a continuum, the responses a person can have to information she or he is given about something fall between certainty of belief and certainty of disbelief. Suspicions, one would have thought, would fall somewhere in the middle. One normally associates a lower degree of reliability with "suspicion," as opposed to "belief." I may suspect something to be the case, but find that I lack the evidence (and consequent moral certainty) to believe it to be true and hence to justify a particular course of action.'[69] Is this a trivial distinction? Perhaps, but I don't think so. One has to wonder whether the test has meaning at all given such careless wording unless the Court really did mean to establish a stiffer-than-*T.L.O.* test.

Judicial deference to school authorities was also implicit in the lower threshold of information required for a student search. However, the Court went on to *explicitly* re-cement its traditional deference in place – shaken loose by the arrival of the *Charter* and the District Court's decision in *J.M.G.* – by stating that school authorities were best positioned to assess whether the information they received gave them reasonable grounds to search. The message to lower courts seems clear enough: there should be no judicial second-guessing of an educator's determination of reasonable cause.

The Supreme Court disposed of the s.10(b) right to counsel argument as easily as the Courts of Appeal in *M.R.M.* and *J.M.G.* had, and for essentially identical reasons; s.10 rights were devised to safeguard individuals against the coercive powers of a criminal investigation and school detentions hardly fit the bill. The Court stated, 'The right to counsel provided in s.10(b) was designed to address the vulnerable position of an individual who has been detained by the coercive power of the state in the course of a criminal investigation, and is thus deprived of his or her liberty and placed at the risk of making self-incriminating statements ... Its application in the school context is inappropriate and would lead to absurd results.'[70]

Embedded in the Court's words is the assumption that a 13-year-old student 'detained' in the office of the principal – the 'boss of the school' to use M.R.M.'s words – on suspicion of committing a criminal offence is somehow neither vulnerable nor in danger of having the full force of the criminal justice system descend on him. It is beyond question that a principal is an agent of the state – after all, this was the reason the Court found the *Charter* applied – with considerable statutory power. The very power to search was inferred by the courts in *J.M.G.* and *M.R.M.* from language in the respective *Education Acts*. Nor can it seriously be thought that in cases such as these administrators do not know full well, when embarking on such searches, that if they find what led them to search the students in the first place, they will be turning both the evidence and the students over to the police and appearing in court as Crown witnesses. Regardless of Justice Grange's idealistic distinguishing of a principal from a police officer because of the former's 'interest in the welfare' of the student-suspect, the reality is that the principal's evidence will often be a, if not *the*, key part of the prosecution's case. This is not the kind of discretionary matter that Justice Grange would have us believe it to be. His comment in *J.M.G.* that finding marijuana on a student might not even warrant calling in the police is completely out of touch with the 'zero tolerance' regimes in place today in schools in Ontario and elsewhere.[71] 'Finally, as I said in "Still Searching for Reason," it is hard to fathom why the application of s.10(b) of the *Charter* in the context of crime-implicated school investigations ... would be any more "absurd" than the application of s.56 of the *Young Offenders Act* [now s.146 of the *Youth Criminal Justice Act*], which protects almost identical interests and which has been held to constrain principals' interrogations of young persons reasonably suspected of having committed criminal offences.'[72] As I said earlier, there are detentions, and there are *detentions*. Crafting a rule based on the supposition that all school detentions are cut from the same cloth is just as nonsensical as crafting a lower standard of search to apply in all schools premised on the assumption that the exigencies possibly justifying such a standard in some schools obtain in every school.

Beyond *M.R.M.*

Although the Supreme Court adopted a conservative stance in *M.R.M.* regarding what it would take to cast a principal as a police agent, and in recognizing a diminished expectation of privacy for students at school, some lower courts have recognized the consequent potential for abuse of students' rights. Two Ontario cases exemplify this concern. In an unreported case,[73] a Guelph judge ruled in 2001 that a search carried out by a vice-principal at the behest of a police officer was not reasonable and that the evidence obtained in the search should be excluded. The police officer testified that he had advised the vice-principal that he wished to speak to a certain student because he believed he had witnessed a drug deal outside the school. The officer did not, however, search the student himself because he did not believe he had requisite cause. Defence counsel's argument that the police officer had recruited the school administrator to search the student was accepted by the judge, who was satisfied that the vice-principal had indeed been acting under the police officer's direction when she asked the student to turn out his pockets.

In the second case, *R. v. A.M.*,[74] a Youth Court judge dealt with a situation that in some ways was the obverse of that in *M.R.M.*, that is, whether the search was conducted under circumstances that would allow the operation of the relaxed standard for reasonable grounds, despite the fact that the police themselves had conducted it. In *A.M.*, the search of a student's backpack had been precipitated by the actions of a drug-detection dog, and had occurred in response to a standing invitation issued to the police by the principal to bring drug-detection dogs to the school whenever they were available. On the day in question, the police arrived without prior notice and, after asking the principal's permission, conducted a general search of the school with the assistance of a drug-detection dog. After they had finished, the police asked the principal whether he wished them to search any particular place. He asked that they search one of the gymnasiums – the location of the backpack that was ultimately found to contain marijuana and psilocybin (magic mushrooms). Neither the principal nor any teacher took any active part in the searches.

Unsurprisingly, the judge found no evidence that the school authorities had been acting as agents of the police. Conversely, because they had adopted a passive role, the school authorities had not been directing the police in the search, precluding the finding that this was a search by school officials that was amenable to the lower threshold for reasonable grounds. Justice Hornblower found that there were no reasonable grounds for the search, regardless of which standard was used – that applying to the police or that applying to the school authorities. The basis for the search was the principal's apparent belief that on any given day there would be drugs in the school, as well as concerns expressed by parents and neighbours based on what they had observed, but not on the day in question. In response to the Crown's attempt, no doubt, to avail itself of the Supreme Court's direction to lower courts to defer to school authorities in determining reasonable grounds to search, the court stated, 'While some flexibility must be extended to school authorities with respect to what information will give them reasonable grounds, I do not believe the intent of the Supreme Court in M.R.M. is to allow a reasonably well educated guess to constitute reasonable grounds.'[75]

In finding that admitting the illegally obtained evidence would bring the administration of justice into disrepute, Justice Hornblower refused to sacrifice meaningful *Charter* rights on the altar of law enforcement expediency simply because the alleged crime happened to take place at a school:

> In a similar case considered by the British Columbia Court of Appeal,[76] concern was expressed by the court that in a school setting it is not an appropriate lesson for students to see the *Charter* as a shield. While that may well be the case, equally important is that the *Charter* must not be seen as something to discard in the interests of expediency. While this case centres on the rights of A.M., 'the rights of every student in the school were violated that day as they were all subject to an unreasonable search ... To admit the evidence is effectively to strip A.M. and any other student in a similar situation of the right to be free from unreasonable search and seizure.'[77]

Upon appeal by the Crown, the Ontario Court of Appeal agreed that Justice Hornblower had decided the case correctly. In upholding his ruling, the appeal court stated that there were no grounds for disturbing his rejection of the evidence in a case that involved such a serious breach of the *Charter* – a random, warrantless, and legally unauthorized search that involved the detention of an entire school body.[78]

As many expected, *R. v. A.M.* found its way to the Supreme Court of Canada, which released its 6 to 3 split decision on 25 April 2008.[79] The Court dealt with several issues in its complex ruling, but the following are the salient points emerging from the majority's reasons for judgment:

1 The subject-matter of the sniff search was not public airspace but the concealed contents of the student's backpack.
2 Briefcases, purses, suitcases, and backpacks bear special consideration because they often hold very personal contents, especially in the case of highly itinerant persons such as students and travellers.
3 Teenagers have an expectation, even at school, that the contents of

their backpacks will not be open to random fishing expeditions by the police. Such an expectation is reasonable and important enough to merit societal support.

4 A warrantless, sniffer-dog search will be constitutional where reasonable suspicion, as opposed to the stricter standard of reasonable belief, can be shown. But the subjectivity implied by the lower standard must be tempered by the requirement that the suspicion be based on 'objectively verifiable indications.'

Particularly poignant in the A.M. case, especially in the judgment of Justice Hornblower, is the focus on the educational message sent to students by how the *Charter* was applied to alleged criminal activity in school. I want to put aside the narrow legal issues in the two cases discussed above and consider the general implications of what the courts were saying. In my view, Justice Hornblower had it exactly right:[80] if any message needs to be delivered to students as part of the formation of their civic character it is that justification for transgressing constitutional rights should never be easy, certainly not merely to facilitate the prosecution of suspects. The British Columbia court's concern that students not see the *Charter* as a shield to criminal activity is misdirected. What is the *Charter* – especially its guarantee of legal rights – if not a shield against the potential abuse of state power? Moreover, it is an accepted legal reality that, far and away, the *Charter* is applied more in criminal cases than in any other kind of legal matters. Is there some reason why students are not to be apprised of this reality and the reasons for it? The operation of the system of justice within a school is a powerful part of the hidden curriculum influencing students. Justice Stevens underscored the particular implications of the hidden curriculum in his dissent in *T.L.O.*:

> The schoolroom is the first opportunity most citizens have to experience the power of government. Through it passes every citizen and public official, from schoolteachers to policemen and prison guards. The values they learn there, they take with them in life … The Court's decision today is a curious moral for the Nation's youth.[81]

Justice is largely about how wisely legal authority is used in both a substantive and procedural sense. Are rules defensible on moral grounds and are they enforced fairly? These are lessons taugh in school day in and day out – largely through the behaviour of people in authority.

Conclusion

One of MacKay's most powerful criticisms of the Ontario Court of Appeal's decision in *J.M.G.* was based on what he termed a 'sin of omission.' That is, the court had failed to probe competing educational theories affecting school discipline and simply adopted unquestioningly the traditional assumption that emphasized 'the value of order [and] educator's [*sic*] discretion' at the expense of theories that stress 'student autonomy and the exercise of individual rights.'[82] Although he acknowledged that he and Justice Grange seemed to agree that educational considerations should condition legal structures in schools, he noted wryly that he suspected that where they disagreed was 'on the proper role of education in Canadian society.'[83] He contended that '[i]t is at least as important to provide students with a model of justice and equality in our schools as it is to teach them the admitted virtue of following rules and accepting the consequences of breaching them.'[84] I would put it this way: teaching students that they must take responsibility for their wrongful acts should not trump their rights as citizens to be protected against the improperly exercised power of the state. That is the lesson that ultimately benefits us all. As former federal Progressive Conservative leader, Robert Stanfield, remarked, 'Civil liberties in Canada will ... continue to depend basically upon the importance Canadians attach to them and upon our willingness to defend them even in times of stress. In our search for protection from violence we must recognize that arbitrary abrogation of individual rights weakens rather than strengthens social order.'[85]

MacKay has also argued that, in *J.M.G.* and *M.R.M.*, the courts wrongfully applied a 'role-based' rather than 'results-oriented' model of analysis. The result was the adoption of legal rules that fail to distinguish situations where administrators are looking for evidence of simple school infractions from those where they are searching for evidence of criminal conduct. The root problem is the courts' obsession with basing the principles governing school searches on the nature or character of the principal and his or her role, rather than the impact of what he or she is actually doing in such cases. The rights afforded students during searches, MacKay argued, should depend on 'the impact a detention or search will have upon the accused, and not upon who is doing the searching or detaining.'[86]

Though not without its own problems, which I briefly point out below, MacKay's impact- or results-based construct makes sense. First, it obviates the problem that there are detentions and there are *detentions*, just as there are searches, and there are *searches*. Looking at the purpose and the potential result of a detention (or search), it is possible to avoid both the absurdity that so concerned the court regarding affording *Charter* rights in trivial school disciplinary matters as well as the diminishment or outright deprivation of those rights in serious matters that implicate the criminal justice system and have significant legal repercussions for students. The role-based test developed in *J.M.G.* and *M.R.M.* has a serious liability: it is based on the subjective *intentions* of the administrator. Justice Grange posited that a principal needed flexibility to exercise his or her discretion whether to implement any of several disciplinary options. Although there may indeed be cases where principals have no idea what they will do and what the overall implications are pending fuller investigation of their suspicions (and therein lies the potential weakness in MacKay's model in some instances), in serious matters where school rule breaches and criminal acts coalesce, discretion becomes a moot point. As I argued above, principals know what the result will be in such cases: school board, if not provincial, policies now largely prescribe their actions.

I suggest that MacKay's objective impact model (a form of which is in place in the *Youth Criminal Justice Act* to prescribe *Miranda*-like[87] responsibilities for a person in authority who has reasonable grounds for believing a young person has committed a criminal offence) is to be preferred over the opaque and potentially inconsistent role-based test. It is preferable for courts to determine, on a case-by-case basis, the question of students' rights based on the objective test of whether there were reasonable grounds to believe there would be criminal consequences. This takes the vagueness of the principal's subjective intention out of play.

The consequences of such a test for educators, in my view, are preferable to navigating the worrisome labyrinth involved in answering the question that courts will always be concerned about with the *J.M.G./M.R.M.* test: 'Have I as a principal done something to transform my role into that of a police agent, thereby imperiling an entire prosecution should I fail to abide by the higher constitutional standards?' This is a serious question for all concerned. The consequence of a results- or impact-oriented approach would be that all investigations, especially searches, involving criminal consequences eventually would fall to the police. There would be no reason for that not to happen inasmuch as there would be no strategic constitutional advantage in having the searches conducted by educators. Ontario policy-makers have recognized the wisdom of such an approach. The *Provincial Model for a Local Police/School Board Protocol* provides that a required element for local school board/police protocols must be that only the police should conduct personal searches.[88] Although one cannot be confident about how faithfully this rule is followed, it is nevertheless sensible and based on sound theoretical, and practical, considerations.

The appellate courts' approach to student discipline, especially search powers, under the *Charter* has simply been to rewrite the old rules using *Charter* language. The traditional emphasis on order and discipline has been used as a judicial platform for adopting a lower expectation of privacy on the part of students at school. Canadian students carry constitutional rights through the schoolhouse gate, but not all those on which they are entitled to rely in the wider community. Furthermore, the attitude that school discipline is a special 'case' (even where the criminal law is implicated) that justifies the awarding of considerable discretion, latitude, and flexibility to administrators, is alive and well in the courts' establishment of a lower threshold for search and in their view that the notion of s.10(b) rights is mostly absurd in a school setting. Finally, the judiciary's traditional pre-*Charter* deference to school disciplinarians could not be more plainly evident than in the Supreme Court's admonition to lower courts to respect educators' subjective views as to whether they had reasonable grounds to search.

It is a trite observation that schools are special places. They are large collectives of vulnerable young people who reflect, act out, and become victims of some of society's worst ills. No one, including me, should go about suggesting that criminal activity in schools should not be treated as a serious matter. The issue is *how* it is handled. I began by quoting the U.S. Supreme Court's recognition that determining student rights was a great and difficult balancing exercise whereby the rights of individual students had to be weighed against those of other students and of the broader society that expects schools to be safe and orderly. No one quarrels with that. But what kind of balance is struck, and what kind of message is sent about the seriousness of *Charter* rights, when judicial reasoning diminishes rights based on broad, stereotypical assumptions and creates a situation which the criminal justice arm of the state views as opportunistic? That the lower courts at least appear to be vigilant about this is heartening, and perhaps all one can do is hope that they continue to be so.

8 Corporal Punishment and Education: Oh Canada! Spare Us!

AILSA M. WATKINSON

In 1995 an Ontario Provincial Court ruled that the physical punishment by an American tourist on his 5-year-old daughter in a restaurant parking lot was 'reasonable under the circumstances' and thus her father was acquitted of assaulting her.[1] At the time I wrote a viewpoint in our local newspaper critical of the defence available to parents and teachers who use force on children.[2] The defence is found in s.43 of the *Criminal Code*[3] of Canada and it states: 'Every school teacher, parent or person standing in the place of the parent is justified in using force by way of correction toward the pupil or child, as the case may be, who is under his care, if the force does not exceed what is reasonable under the circumstances.'[4]

The defence is used by parents, teachers, and others acting in the place of a parent when they are charged with assault. I argued that the s.43 defence may violate at least three sections of the *Canadian Charter of Rights and Freedoms*.[5] First, s.43 discriminates against children on the basis of their age since the defence is only available to those who use force on children (s.15); second, the defence violates a child's right to security of the person (s.7); and third, physical punishment was a form of cruel and unusual punishment (s.12). After the article appeared in the paper, I was encouraged to pursue the argument. I applied for funding through the Court Challenges Program to conduct research into the constitutionality of s.43.[6] The Court Challenges Program then provided funding to take the case forward as a *Charter* challenge. The case eventually wound its way to the Supreme Court of Canada (herein referred to as the Court) and on 30 January 2004 it ruled, in a 6–3 decision that the *Charter* rights of children were not violated by the s.43 defence.[7]

The decision was hailed as 'a strong and balanced landmark ruling' by the Canadian Teachers' Federation (CTF) since the ruling maintained the right of teachers to use reasonable force 'for purposes of restraint, removal of a child from a classroom or to gain compliance with instructions.'[8] The decision of the Court was a disappointment for me both as a parent and teacher, and for others who had worked to bring an end to this legal defence.

The Court, however, significantly limited the protection afforded parents and teachers under s.43 and these limitations have enormous implications for teachers and the education they provide. The purpose of this chapter is to critically analyse and discuss the Supreme Court's decision, the CTF's involvement in the case, and the implications of the decision for teachers and administrators. In this task I am firmly situated within a children's rights framework, one that I consider more conducive to those who provide public education to children and youth, so the perspective I offer in this chapter is quintessentially a personal view.

The Legal Authority for Corporal Punishment

The right of teachers to use force on children to correct their behaviour has been part of our *Criminal Code* since its inception in 1892 and part of civil practice since Roman times. The authority of school officials to administer corporal punishment is passed on to them through the common law doctrine of *in loco parentis*, which means 'in the place of a parent.' The classic statement of this doctrine comes from eighteenth-century legal scholar Sir William Blackstone: '[A parent] may also delegate part of his parental authority during his life, to the tutor or school master of his child; who is the *in loco parentis*, and has such a portion of the power of the parent committed to his charge, viz.: that of restraint and correction, as may be necessary to answer the purposes for which he is employed.'[9]

According to Anne McGillivray, a law professor who has written extensively on the history of corporal punishment of children, the defence of correction of children originated in Roman law over sixteen hundred years ago and was then taken up in ecclesiastical law and urged as a mode of inducing obedience during the Protestant Reformation.[10] Eventually the defence of correction found its way into English common law and was codified together with other common law defences in Canada's first *Criminal Code* in 1892. Section 55 of the original *Code* was placed within a grouping entitled 'Protection of Persons in Authority,' and it stated: 'It is lawful for every parent, or person in the place of a parent, schoolmaster or master, to use force by way of correction towards any child, pupil or apprentice under his care, provided that such force is reasonable under the circumstances.' Other persons entitled to use corporal punishment elsewhere in the 1892 *Code* included the masters of ships 'maintaining discipline', those performing surgical operations, judges, and prison wardens. [11] Over the past number of years we have recognized corporal punishment to be a cruel form of discipline and, with the exception of children, it can no longer be legally administered to any other group of Canadians.

Section 43 of the *Criminal Code* uses the term 'force' which, in the context of s.43, can be either corporal punishment or restraint. Corporal punishment is frequently defined as 'the use of physical force with the intention of causing a child to experience pain but not injury, for purposes of correction or control of the child's behaviour.' [12] It describes many actions, including hitting with the hand or objects such as a belt, wooden paddle, and ruler. It also includes actions that do not involve hitting but cause discomfort for the child – for example, requiring a child to remain in an uncomfortable position, kneel on hard objects, forced physical exertion, isolation in a confined place, or placing foul-tasting substances in the mouth. [13]

Restraint may be used to restrain or remove persons from causing harm to themselves or others. It differs from physical punishment in that the intent is not to cause pain or humiliation. Restraint is defined variously as 'physically restricting movement' [14] and 'the application of external control, not to punish, but to protect the child, or others from physical pain and harm.' [15]

Susan Turner refers to restraint as an intervention rather than a punishment. [16] She describes restraint as having the goal to 'immediately interrupt behaviour which is likely to result in harm to the child or others.' [17] As Turner notes, however, there are times when physical restraint is intended to cause pain or discomfort and thus becomes an incident of corporal punishment. She concludes that when restraint is used in a non-disciplinary and interventionist manner it 'would be widely regarded as morally acceptable.' [18]

The distinction between corporal punishment and restraint is an important one as this distinction was the focus of the Canadian Teachers' Federation defence of s.43. The CTF has a policy prohibiting the use of corporal punishment by its members. [19] Their intervention in this case was to ensure that teachers could use restraint to remove or restrain a student and if, as a result of this action, they were charged with assault, they could defend themselves using s.43. In their factum filed with the Supreme Court of Canada, the CTF expressed concern that if s.43 were

removed teachers would not be able to separate a bully from the class-
mate he is taunting, guide a child by the shoulder to line up in rows, or
remove a disruptive student from the classroom or school bus.[20]

It was our position that there are other defences available to teachers
when caught in these types of situations.[21] The CTF disagreed saying the
other defences available within the *Criminal Code* and at common law
would not 'insulate a teacher from an assault conviction for physically
intervening in ... disciplinary situations.'[22] They said that '[g]iven the fluid
situations that teachers often face, teachers will not know, with any certainty, when the situation has evolved to such an extent that their actions
no longer fall under the applicable defence. This state of law is exacerbated
further by the confused state of law surrounding these defences.'[23]

There is never certainty for any of us when we rely on criminal defences to justify actions initially deemed criminal. The outcome relies
heavily on the circumstances, the ideology of those who sit in judgment, and the context of the lives of those involved. It could be argued
that the later point should make the task of justifying what would
otherwise be viewed as criminal behaviour more onerous considering
the professional nature of teaching. Nevertheless, the Supreme Court
majority agreed with the CTF.

The *Charter* Challenge

On 30 January 2004, the Supreme Court of Canada, in a 6–3 decision,[24]
determined that s.43 of the *Criminal Code* does not violate the constitutional rights of children as enshrined in the *Charter*. Canadian teachers,
represented by the Canadian Teachers' Federation, along with the
Coalition for Family Autonomy,[25] took an active part in defending s.43
before the Supreme Court of Canada.

As noted earlier, s.43 of the *Criminal Code* provides a legal defence
from charges of assault for parents, teachers, and others acting in their
place who use force to correct a child's behaviour. Normally if a person
applies intentional force on another without his or her consent, he or
she is guilty of assault. The victim can charge the perpetrator with assault under the *Criminal Code* and/or pursue civil action and sue for
monetary damages. However, s.43 provides those who use force on
children with a defence if they can show that the force was used for correction and was reasonable under the circumstances. It must be noted
that the *Criminal Code* does not provide a defence for the use of force on
any other identifiable group of people – only children. In fact, the *Criminal*

Code was recently amended to make it a criminal offence to assault an animal,[26] and, as Anne McGillivray points out, there is no defence of moderate correction for training animals.[27]

Section 43 has been used successfully by teachers in Canada for over a hundred years to defend them from charges of assault when they use physical force on children.[28] In recent times it has been used successfully to defend a teacher who used karate moves to discipline four Grade 10 students;[29] to defend a teacher who grabbed a 12-year-old student by the throat with both hands and 'cuffed' him in the stomach;[30] to defend a teacher who grabbed a 13-year-old boy by the arm and throat and pushed him against the wall;[31] and to defend a 260 lb. teacher who lifted a 13-year-old boy off the ground by the chin and head in a wrestling hold.[32]

The Supreme Court of Canada, in upholding the constitutionality of s.43, ruled that the purpose of s.43 was to 'carve out a sphere within which children's parents and teacher may use minor corrective force in some circumstances without facing criminal sanction'[33] and that 'this section provides a workable, constitutional standard that protects both children and parents.'[34] Mark Carter, a law professor, observes that '[n]o other criminal law provisions compares to section 43's sanctioning of the use of violence by private individuals against innocent and uniquely vulnerable third parties – children – based upon the unfortunate accident of the children's relationships to their attackers.'[35]

Legal Arguments

I instigated the *Canadian Foundation* case challenging the s.43 defence by submitting a successful application to the Court Challenges Program in 1995 that resulted in initial funding to challenge s.43. The case was carried forward by the Canadian Foundation for Children Youth and the Law.[36] Our arguments were that s.43 violated the *Charter* rights of children under three sections. First, we claimed that s.43 infringed s.7 of the *Charter* which protects all citizens from invasions of their security, and that the infringement could not be justified within the principles of fundamental justice.[37] We also argued that s.43 violated a child's rights under s.12, which prohibits cruel and unusual treatment.[38] Finally, we argued that s.43 is contrary to the equality rights protected under s.15, which protect all citizens from inequality in law and in the protection afforded by law.[39]

The majority of the Supreme Court judges sided with the Government of Canada, the Canadian Teachers' Federation, and the Coalition for

Family Autonomy and found that while the defence available to parents and teachers under s.43 violates a child's 'security of the person' rights under s.7, it is not done in contravention of the principles of fundamental justice. They found that s.12 of the *Charter* was not offended by s.43 since s.12 applies to the actions of governments and their agents, not to parents. While teachers are considered agents of the state, the Court ruled that s.12 did not apply as the only force teachers could use on students was not 'cruel and unusual.' Finally, the Court found that s.43 did not constitute discrimination against children. They acknowledged that s.43 'permits conduct toward children that would be criminal in the case of adult victims'[40] but the distinction on the basis of age is, they said, designed to protect children by not criminalizing their parents and teachers. Chief Justice McLachlin, writing for the majority said: 'The decision not to criminalize such conduct is not grounded in devaluation of the child, but in a concern that to do so risks ruining lives and breaking up families – a burden that in large part would be borne by children and outweigh any benefit derived from applying the criminal process.'[41]

In the majority's opinion, the benefit to be gained by the existence of s.43 outweighed the deleterious effects of the use of physical force on children.

Section 7

The Canadian Foundation argued that s.43 violated the security of the person rights under s.7 (conceded by the Government of Canada) and further that the violation was not in accordance with the 'principles of fundamental justice.' Those arguing that government action such as legislation contravenes the right to 'life, liberty and security of the person' must clear two hurdles. A claimant must show that the impugned legislation violates the freedoms protected by s.7 and must also provide evidence that the process for abridging those rights is not in accordance with the principles of fundamental justice. The phrase, the 'principles of fundamental justice' has been interpreted to mean, at a minimum, the right to a fair hearing before an impartial adjudicator, to be properly informed of the case against you, and to be given reasonable notice of the actual hearing.[42] The Supreme Court has subsequently recognized other principles, including the first and third of three put forward by the Canadian Foundation.[43] The Foundation argued that s.43 violated the following three principles:

(1) The principle that the child must be afforded independent procedural rights
(2) The principle that legislation affecting children must be in their best interests
(3) The principle that criminal legislation must not be vague or overbroad.[44]

In response to the first principle, the Court said children do not need separate representation of their interests in cases where they are the victim as they are well represented by the Crown and that there 'is no reason to suppose that ... the Crown will not discharge that duty properly.'[45] It noted further that 'jurisprudence has not recognized procedural rights for the alleged victims of an offence.'[46]

The Court found that the third principle of vagueness and overbreadth was not abridged since, as part of the discussion on this point, they limited the scope of s.43. This important discussion and the limitations imposed by the Court are discussed in more detail below.

The Canadian Foundation attempted to introduce a new 'principle of fundamental justice' but this too failed. In a decision issued in December 2003, one month prior to issuing its decision in the *Canadian Foundation* case, the Court outlined three criteria that must be met in order for a principle to be considered a 'principle of fundamental justice.'[47] The first criterion is that it must be a 'legal principle' that 'provides meaningful content for the s.7 guarantee' and avoids the 'adjudication of policy matters.'[48] The Court ruled that the 'best interest of the child' is a legal principle and thus fit the first requirement. It made reference to Canada being 'a party to international conventions that treat "best interest of the child" as a legal principle'[49] as well as the principle being part of domestic law. The second criterion requires consensus that the alleged principle is 'vital or fundamental to our societal notion of justice.'[50] The Court said they are considered shared assumptions, finding meaning 'in the cases and traditions that have long detailed the basic norms for how the state deals with its citizens.'[51] The Court determined that the 'best interest of the child' failed to meet this criterion since it 'may be subordinated to other concerns in appropriate contexts.'[52] While it is an important legal principle, the Court said it 'is not vital or fundamental to our societal notion of justice.'[53] The principle of the 'best interest of the child' also failed to meet the third criterion, which requires it be 'capable of being identified with precision and applied to situations in a manner that yields predictable results.'[54] They found that the principle was dependent on contextual matters and subject to dispute.

Justice Louise Arbour, in her dissenting opinion relied upon the breach of a child's security of the person right under s.7 of the *Charter*, to conclude that s.43 violates the *Charter* rights of children. She argued that the phrase 'reasonable under the circumstances' in s.43 violated the rights of children and the deprivation did not meet the requirements of the principles of fundamental justice because it is 'unconstitutionally vague.'[55] Justice Arbour said: 'Vagueness in defining the terms of a defence, which affects the physical integrity of children, may be even more invidious than is vagueness in defining an offence or a defence in another context, and may therefore call for a stricter standard.'[56]

Justice Arbour also referred to Canada's international obligations regarding the rights of the child and relied on the fact that the United Nations Committee on the Rights of the Child had made similar observations regarding the vagueness or imprecise nature of comparable legislation in the United Kingdom. The U.N. Committee said 'the imprecise nature of the expression of reasonable chastisement as contained in these [United Kingdom] legal provisions may pave the way for it to be interpreted in a subjective and arbitrary manner.'[57]

Section 12

The Court ruled that the prohibition against cruel and unusual punishment under s.12 applies only to governments and their agents. The Court dismissed any connection with parents to government despite the fact that it is an action of government, that is, s.43 of the *Criminal Code*, which provides parents with the authority to use physical force on children. Teachers are employed by the state and their connection to government is clear. The majority, however, found that the conduct permitted by s.43 did not rise to the level of 'cruel and unusual treatment,' nor did it outrage standards of decency thus, the Court concluded, the use of force by teachers could not be considered a violation of s.12.[58] It must be noted that the majority had only just clarified, a few paragraphs earlier in the decision, what conduct would not be permitted under s.43.[59]

Justice Binnie, in his dissenting opinion, found that the inclusion of teachers under s.43 could no longer be justified. He argued that a teacher does not share the same commitment as a parent to a particular child. According to Binnie J, 'The pupil-teacher relationship is closer to the master-apprentice relationship for which s.43 protection was abolished by Parliament in 1955.'[60]

Section 15

In the first s.15 case heard by the Supreme Court of Canada in 1987 the Court said: 's.15 is designed to protect those groups who suffer social, political and legal disadvantage in our society, the burden resting on government to justify the type of discrimination against such groups is appropriately an onerous one.'[61]

The Canadian Foundation maintained that children do suffer social, political, and legal disadvantages.[62] In particular, s.43 does not provide the same legal protection to children who are assaulted as is afforded adults who are assaulted. Section 43 exempts children from the same 'equal protection or equal benefit' of the *Criminal Code*, a federal law that specifically prohibits assaults and applies punitive measures to those who assault adults but does not protect children in the same way.[63] In fact, as pointed out by McGillivray: 'On its plain wording, s.43 justifies the assault of children for correction. This means that the assault is not a wrongful act that should be *excused* in the circumstance but rather a rightful act *justified* by law. The status of children is deeply affected by this. Children are to be cared for, protected from harm, trained in caring behaviour, and socialized as peaceable members of the community, yet their assault is justified by an archaic law. It is a troubling contradiction' (emphasis in original).[64]

Throughout the series of court decisions in this case, the s.15 argument was given surprisingly short shrift. The Superior Court of Ontario found in two short paragraphs that s.15 was not abridged by s.43.[65] The Ontario Court of Appeal found that s.43 appeared to discriminate on the basis of age but acknowledged they were only prepared to admit to such since s.43 could be saved by s.1.[66] They said this without showing how.

Once the matter reached the Supreme Court, McLachlin CJ gave it slightly more attention. The Canadian Foundation argued, among other things, that equality for children can only be assured 'if the criminal law treats simple assaults on children in the disciplinary context the same as it treats simple assaults on adults.'[67] The Chief Justice described the Foundation's argument as equating equal treatment with identical treatment, an interpretation, she said the Court has consistently rejected. Rather, the majority said, the appropriate perspective in considering cases alleging discrimination is the *Law* test,[68] a test developed by the Supreme Court to provide an analysis of substantive equality cases.[69] Substantive equality differs from formal equality, sometimes referred to as equal treatment or identical treatment. The tension between formal and substantive equality has been the focus of numerous legal commentators.[70]

Formal equality is understood to be concerned with 'ensuring that laws or policies do not impose disadvantages on individuals by treating them according to false stereotypes associated with irrelevant personal characteristics.'[71] It is focused on the individual's situation. Ryder et al. use, as an example of formal equality, the debate over same-sex marriage and argue that it violates a formal equality analysis under s.15 in that sexual orientation is irrelevant to the legal objective of marriage.[72] In this example a formal equality analysis works to ferret out the burden placed on gays and lesbians. But as Greschner points out in another example, relying solely on a formal understanding of equality will not work.[73] She uses the case of *Vriend* v. *Alberta*.[74] Mr Vriend, a gay man, taught in a religious college. He was terminated from his position once the college administration became aware of his sexual orientation. He turned to the Alberta Human Rights Commission for help only to find that Alberta's human rights law did not protect individuals from discrimination on the basis of their sexual orientation. In effect it treated homosexuals and heterosexuals the same and therefore within a formal equality analysis '[t]he law did not draw any distinction between heterosexuals and other groups.'[75]

In contrast, substantive equality is concerned with ensuring laws and policies, applied to everyone, do not result in more burdensome consequences to an identifiable group. Substantive equality involves what one writer refers to as 'social equality ... an absence of major disparities in peoples' resources, political and social power well-being, and [an absence] of exploitation and oppressions.'[76] In the case of same-sex marriage the focus is on whether the exclusion from marriage has the effect of further subordinating gays and lesbians in Canada.[77] The focus is on 'the group, and on the impact of the law on their social, economic or political conditions.'[78] Using the same sex-marriage analogy again, Ryder et al. posit that in a substantive equality analysis the focus is 'on whether the exclusion from marriage has the effect of further subordinating gays and lesbians in Canadian society.'[79] Likewise, in the case of *Vriend*, once the Court considered the impact of Alberta's omission of 'sexual orientation' in their human rights legislation 'it could only conclude that the impact of the legislative omission on gay men and lesbians was far more severe than on heterosexuals.'[80]

Ryder et al. note that in many cases, such as the same sex marriage case, both formal and substantive equality 'will work together to lead to the same conclusion.'[81] But, as in *Vriend*, a formal equality analysis will leave in place practices that impact more profoundly on a specific group. The common thread in identifying either formal or substantive inequality is the eradication of any further subordination of an already disadvantaged group in order to make their conditions better.

Mark Carter, a law professor, finds Chief Justice McLachlin's reasoning troublesome. Substantive equality acknowledges that meeting the principle of equality sometimes requires different treatment in order to improve the situation for a disadvantaged group – not make it worse. He said, 'the suggestion that the corporal punishment defence which propagates and retains the vulnerability of children is the kind of different treatment that advances substantive equality can only be characterized as bizarre.'[82] As noted by Justice Binnie in his dissent, the Chief Justice's view, that children's needs and circumstances are such that diminishing their right to protection under s.43 is essential, corrupts our understanding of substantive equality in such a way that 'the objective of substantive equality (as distinguished from formal equality) justifies the differential treatment of children.'[83]

The Court turned to the *Law* test to consider whether a distinction in law, that is, s.43, is discrimination and thus a violation of s.15. The *Law* test sets out three steps necessary to prove a violation of s.15. First, does the law create a distinction; second, is the distinction based on an enumerated or analogous ground; and third, is the distinction discriminatory? The third step requires the courts to look at the contextual factors to determine if the distinction is discriminatory. There are four factors to be considered:

(1) Pre-existing disadvantage
(2) Correspondence between the distinction and the claimants' characteristics or circumstances
(3) The existence of ameliorative purposes or effects
(4) The nature of the interest affected.[84]

Chief Justice McLachlin said the first factor was met as children are clearly a 'highly vulnerable group.'[85] The third factor does not apply to this case, and the fourth factor is met since 'the interest affected – physical integrity – is profound.'[86] However, it was the second factor that convinced the majority of the Court that s.43 was not discriminatory.[87] 'This factor acknowledges that a law that "properly accommodates the claimant's needs, capacities, and circumstances" will not generally offend s.15(1).'[88]

The majority ruled that while children need to be protected from abuse they also need their parents and teachers. The Court said '[a] stable and secure family and school setting is essential to this growth process.'[89] The Chief Justice said it made little sense to 'bring the blunt hand of the criminal law down on minor disciplinary contacts,'[90] which it must be remembered, the Court had only just described as 'minor' a few paragraphs earlier. The rationale for s.43 is based, she said 'on the interest of the child and on family and school relationships.'[91] The benefit to be gained for children was the assurance that their family setting would not be ruptured nor their teacher 'detained pending bail, with the inevitable harm to the child's crucial educative setting.'[92] Mossoff and Grant describe the majority's discussion of possibilities arising from the repealing of s 43 as *in terrorem* arguments. They note: 'It is not clear why a teacher would be denied bail in such a circumstance and this example further demonstrates the approach of the majority in creating unlikely counter-factual scenarios to support its argument.'[93] The Chief Justice remarked further, 'Parliament's choice not to criminalize this conduct does not devalue or discriminate against children, but responds to the reality of their lives by addressing their need for safety and security in an age-appropriate manner.'[94]

Justice Binnie in his dissent strongly disagreed with the majority's application of the second contextual factor. He said: 'I do not accept that the use of force against a child (that in the absence of s.43 would result in a criminal conviction) can be said to "correspond" to a child's "needs, capacities and circumstances" ... I have difficulty with the proposition that a child "needs" correction through conduct that, but for s.43 amounts to a criminal assault that exceeds the *de minimis* threshold.'[95]

Carter summarized the majority's development of sections 7, 12, and 15 of the *Charter* as a 'disturbing development in our understanding of how law directly and indirectly allows children to be the victim of violence.'[96] He states: 'There is cruel irony in the extent to which the majority decision in the *Canadian Foundation* case is characterized by the identification of teachers and parents as the most deserving recipients of our concern about victimization in the debate over the retention of the corporal punishment defence ... Equally troubling is the Court's willingness to compromise the constitutional standard of children's equality in the interests of vague concepts of family integrity. The majority does so by usurping the language of substantive equality.'[97]

Interpreting s.43 and Taking the Law to Where It Ought to Be

In *Canadian Foundation*, Chief Justice McLachlin, writing for the majority, said: 'the purpose of s.43 is to delineate a sphere of non-criminal conduct within the larger realm of common assault. It must, as we have seen, do this in a way that permits people to know when they are entering a zone of risk of criminal sanction and that avoids ad hoc discretionary decision-making by law enforcement officials.'[98] The Chief Justice then, as Justice Arbour noted, undertook 'a laudable effort to take the law where it ought to be.'[99] An effort that though laudable was, in Justice Arbour's opinion, beyond the proper role of the Court since the process has enlarged 'criminal responsibility by limiting defences enacted by Parliament.'[100] The limitations are those set down by the Court in their determination of the kind of conduct that will not be protected under s.43. Section 43, the Chief Justice said, is less precise in 'what conduct falls within its sphere.'[101] Even so, s.43 provides some guidance by defining the conduct of physical punishment in two ways, first the force is to be 'by way of correction' and it is to be 'reasonable under the circumstances.'[102]

By Way of Correction

Chief Justice McLachlin noted that the requirement that the force be 'by way of correction' sets two limitations on the type of conduct protected by s.43. First, the force used must be for 'educative or corrective purposes' and cannot be justified by outbursts of anger or frustration.[103] Second, the child upon whom the force is applied must be capable of understanding why they are being hit and be able to benefit from the correction. This eliminates children under the age of 2 and children who, due to a disability, are 'incapable of learning from the application of force.'[104]

Reasonable under the Circumstances

The second requirement of conduct is that the force be 'reasonable under the circumstances.' This phrase has been roundly criticized for its vagueness and the fact its interpretation by police, judges, and prosecutors is often based on what they went through as children.[105] Chief Justice McLachlin acknowledged that the words were broad and used the case before her to provide precision. She turned for assistance to selected international human rights documents and to what she referred to as social consensus and expert evidence to determine what constitutes reasonable corrective discipline.[106] The first limitation is that the behaviour for which s.43 provides an exemption is the 'non-consensual application of force that results neither in harm nor in the prospect of bodily harm. This limits its operation to the mildest forms of assault.'[107] She said that 's.43 exempts from criminal sanction only minor corrective force of a transitory and trifling nature.'[108]

Canada's international obligations direct that physical correction can be neither harmful nor degrading to children. Chief Justice McLachlin quoted from Articles 5, 19, and 37 of the United Nations *Convention on the Rights of the Child* and also made reference to the *Covenant on Civil and Political Rights*.[109] She noted that the Human Rights Committee of the United Nations 'has expressed the view that corporal punishment of children in schools engages Art. 7's prohibition of degrading treatment or punishment ... [but] the committee has not expressed a similar opinion regarding parental use of mild corporal punishment.'[110] Despite the United Nations' Committee's conclusions, the Chief Justice did not remove teachers from the scope of s.43, but said that when a teacher uses corporal punishment it is 'unreasonable.'

As noted earlier, the Chief Justice turned to international human rights documents to assist her, but for some reason, she did not refer to the latest report from the United Nations Committee on the Rights of the Child regarding Canada's compliance with the *Convention on the Rights of the Child*. Justice Arbour, in her dissenting opinion, relied directly on the commission's report, which recommended that Canada adopt 'legislation to remove the existing authorization of the use of "reasonable force" in disciplining children and explicitly prohibit all forms of violence against children, however light, within the family, in schools and in other institutions where children may be placed.'[111] The committee further recommended that Canada improve the quality of its education by 'adopting appropriate legislative measures to forbid the use of any form of corporal punishment in schools and encouraging child participation in discussions about disciplinary measures.'[112]

The majority of the Court expanded on the limitations to s.43 specifically listing actions that will not be considered 'reasonable.' These actions enter what the Court called a 'zone of risk' meaning that the s.43 defence will not be available in certain circumstances. The Court said it is never reasonable to use corporal punishment on children under 2 years of age because they do not have the capacity to understand 'why they are hit.'[113] Similarly, a child with a 'disability or some other contextual factor' will not understand the reasons for the use of force.[114] The Court said, '[i]n these cases, force will not be 'corrective' and will not fall within the sphere of immunity provided by s.43'[115] since children must be capable of learning and have the capacity to successfully correct their behaviour.[116] Corporal punishment is not to be used on teenagers as it can induce aggressive or antisocial behaviour in them.[117] Corporal punishment cannot be justified under s.43 when an object or weapon is used such as a ruler or belt[118] nor in cases involving slaps or blows to the head[119] or when the force is 'degrading, inhuman or harmful conduct.'[120] Section 43 cannot be used as a defence to charges of assault when corporal punishment is applied in anger stemming from 'frustration, loss of temper or abusive personality.'[121]

In summary, those who use corporal punishment on children risk criminal sanctions when:

- It is used by teachers
- It is used on children under the age of 2
- It is used on teenagers
- It is used on children with disabilities
- A child is hit on the head
- The force is degrading or inhuman
- It is applied in anger
- An object is used
- It exceeds minor corrective force of a transitory and trifling nature.

Implications for Teachers

The majority of the Court found that teachers remain within the parameter of s.43. However, the Court also said that s.43 is not available as a defence for teachers who use corporal punishment on students. It noted: 'Substantial societal consensus, supported by expert evidence and Canada's treaty obligations, indicates that corporal punishment by teachers is unreasonable.'[122] Section 43 will protect teachers from charges of assault only when 'a teacher uses reasonable, corrective force to restrain or remove a child in appropriate circumstances.'[123] In other words, teachers are in the 'zone of risk' whenever they use corporal punishment on their students. Section 43 can only be used to defend teachers from charges of assault when they use corrective force to restrain or remove a child. The majority of the Court did not remove teachers from s.43 as was called for by Justice Binnie, and it is obvious that the reason teachers were not removed was the Court's concern that if this happened teachers would not be able to use restraint to control disruptive students.[124]

But even the use of restraint by teachers is tricky. In a number of cases teachers may have thought they were using restraint but found too late that it can lead to injuries – some of them serious. In a case recently decided, a day care worker forced a 3-year-old boy to sit down injuring the child's leg. The day care worker was found guilty of assault under the new interpretation of s.43 since force can only be used for educational purposes not out of anger or frustration. The court found that an experienced 'educatrice de garderie' should have foreseen the child's resistance and the resultant risk of injury.[125]

Restraint is considered a security measure designed to protect the student, others, and property. Authors of a review on the use of restraints on patients reported on one U.S. government report that 'found conclusively that children are especially targeted by facility staff for this unsafe practice (restraints), and are at greater risk of injury and death.'[126] Ironically, they noted that most injuries occur to staff and the subject of the restraint during the process of restraint or seclusion,[127] which raises questions about the utility of restraints as opposed to other less physical forms of intervention. The authors recommend that alternative interventions be used such as 'promoting self-management for some children ... with poor self-control'[128] and appropriate protection be provided to others from acutely aggressive individuals. If restraint is to be used it is to be carried out by judicious and well-trained staff. While this review was focused on patients it provides useful advice and warnings for teachers as well.

For Private/Independent Schools

Some private schools use corporal punishment. In fact, the principal of one such school was featured in a 1997 issue of a Canadian national magazine holding a 'paddle' used in his school to administer corporal punishment to students.[129] If this practice is still in place, the school administration is sitting firmly within the 'zone of risk' of prosecution without benefit of the s.43 defence. First and foremost, teachers cannot use corporal punishment only restraint; second, the administration is using an instrument – a paddle, and; third, if it is applied on teenagers, it is again contrary to the court's limitations.

Physical punishment of children is often supported with reference to the Bible. Solomon is quoted in this regard: 'Do not withhold discipline from a boy; take the stick to him, and save him from death. If you take the stick to him yourself, you will preserve him from the jaws of death'[130] leading eventually to the maxim 'spare the rod and spoil the child.'[131]

A number of private religious schools and parents are influenced by the teachings and writings of Focus on the Family founder, Dr James Dobson. Focus on the Family Canada is affiliated with Focus on the Family in the United States and was one of the members of the Coalition for Family Autonomy, an intervenor in the *Canadian Foundation* case. In his best-selling book *Dare to Discipline*,[132] James Dobson advises parents and teachers to use corporal punishment on children using an object such as a switch or paddle.[133]

Recently, the principal and a teacher of a religious private school in Aylmer, Ontario, have been charged with assault with a weapon arising from incidences of corporal punishment. The case involved seven 9- and 10-year-old students of the Old Colony Christian School, which is located in the basement of the Old Colony Mennonite Church in Malahide Township.[134]

For the Provincial Government's Responsibility

Currently, the provinces and territories of British Columbia, Quebec, Nova Scotia, New Brunswick, Prince Edward Island, Newfoundland, Saskatchewan, Yukon, Northwest Territories, and Nunavut prohibit, within their *Education Act*s, the use of corporal punishment in schools. In order to clarify the Supreme Court's decision it is recommended that each province clearly state within its *Education Act* that corporal punishment is no longer allowed. This requirement is all the more urgent bearing in mind that practices once considered inappropriate but legal are now criminal.

Canada, as a signatory to many international human rights documents, is obliged to provide education on human rights. The obligation to provide human rights education is consistently referred to in every major human rights document including the *Universal Declaration of Human Rights*,[135] the *International Covenant on Economic, Social and Cultural Rights*,[136] the *Convention on the Rights of the Child*,[137] the *Convention on the Elimination of all Forms of Discrimination Against Women*,[138] and the *Convention on the Elimination of All Forms of Racial Discrimination*.[139]

Thus provincial departments of education are obliged to ensure that their curriculum provides information that develops within the child a respect for human rights. Within this framework comes a duty on the part of educators to provide students with an understanding of their rights to physical and mental integrity including their right to be free from forms of physical punishment that are outside of the limits placed on s.43. A clear understanding of the limits placed on the use of corporal punishment on children is important not only to children as students in school but as members of families in society.

Research has consistently shown that children raised with corporal punishment display more aggressive tendencies to others.[140] This has important implications for their interactions with peers at schools. A recent study reporting on a national longitudinal survey found: 'Children showed higher levels of aggressive behaviour when their parents were more punitive. They also showed higher levels of anxiety and lower levels of pro-social behaviour, the later being defined as actions that benefit another person with no reward for oneself.'[141] In an earlier report from the same study, Statistics Canada reported that 'children aged two to three years who were living in punitive environments in 1994 scored 39% higher on a scale of aggressive behaviours, such as bullying or being mean to others, than did those in less punitive environments. The difference was even more pronounced six years later in 2000, when the children were eight to nine years old. Those who lived in punitive homes scored 83% higher on the aggressive behaviour scale than those in less punitive homes.'[142]

Other studies have demonstrated that incidents of violence are more prevalent in schools that use corporal punishment,[143] that the use of corporal punishment has a negative and statistically significant relationship to academic achievements,[144] and that high school dropout rates were higher among students who experienced moderate to severe corporal punishment.[145] Other studies have found a positive association between the frequency of corporal punishment and both psychological distress and depression.[146]

Conclusion

Teachers and students have a great deal to benefit from the elimination of corporal punishment in schools and in families. Despite the overwhelming evidence detailing the negative impact of corporal punishment on children, the Supreme Court of Canada did not go as far as to declare s.43 of the *Criminal Code* unconstitutional. It did, however, limit its scope as a defence for parents and teachers who use force on children as a means of correction. Teachers can only use s.43 as a defence if they are charged with assault arising from restraining or removing a student. It is simply 'unreasonable ' for a teacher to use any form of corporal punishment on a student; if they do and are subsequently charged with assault, they can no longer rely on s.43 to exculpate their behaviour. Therefore, provincial governments are being called on to amend their legislation to reflect these changes. In addition, provincial educational curricula must reflect Canada's obligation to teach about human rights with obvious attention paid to the limitations on the use of corporal punishment of children.

The Supreme Court's decision side-stepped the issue of the rights of children but curtailed the authoritative entitlement of parents and teachers. It is a disappointing conclusion to a long and, I would argue, principled endeavour, in that the Supreme Court shied away from truly recognizing children as individuals endowed with rights, including the fundamental right to personal integrity and security of the person.

9 Children's *Charter* Rights: A Slogan Still in Need of Judicial Definition

CHERYL MILNE

> Children's rights and attention to their interests, are central humanitarian and compassionate values in Canadian society.[1]

> Canadian society has always recognized that children are deserving of a heightened form of protection. This protection rests on the best interests of the child.[2]

A review of cases at the Supreme Court of Canada that have invoked the rights of children under the *Canadian Charter of Rights and Freedoms*[3] illustrates the commonly identified tension between society's obligation to protect children (not often described as a right) and children's rights to participation and autonomy. Where children's rights are specifically identified those rights are most often mentioned simply in obiter. Where their rights are the central issue of the case, the Court generally acknowledges them when there is no apparent conflict with the interests of their caregivers, be they parents or teachers, or with the Court's inclination to protect the health and welfare of the child. Additionally, Canadian courts are most willing to acknowledge children as rights bearers when imposing adult-like responsibility on children through criminal law or state control for protection and treatment.

This chapter focuses on Supreme Court of Canada cases in an attempt to analyse the significance of children's rights rhetoric in constitutional cases involving children. Since the coming into force of the *Charter* children's rights have received even greater prominence through the ratification of the United Nations *Convention on the Rights of the Child*[4] and the Court's greater acceptance of the impact of international law on human rights more generally. Unfortunately, despite the superficial recognition of the concept of children as rights bearers, the cases, in this writer's opinion, lack coherence and perpetuate the oft-quoted thirty-year-old aphorism that the concept of children's rights is 'a slogan in search of a definition.'[5]

Recognition of Children's Rights

The legal foundation for children's rights rhetoric lies, not only in *Charter* jurisprudence, but also in civil and international law. The concept of children as rights holders finds its way into the language of many decisions of the Supreme Court of Canada involving children, especially in the context of family law. The Court has stated, for example, that parental access to a child[6] and, most recently, the obligation of a parent to financially support a child[7] are rights of the child, not the parent. Neither of these cases involved the assertion of *Charter* rights by or on behalf of the child. In *Baker,* a case invoking international law, L'Heureux-Dubé J acknowledged the importance of children's rights in Canadian society and recognized the significance of the United Nations *Convention on the Rights of the Child,* a case involving the deportation of a mother, and the importance of considering the best interests of her Canadian-born children when making this type of decision.

Baker is often cited as a ground-breaking children's rights case because the majority of the Court held that in making a decision under the *Immigration Act*[8] (as it then was) on humanitarian and compassionate grounds, the decision-maker must take into consideration the best interests of the affected Canadian-born children. In so doing, L'Heureux-Dubé J, speaking for the majority, held that the *Convention on the Rights of the Child* informed the contextual approach to statutory interpretation of what was meant by humanitarian and compassionate values. Despite this, the background to the decision is problematic from the point of view of the right of children to be heard in proceedings that affect them (Art. 12 of the *Convention*), and alternatively, their rights under s.7 of the *Charter*. The Court declined to rule on the various *Charter* issues raised by the appellant and interveners. Thus, children's security interests under s.7 and their right to procedural fairness within the concept of fundamental justice were not addressed.[9]

In *R. v. M.(M.R.),*[10] another case in which the Supreme Court of Canada arguably paid lip-service to the *Charter* rights of children (in this instance students), Cory J speaking for the Court noted the importance in a school setting of modelling respect for the rights of all members of society by respecting the rights of students. Almost without pause, the Court then proceeded to devalue those rights by finding that students have a lower expectation of privacy in school settings and are not entitled to the same right to be free from unreasonable search and seizure as adults, even when a police officer is in the room. Subsequently, the majority of the Court appeared to have more clearly defined this position in its strongly divided decision in the case of *R.* v. *A.M.*[11], which involved the use of sniffer dogs in schools. The majority of the Court acknowledged the privacy rights of students in school and in respect of their personal belongings such as a backpack, in relation to random searches by police.

In contrast, the Supreme Court of Canada completely ignored the *Charter* rights of children in *Trociuk* v. *British Columbia (Attorney General)*,[12] asserting the right of a father to have his name included on the birth registration of his children. The father successfully argued that his rights were violated under s.15 of the *Charter* by his exclusion from a form of meaningful participation in the children's lives, that of having his particulars included in the children's birth registration and participating in the naming of his children. Nothing was stated in respect of the children's right to include their father's identity as a component of their own identity, except that this exclusion of the father could not be presumed to be in the children's best interests.[13]

The *Charter* does not on its face distinguish between the rights of adults and the rights of children. It is presumed that children have *Charter* rights. Despite the fact that age is an enumerated ground of discrimination under s.15 of the *Charter*, however, the treatment of children by the courts in respect of rights-based claims demonstrates a clear distinction between adults and children. How that plays out in the assertion of *Charter* rights by and on behalf of children is difficult to predict and at times contradictory. For example, in contrast to the decision in *M.(M.R.)*, the Court has recently ruled in *R.* v. *R.C.*[14] that young people's privacy rights deserve a more heightened protection within the criminal justice system, relying on legislative interpretation of the *Youth Criminal Justice Act*[15] in light of its 'incorporation by reference' of the U.N. *Convention*.[16] In *R.* v. *D.B.*,[17] its most recent *Charter* decision in respect of children, a majority of the Court held that it was a principle of fundamental justice under s.7 that young people are entitled to a presumption of diminished moral blameworthiness or culpability flowing from the fact that, because of their age, they have heightened vulnerability, less maturity, and a reduced capacity for moral judgment.

Right to Equality

There has yet to be a case in which the equality rights of children, as defined by age, have been clearly recognized by the Supreme Court of Canada. The case that comes closest to doing so is *Eaton* v. *Brant County Board of Education*,[18] in which the Supreme Court of Canada acknowledged that children with disabilities have equality rights in the school setting that are accommodated by an approach that takes a subjective, child-centred perspective, that is, the best interests of the child govern. The court clearly stated that in determining what is in the child's best interests, the views and wishes of the child, if ascertainable, must be taken into account. This decision has been criticized, however, for its emphasis on the best interests test, which itself is biased towards professional opinions and away from the views and preferences of children and parents.[19] It also confounds rights rhetoric with paternalism, highlighting the tension between protection and autonomy in children's rights analysis.

Unfortunately, from the perspective of children's rights advocates, the Court's next pronouncement on the equality rights of children is found in *Canadian Foundation for Children, Youth and the Law* v. *Canada (Attorney General)*[20] in which the Foundation challenged the constitutionality of the criminal defence for assault in the context of physical discipline of children. McLachlin CJ, for the majority, stated that the best perspective one can adopt in respect of a child's equality rights claim is not that of the *child* but that of the 'reasonable *person* acting on behalf of a child, who seriously considers and values the child's views and developmental needs' (emphasis added).[21] As the Court stated in *Andrews* v. *Law Society of British Columbia*,[22] not every distinction or differentiation in law will amount to discrimination,[23] but there is indeed some distance to go before children's equality rights can be recognized if we need to first convince the court that a child is a person. Also, in a manner consistent with the Court's approach to children's rights in *R.* v. *M.(M.R.)*, the majority in the *Canadian Foundation* case valued children's equality rights less than those enjoyed by adults by viewing children as being inherently disempowered and vulnerable with a diminished sense of dignity.[24] Thus, their loss of dignity matters less than the loss of dignity to an adult person in the equality analysis.

The Court set the stage in *Andrews* for differential treatment of children based upon personal characteristics and capacity, linked to presumed developmental differences between adults and children.[25] We have come to accept such absolute distinctions in the law despite their being artificial and, in some instances indefensible, in part due to a tendency to favour absolute categories and formal rules.[26] The *Canadian Foundation* case relies considerably on this approach by reinterpreting the definition of the defence for physical punishment of reasonable force in terms of the age of the child. Although ostensibly an attempt to better protect children from abusive physical punishment, the redefining of the perimeters of the defence to a list of prohibitions does not speak to the issue of how the court approaches children's rights per se. Rather, the majority created a list of behaviours that are not to be considered reasonable. One item on the list is particularly troubling – that only children aged 3 to 12 may be subject to force by way of correction. We are accustomed to arbitrary cut-offs in respect of liberty interests of children, but such an arbitrary age-based authorization for the imposition of physical assault for which there is no evidence of benefit to the child is bizarre. As Mark Carter notes, '[i]t is necessary to accept arbitrary age distinctions as a pragmatic way of facilitating the work of the law in many areas. These would include, for example, laws that establish minimum ages for the enjoyment of privileges such as obtaining a driver's licence. Pragmatic rationales lose their force, however, when vulnerability to physical assault and the enjoyment of constitutionally protected rights become relative to a calendar date.'[27]

In *Fitzgerald (Next friend of)* v. *Alberta*,[28] a case that the Supreme Court of Canada declined to hear, the Alberta Court of Appeal endorsed an arbitrary age cut-off of 18 years in the respect of voting rights. Without considering the evidence of the developmental capabilities of children, the Court below held that, although the age restriction amounted to discrimination, it was a justifiable limit on children's equality rights. The Court quoted the obiter of the Supreme Court of Canada in *Sauvé* v. *Canada (Chief Electoral Officer)*,[29] implying that a youth voting restriction is legitimate because of the basic fact that children mature as they get older [30] and that 'Parliament is making a decision based on the experiential situation of all citizens when they are young.'[31] McLachlin CJ for the majority in *Sauvé* also stated that '*Charter* rights are not a matter of privilege or merit, but a function of membership in the Canadian polity that cannot lightly be cast aside,'[32] which begs the question of the degree of membership that children enjoy in Canadian society, if their participation is simply disregarded without evidence of their abilities.

Liberty and Autonomy

In respect of the most basic concept of liberty, that is, freedom from con-
finement or incarceration, children are viewed as perpetually in some
form of custody, and therefore, less in need of procedural protections
when faced with the prospect of a different form of custody.[33] The only
real exception to this is the treatment of children as accused persons
under youth criminal justice legislation[34] that more closely resembles the
adult system, with adult-like penalties and corresponding rights. Even in
that context, however, children's rights differ to the extent that the legislation and the courts provide greater protections to young people.[35] One
queries what the implications of the Court's decision in *D.B.* might be in
respect of a child's right to make autonomous decisions under s.7. There
the Court, drawing on the view that 'age plays a role in the development
of judgment and moral sophistication'[36] found that it is a principle of
fundamental justice that there is a presumption of diminished moral
culpability in the youth justice context. Where children are permitted to
participate in decision-making on civil issues, those rights are rarely derived from constitutional law, although increasingly lower courts are
making reference to the United Nations *Convention on the Rights of the
Child* to support a child's participation in proceedings through a canvas-
sing of the child's own views and wishes.[37]

Inherent in the concept of liberty is the ability and capacity to make
choices, a presumption of autonomy that is by definition not available to
children, whether through laws or the fact of their emotional and physical dependency on adults. Instead, Michael Freeman has theorized that
one way to uphold children's autonomous rights is to view the responsibility of adults as that of being required to act to preserve the future autonomy of children.[38] The Supreme Court of Canada has recognized a
parent's liberty interest in making fundamental decisions about education[39] and medical health,[40] but we currently await the Court's pronouncement on the same assertion by a young person.[41] The Court has been
consistently clear until most recently, however, that parental duties are to
be discharged in accordance with the 'best interests of the child.'[42] The
child's own perception of her or his best interests rarely is discussed in
such cases. Unless the best interests test incorporates a measure of child
autonomy, arguably the child remains an object rather than an individual
worthy of respect as a rights holder.[43] The Supreme Court of Canada did
acknowledge the importance of a child's own views and wishes in respect

of the accommodation for disabilities in education placements in *Eaton*[44] but that case appears to be the high-water mark on this point.

In the 2004 case of *C.U.* v. *McGonigle*,[45] the Supreme Court of Canada declined to hear as moot a case in which a 16-year-old girl sought the right to refuse medical treatment on religious grounds. The Alberta Court of Appeal's ruling[46] in that case stands as authority for the power of the legislature, through child protection laws, to override the common law rules in respect of consent to treatment rather than a ruling on the constitutional rights of the child under s.7. The Supreme Court of Canada heard argument in May 2008, on an appeal of a similar ruling from the Manitoba Court of Appeal, in which a 14-year-old girl has asserted her own rights under sections 7, 15, and 2(a) to make a religiously motivated decision to refuse blood transfusions.[47] As Carole Smith notes, 'it is understandable [in such cases] that the judiciary has struggled with respecting children's rights in the anticipation of negative, or sometimes devastating, consequences for their welfare.'[48]

In *Multani* v. *Commissions scolaire Marguerite-Bourgeoys*,[49] a case involving less controversial consequences to a religious-based decision, the Supreme Court of Canada recognized the religious freedom of a Sikh high school student whose parent claimed that his right to religious freedom pursuant to s.2(a) of the *Charter* was infringed when a Council of Commissioners of the school board prohibited him from wearing his kirpan to school. The Court accepted as an undisputed fact that the 12-year-old student sincerely held the religious belief that he was required to wear the kirpan as part of the Sikh religion. It is noteworthy that the right was being asserted by the parent, albeit consistent with and on behalf of the child who was not a party to the proceedings. As discussed above, however, this case did not involve a conflict with the Court's inclination to protect the health and welfare of the child asserting the right, although the school argued that the safety of other students was at issue. It remains to be seen whether this decision will have any bearing on serious health-related decisions that might be challenged in the future on the basis of interference with religious freedom, since at 17 a young person can be found capable of having a religion, and therefore, a constitutional right to express it.

Life and Security

A child's assertion of the right to life and security of the person appears, superficially at least, to be more accepted by the Court than liberty.

When one looks at the cases that have invoked s.7 of the *Charter*, we see a clear statement that children have the right to life and health when others are required to make decisions on their behalf, but the rights to liberty and, depending on its definition, security of the person are more elusive. An obvious explanation might be found in the inherent elements of personal choice and capacity for decision-making in liberty interests, and the child's relationship of dependency on adults within the concept of security for children in particular. One might expect that the rationale for not fully recognizing the rights of children in this regard would rest on a protective obligation to act in a child's best interests. An analysis of the cases to date does not, however, consistently support this as an explanation for the failure of our courts to recognize that children as individuals are entitled to *Charter* rights in general, and s.7 rights in particular.

Not surprisingly, the majority of cases involving children's rights are argued within the context of the assertion of a parental right, often to liberty or security of the parent. In the case of *B.(R.)*,[50] the parents of Sheena B. asserted their rights to liberty and to religious freedom in the exercise of their parental decision-making power over medical treatment for their daughter. La Forest J, for the majority, stated that 'children undeniably benefit from the *Charter*, most notably in its protection of their rights to life and to the security of their person'[51] and went on to state that children are unable to assert such rights on their own behalf. He also described a child's right to life and health as an obligation and power of the state.[52]

La Forest's reasoning for the majority demonstrates a willingness to recognize a child's s.7 rights when they more closely mirror the state's paternal duty to protect. The view of children's fundamental rights as grounded in the fundamental obligations of others is supported by some theorists[53] and by judgments of various levels of court. For example, the Court has been less likely to find a breach of a child's s.7 rights to liberty and security of the person when those rights have appeared to conflict with the adults' perceptions of their protective obligations, often described as parental rights. As to the limits of a rights-based approach to children Onora O'Neill has stated:'Theories of rights were born and developed in large part in repudiation of paternalistic models of just political and social relations. Their proponents have repudiated the justice of familial analogies which liken kings to fathers, see colonial powers as mother countries, women and underdeveloped peoples as childlike, and just social relations as patriarchal. However, it is no mere analogy when we speak of mothers and fathers as parents, and children are not just metaphorically childlike. There are good reasons to think that paternalism may be much of what is ethically required in dealing with children, even if it is inadequate in dealings with mature and maturing minors.'[54]

In *B.(R.)*, Justices Iacobucci and Major were critical of Justice La Forest's focus on parental liberty finding in it a failure to fully acknowledge the child's rights under s.7 to life and security of the person, and a suggestion that the child's rights were reduced to 'a limitation on the parents' constitutionally protected ability to deny that child the necessities of life owing to parental liberty and freedom of religion.'[55] They preferred to 'view an exercise of parental liberty which seriously endangers the survival of the child as falling outside s.7.'[56] The preference is worth noting when reviewing the Court's approach to similar cases invoking a child's own liberty interest, such as in *McGonigle* and *A.C.*, cited above.

The *Canadian Foundation* case makes it more difficult to formulate a consistent theory of how the Court approaches children's protective rights. It was undisputed in the case that the impugned defence for the physical punishment of children (s.43 of the *Criminal Code*) infringed children's right to security of the person. Hitting people will do that. The lack of evidence of benefit to children in that case negates the argument that courts, and the state, are more concerned about obligations and responsibilities to children than about giving effect to their rights. The reality was that the Court focused, not on children, but on the adults who they deemed to be in need of protection from state interference. Despite the fact that the Supreme Court of Canada in *R. v. Ogg-Moss*[57] held that the purpose of the section was for 'the benefit of the education of the child,' Susan Turner noted, 'Section 43 is first and foremost a defence. As such, while its ultimate purpose may be to ensure the civilization of children, its specific aim is to protect those whose prima facie criminal behaviour falls under its purview.'[58] This focus on parents and teachers led to a disregard for the evidence about the lack of efficacy of the physical discipline practice. It also justified the discounting of the importance of the principle of the best interests of the child. The section was not viewed by the majority of the court in its s.7 of the *Charter* analysis as having much to do with children's interests at all.

The concept of security of the person is broader than simply protection of one's physical integrity and includes one's psychological and emotional integrity.[59] In child welfare cases, the Supreme Court of Canada has recognized that the parental right to security of the person is infringed when a child is removed from a parent's custody.[60] In *K.L.W.*, Arbour J in dissent, noted that the child's interest in remaining with his or her parents is a significant security interest of the child,[61] echoing Lamer CJ in *G.(J.)*. The right of the child in this respect is simply the flip side of the parental right.

Decisions in cases in which the child's right to psychological integrity might play a role all too often simply ignore this aspect of the context in which parents or other adults are asserting their own rights. For example, in *Trociuk,* the Supreme Court of Canada recognized that the biological tie between a parent and child is a significant mode of participation in a child's life and that the denial of the father's particulars on a child's birth registration was harmful to his dignity in the context of a s.15 claim by a father, no s.7 argument being advanced. At the British Columbia Court of Appeal, the children's interests were represented by an *amicus curiae*, who supported the father's position. No one representing the children's interests was present, however, at the Supreme Court of Canada. Thus, no arguments were acknowledged by the Court as to the impact on the rights of the children of the denial of biological information about their father. Similarly, in *Louie* v. *Lastman*,[62] the Ontario Court of Appeal dismissed the Canadian Foundation for Children, Youth and the Law's assertions of a right to know one's biological identity as irrelevant to the case in which adult children sought retroactive child support and a declaration of paternity on the basis of a fiduciary obligation by the parent.

Best Interests

Despite the promising rhetoric of the *Baker* judgment requiring a decision-maker to look at the best interests of the child as one factor in a humanitarian and compassionate application,[63] *Baker* falls seriously short of recognizing children as individual rights bearers. More alarmingly, the Federal Court of Appeal has since adopted a narrow definition of 'best interests of the child' such that immigration officials need only consider whether the child would suffer 'undue hardship' should a parent be deported,[64] begging the question of what hardship children might deserve in this context.

McLachlin CJ's reasoning in the *Canadian Foundation* case further complicates any attempt to develop a cohesive theory of how children's interests are protected within Canadian society through the best interests principle. Decisions that override the psychological security of the child in the familial relationship generally rely on a paternalistic approach that seeks to act in a child's best interests. And while the *Baker* and *Hawthorne* decisions water that down somewhat, the child's best interests test could still be said to be the operative principle. In the *Canadian Foundation* case, however, the Attorney General conceded that the child's security interests were infringed while the Court refused to consider what was in a child's best interests. In deciding that the principle of the best interests of the child is not a principle of fundamental justice, McLachlin CJ held that the principle failed to meet the criteria because it is not 'vital or fundamental to our societal notion of justice.'[65] This sweeping statement has serious implications for future cases involving children. It calls into question the Quebec Court of Appeal's decision in *Quebec (Ministre de la Justice)* v. *Canada (Ministre de la Justice)*[66] that it is a principle of fundamental justice that the youth criminal justice system consider the best interests of the child. This pronouncement by the majority of the Court leaves in doubt the role of this principle in laws affecting children. The principle is certainly fraught with problems in that its imprecise nature leaves it up to courts to fill in the blanks and impose subjective adult-focused views on what is best for a child. Jeffery Wilson in his criticism of the varying laws that affect children states:

> [T]hese laws, unlike those for other constituencies, find their political validity in what is deemed to be in children's 'best interests' as opposed to what the particular constituency is directly demanding for itself. This difference may be due to the dependent status of children, which compels adults in democratic society to legislate for children those rights which children would pursue for themselves if they were capable. However, by this very approach, which is theoretically highly moral and admirable, the legislation and its method of implementation more often reflects the interests of every other constituency but children ... Further, even if the motivation is pure, the assumptions underlying 'best interests' may unconsciously have more to do with an adult's biases, prejudices and myths about childhood than with any objective, empirical evidence.[67]

The Future for Children's *Charter* Rights

Without a clear trend in the past judgments of the Supreme Court of Canada, it is difficult to predict the approach the Court is likely to take in the cases destined to come before it. The general tendency, with some notable exceptions, has been either a disregard for children's rights altogether[68] or a somewhat reluctant acknowledgment of them although in a diminished form. Martha Minow observes that 'children simply are not the real focus of the varied laws that affect them. Instead, other powerful social goals are the focus of these laws.'[69] She notes that child labour laws did not pass legislatures until organized labour supported such legislation in their own self-interest. Advocates for the elimination of the physical punishment of children, for example, might do well to take a more utilitarian approach that might appeal to the interests of adults[70] by pointing to the significant association between the use of physical punishment and poor relationships between parents and their children as well as increased aggression by children. Perhaps a more reliable indicator is to be found in an analysis of *Charter* cases more generally which have been criticized as making *Charter* claims more difficult for marginalized or vulnerable claimants, children being just one group among many.[71]

The difficulty in predicting future decisions is exacerbated by an analysis of the Court's past reliance on the best interests principle as an acknowledgment of children's legal interests, not of their legal rights. Although our courts have recognized the obligation of educators to act in the best interests of exceptional students, children's rights have continued to be given a back seat to perceptions about order and discipline or to the rights of parents as decision-makers on behalf of children. The Supreme Court of Canada's decision in *Canadian Foundation* has created a huge black hole in children's rights jurisprudence. The majority's reasoning that a law which justifies assaults on children (with no evidence of benefit of these assaults on them) does not infringe the *Charter* or *Convention* rights of children in any way, and that the principle of the best interests of the child is not part of our societal notion of justice, leaves little ammunition for those arguing for the rights of children in other contexts whether based on protection or autonomy.

We have a long way to go to recognizing children's rights as set out in the UN *Convention on the Rights of the Child*. The Court's general acceptance of the U.N. *Convention* as an integral part of the legal analysis of issues affecting children is, however, a move towards a more fundamental incorporation of children's rights rhetoric in future cases invoking the *Charter*. In this regard the *Baker* decision and even the Court's comments on the international law in the *Canadian Foundation* case are positive indicators of what is to come. The impact of incorporating the *Convention* into legislation, albeit only in the preamble of the *Youth Criminal Justice Act*, has already been felt; it remains to be seen, however, what its influence might be on interpreting and upholding the *Charter* rights of children in other contexts.

10 The Judicial Contours of Minority Language Educational Rights under the *Charter*

PAUL T. CLARKE

In *Reference re Manitoba Language Rights*,[1] the Supreme Court of Canada noted that our constitutionally enshrined language rights reflect the seminal role language occupies in human flourishing: 'The importance of language rights is grounded in the essential role that language plays in human existence, development and dignity. It is through language that we are able to form concepts; to structure and order the world around us. Language bridges the gap between isolation and community, allowing humans to delineate the rights and duties they hold in respect of one another, and thus to live in society.'[2] More specifically, sections 16 through 23 of the *Canadian Charter of Rights and Freedoms*[3] offer constitutional protection for English and French, the two official languages in Canada (see Appendix).These sections provide language protection in a broad spectrum of public life, including legislatures, courts, government offices, and public schools.[4]

In this chapter, I explore the contours of the minority language educational rights jurisprudence by focusing primarily on the Supreme Court of Canada's judicial treatment of s.23 since the advent of the *Charter* in 1982. I do this by examining the following topics: (1) the special nature of s.23 rights; (2) the general interpretive principles relevant for the purposes of defining minority language educational rights; (3) the judicial interpretation of the leading s.23 cases; and (4) future legal challenges in the context of minority language educational rights. I then offer some concluding thoughts.

Special Nature of Language Rights

The rights set out in s.23 are of a special breed. As the Supreme Court of Canada (SCC) stated in *Mahe* v. *Alberta*:[5] 'Section 23 provides a comprehensive code for minority language educational rights; it has its own internal qualifications and its own method of internal balancing. The provision provides for a novel form of legal right, quite different from the type of legal rights which courts have traditionally dealt with. Both its genesis and its form are evidence of the unusual nature of s.23.'[6] These rights are unique in a number of ways. First, s.23 rights are positive rights because they require the state to do something.[7] In *Ford* v. *A.G. Quebec*,[8] the SCC declared: 'The central unifying feature of all of the language rights given explicit recognition in the Constitution of Canada is that they pertain to governmental institutions and for the most part they oblige the government to provide for, or at least tolerate, the use of both official languages.'[9] Consequently, provincial and territorial governments must implement their positive constitutional responsibility to offer minority language instruction to their minority language community.[10]

Second, s.23 rights are unusual because they protect both group[11] and individual rights. In *Solski (Tutor of)* v. *Quebec (Attorney General)*,[12] the SCC framed this dual nature as follows: 'Section 23 is clearly meant to protect and preserve both official languages and the cultures they embrace throughout Canada; its application will of necessity affect the future of minority language communities. Section 23 rights are in that sense collective rights ... Nevertheless, these rights are not primarily described as collective rights, even though they presuppose that a language community is present to benefit from their exercise. A close attention to the formulation of s.23 reveals individual rights in favour of persons belonging to specific categories of rights holders.'[13]

Third, language rights, such as those in s.23 of the *Charter*, are not considered 'fundamental' rights because they are not available to all members of the human family. The section only grants special constitutional status to minority English and French communities in Canada. The SCC highlighted this in *Quebec (Attorney General)* v. *Quebec Assn. of Protestant School Boards*:[14] 'Section 23 of the *Charter* is not, like other provisions in that constitutional document, of the kind generally found in such charters and declarations of fundamental rights. It is not a codification of essential, pre-existing and more or less universal rights that are being confirmed and perhaps clarified, extended, or amended, and which, most importantly, are being given a new primacy and inviolability by their entrenchment in the supreme law of the land. The special provisions of s.23 of the *Charter* make it a unique set of constitutional provisions, quite peculiar to Canada.'[15]

In *Société des Acadiens du Nouveau-Brunswick Inc.* v. *Association of Parents for Fairness in Education*,[16] Justice Beetz of the SCC posited that language rights, unlike legal rights that are 'seminal in nature because they are rooted in principle' are 'founded on political compromise.'[17] More recently, however, the SCC has moved away from the position that language rights are simply compromise-based rights. The Court has even gone so far to state that the historical pedigree of language rights, including s.23 rights, does not make them unprincipled. In *Reference re Secession of Quebec*,[18] the SCC ruled: 'There are a number of specific constitutional provisions protecting minority language, religion and education rights. Some of those provisions are, as we have recognized on a number of occasions, the product of historical compromises. However, we highlight that even though those provisions were the product of negotiation and political compromise, that does not render them unprincipled. Rather, such a concern reflects a broader principle related to the protection of minority rights ... We emphasize that the protection of minority rights is itself an independent principle underlying our constitutional order. The principle is clearly reflected in the *Charter*'s provisions for the protection of minority rights.'[19]

In sum, s.23 is distinct in a variety of ways. It is an expression of positive rights; it protects both collective rights and individual rights; and it is anchored in historical compromise yet reflects an independent constitutional principle, namely, the protection of minority rights.

General Interpretive Principles and s.23

A review of the SCC jurisprudence suggests a number of key interpretive principles relevant for the purposes of defining s.23 rights. First, courts should take a purposive approach to interpreting s.23 rights. This means considering the underlying rationale or raison d'être of the provision. As the late Chief Justice Dickson noted in *Société des Acadiens*: 'To give effect to a purposive approach in the language context, it is important to consider the constitutional antecedents of the *Charter* language protections, the cardinal values and purpose of the guarantees, the words chosen to articulate the rights, the character and larger objects of the *Charter*, and the purpose and meaning of other relevant *Charter* rights and freedoms.'[20] In *Mahe*, a unanimous SCC articulated the purpose of s.23 in these terms: 'The general purpose of s.23 is clear: it is to preserve and promote the two official languages of Canada, and their respective cultures, by ensuring that each language flourishes, as far as possible, in provinces where it is not spoken by the majority of the population.'[21]

Second, courts should be mindful of the remedial nature of s.23 rights. According to the SCC in *Solski*: 'The minority language education rights entrenched in s.23 are national in scope and remedial in nature. At the time the section was adopted, the framers were aware of the various regimes governing the Anglophone and Francophone linguistic minorities throughout Canada and perceived these regimes as inadequate. Section 23 was intended to provide a uniform solution to remedy these inadequacies.'[22]

Third, the SCC has consistently rejected a narrow construction of s.23. In *Doucet-Boudreau* v. *Nova Scotia (Minister of Education)*,[23] the SCC stated: 'It is well accepted that the *Charter* should be given a generous and expansive interpretation and not a narrow, technical, or legalistic one ... The need for a generous interpretation flows from the principle that the *Charter* ought to be interpreted purposively. While courts must be careful not to overshoot the actual purposes of the *Charter*'s guarantees, they must avoid a narrow, technical approach to *Charter* interpretation which could subvert the goal of ensuring that rights holders enjoy the full benefit and protection of the *Charter*.'[24] In the specific context of s.23, the same Court held that 's.23 must be given the same large and liberal interpretation as all *Charter* rights.'[25]

Fourth, the SCC in *Solski* stressed the need for a contextual approach to s.23: '[L]anguage issues are related to the development and existence of the English-speaking minority in Quebec and the French-speaking minorities elsewhere in Canada. They also inevitably have an impact on how Quebec's French-speaking community perceives its future in Canada, since that community, which is in the majority in Quebec, is in the minority in Canada, and even more so in North America as a whole. To this picture must be added the serious difficulties resulting from the rate of assimilation of French-speaking minority groups outside Quebec, whose current language rights were acquired only recently, at considerable expense and with great difficulty.'[26]

It then went on to add: 'Thus, in interpreting [s.23] rights, the courts have a responsibility to reconcile sometimes divergent interests and priorities, and to be sensitive to the future of each language community. Our country's social context, demographics and history will therefore necessarily comprise the backdrop for the analysis of language rights. Language rights cannot be analysed in the abstract, without regard for the historical context of the recognition thereof or for the concerns that the manner in which they are currently applied is meant to address.'[27]

In essence, s.23 rights should be interpreted purposively, remedially, generously, and contextually.

Judicial Interpretation of the Specific Provisions of s.23

Judicial decisions concerning s.23 typically address one, or both, of the following two key questions. Who qualifies for s.23 protection? What does minority language instruction mean? A few cases highlight other *Charter* provisions, namely, sections 1, 29, and 24. These sections deal respectively with 'reasonable limits' on s.23 rights, denominational rights, and remedies.

Who Qualifies?

The legal text of s.23 is the starting point for determining who qualifies for s.23 protection. The provision states that only Canadian citizens are covered by s.23. Subsections 1 and 2 provide further clarification. According to paragraph 23(1)(a): 'Citizens of Canada: whose first language learned and still understood is that of the English or French linguistic minority population of the province in which they reside ... have the right to have their children receive primary and secondary school instruction in that language in that province.' Paragraph 23(1)(b) offers a similar entitlement for citizens: 'who have received their primary school instruction in Canada in English or French and reside in a province where the language in which they received that instruction is the language of the English or French linguistic minority population of the province.' Subsection 23(2) states that citizens with any child who 'has received or is receiving primary or secondary school instruction in English or French in Canada, have the right to have all their children receive primary and secondary school instruction in the same language.' Under s.23(1), the qualifying standard is based on either the parents' proficiency in the minority language or their primary instruction. Under s.23(2), however, the standard focuses on the child's education. As for who exercises minority language educational rights, the SCC has ruled in *Mahe*[28] that the only rights holders under s.23 are minority language parents or their representatives.

It is noteworthy that paragraph 23(1) (a) does not apply in Quebec. This is because of s.59 of the *Constitution Act, 1982*[29] which states: '(1) Paragraph 23(1)(a) shall come into force in respect of Quebec on a day to be fixed by proclamation issued by the Queen or the Governor

General under the Great Seal of Canada. (2) A proclamation under subs. (1) shall be issued only where authorized by the legislative assembly or government of Quebec.'

So far, neither the National Assembly nor the Quebec government has given such authorization. The SCC offered a possible explanation for this anomaly in *Quebec (Attorney General)*: 'It may be possible to suggest a reason for this exception: so far as Quebec is concerned, s.23(1)(a) applies to Canadian citizens whose first language is English but who did not receive their primary school instruction in that language in Canada; that is, in practice, largely immigrants whose first language is English and who have become Canadian citizens. It is therefore plausible to think that this particular provision of the *Charter* was suspended for Quebec in part so as to calm the concerns regarding immigration, that, long before Bill 101 was adopted, were expressed in Quebec because of the minority status of French in North America.'[30]

To date, court decisions about the relevant qualifying standard for s.23 have focused on unsuccessful attempts to redefine the class of persons entitled to minority language educational rights as well as clarifying the scope and application of s.23(2).

Attempts at Redefinition

In *Quebec (Attorney General)*, a group of Protestant School Boards challenged the constitutionality of Chapter VIII of the *Charter of the French Language* (CFL). At the heart of the challenge were sections 72 and 73 of the *CFL*. Section 72 stated: 'Instruction in the kindergarten classes and in the elementary and secondary schools shall be in French, except where this chapter allows otherwise.' Section 73 stated: 'In derogation of s.72, the following children, at the request of their father and mother, may receive their instruction in English: (a) a child whose father or mother received his or her elementary instruction in English, in Québec; (b) a child whose father or mother domiciled in Québec on 26 August 1977, received his or her elementary instruction in English outside Québec; (c) a child who, in his last year of school in Québec before 26 August 1977, was lawfully receiving his instruction in English, in a public kindergarten class or in an elementary or secondary school; (d) the younger brothers and sisters of a child described in paragraph c.'

Under s.23(1)(b) of the *Canadian Charter of Rights and Freedoms*, citizens who have received their primary school instruction in *Canada* in English have the right to have their children receive primary and secondary education in the same language in Quebec. Subsection 73(a) and (b) of the *CFL*, however, further reduced the ambit of s.23(1)(b) by placing geographical (Quebec) and temporal (26 August 1977) restrictions on the parent's elementary education. Under s.23(2), citizens whose child has received or is receiving primary or secondary schooling in English in *Canada* are entitled to have all their children receive the same instruction in the same language in Quebec. But subsection 73(c) and (d) of the *CFL* qualified this, once again, with geographical and temporal limitations. The net effect of s.73 was to make an exception to s.23(1)(b) and s.23(2) of the *Charter* by further restricting who is entitled to English language instruction in Quebec.

The SCC struck down the Quebec legislation, holding that it was inconsistent with the minority language educational rights guarantee contained in s.23. Commenting on the Quebec government's failed attempt under s.73 to redefine the classes of persons entitled to s.23 protection, the Court stated: 'The rights stated in s.23 of the *Charter* are guaranteed to very specific classes of persons. This specific classification lies at the very heart of the provision, since it is the means chosen by the framers to identify those entitled to the rights they intended to guarantee. In our opinion, a legislature cannot by an ordinary statute validly set aside the means so chosen by the framers and affect this classification. Still less can it remake the classification and redefine the classes.'[31]

The SCC noted that redefining the classes of persons protected by s.23 would require an amendment to the Constitution of Canada.[32] The Court also ruled against using equality arguments[33] or multicultural arguments[34] to amend the categories of rights holders under s.23. As the SCC in *Mahe* stated: 'A notion of equality between Canada's official language groups is obviously present in s.23. Beyond this, however, the section is, if anything, an exception to the provisions of ss. 15 and 27 in that it accords these groups, the English and the French, special status in comparison to all other linguistic groups in Canada ... it would be totally incongruous to invoke in aid of the interpretation of a provision which grants special rights to a select group of individuals, the principle of equality intended to be universally applicable to "every individual."'[35]

Most recently, in *Gosselin (Tutor of)* v. *Quebec (Attorney General)*,[36] a group of French parents in Quebec sought access, for their children, to English-language schools in their province. Under Quebec's *Charter of the French Language*, these schools only accept children who have received or are receiving English language instruction in Canada or whose parents studied in English in Canada at the primary level. The parents argued that Quebec's language law violated their equality rights by discriminating between children who qualify and the majority of French-speaking Quebec children, who do not. Relying on the equality guarantees set out in both the *Charter* and Quebec's *Charter of Human Rights and Freedoms*, they maintained that all children in Quebec should be given access to publicly funded English-language education. The SCC rejected this claim:

> If adopted, the practical effect of the appellants' equality argument would be to read out of the Constitution the carefully crafted compromise contained in s.23 of the *Canadian Charter of Rights and Freedoms*. This is impermissible. As the Court has stated on numerous occasions, there is no hierarchy amongst constitutional provisions, and equality guarantees cannot therefore be used to invalidate other rights expressly conferred by the Constitution. All parts of the Constitution must be read together. It cannot be said, therefore, that in implementing s.23, the Quebec legislature has violated either s.15(1) of the *Canadian Charter of Rights and Freedoms* or ss. 10 and 12 of the Quebec *Charter*. The appeal should therefore be dismissed.[37]

The Court noted that the parents were 'attempting to accomplish precisely that which *Mahe* prohibited, namely the use of equality guarantees to modify the categories of rights holders under s.23.'[38]

Scope and Application of s.23(2)

According to s.23(2): 'Citizens of Canada of whom any child has received or is receiving primary or secondary school instruction in English or French in Canada, have the right to have all their children receive primary and secondary school instruction in the same language.'

In *Whittington* v. *Saanich School District No. 63*,[39] a group of anglophone parents in British Columbia petitioned for an order to set aside the local school board's decision to discontinue its French immersion program in Kindergarten and for a declaration of educational-language rights. The parents claimed that the *Charter* guaranteed them the right to a French immersion program in an English linguistic majority province, by virtue of the words 'instruction in French' found in s.23(2). The B.C. Supreme Court refuted this argument: 'The Petitioners' interpretation, if accepted, would be that those words "instruction in French" in the section refer to the linguistic majority; that simply cannot be correct. Section 23 does not guarantee majority rights, which they already have, rather it guarantees rights to the English or French linguistic minority populations residing in each province to have their children receive education in the language of their minority.'[40]

In essence, the English-linguistic majority in British Columbia had no constitutionally protected right, under s.23(2), to a French immersion program.

In *Abbey* v. *Essex County Board of Education*,[41] an anglophone mother in Ontario had three children who received practically their entire primary school education in French first language schools. Until 1996, the local public school boards had acquired this service for Ms. Abbey's children through a purchase-of-services arrangement with the separate school boards. In 1996, the Essex County Board of Education refused to enter into such an agreement for her children, relying on s.23(1). The Board claimed that Ms. Abbey had no constitutional entitlement under s.23 because her first language was not that of the linguistic minority population of the province where she resided, namely, Ontario. She applied for judicial review of that decision, relying on s.23(2) of the *Charter*. She argued that since her children had already received French first language instruction, they were thus qualified to further instruction under s.23(2). The Divisional Court rejected her claim maintaining that she was not a member of the minority linguistic community. The Court of Appeal reversed this decision.

The appellate court noted that the entitlements set out in sections 23(1) and (2) are 'conceptually related, but independent from each other.' Ms. Abbey had no claim under s.23(1) because she was an anglophone living in Ontario. She did, however, qualify under s.23(2). The court observed, pursuant to this section, that children who have received – or are receiving – their education in the language of the linguistic minority have the right to continue receiving their primary and secondary school education in that language. Their siblings, likewise, enjoy the same continuous right.

In *Solski*,[42] the SCC had to ascertain whether s.73(2) of Quebec's *Charter of the French Language* (*CFL*) conforms with s.23(2) of the *Charter*. According to s.73(2) '[t]he following children, at the request of one of their parents, may receive instruction in English: a child whose father or mother is a Canadian citizen and who has received or is receiving elementary or secondary instruction in English in Canada, and the brothers and sisters of that child, provided that that instruction constitutes the *major part* of the elementary or secondary instruction received by the child in Canada' (emphasis added).

The case came to the courts after three families unsuccessfully requested certificates of eligibility to allow their child or children to attend public English-language schools in Quebec pursuant to s.73(2) of the *CFL*. The requests were denied on the ground that the child or children had not completed the 'major part' of their instruction in the minority language.

The SCC characterised the minister of education's interpretation of 'major part' in the following manner: 'The Minister has interpreted the "major part" requirement in a disjunctive and strictly mathematical manner. The Minister will consider either the child's primary school attendance or the child's secondary school attendance, but will not consider them cumulatively ... Further, the Minister will determine eligibility solely on the basis of the number of months spent in each language. Other factors, including the availability of linguistic programs and the presence of learning disabilities or other difficulties ... are not considered.'[43]

The Administrative Tribunal of Quebec (ATQ) embraced the minister's narrow interpretation. Yet, the Supreme Court rejected this rigid mathematical approach. It maintained that this approach could not be reconciled with a broad interpretation of s.23(2), whose constitutional objective is to protect minority language communities and must be defined in a *qualitative* way rather than in a *quantitative* manner: 'Based on the proper interpretation of s.23(2) ... we are of the view that in order to comply with this constitutional provision, the *CFL*'s "major part" requirement must involve a qualitative rather than a strict quantitative assessment of the child's educational experience through which it is determined if a significant part, though not necessarily the majority, of his or her instruction, considered cumulatively, was in the minority language. Indeed, the past and present educational experience of the child is the best indicator of genuine commitment to a minority language education.'[44]

At the same time, the Court acknowledged that provincial governments are authorised 'to verify that registration and attendance in the program, the past and present educational experience of the child, are consistent with participation in the class of beneficiaries defined in s.23(2).'[45] This verification would help furnish the evidence necessary to ascertain whether or not there existed a genuine commitment to a minority language educational experience.

The SCC then had to determine whether the three families qualified for minority language instruction. Since the Solskis abandoned their appeal after the trial judgment, the Court did not deal with their particular circumstances. As for the Lacroix children, Eve and Amelie, the SCC ruled that they were both eligible for English education on the basis of

Amelie's prior schooling in Quebec. She completed Grades 1 and 2 in a private French school. Amelie then attended an unsubsidized private school that provided 60 per cent English instruction and 40 per cent French instruction. With respect to the Casimir children, Shanning and Edwin, the Court held that they were also entitled to attend English schools in Quebec. Shanning attended Grades 1 and 2 in a French immersion school in Ottawa administered by an English school board. She received 50 per cent of her education in French and 50 per cent of her education in English. In July 2000, the family moved to Quebec. The SCC ruled that Shanning's prior schooling, including her instruction in French, constituted English education because she received this education in a French immersion program while in an English-language setting.

Ultimately, the SCC ruled that the Quebec Administrative Tribunal's narrow construction of 'major part' in s.73(2) of the *Charter of the French Language* was under-inclusive.[46] Rather than striking down the legislation, by declaring it unconstitutional, the Court chose to interpret the word 'major' in a qualitative rather than a quantitative way. The Court thus found s.73(2) to be constitutional, thereby ensuring compliance of s.73(2) with s.23(2) of the *Charter*.

In *Solski*, the SCC acknowledged that the correct interpretation of 'major part' is still the subject of ongoing litigation in other circumstances. The Court noted that the Quebec legislature introduced *Bill 104*,[47] in 2002 amending s.73 of the *Charter of the French Language*. When calculating the 'major part' requirement, the new legislation disqualifies both education in private unsubsidized English schools and any English education occurring during the granting of a temporary stay certificate for immigrant children. Since Bill 104 was not in existence when the three families in *Solski* brought their lawsuit, the SCC concluded that the Quebec legislature must be taken to have accepted attendance at a private unsubsidized English school, as well as time spent in an English school under the aegis of a temporary stay certificate, as valid when calculating the major part of a child's education. The Court noted that the constitutionality of the changes brought about by *Bill 104* were the subject of other judicial proceedings and, consequently, would be dealt with in due course.[48]

What Does Minority Language Instruction Mean?

Case law also exists that considers the meaning of *minority language instruction* in the context of s.23. These judicial decisions focus on the proper interpretation of minority language instruction, the meaning of management and control, the definition of *where numbers warrant* and the location of minority language instruction.

General Analytical Approach to s.23(3)

According to s.23(3) of the *Charter*: 'The right of citizens of Canada under subsections (1) and (2) to have their children receive primary and secondary school instruction in the language of the English or French linguistic minority population of a province (a) applies wherever in the province the number of children of citizens who have such a right is sufficient to warrant the provision to them out of public funds of minority language instruction; and (b) includes, where the number of those children so warrants, the right to have them receive that instruction in minority language educational facilities provided out of public funds.'

The SCC's landmark decision in *Mahe*[49] established, for the first time, the general analytical approach all subsequent courts have taken to interpreting the right to minority language instruction enshrined under s.23. Speaking for a unanimous Court, the late Chief Justice Dickson declared: 'The proper way of interpreting s.23, in my opinion, is to view the section as providing a general right to minority language instruction. Paragraphs (a) and (b) of subs. (3) qualify this general right: para. (a) adds that the right to instruction is only guaranteed where the "number of children" warrants, while para. (b) further qualifies the general right to instruction by adding that where numbers warrant it includes a right to "minority language educational facilities."'[50]

The Chief Justice described this approach as the 'sliding scale' requirement, with the term *minority language educational facilities* in subsection (3)(b) indicating the upper level of this range and the term *instruction* in subsection (3)(a) indicating the lower level.[51] As he declared: 'The idea of a sliding scale is simply that s.23 guarantees whatever type and level of rights and services is appropriate in order to provide minority language instruction for the particular number of students involved.'[52]

Management and Control

Chief Justice Dickson went on to hold that s.23 encompasses a degree of *management and control*. While recognizing that this concept was imprecise and required further clarification, the Chief Justice noted that to satisfy the purpose of s.23, the minority language group must 'have control over those aspects of education which pertain to or have an effect upon their language and culture.'[53] He also acknowledged that precision concerning the nature of the scope of management and control was neither possible nor desirable given the infancy of the jurisprudence around s.23: 'It is not possible to give an exact description of what is required in every case in order to ensure that the minority language group has control over those aspects of minority language education which pertain to or have an effect upon minority language and culture. Imposing a specific form of educational system in the multitude of different circumstances which exist across Canada would be unrealistic and self-defeating. The problems with mandating "specific modalities" have been recognized by all of the courts in Canada which have considered s.23. At this stage of early development of s.23 jurisprudence, the appropriate response for the courts is to describe in general terms the requirements mandated.'[54]

Consequently, he proposed some guidelines to help determine the requisite level of management and control in different circumstances. At the upper end of the sliding scale, numbers might warrant an independent school board. Where numbers did not justify this kind of control, they might still require linguistic minority representation on an existing school board. In this scenario, Chief Justice Dickson ruled that the following criteria should apply:

> The representation of the linguistic minority on local boards or other public authorities which administer minority language instruction or facilities should be guaranteed;
>
> The number of minority language representatives on the board should be, at a minimum, proportional to the number of minority language students in the school district, i.e., the number of minority language students for whom the board is responsible;
>
> The minority language representatives should have exclusive authority to make decisions relating to the minority language instruction and facilities, including:
> (a) expenditures of funds provided for such instruction and facilities;
> (b) appointment and direction of those responsible for the administration of such instruction and facilities;
> (c) establishment of programs of instruction;
> (d) recruitment and assignment of teachers and other personnel; and
> (e) making of agreements for education and services for minority language pupils.[55]

He concluded by adding the following six qualifications. First, quality education in a minority context embraces the notion of equality. Second, s.23 sets out a minimalist approach to management and control which does not preclude governments from offering minority language communities more control over their own education. Third, there are a variety of different forms of institutional structures, which governments may choose from to satisfy the requirements of s.23. Fourth, s.23 parents, or their representatives, are responsible for exercising the appropriate level of management and control. Fifth, other degrees of management and control might be necessary where the numbers do not justify granting full rights of management and control. Sixth, provincial regulation of minority language education is permissible to the extent that it respects the linguistic and cultural concerns of the minority language community.[56]

It is worth noting that the lower levels of the sliding scale approach have not really worked in practice and have in fact lead to more problems associated with assimilation.[57] As a result of this, all provinces have now moved to provide the first-language minorities, be they French or English, with their own school boards. In some provinces with small and geographically dispersed minorities there is only one board for the entire province. Examples of this include British Columbia, Prince Edward Island, Newfoundland and Labrador, and Saskatchewan. Other provinces have multiple boards and, in some of these with denominational rights, French-language boards have split along denominational lines. This is the case in Alberta and Ontario but not yet in Saskatchewan.

Where Numbers Warrant

The language of s.23(3) makes it clear that the provision of minority language instruction is subject to the caveat *where numbers warrant*. In *Mahe*,[58] the SCC stated that the meaning of the phrase must be determined on a case-by-case basis with reference to the purpose of s.23: '[T]he phrase "where numbers warrant" does not provide an explicit standard which courts can use to determine the appropriate instruction and facilities ... in every given situation. The standard will have to be worked out over time by examining the particular facts of each situation which comes before the courts, but, in general, the inquiry must be guided by the purpose of s.23.'[59] Nonetheless, the Court noted that the 'relevant figure for s.23 purposes is the number of persons who will eventually take advantage of the contemplated programme or facility.'[60] It went on to suggest that this number could be 'roughly estimated by considering the parameters within which it must fall – the known demand for the service and the total number of persons who potentially could take advantage of the service.'[61]

In *Mahe*, the SCC also ruled that any discussion of *where numbers warrant* must consider two key criteria: pedagogy and costs. As for pedagogical considerations, the Court stated that 'a threshold number of students is required before certain programmes or facilities can operate effectively.'[62] If the threshold is not met, the SCC reasoned, the programmes and facilities are not required. With respect to costs, the Court acknowledged that s.23 'must be subject to financial constraints, for it is financially impractical to accord to every group of minority language students, no matter how small, the same services which a large group of s.23 students are accorded.'[63] In *Mahe*, the SCC found that if there are 'too few students' to justify a program of minority language instruction, 'then s.23 will not require any programmes be put in place.'[64] Ascertaining what constitutes 'too few students' has yet to be judicially determined.[65]

In *Arsenault-Cameron* v. *Prince Edward Island*,[66] a group of s.23 rights holders initiated proceedings against the Prince Edward Island government seeking a declaration of their right to have their children receive French first language instruction at the primary level in a school located in Summerside. When the action commenced, the children were being bussed to an existing French-language school in Abram's Village. The SCC held that the parents were entitled to a new school in Summerside. One of the key issues the Court addressed was the question of *where numbers warrant*. Based on expert evidence, the SCC ruled that there were between 49 actual students and 155 potential s.23 students who could take advantage of the new school in Summerside. These numbers led the Court to conclude that 'the threshold number of "fifteen s.23 children over two consecutive grade levels, who can reasonably be assembled for the purposes of providing French language instruction," in s.6.01(f) of the Regulations, was met in this case and that the Board complied with the requirements of s.6.08 in evaluating the need for local classes.'[67]

In addition, the SCC found that the minister of education's decision to deny the request for a new French school could not be justified on pedagogical grounds:

Despite the Minister's testimony that small schools generally have more difficulty meeting all curriculum requirements, we note that there was no evidence that pedagogical concerns could not be met, or that a small school would mean an education that is substandard. It was not shown that the Board would not be able to meet these requirements in the instant case ... Instead of providing a rationale for refusing the creation of a school based on the reasoning of the [French Language] Board, the Minister announced a minimum requirement of 100 students for a school to be viable. This number was based solely on the personal experience of the Minister as an educator. He testified that the provision of a full range of educational services, including guidance, music, gym and resource teaching is difficult in small schools. However, the number of students suggested by the Minister is unrelated to the specific circumstances and needs of the official language minority in the Summerside area. There was also evidence that a number of English language schools with less than 100 students existed in the Eastern school district, but the Minister was not willing to close them or to say they did not meet the department's pedagogical standards.[68]

The Court also noted that costs were not a consideration in the minister's decision. His sole opposition to the construction of the new facility was based on pedagogical considerations.

Location of Instruction

Typically, minority language instruction occurs within the province where the minority language students live. But, this may not always be the case. In *Chubbs* v. *Newfoundland and Labrador*,[69] the government of Newfoundland entered into an agreement with the government of Quebec whereby seventeen minority language children who lived in L'Anse au-Clair in Southern Labrador were bussed a few kilometres across the border into Quebec to attend school in Lourdes de Blanc-Sablon. The province of Newfoundland paid all the costs associated with the arrangement. Given the small number of children involved, the government refused to create a separate school in Labrador because there was a satisfactory agreement with the Quebec school, both pedagogically and culturally, which offered a quality education to the Newfoundland students.

A group of parents brought an application to have their children educated in French in their southern Labrador community. The court rejected the application. It noted that the province was providing a totally

French educational environment for the students who did not have to reside away from their home and community. In addition, the students did not have to incur any tuition or travel expenses. Moreover, in comparative terms, the court reasoned that the educational experience in Quebec would be clearly superior to what could be offered in the students' home community – a two-room school with two teachers in a multigrade environment. Evidence also suggested that some Newfoundland minority language parents would still send their children to Quebec even if a local school was built, further reducing the small number of qualified students. Judge Fowler consequently refuted the argument that s.23 instruction in Newfoundland had to occur within the province's own borders:

> It would appear to be an extremely narrow view of s.23 of the *Charter* and counterproductive to its purpose to interpret that section as intending to restrict actual French language instruction as being provided solely within the actual borders of the Province. The Province has a clear obligation to facilitate that instruction, such that it meets the s.23 requirements of the *Charter*. I find that the arrangement made by the Province of Newfoundland and Labrador to make available full French language instruction in a fully equipped French school in a French cultural environment is a novel remedy that promotes and preserves in the best possible manner the French language in the region and satisfies those purposes under s.23 of the *Charter*.[70]

In *Arsenault-Cameron*, location of the school was also a relevant consideration in the SCC's analysis. The Court highlighted the special challenges confronting the minority francophone community in Summerside which had to decide whether or not to bus their elementary school aged children, on average 57 minutes one way, to Abram's Village. The SCC noted that s.23 children were faced with a choice between a locally accessible school in Summerside in the majority language and a less accessible school in the minority language in Abram's Village. Some parents chose the local English school because of the excessively long travel times for their young children. The Court remarked that even among those children attending *École Évangéline* in Abram's Village, most were not able to participate in any extracurricular school activities owing to the distance between their home and the school.

The Court also observed that the choice of travel would have an impact on the assimilation of the minority language children, while travel arrangements had no cultural impact on majority-language children:

'For the minority, travel arrangements were in large measure a cultural and linguistic issue; they involved not only travel times but also a consideration of distances because of the impact of having children sent outside their community and of not having an educational institution within the community itself.'[71] Where numbers warrant, the location of instruction cannot be dissociated from the notion of the school as a community centre and thus as an engine of community growth. In this regard, the SCC in *Arsenault-Cameron* stated: 'It is ... important to note that the s.23 standard is not neutral but favours community development.'[72]

Other Charter Provisions

Although judicial analysis of s.23 tends to focus on who qualifies for minority language educational rights and the meaning of minority language instruction, sections 1 and 29 of the *Charter* are still potentially relevant in the analysis. Section 1 places 'reasonable limits' on all *Charter* rights while s.29 protects denominational rights. Most recently, the remedial section of the *Charter*, being s.24, has assumed special significance in the context of s.23.

Section 1 – Reasonable Limits

In *R. v. Oakes*,[73] the SCC set out the analytical guidelines (known as the *Oakes* test) to help ascertain whether government infringements of *Charter* rights, including s.23 rights, can be justified under s.1. Two basic requirements must be satisfied to establish that a limit is reasonable and demonstrably justified in a free and democratic society. First, the legislative objective, which the limitation is designed to promote, must be of sufficient importance to warrant overriding a constitutional right. It must bear on a 'pressing and substantial concern.' Second, the means chosen to attain those objectives must be proportional or appropriate to the ends.[74]

Prior to the adoption of the *Oakes* test, the SCC struck down parts of a Quebec statute in *Quebec (Attorney General)*. These provisions could not be saved under s.1 because they constituted exceptions from, or amendments to, s.23. In the post-*Oakes* era, it appears that no cases have been adjudicated where the courts have used s.1 to limit, or outright deny, an individual's s.23 rights. Nevertheless, in *Mahe*, the SCC stated that reasonable limitations of s.23 rights are permissible under a s.1 analysis. In general terms, the Court expressed this ability to place limits on minority language educational rights in the following manner: '[I]t should be noted that the management and control accorded to s.23 parents does not preclude provincial regulation. The province has an interest both in the content and the qualitative standards of educational programmes. Such programmes can be imposed without infringing s.23, in so far as they do not interfere with the linguistic and cultural concerns of the minority.'[75]

More specifically in the *Mahe* case, the late Chief Justice Dickson considered the claim by minority rights holders that a provincial regulation, mandating a minimum of approximately 20 per cent of class time be spent on English-language education, violated their s.23 rights. He noted that this restriction infringed s.23 and ran afoul of parental desires to have their children's instruction conducted exclusively in French. Notwithstanding the s.23 violation, the Chief Justice acknowledged that some mandatory English-language training constituted a reasonable limit under s.1:'I am prepared to agree with the Alberta courts that a certain amount of mandatory English language instruction is a reasonable limitation on s.23. It seems indisputable that some English language education is important for all students in Alberta.'[76] He was not convinced, however, that the 20 per cent requirement of the regulation, being 300 minutes a week of English instruction, was necessary in francophone schools. Since the Alberta government did not demonstrate, pursuant to the *Oakes* tests, that 'this limit infringes the s.23 right no more than is necessary,'[77] the Chief Justice struck down the regulation because it could not be saved by s.1. He left open, however, the possibility that the government might rely on s.1 in the future to justify an infringement on s.23 rights by adducing evidence and argument in favour of some form of English-language education: 'This conclusion does not, of course, preclude the respondent from attempting in the future to prove that some mandatory English instruction, perhaps even 300 minutes per week, is a reasonable limit under s.1.'[78]

The paucity of case law under s.1 leaves a number of questions unanswered. As Power and Foucher observe:

> The question of whether impugned legislation which has the effect of limiting an individual's s.23 *Charter* right may be justified under s.1 remains unsettled. For instance, what is the impact of the fact that Quebec is the only province where the language of the majority is French on the determination of whether an impugned legislation's objective is sufficiently important? May limits to s.23 be justified in an attempt by the government

to save money? How may preventing entitled persons from having their children receive instruction in the minority language be properly characterized as impairing as little as possible their constitutional right to do so? Could a minimum period of continuous minority language instruction constitute a reasonable limit to entitlement under subsection 23(2)?[79]

These important queries remain to be addressed in future litigation. In any event, governments should not be entitled to limit s.23 rights unless they can show that there exist good reasons for doing so by meeting the specific exigencies of the *Oakes* test in the context of s.1.

Section 29 – Denominational Considerations

Any interpretation of s.23 rights must be consistent with the denominational guarantees set out in s.29 of the *Charter*. This section states:'Nothing in this *Charter* abrogates or derogates from any rights or privileges guaranteed by or under the Constitution of Canada in respect of denominational, separate or dissentient school.'

The rights of denominational, separate, or dissentient schools referred to in s.29 are generally provided for in s.93(1) of the *Constitution Act, 1867*, as follows: '93. In and for each Province the Legislature may exclusively make Laws in relation to Education, subject and according to the following Provisions: (1) Nothing in any such Law shall prejudicially affect any Right or Privilege with respect to Denominational Schools which any Class of Persons have by Law in the Province at the Union.'

In *Mahe*, initial concern was expressed that the right of management and control under s.23 might clash with the denominational rights affirmed in s.29.[80] After all, most of the rights holders in *Mahe* were Roman Catholic and a separate school board had responsibility for the school at the heart of the case. The SCC allayed fears in this regard. The Court noted that minority language trustees on a denominational school board were simply required to wear two hats: one as minority language trustees with s.23 powers over management and control of minority language education and one as denominational trustees with power to manage and control things denominational. The Court held that this arrangement would neither interfere with a denominational board's power to manage and control nor alter its denominational character. Moreover, as the SCC observed, a denominational board's ceding of authority over minority language education 'amounts to the regulation of a non-denominational aspect of education, namely, the language of instruction, a form of regulation which the courts have long held to be valid.'[81]

Section 24 – Remedies

Section 24(1) entitles courts to grant rights holders a host of different, and potentially new, remedies to ensure that governments make good on their constitutional obligations under the *Charter*. As the SCC in *Mahe* ruled, courts should not 'avoid implementing the possibly novel remedies needed to achieve'[82] the purposes of s.23.

More recently, in *Doucet-Boudreau*, the SCC demonstrated that it is prepared to embrace the crafting of exceptional remedies, pursuant to s.24(1) of the *Charter*, to correct government inaction and neglect which jeopardize s.23 rights. In this case, a group of francophone parents living in five school districts[83] in Nova Scotia applied for an order directing the province and the province's francophone school board[84] to provide homogeneous French-language facilities and programs at the secondary school level out of public funds. Judge Leblanc, the trial judge, noted that the government did not deny the existence or content of the parents' rights under s.23. He held that the government had failed to prioritize those rights and delayed fulfilling its obligations, despite clear reports showing that assimilation was 'reaching critical levels.' Judge LeBlanc found a s.23 violation and ordered the province and the minority board to use their 'best efforts' to provide school facilities and programs by particular dates. He retained jurisdiction to hear reports on the status of the efforts. The province appealed the part of the order where Judge LeBlanc retained his jurisdiction to hear reports. A majority of the SCC[85] upheld the trial judge's order, thereby rejecting the province's appeal.[86]

In its judgment, the majority underlined the stonewalling and unfulfilled promises that s.23 rights holders faced from the provincial government:

> Through the mid-1990s, s.23 parents had pressured the government to provide homogeneous French-language facilities in presentations to Legislative Committees and in written and oral submissions to Ministers of Education. They had submitted petitions, letters, and expert analyses on assimilation to the Province. In 1996, amendments to the *Education Act* provided for a French-language school board, the Conseil scolaire acadien provincial, geared toward the fulfilment of the Province's s.23 obligations. The school board then decided to provide the facilities at issue in this appeal. From 1997 to 1999, the provincial government announced the construction of homogeneous French-language schools in Petit-de-Grat, Clare, and Argyle. The schools were never built, and the construction projects were officially put on hold in September 1999.[87]

The government argued that its decision to put the school construction projects on hold pending cost-benefit reviews could be defended on three grounds: a lack of consensus in the community, a consequent fear that enrolment would drop, and a lack of funds. The majority of the Court agreed with Judge LeBlanc that none of these reasons justified the government's failure to fulfil its obligations under s.23.

The majority also highlighted the nefarious effect government delay could have on the 'numbers warrant' provision of s.23: '[T]he "numbers warrant" requirement leaves minority language education rights particularly vulnerable to government delay or inaction. For every school year that governments do not meet their obligations under s.23, there is an increased likelihood of assimilation which carries the risk that numbers might cease to "warrant." Thus, particular entitlements afforded under s.23 can be suspended, for so long as the numbers cease to warrant, by the very cultural erosion against which s.23 was designed to guard.'[88]

The majority of the Court then examined whether the trial judge had the authority to retain jurisdiction to hear reports from the province, about the government's best efforts to comply with s.23, as part of its remedy under s.24(1) of the *Charter*. It held that Judge LeBlanc's order was within the jurisdiction of a superior court. The majority noted that a 'court of competent jurisdiction' envisaged by s.24(1) is a superior court established under s.96 of the *Constitution Act, 1867*. It then declared: 'There is nothing in s.96 to limit the inherent jurisdiction of the superior courts or the jurisdiction that can be conferred on them by statute ... and, *a fortiori*, nothing to limit the jurisdiction of a superior court under s.24(1) of the *Charter*.'[89]

According to s.24, a court of competent jurisdiction has the authority to grant a remedy that it considers appropriate and just in the circumstances. The majority of the Court outlined five general principles that courts should follow when assessing the appropriateness and justice of a potential remedy.

First, an appropriate and just remedy in the circumstances of a *Charter* claim is one that meaningfully vindicates the rights and freedoms of the claimants. Second, this remedy must employ means that are legitimate within the framework of our constitutional democracy. Third, this remedy must be a judicial one, which vindicates the right while invoking the function and powers of a court. Fourth, this remedy is one that, after ensuring that the right of the claimant is fully vindicated, is also fair to the party against whom the order is made.

Fifth, s.24 is part of a constitutional scheme for the vindication of fundamental rights and freedoms enshrined in the *Charter*. As such, s.24, because of its broad language and the myriad of roles it may play in cases, should be allowed to evolve to meet the challenges and circumstances of those cases.[90] On all five principles, the majority of the Court concluded that Judge LeBlanc's remedy was just and appropriate in the circumstances.

In the final analysis, *Doucet-Boudreau* clearly establishes a new judicial benchmark for the application of appropriate and just remedies in the context of s.23. Rights holders may now seek the help of the courts, in novel ways, to enforce 'the full and prompt vindication of their rights after a lengthy history of government inaction.'[91] Moreover, the majority's approval of the trial judge's decision to monitor ongoing government efforts to comply with s.23 is significant. One can argue that this ruling gives courts more of a 'hands on' approach, normally reserved to the executive branch of government, to ensure compliance with s.23 in the face of government delay. After all, the majority held: '[A] court ordering a *Charter* remedy must strive to respect the relationships with and separation of functions among the legislature, the executive and the judiciary. This is not to say that there is a bright line separating these functions in all cases. A remedy may be appropriate and just notwithstanding that it might touch on functions that are principally assigned to the executive.'[92] The majority cautioned, however, that this departure from the courts' traditional role must not imperil its adjudicative functioning: 'The essential point is that the courts must not, in making orders under s.24(1), depart unduly or unnecessarily from their role of adjudicating disputes and granting remedies that address the matter of those disputes.'[93]

Future Challenges

As we have seen, it is reasonable to anticipate that future litigation will help clarify a number of unresolved issues. Chief among these are what constitutes reasonable limits on s.23 rights under s.1? In terms of too few students, what does the phrase *where numbers warrant* mean? What novel remedies, under s.24(1), are available to ensure that governments satisfy their obligations under s.23? In Quebec, do recent changes under *Bill 104* concerning private unsubsidized English schools and English education acquired while holding a temporary stay certificate violate minority language educational rights protected by the *Charter*?

On another front, questions about funding and the quality of the educational experience are now surfacing. In Saskatchewan, for instance, two minority language parents and the province's minority language school board, le Conseil scolaire Fransaskois (CSF), have recently filed a statement of claim in the Court of Queen's Bench[94] to seek additional funding to meet the CSF's operating budget and capital budget needs. The claimants maintain that inadequate government funding is violating their s.23 rights. Consequently, they are seeking judicial redress to ensure 'une égalité des résultats en éducation.'[95]

The CSF is responsible for twelve schools and one program in twelve different communities throughout the province of Saskatchewan. It represents a total student population of 1,068 students in classes from Kindergarten to Grade 12. The distance between the CSF's two closest schools is 50 kilometres. The distance between its two farthest schools is 670 kilometres.[96]

The CSF alleges that the effects of underfunding have led the minority language school board to draw on its reserve, as it no longer has a surplus, and to run an operating deficit since 1999. Furthermore, it notes that parents are withdrawing their children from minority language programs because the quality of educational services is not comparable to the services offered elsewhere, notably in the English-speaking majority language schools. Under these circumstances, the CSF maintains that it can no longer fulfil its mandate of offering minority language instruction in conformity with s.23. This, in turn, the board argues, leads to an assimilation of the minority language community.

In essence, the claim is about educational equality. The rights holders and the minority board are arguing that they cannot offer educational services and guarantee educational results comparable to those offered and guaranteed by the majority English-language boards in Saskatchewan because of inadequate funding. The quality of the educational experience in minority language communities is certainly something the SCC was alive to in *Mahe*. As the Court observed: '[T]he quality of education provided to the minority should in principle be on a basis of equality with the majority.'[97] The Court went on to clarify that additional funding may be required to guarantee equality between the minority and majority communities: 'It should be stressed that the funds allocated for the minority language schools must be at least equivalent on a per student basis to the funds allocated to the majority schools. Special circumstances may warrant an allocation for minority language schools that exceeds the per capita allocation for majority schools.'[98]

This differential treatment rejects the notion of formal equality, which means treating the majority and the minority official language groups in an identical manner. Instead, as the SCC explained in *Arsenault-Cameron*, s.23 embraces the concept of substantive equality: 'Section 23 is premised on the fact that substantive equality requires that official language minorities be treated differently, if necessary, according to their particular circumstances and needs, in order to provide them with a standard of education equivalent to that of the official language majority.'[99]

Notwithstanding the articulation of these principles, difficult questions remain. In the Saskatchewan context, for instance, how much additional funding is really needed? The claimants are asking for $1.7 million. Is this adequate? Is this a realistic number given the numerous and varied demands on the province's treasury? How will we know when we have achieved equality between the minority and majority language communities when it comes to the delivery of educational services? What about equality of outcomes? Is this measurable? If so, how? And at what cost? It is unlikely that these thorny and vexatious questions will go away any time soon. If these issues cannot be resolved politically, however, minority rights holders will ask the courts to make important decisions about funding, the quality of the educational experience in a minority context, and, ultimately, what equality means in the context of the minority/majority dynamic.

Concluding Remarks

Judicial interpretation of s.23 rights recognizes that the French and English linguistic minority communities in Canada have a unique and privileged place in the Canadian constitution. The justification for these rights is, in part, founded in realpolitik. As the SCC has often noted, language rights are rooted in historical compromise. This compromise reflects the trade-offs, negotiations, and bargaining that Canada's two official language communities have engaged in for some time. The efforts of this bargaining culminated in the adoption of the language provisions, including minority language educational rights, in the *Charter*.

Entrenchment of language rights, including s.23, in the Constitution requires us as Canadians to remain true to our constitutional commitments. As Joseph Magnet states: 'We have to respect our constitutional promises, subject always to amending procedures. If we did otherwise, constitutional bargaining would be hollow. We would deprive ourselves of organizing our affairs by making constitutional settlements, and weaken our ability to live under a constitution at all.'[100]

Yet, realpolitik and the need to respect our constitutional promises do not tell the whole story when it comes to justifying language rights. In *Quebec Secession Reference*, the SCC ruled that the historical compromises underpinning minority language rights, including s.23 rights, do not render these rights unprincipled. The Court held that constitutionally entrenched language provisions are an expression of a broader and independent principle, notably, the protection of minority rights. While the SCC did not elaborate this point, its position begs the question why we should protect minority communities and minority rights in the first place. Magnet suggests, as a matter of principle, that two reasons explain why the state should compensate internal minority nations,[101] including Canada's official linguistic minorities, with a package of minority rights where the state favours one national culture or language.

His first reason focuses on the enjoyment of minority culture and the state's duty of fairness: 'First, enjoyment of its national culture is an important source of the good life for many minority nations. The state's action devalues the minority culture, and thus threatens continued enjoyment of it. It is only fair that the state bring any costs imposed on the status of the minority nations to zero balance by removing those costs through a grant of minority rights.'[102]

His second reason is related to the state's own interests, including its continued existence: 'Second, it is in the state's interest to grant minority rights. The state's action threatens to depreciate the status of its component minority nations. If the state does not act to protect their status with a package of minority rights, the reaction of the minority nations is almost certainly to be a vigorous program of nationalist activity, which may destabilize the state. It is in the state's interest to counter this development by granting minority rights that are fair and responsive to the situation of the minority nations. This is the best way to retain the loyalty of interior nations and so to strengthen the state.'[103]

In sum, a defence of minority language educational rights under s.23 of the *Charter* can be found in both pragmatic and principled considerations.

Even if legitimate reasons exist to defend the existence of s.23 rights, these rights do not exist or operate in an abstract legal void. Successful protection and promotion of minority language and culture in a given context depends on a number of institutional players making concerted efforts to fulfil the purposes and promises of s.23. Chief among these actors are governments, courts, and schools.

Provincial and territorial governments have a constitutional obligation to offer minority language instruction to their minority English
and French language communities. Governments must continue to fulfil their constitutional duties and be responsive to the needs of the minority communities as new circumstances and challenges arise. To date,
much progress has been made and, in part, as a result of government
policy and initiative there are now minority language school boards
and basic governance structures in every province and in both the
Northwest Territories and the Yukon Territory.[104]

Unfortunately, government commitment to respecting s.23 rights has
not always been a success story. In *Doucet-Boudreau*, a majority of the
SCC highlighted government neglect around the construction of five
high schools for Nova Scotia's minority Acadian and francophone
population. The Court noted that this neglect lasted over a period of
years and contributed directly to the assimilation of Nova Scotia's minority language rights holders. In Saskatchewan, rights holders and the
minority language school board are currently claiming that underfunding and government inaction are violations of s.23 and are leading to
unsustainably high levels of assimilation

Although negotiated settlements and political resolutions of impasses
around s.23 questions between rights holders and governments are preferable, recourse to the courts must always remain an option. The judiciary
has a key role to play in ensuring that governments make good on their
Charter responsibilities under s.23. When claims alleging *Charter* violations of minority language educational rights come before the courts, the
judiciary must ascertain whether the plaintiffs are entitled to the appropriate and just relief they are seeking pursuant to s.24 of the *Charter*. In
their analysis, the courts must continue to interpret s.23 rights purpose-
fully, remedially, liberally, and contextually. In certain circumstances, governments may attempt to justify violations of s.23 on the grounds that
their legislation, policies, and actions constitute reasonable limits under
s.1. Courts must be prudent to ensure that violations will only be justified
by meeting the strict exigencies of the *Oakes* test and not as a means of
frustrating the minority language educational rights guaranteed under
s.23. When governments fail to live up to their constitutional commitments, courts must be willing to craft just and appropriate remedies under
s.24(1) to force governments to comply with the requirements of s.23. This
may even require the crafting of novel remedies, including some degree
of court supervision à la *Doucet-Boudreau*, to prevent cultural erosion and
assimilation resulting from undue government delay.

Let us not forget, however, that the courts can only do so much to protect s.23 rights. They can only adjudicate actual cases, which come before them. They cannot compel rights holders to appear in front of them. Consequently, other minority language institutions must continue to fight the linguistic and cultural assimilation that threatens to destroy them, especially in minority francophone communities outside Quebec that are often small and isolated.[105] In *Arsenault-Cameron*, the SCC noted that the school is 'the single most important institution for the survival of the official language minority.'[106]

In liberal democracies, schools are responsible for educating and enlightening individual students. Respect for personhood requires educators to impart, among others, the values of rationality, autonomy, and critical thinking to each student. Here, the focus is on the worth and dignity of the individual. At the same time, schools must teach students about the limits of freedom, caring, citizenship, and the needs of others. Here, the focus is on community and the individual's relationship to others. Canada's minority language schools are not exempt from this educational imperative that requires constant negotiation between self-fulfilment and social responsibility.

At the same time, minority language schools are called to do more. As the SCC in *Solski* declared: 'Minority language education is a requisite tool to encourage linguistic and cultural vitality. Not only do minority schools provide basic language education, they also act as community centres where the members of the minority can meet to express their culture. Thus, the education rights provided by s.23 form the cornerstone of minority language rights protection.'[107]

Linguistic vitality is only possible for minority communities when enough people are willing, able, and encouraged to speak to each other in their mother tongue. Minority language schools exist to facilitate this vitality. At the same time, the provision of basic language education in minority schools is more than just linguistic training. It is also a cultural act. In *Ford*, the SCC expressed the link between language and culture in these terms: 'Language is not merely a means or medium of expression; it colours the content and meaning of expression. It is, as the preamble of the *Charter* of the French Language itself indicates, a means by which a people may express its cultural identity.'[108]

Cultural vitality, like linguistic vitality, ultimately depends on numbers. Are there enough people to continue to etch the daily practices, customs, traditions, beliefs, and assumptions deep enough into the minority community's memory and soul to allow it to survive? Where numbers are sufficient, the minority culture will continue. Where they are not, it will die. In borderline cases, the school as community centre, where members of the minority community gather to express, affirm, and celebrate their identity, may offer a glimmer of hope as the minority community struggles for its very existence. In the face of constant majoritarian pressures, linguistic minorities must always struggle against assimilation for survival. In this struggle, the role of the s.23 minority language school can never be underestimated. Maintaining robust and healthy schools is our best chance of preserving and promoting Canada's two official language communities.

11 The Courts and the School: The Judicial Construction of the School

CESARE OLIVERIO AND
MICHAEL MANLEY-CASIMIR

> At the same time, the judiciary will have to grapple with the fact that the
> school is a particular kind of social institution with a particular purpose
> and as such, courts will have to search for that delicate balance between
> constitutional interests and the special nature of education.[1]

Since the introduction of the *Canadian Charter of Rights and Freedoms*,[2]
Canadian courts have dealt with a significant number of cases involving
educational issues. No case, however, has dealt specifically with the institutional role of the school as the main question requiring judicial interpretation. Yet, as the above quotation from *Courts in the Classroom* predicted,
the issue of the special nature of the school as a social institution charged
with educational purposes would inevitably require judicial attention.
While such has proved to be the case, any discussion of the role of the
school is usually ancillary to other issues before the court, frequently dealing with the actions of the players in the education arena: teachers, administrators, students, and parents to name the most obvious. In some of these
cases, however, judges do attempt to define the role of the school as a
means of contextualizing and assessing the actions of its players.

In an earlier paper, 'The Judicial Construction of the Role of the
Teacher,'[3] we examined the evolving Canadian jurisprudence at the appellate court level to extract an emerging definition of the role of the
teacher judicially defined. In that analysis, we found that appellate
court judges have constructed the role of the teacher in ways that extend beyond the legislatively mandated duties and responsibilities expected of all members of the teaching profession. In cases of alleged
teacher misconduct, the courts include a discussion of the social role of

the school to define the context of judicial scrutiny in assessing teacher behaviour. In such cases, the school is often recognized as an institutional hierarchy with strongly embedded normative expectations respecting the appropriate behaviour of all its players. This behaviour must in general accord with the prevailingly accepted normative standards of Canadian society but may also acknowledge and respect the differences that are present in a multicultural society. From this perspective, a number of obvious problems emerge as courts struggle to render decisions based on judicially conceived notions of what Canadian society defines as the role of the school.

Given the heterogeneous character of Canadian society, it becomes increasingly difficult to derive a homogeneous definition or discover a publicly agreed consensus on the role of the school. An examination of provincial legislation shows that most educational statutes are conceptually similar, in that they all essentially deal with those issues necessary to establish and maintain systems of public education. Whereas some provinces have attempted to provide some guidance in understanding the role of the school as a social and formative institution, most have only provided a basic definition of what a school is and have overlooked altogether its role or function in their particular segment of society. It is in this stark context that the judiciary is called upon to operate and appreciate the role of the school as an institution encompassing all aspects of education. Even though lower courts and provincial courts of appeal operate within the context of their particular provincial legislation, their task becomes onerous when they are called upon to define and elaborate the role of the school when the desired characteristics of the school are missing from the statutes and regulations. The Supreme Court of Canada has an even more difficult task in trying to provide a pan-Canadian perspective applicable to all jurisdictions within the context described by provincial legislation.

This chapter focuses on the judicial conception of the school as a social institution in a democratic society and examines the way that the courts have conceived of the school as a formative institution in Canadian society. First, we examine the education legislation of a number of different provinces to highlight the presence or absence of a definition of the institutional role of the school. In the absence of a clear definition, those sections that provide the principles governing school conduct are analysed to extract guidelines for the articulation of a definition of the role of the school. Second, we carefully assess recent lower court and provincial appellate court decisions to demonstrate how courts in several provinces have dealt with an array of issues concerning publicly funded education. Finally, we outline and examine four Supreme Court of Canada decisions to show how over a short period of time the Supreme Court has begun to delineate legal principles describing the role of the school in a Canadian context.

Provincial Legislation

A close examination of the Acts governing education in different provinces shows that, with the exception of Quebec, most statutes and regulations do not provide a direct definition of the role of the school as a social, educational, and developmental institution for Canadian children. Most provincial legislation includes a rudimentary definition of 'school' in the section that provides meaning to the terminology used throughout. In such cases, the school is defined according to the people involved in the education process (pupils, teachers, and other staff members) and/or the lands and premises where the unit is physically located. The Ontario *Education Act*[4] provides the following definition: '"school" means, (a) the body of elementary school pupils or secondary school pupils that is organized as a unit for educational purposes under the jurisdiction of the appropriate board, or (b) the body of pupils enrolled in any of the elementary or secondary school courses of study in an educational institution operated by the Government of Ontario, and includes the teachers and other staff members associated with the unit or institution and the lands and premises used in connection with the unit or institution.' Although there is mention of words like 'educational purposes' and 'institution,' the legislation itself does not offer any insight into what is meant by the 'educational purposes that the institution serves.' This type of language is also used in the statutes governing education in the provinces of British Columbia,[5] Newfoundland,[6] Prince Edward Island,[7] and New Brunswick.[8] What is glaringly missing from all of these definitions is an explication of the role that the school serves as an institution providing educational services to the public. It is left to Regulations and provincial policy and curriculum documents to explicate the issues more fully.

By contrast, s.36 in Chapter III, Division I of the Quebec *Education Act*,[9] dealing with the establishment of schools, the Quebec legislature provides a comprehensive definition of 'school' which details the role that this institution plays in the educational development of students within a cultural and social background: 'A school is an educational institution whose object is to provide ... the educational services provided for by this Act ... and to contribute to the social and cultural development of the community. A school shall, in particular, facilitate the spiritual development of students so as to promote self-fulfillment.' And in the next paragraph it states: 'In keeping with the principles of equality of opportunity, the mission of a school is to impart knowledge to students, foster their social development and give them qualifications, while enabling them to undertake and achieve success in a course of study.'

The wording used in s.36 of the Act makes specific reference to the role that the school should play in providing the necessary environment to nourish students' spirituality, self-fulfilment, social development, knowledge development, and overall success. This view of the school extends beyond the obvious players and premises. In some ways, it undergirds the definitions provided by the statutes of other Canadian provinces. The Quebec legislation advances a set of criteria that function as guidelines for the public perception of the role of the school as a social and formative institution in society. It also provides a point of departure for judicial interpretation of issues related to the position that the school and its players occupy in the context of Quebec society. The courts in the province of Quebec can turn to this section and use these criteria in providing their interpretation of the role of the school.

Nevertheless, in many provincial statutes dealing with education, legislatures do provide some guidelines about the functions the school is expected to play in the lives of its students and in society as a whole. In the Ontario *Education Act*, for example, s.264(1) deals with the duties of teachers and states: 'It is the duty of a teacher and a temporary teacher, (a) to inculcate by precept and example respect for religion and the principles of Judaeo-Christian morality and the highest regard for truth, justice, loyalty, love of country, humanity, benevolence, sobriety, industry, frugality, purity, temperance and all other virtues.' The imposition of this duty on classroom instructors reflects, even if in an indirect manner, the expectations attached to the role that the school plays in shaping the lives of individual students. This role can be described as an obligation to provide an environment that exemplifies the qualities listed above and to guide students in the attainment of such characteristics. Although this section sheds some light on the role of the school, however, it is not a comprehensive and direct reference to such a role.

The British Columbia *School Act* includes the same sort of indirect reference to the role of the school. The Preamble states that 'whereas it is the goal of a democratic society to ensure that all its members receive an education that enables them to become personally fulfilled and publicly useful, thereby increasing the strength and contributions to the health and stability of that society,' and continues with 'and whereas the purpose of the British Columbia school system is to enable all learners to develop their individual potential and to acquire the knowledge, skills and attitudes needed to contribute to a healthy, democratic and pluralistic society and a prosperous and sustainable economy.'

This language yields the inference that the goal of the Legislative Assembly of British Columbia is to establish formative and social institutions to educate students and prepare them to live a purposeful and fulfilled life, thereby contributing to the welfare of the province. In s.76(1) and (2), the Act also provides rules on how schools must be conducted in order to achieve these goals: '(1) All schools and Provincial schools must be conducted on strictly secular and non-sectarian principles. (2) The highest morality must be inculcated, but no religious dogma or creed is to be taught in a school or Provincial school.' It is obvious from the wording of this section that schools are expected to instil a high sense of morality within the student population, without relying on any religious dogma.

A close look at the statutes governing education in the provinces of Quebec, Ontario, and British Columbia makes it clear that only the Quebec statute directly addresses the role of the school as a social and formative institution. This is not to say that the other provinces do not deal at all with providing such a definition. A close examination of their respective statutes reveals that these legislatures have provided some insight on the role of the school in their particular provincial contexts. The judiciary can use the sections that deal with this subject in an indirect manner, when trying to define the function of the role of the school in contexts that require such an interpretation. Problems arise when the courts are expected to use these inadequate guidelines in constructing an all-encompassing definition of the role of the school as a social and educational institution. These problems are exacerbated when the definition is one that must apply not only in the context of each particular province but in the context of Canadian society as a whole.

Recent Provincial Court and Provincial Appellate Court Decisions

At the provincial level, a number of post-*Charter* cases have required the courts to address and define the role of the school in a Canadian context. The main issue in these cases was not to decide whether or not any particular legislation contained the necessary guiding principles to define the role of schools; nor were the courts asked to determine if any school had failed to fulfil its mandated role. In all these cases, the role of the school was supplementary to the main issues being adjudicated. At the same time, it was necessary for the court to define and in certain cases construct this role in order to properly deal with the issues at hand. Such diverse issues include French language instruction, government funding for Cree education, the nature and powers conferred on Roman Catholic schools, and relationships between teachers and students. In these cases the courts look not only at the role that the school plays in Canada, but also at the role that education plays in cultural transmission.

Lower Court Decisions

In *Marchand* v. *Simcoe County Board of Education et al.*[10] the Ontario High Court of Justice had to decide whether the plaintiffs had a right to receive secondary school instruction in French, according to s.23 of the *Charter*. The judge found for the plaintiffs stating: 'The French language school provides a setting within which the Francophone students will have a better opportunity to come to know and to understand and to strengthen and develop their own culture and heritage ... [T]he school occupies a central role in the cultural life and linguistic community ... [T]he French language schools must truly be community schools and easily accessible to the general population of the linguistic group they exist to serve.'[11]

To determine whether to grant the plaintiff's request and require the defendant Board of Education to provide secondary school French language instruction, the court began by considering the need for students to develop a sense of culture and heritage. Having established the primacy of this goal, the judge then defined the role of the school, in a cultural and linguistic context, to emphasize the importance of French language education for the francophone community. Essentially, the court devised a definition of the role of the school to provide the framework within which to decide the issue at hand – that the plaintiffs had a right to secondary instruction in the French language, pursuant to s.23 of the *Charter*.

In *Casagrande* v. *Hinton Roman Catholic Separate School District*,[12] the Alberta Court of Queen's Bench was asked to decide whether the defendant Roman Catholic School Board had the right to dismiss a teacher on the grounds that she had had premarital sex, contrary to Catholic doctrine. The court's depiction of the way that Catholic School education is structured can be surmised from the following quote from *Caldwell et al.* v. *Stuart et al.*:[13] 'The relationship of the teacher to the student enables the teacher to form the mind and attitudes of the student and the Church depends not so much on the usual form of academic instruction as on the teachers who, in imitation of Christ, are required to reveal the Christian message in their work and as well in all aspects of behaviour.'[14] This passage highlights the importance of the role model of authentic Catholicity expected of Catholic teachers in the context of Catholic education. As a result, the judge explained that the role of Catholic schools is to impart the Christian message to all its pupils, so that it can pervade all aspects of their behaviour and imbue their lives.

This point is made clear by the court's view that the Catholic School 'is a genuine community bent on imparting, over and above an academic education, all help it can to its members to adopt a Christian way of life.'[15] This case demonstrates how a court can use the socially ascribed conception of the school as a framework within which to place and scrutinize the role of all the players in the education arena. In this particular case, the conception of a Catholic school provided the judicial justification to deny the plaintiff's claim of discrimination that she was fired for engaging in premarital sexual activity. Such a judicial disposition of the case relied on the well-established legal doctrine of *denominational cause*. The position that a teacher fills in Catholic education dictates that she live as a role model for the students and the community. Her departure from proper Catholic conduct meant that she could not as a result serve as an authentic role model within the context of Catholic education.

The role of the Catholic school was also described in the recent case of *Hall (Litigation guardian of)* v. *Powers*.[16] This case dealt with an application for an interlocutory injunction restraining the defendant Board of Education from preventing the applicant from attending the graduation prom with his boyfriend. In allowing the application, the judge stated: 'School is a fundamental institution in the lives of young people. It often provides the context for their social lives both in and outside of school hours. Recreational activities such as sports, clubs and dances, which are important in the development of a student's development, are often experienced within the school setting. Exclusion of a student from a significant occasion of school life, like the school prom, constitutes a restriction in access to a fundamental social institution.'[17]

In this passage, McKinnon J provides a definition of school as a social institution, which shapes the development of young people. School is seen as the setting for social interaction, which provides context for the social life of all students. The judge does not apply a definition of the role of a Catholic school. Instead, he applies a general definition of the role of the school, one which encompasses social activities, and hence the prom. Later in his decision, however, he does not view the prom as a component of education. He states: 'It is important to note that the prom in question is not part of a religious service (such as a mass), is not part of the religious education component of the Board's activity, is not held on school property, and is not educational in nature.'[18] In other words, the prom is part of the social role of school, but not educational. As such, the court effectively finds a way to allow an application that is in direct contrast with Catholic doctrine.

In the *Casagrande* case, the Catholic school played a central role in the lives of all its students. This role transcended all educational and social boundaries, and functioned at a cultural and spiritual level. Everything within the Catholic school must transmit the Catholic message. The teacher, who had behaved contrary to Catholic dogma, was justifiably removed from her position, and hence excluded from the Catholic school environment. In *Hall*, although the judge dealt with the Catholic dimension of the defendant school board, he chose to apply a general definition of the role of any public school, in order to find justification for his decision, which needed to be made promptly before the prom. While he upheld the importance of the role Catholic schools play in their communities, he distanced the issue at hand from the Catholic arena and placed it in a public forum. Moreover, he distanced the prom from the social component of education. Researchers Peter Pound and Iain Benson[19] discuss the judge's decision and point out that distancing the prom from education cannot be justified in a Catholic school context: 'McKinnon J. claimed that *"...the role of a school is to enlighten and guide students – not to control their private thoughts or behaviour"* and claimed that the prom *"is not part of the religious education component of the Board's activity"* and *"...is not educational in nature."* While the prom is clearly not a spelling lesson, Catholic education is very much about forming students by shaping a coherent view of human life consistent with the teachings of the Catholic Church, specifically with a view to influencing private thought and private and public behaviour. Catholic education, like most religious education, is about inculcating the faith. This requires a congruency between teaching and conduct, and examples that demonstrate the institution's faith commitment'[emphasis added].[20] The Catholic faith is present in every aspect of a person's life. As such, the role of the Catholic school is one that incorporates this faith aspect in the formative, social, cultural, and spiritual dimension.

These lower court cases essentially illustrate different dimensions of the role of the school as a social and formative institution. Whereas *Casagrande* and *Hall* both deal with the role of the Catholic school in the spiritual growth of its community, *Marchand* deals with the role of the school as a linguistic and cultural centre for the francophone community. These cases make evident the different dimensions of the role of the school in Canadian society. As well, they demonstrate how the judiciary utilizes the essential aspects of the role of a school to arrive at decisions that uphold their own personal view of the purpose that schools serve in our communities.

Court of Appeal Decisions

A number of provincial Court of Appeal decisions address issues related to school and education. Two cases in particular have individually delineated the role of the school and merit consideration here. The first case, *Commission scolaire crie c. Canada (Procureur General)*,[21] heard by the Quebec Court of Appeal, dealt with the right of members of the Cree nation to receive education funding from both the provincial and the federal governments, as stipulated in a previously negotiated agreement. In upholding the appellants' argument that they needed funding according to their budget for the continued existence of their own schools, the court examined the importance of education as a cultural process: 'Education is the instrument through which cultures perpetuate themselves. It is the process through which the members of a society assure themselves that the behaviour necessary to continue their culture is learned. Since education is a cultural process, it is important for educators to have a clear conception of the meaning of culture. Confusion over this meaning is an important factor in confusion and conflict concerning the proper role of the school.'[22]

Here the court emphasized the central importance of the school as the social mechanism though which cultures perpetuate themselves and recognized the need of the Cree to establish, maintain, and control their own schools to ensure the survival of their culture. Education is the vehicle of cultural transmission. For this reason, the Cree need to manage their own education process, so that their culture is not assimilated or overlooked by the provincial government. The judges then emphasized that in order to define the role of the school, there must be no confusion about the meaning of culture: 'The school is concerned with the transmission, conservation, and extension of culture. Cultural transmission and personality formation are perhaps the two most important functions of the school.'[23]

Although this reference to the role of the school is particular to the facts of this case, dealing as it does with the transmission of a cultural heritage, it can be applied to any community within Canada. As such, it exemplifies the purpose that the school serves as an institution where students gain knowledge of their particular culture and form their personality accordingly.

In the second case, *Young* v. *British Columbia College of Teachers*,[24] the British Columbia Court of Appeal dealt with an altogether different set of facts. This case involved the question of the appropriate penalty to be imposed by the British Columbia College of Teachers on a young teacher who began a sexual relationship with a student. The court placed a great deal of emphasis on the fact that the girl's mother accepted the relationship, which continued and was strong at the time of appeal. In other words, this was not a clear-cut case of teacher sexual misconduct and no criminal charges were ever laid.

The court engaged in an examination of relevant case law dealing with the role of education in general and the role of the school in particular. It began by applying the concepts related to educational institutions enunciated by the Supreme Court of Canada in *Ross* v. *New Brunswick School District No. 15*.[25] In this case the Supreme Court of Canada stated: 'A school is a communication centre for a whole range of values and aspirations of a society. In large part, it defines the values that transcend society through the educational medium. The school is an arena for the exchange of ideas and must, therefore, be premised upon principles of tolerance and impartiality so that all persons within the school environment feel equally free to participate.'[26] With these words, Chief Justice La Forest provided the most comprehensive, all-encompassing legal definition of the role of school, a definition that forms the basis for the judicial construction of the role of educational institutions in modern Canadian jurisprudence. Although this case is dealt with in detail in the next section, it is important to note here that the school is seen as the forum where values are communicated and ideas exchanged so that the essence of society is perpetuated. Because its function is to promulgate the main goals of culture from the point of view of the society with which it is associated, the school can only operate as an extension of this society, in harmony with its rules. Any deviation that upsets this balance will undermine the system.

The facts of the case at hand, involving the sexual relationship between a teacher and a student, are a clear example of elements that create a negative environment within the school. The British Columbia Court of Appeal dealt directly with the issue of the integrity of the education system in identifying the need to protect children from these type of relationships: 'an education system that functions appropriately fulfills the educational needs of children. Misconduct by a teacher that undermines the education system should thus be subjected to discipline ... Public confidence in the school system is important. If parents cannot send their children to school in the confidence that they will be guided by morally responsible and trustworthy teachers, they cannot be expected to support the system and encourage their children to take maximum advantage of it.'[27]

Teacher sexual misconduct has a direct negative impact on all the students and erodes public confidence in the system as a whole. Society deems such behaviour to be reprehensible because sexual relationships between teachers and students, however volitional, fundamentally distorts the educational purpose of the school. For this reason, teacher misconduct must be condemned or the administration of the school system is brought into disrepute.

Although the two Court of Appeal cases outlined in this section are from two separate provinces and deal with very different sets of facts, they proclaim the same message as it relates to the role of the school within Canadian society. *Commission scolaire* describes education as the instrument that allows for the transmission of culture. School is the educational instrument that facilitates this task, and allows students to grow in a manner consistent with their particular cultural tradition. *Young* takes this dialogue to a different level and labels the school as the milieu that allows for the exchange of ideas and the communication of values that define a specific society. Both cases describe the school as a formative institution, a learning environment that allows students to grow intellectually. As well, both cases view the school as a social institution whose function is to transmit the cultural message inherent in the cultural context of the school and to help students understand the values cherished by their society.

Supreme Court of Canada Decisions

The Supreme Court of Canada has dealt with a number of issues centred on the role of the school. What emerges from a careful reading of these decisions is a view of the school having a multifaceted and diverse role, concerned with the physical, emotional, social, cultural, and intellectual development of its pupils. Three of these cases question the fitness of teachers or student teachers who have engaged in behaviour deemed inappropriate by an administrative body. The fourth case deals with a school board resolution prohibiting the use of books that depicted same-sex families, as supplementary classroom resources. All these cases inevitably discuss the role of the school and the importance of establishing an educational environment that is welcoming to all members of a community and is free of negative attitudes towards any sector of society.

The first case, *Ross*, dealt with allegations that the School Board failed to take appropriate action against one of its teachers, Mr Ross, who had made public statements discriminating against people of the Jewish faith. The School Board hesitated to discipline Mr Ross and was held responsible for discriminating against Jewish people and other minorities within the educational system: 'The Board [of Inquiry] concluded that the School Board discriminated by failing to discipline the respondent meaningfully in that, by its almost indifferent response to the complaints and by continuing his employment, it endorsed his out-of-school activities and writings. This, it held, resulted in an atmosphere where anti-Jewish sentiments flourished and where Jewish students were subject to a "poisoned environment" within the School District "which has greatly interfered with the educational services provided" to the appellant Attis and his children.'[28]

The Board of Inquiry established by the Human Rights Commission, made an initial finding that Mr Ross' misconduct created a 'poisoned environment' that interfered with the provision of educational services. The School Board's failure to reprimand Mr Ross contributed to the creation of this poisoned environment to the detriment of the students. The Board of Inquiry essentially found that the School Board's inaction had a negative effect on the role of the school as an educational environment. In other words, it effectively interfered with its own mandate to provide the best educational setting to promote the values of the community. The Board of Inquiry stated: 'Education of students must be viewed in the broad context of including not only the formal curriculum but the more informal aspects of education that come through interchange and participation in the whole school environment.'[29] The informal curriculum is made up of all the activities and interactions that occur within the school community, among all the people involved in the education process – students, teachers, administrators. When one player makes others feel uncomfortable, an important aspect of education becomes restricted, and the integrity of the school system is seriously compromised.

In their examination of the role of the teacher, the Supreme Court of Canada makes it clear that the teacher is 'inextricably linked' to the school system, and when the teacher's image is tarnished, the whole education system is discredited. The School Board has an obligation to avoid impairment of the education process, and should therefore enforce appropriate disciplinary action against any member of the system who engages in inappropriate behaviour. The Court found that a school board has a duty to maintain a positive school environment for all persons served by it, and it must be ever vigilant of anything that might interfere with this duty.[30]

In emphasizing the importance of education, the court quoted *Brown* v. *Board of Education of Topeka*:[31] 'Today, education is perhaps the most important function of state and local governments ... It is the very foundation of good citizenship. Today it is a principal instrument in awakening the child to cultural values, in preparing him for later professional training, and in helping him to adjust normally to his environment.'[32] The school's role, to fulfil the task of instilling the values of a culture in the young, must not be hampered, lest the development of a society be inhibited. The school must ensure that the educational message that young and impressionable children receive is one that exemplifies the cultural values it is trying to inculcate, free of intolerance and discrimination.

The second case occurred in 1997 with the Supreme Court decision in *Toronto Board of Education* v. *Ontario Secondary School Teachers' Federation, District 15*.[33] This case dealt with a teacher who was discharged from his duties because of his destructive and threatening behaviour towards board officials. The Court looked at the Ontario *Education Act*, specifically at subsection 264 (1)(c), which declares that every teacher must inculcate by precept and example the highest regard for truth, justice, loyalty, love of country, humanity, and benevolence. These are cultural and social values that are transmitted to students by the education medium, through the teacher, in the school. When the teacher fails in role modelling these values, the school fails in its duty to the students, and must redress the situation by imposing appropriate disciplinary action against the teacher.

In this case, the Toronto Board of Education discharged the teacher in question. In deciding whether this discharge was appropriate, the Court once again argued for the integrity of the education system and stated: 'it is essential that arbitrators recognize the sensitivity of the educational setting and ensure that a person who is clearly incapable of adequately fulfilling the duties of a teacher both inside and outside the classroom is not returned to the classroom. Both the vulnerability of students and the need for public confidence in the education system demand such caution.'[34] If a teacher cannot provide the emotional growth and positive self-esteem necessary for teaching young students, he must be removed so that the education system does not fall into disrepute.

The third Supreme Court of Canada case dealing with the role of the school in Canadian society is *Trinity Western University* v. *British Columbia College of Teachers*.[35] In this case, the British Columbia College of Teachers denied Trinity Western University (TWU) its application to establish its own College of Education. The denial was based on a document, which all staff and students of TWU had to sign, and which discriminated against homosexuals. The role of the school became an important aspect of the litigation because at issue was the question of whether graduates of TWU would be prepared to work in a public school environment that requires all its players to be free of discriminatory views and practice. The majority of the Supreme Court of Canada agreed that schools teach much more than skills and knowledge. Schools are meant to develop civic virtue and responsible citizenship, to educate in an environment free of bias, prejudice, and intolerance.[36] In the facts of this case, however, they found that there was no evidence that TWU would in fact produce teachers unable to accept and embrace the diversity of public school students.

In her dissent, L'Heureux-Dubé J considered that at stake was the best possible educational environment for public school students. She referred often to *Ross* and stated: 'In short there is a vital public interest in maintaining and improving supportive environments in the classrooms of our country, which are the intellectual incubators of Canada's most vulnerable and impressionable citizens. The educational process "awakens children to the values a society hopes to foster and to nurture."'[37]

It is the role of the school to ensure that children are provided with the best learning situations. In the case of children who need extra support or even protection, such as children dealing with issues of sexual orientation, it is imperative that the school provides the necessary safe and welcoming environment. In many of these cases, the school is the only place where children are able to escape the hostility that they may be subjected to at home, due to their personal dilemmas. Thus, the school board has a duty to maintain a positive learning environment where these children have the opportunity to develop their sense of being without fear and harassment.

In the final case, *Chamberlain* v. *Surrey School District No. 36*,[38] the Supreme Court of Canada dealt with whether or not a School Board resolution prohibiting certain books from being used as classroom resources, contravened s.76 of the British Columbia *School Act*. Section 76 provides that all schools and provincial schools must be conducted on strictly secular and non-sectarian principles. It also emphasizes that the highest morality must be inculcated, but no religious dogma or creed is to be taught in a school or provincial school.[39] In this case, Mr Chamberlain, a primary school teacher, had asked the Board to approve three books depicting same-sex families to be used as resources for the Kindergarten and Grade 1 curriculum. When the Board refused to approve these books, Mr Chamberlain began court proceedings arguing that the Board's decision was influenced by religious-based beliefs against homosexuality.

The majority of the Supreme Court of Canada has interpreted s.76 to mean that religious-based concerns and views can be brought to the deliberation process but cannot be used to deny equal treatment and respect for any sector of society. In other words, during deliberations, all views, even those that condemn homosexuality can be brought to the table; those who adhere to these views cannot, however, use their concerns to exclude those who do not adhere to them. Every person in Canada has the right to be free from discrimination of any sort. The education process must mirror this belief and provide an environment free of all bias: 'if the school is to function in an atmosphere of tolerance and respect, in accordance with s.76, the view that a certain lawful way of living is morally questionable cannot become the basis of school policy. Parents need not abandon their own commitments, or their view that the practices of others are undesirable. But where the school curriculum requires that a broad array of family models be taught in the classroom, a secular school system cannot exclude certain lawful family models simply on the ground that one group of parents finds them morally questionable.'[40]

It is obvious that the school must adopt a curriculum respecting diversity and avoiding at all costs the creation of a 'poisoned atmosphere' where any segment of society is devalued. Although not specifically stated in these words, the Preamble to the *School Act* defines the goals of the British Columbia school system in terms that empower all sectors of society to develop their potential and thereby contribute to the welfare of the province. In discussing the message of the Preamble, the Supreme Court of Canada states that the British Columbia public school system is open to all children of all cultures and family backgrounds. All are to be valued and respected.[41] This clearly calls for the embracing of all family models, regardless of the moral objection of some members of the community. The Board has the responsibility to provide inclusive learning materials that acknowledge all the realities within society. One such reality is that of families with same-sex parents, whose children cannot be treated in ways that make them feel invisible or unequal to other children. The Board has a mandate to provide gender equitable education: 'Gender equitable education involves the inclusion of the experiences, perceptions, and perspectives of girls and women, as well as boys and men, in all aspects of education; all students have the right to a learning environment that is gender equitable; gender equity incorporates a consideration of social class, culture, ethnicity, religion, sexual orientation, and age; gender equity requires sensitivity, determination, commitment, and vigilance over time.'[42]

Basically, the Board must promote respect and tolerance for all the people in the community that it serves. The Supreme Court outlines the requirements of the School Board to adhere to a strictly secular model, which they interpret as demanding that children are made aware of all family models that exist in society without the interference of any religious dogma:

> In summary, the Board was required to act in accordance with the Act and its own regulation. This meant that the Board was required to do three things: (1) to operate in a strictly secular manner, not allowing the concerns of one group of parents to deny equal recognition to the family models of other members of the school community; (2) to act in accordance with its own general regulation requiring that supplementary materials be relevant to the learning objectives, appropriate to the age, maturity and learning needs of the students, fair and free from discrimination, and readable, interesting and manageable in the teaching situation; and (3) to apply the criteria for supplemental resources indicated by the curriculum goals for K-1 students, which included the objectives of permitting all K-1 students to discuss their particular family models in class, and of making all students aware of the broad array of family models that exist in our society.[43]

Parental concerns, about what is in the best interests of their own children, cannot be used to influence the Board's decision, if they are based on religious views, and deny recognition of other models in society. The Court did not engage in an examination of the ability of children at the K-1 level to understand the information provided to them. Nor did the Court inquire about the prevalence of the family model that is the subject of the books in the community served by the School Board. In fact, this case did not arise from the complaint of same-sex parents who felt that they were being denied equal recognition.

In his dissent, Gonthier J points out that this case really involves an issue of competing *Charter* rights – those of the homosexuals to be free from discrimination and those of parents to look after their children's well-being and moral education. Although the school must provide an environment that teaches about tolerance, it does not automatically endorse every book or publication that depicts minorities. Gonthier's view encompasses a school environment espoused in *Ross*, premised upon principles of tolerance and impartiality. Tolerance does not, however, mean tacit approval: 'to suggest that "tolerance" requires the mandatory approval of the Three Books, which is what the appellants seek as a remedy, begs the question as to what the books portray and the capability of children to receive the messages in the books in a manner which is consistent with the parental determination of what is in their best interests.'[44]

Gonthier J interprets the need for strict secularism in the schools to include all moral positions, irrespective of whether or not they emanate from a religiously informed mind. Whereas the majority of the Supreme Court views basically restrict the use of religious notions to the deliberation process, Gonthier J takes the position that any moral view, regardless of its basis, must be given standing in the public square. Parental concerns about what is in the best interests of their children, and the ability of children to receive and understand the messages provided in learning materials should form the basis of whether or not these materials should be made available: 'it is well established in Canadian law that parents have the primary authority and responsibility for the moral and religious education of their children, and that responsibility is then delegated to teachers, administrators, and schools: the state's interest is secondary. In the context of the case at bar, the School Board is an instrument by which, in the absence of an already clearly developed consensus at the provincial level (whether pertaining to curriculum subject matter or to education resource materials), consensus is developed locally, a reflection of what parents deem is in their children's best interests.'[45]

Gonthier J describes a pluralist view of what the legislature intended the words 'strictly secular.' He argues that parental authority regarding the education of their children cannot be eroded by a strict non-religious requirement. Opinions and beliefs formed by religion have just as much standing in curriculum deliberations as those that are not based on any religious doctrine. He emphasizes the importance of allowing School Boards to arrive at local consensus regarding the best interests of the children in their particular community. Although he envisions a school environment free of discrimination, he does not believe this can be established simply by denying parents the ability to make decisions about their own children's education, if they adhere to religious beliefs.

In recent years, the Supreme Court of Canada has dealt with an array of cases involving the role of the school. Although the facts of the cases involve diverse issues, a definition of the role of the school becomes an essential element in finding appropriate resolutions. The school is concerned with the development of all pupils encompassing all aspects of life – physical, emotional, social, cultural, and intellectual. In order to establish the necessary positive environment that fosters such growth, the school must become a milieu free of actual or apprehended discrimination. Central to this mandate is the role of the teachers, who must conduct their lives in ways that do not oppose the views of the school. Through role modelling, teachers must transmit to their students all values intrinsic to their culture and society. Failure in this task results in a 'poisoned environment' that hinders the transmission of values deemed important in society, and places certain community groups in a vulnerable and disadvantaged position. School Boards have a duty to supervise their employees and discipline them appropriately when they act in a manner inconsistent with community standards. As well, School Boards must provide gender equitable education that is sensitive to the constitution of the community that they serve. In this manner they must adopt a curriculum that respects diversity, and they must avoid making any morally questionable decisions regarding the contents of the curriculum.

Conclusion

In recent years, Canadian courts, both appellate and of first instance, have begun to lay the foundation for a working definition of the role of the school as a social and formative institution. The process has proved to be difficult. Most provincial statutes and regulations governing education do not provide an explicit working definition of the cultural and social role that a school is expected to play in the life of the community where it is situated. As a result, courts have relied on very general terms laid out in the legislation and have extrapolated from these terms to construct a meaningful explanation of the role of the school. This is rendered more difficult by the fact that each province has its own legislation governing education. Providing a definition that encompasses Canadian society is indeed an arduous task. As well, most cases at bar have not dealt directly with the role of the school but with the role of individual players within the school community – teachers, students, and parents. The courts have had to invoke interpretations of the role of the school to enable them to contextualize the adjudication of the particular issues before them.

In *Ross*, however, the Supreme Court of Canada articulated a comprehensive definition of the role of the school, one that views the school both as a communication centre where social values are transmitted to the students, and as an arena for the exchange of ideas premised upon principles of tolerance and impartiality. This conception of the school combines the ideals embedded in the legislation and the case law, and provides a broader, more detailed construction of the role the school plays in Canadian society.

The construction of the school provided in *Ross* has two major parts. The first part states that 'a school is a communication centre for a whole range of values and aspirations of a society. In large part it defines the values that transcend society through the educational medium.'[46] This section makes it clear that an important function of the school is to provide the means for society to transmit its values to children. These values, which define the community, encompass much more than a social aspect. They also include cultural, linguistic, spiritual, and moral components. The school is expected to reflect these values in its educational objectives and programs.

Other Canadian cases both before and after *Ross* and at least one provincial statute have affirmed this aspect of the role of the school. The *Marchand* case dealing with the right of the francophone community to receive secondary education in French declares that the French language school occupies a central role in the cultural life and the linguistic community. In fact, it helps students to understand, strengthen, and develop their own culture and heritage. The *Casagrande* case dealing with a Catholic school board's power to dismiss a teacher for conduct contrary to Catholic doctrine, maintains that Catholic education requires all teachers to be role models in imparting the Christian message to the pupils. Thus, much like the cultural and social aspect of education, the religious and spiritual message must be transmitted to the members of the Catholic community. In *Commission scolaire*, the Quebec Court of Appeal recognizes the importance that the Cree nation receive funding for the continued existence of its schools. Education is viewed as the central vehicle enabling the perpetuation of cultures. In turn, the school concerns itself not only with the transmission of culture, but also with its conservation and extension. The Quebec *Education Act* provides a similar concept in stating that the object of the school is to contribute to the social and cultural development of the community.

The second part of the definition provided in *Ross* maintains that 'the school is an arena for the exchange of ideas and must, therefore, be premised upon principles of tolerance and impartiality so that all persons within the school environment feel equally free to participate.'[47] This component is concerned with the establishment of a forum free of any type of discrimination, where all students feel at liberty to be who they are without fear of judgment, negative attention, or even violence. The Supreme Court of Canada in *Trinity Western University* clearly states that the school environment must be free of bias, prejudice, and intolerance so that students can be educated in a responsible way. The court in *Hall* held that school provides the context for the lives of the students and its role is to enlighten and guide students, not to control their private thoughts or behaviours. Essentially, the school must provide the proper environment where students can be themselves without worrying about prejudicial views demeaning the core of their being. Any discrimination will not be tolerated in the educational environment. Much like *Ross*, the message in this particular case seems to be that depriving a person from attending a social function, based on his sexual orientation, would create an environment where other people of the same group would feel unequal to participate.

The Supreme Court of Canada adopted a similar stance in *Chamberlain* where a school board's resolution to prohibit same-sex family books in the classroom was found to be unreasonable. Schools must function in an atmosphere of tolerance and respect. School boards cannot adopt policies that discriminate against certain individuals who are involved in lawful relationships. One person's beliefs cannot be used to deny another person the same status in the school and therefore in the community. If children from same-sex families cannot be allowed to share their reality, they are not equally free to participate in the school.

All people who work in education must ensure that their actions never compromise the integrity of the learning environment lest they create a 'poisoned environment' where students feel threatened and under attack. If employees behave in a way that brings the school into disrepute, the school board has the responsibility to discipline these individuals, including discharging them, to avoid being perceived as endorsing their inappropriate behaviour. Failure to take the necessary steps will result in the establishment of a negative learning environment that fails in its mandate and obstructs the learning process.

In *Young*, a case dealing with teacher sexual misconduct, the British Columbia Court of Appeal adopted the reasoning in *Ross* and stated that it is important to maintain public confidence in the school system. Misconduct by a teacher impairs the education system in the eyes of the public. Parents do not feel free to send their children to school, afraid that they will be victims of irresponsible and immoral behaviour. Teacher misconduct creates the 'poisoned environment' described in Ross, and will bring the education system into disrepute. This line of reasoning is also adopted in *Toronto Board of Education* where the court states that the vulnerability of students and the need for public confidence in the education system demand that teachers who are unable to fulfil their duties must not be allowed in the classroom. Teachers must not only teach by example but also live by example. Any deviation from appropriate conduct will inevitably lead to the failure of the educational institution. A community will certainly lose respect and confidence for a system that falls short in establishing a setting premised on 'principles of tolerance and impartiality, where all students feel equally free to participate.' The school must be a safe and welcoming environment where society can transmit its core values to children and foster all aspects of their lives so that their learning will not be repressed by feelings of fear or inequality.

Appendix: *Constitution Act, 1982*
Charter of Rights and Freedoms

SCHEDULE B: CONSTITUTION ACT, 1982

PART I: CANADIAN CHARTER OF RIGHTS AND FREEDOMS

Whereas Canada is founded upon the principles that recognize the supremacy of God and the rule of law:

Guarantee of Rights and Freedoms

1. The Canadian Charter of Rights and Freedoms guarantees the rights and freedoms set out in it subject only to such reasonable limits prescribed by law as can be demonstrably justified in a free and democratic society.

Fundamental Freedoms

2. Everyone has the following fundamental freedoms:

(*a*) freedom of conscience and religion
(*b*) freedom of thought, belief, opinion and expression, including freedom of the press and other means of communication.
(*c*) freedom of peaceful assembly; and
(*d*) freedom of association.

Democratic Rights

3. Every citizen of Canada has the right to vote in an election of members of the House of Commons or of a legislative assembly and to be qualified for membership therein.

4. (1) No House of Commons and no legislative assembly shall continue for longer than five years from the date fixed for the return of the writs at a general election of its members.

(2) In time of real or apprehended war, invasion or insurrection, a House of Commons may be continued by Parliament and a legislative assembly may be continued by the legislature beyond five years if such continuation is not opposed by the votes of more than one-third of the members of the House of Commons or the legislative assembly, as the case may be.

5. There shall be a sitting of Parliament and of each legislature at least once every twelve months.

Mobility Rights

6. (1) Every citizen of Canada has the right to enter, remain in, and leave Canada.

(2) Every citizen of Canada and every person who has the status of a permanent resident of Canada has the right

(*a*) to move to and take up residence in any province; and
(*b*) to pursue the gaining of livelihood in any province.

(3) The rights specified in subsection (2) are subject to

(*a*) any laws or practices of general application in force in a province other than those that discriminate among persons primarily on the basis of present or previous residence; and
(*b*) any laws providing for reasonable residency requirements as a qualification for the receipt of publicly provided social services.

(4) Subsections (2) and (3) do not preclude any law, program or activity that has as its object the amelioration in a province of conditions of individuals in that province who are socially or economically disadvantaged if the rate of employment in that province is below the rate of employment in Canada.

Legal Rights

7. Everyone has the right to life, liberty and security of the person and the right not to be deprived thereof except in accordance with the principles of fundamental justice.

8. Everyone has the right to be secure against unreasonable search or seizure.

9. Everyone has the right not to be arbitrarily detained or imprisoned.

10. Everyone has the right on arrest or detention

(*a*) to be informed promptly of the reason therefore;
(*b*) to retain and instruct counsel without delay and to be informed of that right; and
(*c*) to have the validity of the detention determined by way of habeas corpus and to be released if the detention is not lawful.

11. Any person charged with an offence has the right

(*a*) to be informed without unreasonable delay of the specific offence;
(*b*) to be tried within a reasonable time;
(*c*) not to be compelled to be a witness in a proceedings against that person in respect of the offence;
(*d*) to be presumed innocent until proven guilty according to law in a fair and public hearing by an independent and impartial tribunal;
(*e*) not to be denied reasonable bail without cause;
(*f*) except in the case of an offence under military law tried before a military tribunal, to the benefit of trial by jury where the maximum punishment for the offence is imprisonment for five years or a more severe punishment;
(*g*) not to be found guilty on account of any act or omission unless, at the time of the act or omission, it constituted an offence under Canadian or International law or was criminal according to the general principles of law recognized by the community of nations;
(*h*) if finally acquitted of the offence, not to be tried for it again and, if finally found guilty and punished for the offence, not to be tried or punished for it again; and

(*i*) if found guilty of the offence and if punishment for the offence has been varied between the time of commission and the time of sentencing, to the benefit of the lesser punishment.

12. Everyone has the right not to be subjected to any cruel or unusual treatment or punishment.

13. A witness who testifies in any proceedings has the right not to have any incriminating evidence so given used to incriminate that witness in any other proceedings, except in a prosecution for perjury or for the giving of contradictory evidence.

14. A party or witness in any proceedings who does not understand or speak the language in which the proceedings are conducted or who is deaf has the right to the assistance of an interpreter.

Equality Rights

15. (1) Every individual is equal before the and under the law and has the right to the equal protection and equal benefit of the law without discrimination and, in particular, without discrimination based on race, national or ethnic origin, colour, religion, sex, age, or mental or physical disability.

(2) Subsection (1) does not preclude any law, program or activity that has as its object the amelioration of conditions of disadvantaged individuals or groups including those that are disadvantaged because of race, national or ethnic origin, colour, religion, sex, age, or mental or physical disability.

Official Languages of Canada

16. (1) English and French are the official languages of Canada and have equal rights and privileges as to their use in all institutions of the Parliament and government of Canada.

(2) English and French are the official languages of New Brunswick and have equality of status and equal rights and privileges as to their use in all institutions of the legislature and government of New Brunswick.

(3) Nothing in this Charter limits the authority of Parliament or a legislature to advance the equality of status or use of English and French.

16.1 (1) The English linguistic community and the French linguistic community in New Brunswick have equality of status and equal rights and privileges, including the right to distinct educational institutions and such distinct cultural institutions as are necessary for the preservation and promotion of those communities.

(2) The role of the legislature and the government of New Brunswick to preserve and promote the status, rights and privileges referred to in subsection (1) is affirmed.

17. (1) Everyone has the right to use English or French in any debates or other proceedings of Parliament.

(2) Everyone has the right to use English or French in any debate and other proceeding of the legislature of New Brunswick.

18. (1) The Statutes, records and journals of Parliament shall be printed and published in English and French and both language versions are equally authoritative.

(2) The Statutes, records and journals of New Brunswick shall be printed and published in English and French and both language versions are equally authoritative.

19. (1) Either English or French may be used by any person in, or in any pleading in or process issuing from any court established by Parliament.

(2) Either English or French may be used by any person in, or in any pleading in or process issuing from any court of New Brunswick.

20. (1) Any member of the public of Canada has the right to communicate with, and to receive available services from, any head or central office of an institution of the Parliament or government of Canada in English or French, and has the same right with respect to any other office of any such institution where (*a*) there is significant demand for communications with and services from that office in such language; or

(*b*) due to the nature of the office, it is reasonable that communications with and services from that office be available in both English and French.

(2) Any member of the public in New Brunswick has the right to communicate with, and to receive available services from, any office of an institution of the legislature or government of New Brunswick in English or French.

21. Nothing in sections 16 to 20 abrogates or derogates from any right, privilege or obligation with respect to the English and French languages, or either of them, that exists or is continued by virtue of any other provision of the Constitution of Canada.

22. Nothing in sections 16 to 20 abrogates or derogates from any legal or customary right or privilege acquired or enjoyed either before or after the coming into force of this Charter with respect to any language that is not English or French.

Minority Language Educational Rights

23. (1) Citizens of Canada

(*a*) whose first language learned and still understood is that of the English or French linguistic minority population of the province in which they reside, or

(*b*) who have received their primary school instruction in Canada in English or French and reside in a province where the language in which they received that instruction is the language of the English or French linguistic minority population of the province, have the right to have their children receive primary and secondary school instruction in that language in that province.

(2) Citizens of Canada of whom any child has received or is receiving primary or secondary school instruction in English or French in Canada, have the right to have all their children receive primary and secondary school instruction in the same language.

(3) The right of citizens of Canada under subsections (1) and (2) to have their children receive primary and secondary school instruction in the language of the English or French linguistic minority population of a province

(*a*) applies wherever in the province the number of children of citizens who have such a right is sufficient to warrant the provision to them out of public funds of minority language instruction; and
(*b*) includes, where the number of children so warrants, the right to have them receive that instruction in minority language educational facilities provided out of public funds.

Enforcement

24. (1) Anyone whose rights or freedoms, as guaranteed by this Charter, have been infringed or denied may apply to a court of competent jurisdiction to obtain such remedy as the court considers appropriate and just in the circumstances.
(2) Where, in proceedings under subsection (1), a court concludes that evidence was obtained in a manner that infringed or denied any rights or freedoms guaranteed by this Charter, the evidence shall be excluded if it is established that, having regard to all the circumstances, the admission of it in the proceedings would bring the administration of justice into disrepute.

General

25. The guarantee in this Charter of certain rights and freedoms shall not be construed so as to abrogate or derogate from any aboriginal, treaty or other rights or freedoms that pertain to the aboriginal peoples of Canada including

(*a*) any rights or freedoms that have been recognized by the Royal Proclamation of October 7, 1763; and
(*b*) any rights or freedoms that may be acquired by the aboriginal peoples of Canada by way of land claims settlement.

26. The guarantee in this Charter of certain rights and freedoms shall not be construed as denying the existence of any other rights and freedoms that exist in Canada.

27. This Charter shall be interpreted in a manner consistent with the preservation and enhancement of the multicultural heritage of Canadians.

28. Notwithstanding anything in this Charter, the rights and freedoms referred to in it are guaranteed equally to male and female persons.

29. Nothing in this Charter abrogates or derogates from any rights or privileges guaranteed by or under the Constitution of Canada in respect of denominational, separate or dissentient schools.

30. A reference in this Charter to a province or to the legislative assembly or legislature of a province shall be deemed to include a reference to the Yukon Territory and the Northwest Territories, or to the appropriate legislative authority thereof, as the case may be.

31. Nothing in this Charter extends the legislative powers of any body or authority.

Application of Charter

32. (1) This Charter applies

(*a*) to the Parliament and government of Canada in respect of all matters within the authority of Parliament including all matters relating to the Yukon Territory and Northwest Territories; and
(*b*) to the legislatures and governments of each province in respect of all matters within the authority of the legislature of each province.

(2) Notwithstanding subsection (1), section 15 shall not have effect until three years after this section comes into force.

33. (1) Parliament or the legislature of a province may expressly declare in an Act of Parliament or of the legislature, as the case may be, that the Act or a provision thereof shall operate notwithstanding a provision included in section 2 or sections 7 to 15 of this Charter.

(2) An Act or a provision of an Act in respect of which a declaration made under this section is in effect shall have such operation as it would have but for the provision of this Charter referred to in the declaration.

(3) A declaration made under subsection (1) shall cease to have effect five years after it comes into force or on such earlier date as may be specified in the declaration.

(4) Parliament or the legislature of a province may re-enact a declaration made under subsection (1).

(5) Subsection (3) applies in respect of re-enactment made under subsection (4).

Citation

34. This Part may be cited as the Canadian Charter of Rights and Freedoms.

Notes

Introduction

1 M. Ignatieff, *The Rights Revolution* (Toronto: Anansi, 2000), 7.
2 Karl N. Llewellyn & E. Adamson Hoebel, *The Cheyenne Way* (Norman: University of Oklahoma Press, 1941) 28–9.
3 [1984] 2 S.C.R. 145.
4 *Re s. 24 of BNA Act; Edwards* v. *A.G. Can.*, [1930] 1 DLR 98 (P.C.).

1 Equality in the Schoolhouse: Has the *Charter* Made a Difference?

1 Cited in *Report of the Royal Commission on Aboriginal Peoples, vol. 4, Perspectives and Realities* (Ottawa: Canada Communication Group, 1996) [hereinafter *RCAP*] at 164.
2 See *World Declaration on Education for All and Framework for Action to Meet Basic Learning Needs*, adopted by the World Conference on Education for All: Meeting Basic Learning Needs, Jomtien, Thailand, March 1990 (Paris: UNESCO, 1994) [hereinafter *World Declaration on Education*].
3 Part I of the *Constitution Act, 1982*, being Schedule B of the *Canada Act, 1982* (U.K.), 1982, c. 11 [hereinafter *Charter*].
4 M.E. Manley-Casimir & T.A. Sussel, eds., *Courts in the Classroom: Education and the Charter of Rights and Freedoms* (Calgary: Detselig, 1986) [hereinafter *Courts in the Classroom*].
5 Ibid., at 3.
6 In accordance with s.32(2), the equality provisions only came into force on 17 April 1985, three years after the proclamation of the *Charter*.
7 For a detailed discussion of the part played by the codes in the development of the normative guidelines for equality rights and their application in schools, see W.J. Smith & W.F. Foster, 'Equal Opportunity and the School

House: Part I – Exploring the Contours of Equality Rights,' (2003) 13 *Education & Law Journal* 1 [hereinafter Smith & Foster Part I]; and Foster & Smith, 'Equal Opportunity and the School House: Part II – Access to and Benefit from Education for All,' (2003) 13 *Education & Law Journal* 173 [hereinafter Smith & Foster Part II].

8 To avoid duplication, we do not deal with equality rights in relation to: (a) minority language education rights; (b) denominational education rights; (c) other religious issues; or (d) inclusion versus segregated placements of students with disabilities. Finally, our equal educational opportunity focus on students excludes any treatment of other school-related equality rights such as teacher employment rights.

9 See discussion below, surrounding n45, regarding the application of the *Charter* to independent schools.

10 For purposes of this chapter, the expression 'special purpose schools' includes all those with a vocation that distinguishes them from regular schools, including schools that target particular groups of students, such as dropouts or gifted students, and those offering particular programs, such as fine arts or sports. The expression also applies to a 'school within a school' or special purpose programs of a similar nature.

11 *Universal Declaration of Human Rights*, G.A. res. 217A (III), U.N. Doc A/810 at 71 (1948), art 1.

12 *Charter*, s.15(1).

13 M.E. Manley-Casimir & T.A. Sussel, 'The Equality Provisions of the Canadian Charter of Rights and Educational Policy: Preparations for Implementation,' (1986) 17(3) *Interchange* 1, at 1.

14 A.F. Bayefsky, 'Defining Equality Rights,' in Bayefsky & M. Eberts, eds., *Equality Rights and the Canadian Charter of Rights and Freedoms* (Toronto: Carswell, 1985) 1, at 27. As a general rule, human rights codes in Canada prohibit discrimination rather than providing a right to equality.

15 See, e.g., J.S. Coleman, 'The Concept of Equality of Educational Opportunity,' (1968) 38 *Harvard Education Review* 7.

16 K.R. Howe, *Understanding Equal Educational Opportunity: Social Justice, Democracy, and Schooling* (New York: Teachers College Press, 1997), at 22.

17 *Courts in the Classroom*, supra n4 at 3–4.

18 *Brown v. Board of Education*, 347 U.S. 483 (1954) [hereinafter *Brown*].

19 *Plessy v. Ferguson*, 163 U.S. 537 (1896) [hereinafter *Plessy*].

20 *Bouchard v. School Commissioners of Saint-Mathieu-de-Dixville*, [1950] S.C.R. 479 [hereinafter *Bouchard*].

21 Ibid., at 481.

22 *Bouchard* is still cited in Quebec cases in support of this position; see, e.g., *Picard* v. *Commission scolaire Prince-Daveluy*, [1991] R.J.Q. 167 (Que. Sup. Ct.) [hereinafter *Picard*], aff'd [1992] R.J.Q. 2369 (Que. C.A.) [hereinafter *Picard Appeal*].

23 *Constitution Act, 1867* (U.K.), 30 & 31 Vict., c. 3 .

24 In the interval, the *Canadian Bill of Rights*, S.C. 1960, c. 44, reprinted in R.S.C. 1985, App. III, had been adopted but it applied only to federal legislation. Similarly, human rights legislation was expanding, but with no constitutional foundation.

25 D. Cruickshank, 'Charter Equality Rights: The Challenge to Education Law and Policy,' in *Courts in the Classroom*, supra n4 at 51. In U.S. case law, discrimination based on race, religion, or nationality is inherently suspect and subject to 'strict scrutiny.' By contrast, discrimination based on social or economic reasons is subject to 'minimal scrutiny,' where the court only seeks to determine whether there is a rational relationship between the impugned law and government objectives. In between are cases of gender-based discrimination subject to 'intermediate scrutiny,' which Cruickshank describes as an upgraded version of minimal scrutiny.

26 Ibid., at 66. The phrase refers to an unreported Alberta case, *Carrière* v. *County of Lamont* (1978), Edmonton 107/134 (Alta. S.C.T.D.) [hereinafter *Carrière*], which held that it was not up to the courts to determine what happened in school, merely to assure that students had access to school.

27 Ibid., at 69.

28 See infra n37.

29 Moreover, the pursuit of a human rights complaint under the codes is much easier and less costly to individual complainants than a private action taken under the aegis of the *Charter*. As a general rule, complaints are investigated by staff of the human rights commission with unresolved disputes adjudicated by a human rights panel or tribunal at no cost to the individual complainant.

30 Many human rights codes also contain their own form of derogations; see infra, nn36, 37, & 38.

31 The *Charter* is part of the Constitution which, according to the *Constitution Act, 1982*, s.52(1): 'is the supreme law of Canada, and any law that is inconsistent with the provisions of the Constitution is, to the extent of the inconsistency, of no force or effect.'

32 W.F. Pentney, *Discrimination and the Law Including Equality Rights under the Charter*, loose-leaf with supplements (Toronto: Carswell, 1994–2005), at 4–102.11.

33 Generally, these rights are framed as a prohibition against discrimination, which P. Hogg, *Constitutional Law of Canada*, 4th ed. loose-leaf with supplements (Toronto: Carswell, 1997–2005), at 52–17, argues is the 'operative concept' of the *Charter* right to equality.

34 The codes do not have constitutional status and can be amended like any statute. However, they are viewed as 'special' quasi-constitutional laws, deserving of the same purposive interpretation given to *Charter* provisions.

35 For example, contrast the *Charter* right to 'equality before the law' with the right to attend school from the age of 5.

36 A derogation is understood as an abrogation of a human right, as opposed to a *restriction* or *limitation* of a right.

37 Section 33 of the *Charter* permits the government to adopt a law that is contrary to certain *Charter* rights and freedoms: fundamental rights (s.2), legal rights (ss.7–14), and equality rights (s.15). However, to do so, a government must declare in the law that it shall operate *notwithstanding* one of these provisions. Such a declaration is valid for a period of five years but may be renewed for an indefinite number of five-year periods.

38 A review of human rights codes in Canada reveals three distinct situations depending on the existence and type of *primacy* clause, a provision that states that the code prevails or has 'paramountcy' over other legislation: (a) the code contains a primacy clause that does not allow override; (b) the code contains a primacy clause permitting override; or (c) the code contains no primacy clause.

39 First, the best interests of the child must be a primary consideration, such interests being determined from a subjective, child-centred perspective, which attempts to make equality meaningful from the child's point of view. Second, the evolving capacities of the child must be taken into account, recognizing the progressive maturity of children and their evolving capacity to speak for themselves (see n117).

40 [1986] 1 S.C.R. 103, 26 D.L.R. (4th) 200 [hereinafter *Oakes*]. To pass this test a law must: (1) pursue an objective that is sufficiently important to justify limiting a *Charter* right; (2) be rationally connected to the objective; (3) impair the right no more than is necessary to accomplish the objective; and, (4) not have a disproportionately severe effect on the persons to whom it applies.

41 *Eaton v. Brant (County) Board of Education*, [1997] 1 S.C.R. 241, 142 D.L.R. (4th) 385, rev'g (1995), 22 O.R. (3d) 1, 123 D.L.R. (4th) 43 (Ont. C.A.) [hereinafter *Eaton*].

42 No discussion of Step 1 (using override provisions to pre-empt equality rights) is included as, excluding derogations relating to denominational

rights, we did not identify any such recourse in existing legislation. For details on all normative guidelines, see supra n7.

43 *Charter*, s.32.

44 W.J. Smith, 'Rights and Freedoms in Education: The Application of the Charter to Public Schools,' (1992–93) 4 *Education & Law Journal* 107.

45 *Eldridge* v. *British Columbia (Attorney General)*, [1997] 3 S.C.R. 624, 151 D.L.R. (4th) 577 [hereinafter *Eldridge* cited to S.C.R.].

46 In *Eldridge*, ibid., at § 42, the Supreme Court of Canada recognized that hospitals were private actors and, therefore, not generally bound by the *Charter*, as per *Stoffman* v. *Vancouver General Hospital*, [1990] 3 S.C.R. 483, 76 D.L.R. (4th) 700 [hereinafter *Stoffman*]. However, it held that they are subject to the *Charter* 'in so far as they act in furtherance of a specific governmental program or policy.'

47 Manitoba does mention education, while Quebec and Saskatchewan include education as a human right in the code: *Human Rights Code*, S.M. 1987–88, c. 45, s.1 [hereinafter *Manitoba Code*]; *Charter of Human Rights and Freedoms*, R.S.Q., c. C-12, s.40 [hereinafter *Quebec Code*]; *Saskatchewan Human Rights Code*, R.S.S. 1978, c. S-24.1, s.13(1) [hereinafter *Saskatchewan Code*]. The lack of specificity in other codes, once seen as problematic, is no longer an issue; see *University of British Columbia* v. *Berg*, [1993] 2 S.C.R. 353, 102 D.L.R. (4th) 665 [hereinafter *Berg*].

48 All these listed grounds can be found in most human rights codes; the absence of socioeconomic conditions as a listed ground is also true of most codes.

49 See Coleman, supra n15.

50 See W. Black & L. Smith, 'Equality Rights,' in W.A. Tarnopolsky, G.-A. Beaudoin, & E. Mendes, eds., *Canadian Charter of Rights and Freedoms*, 4th ed. (Markham: LexisNexis, 2005) 925, at 1008–11.

51 See, e.g., *Québec (Commission des droits de la personne)* v. *Commission scolaire Deux-Montagnes*, [1993] R.J.Q. 1297, 19 C.H.R.R. D/1 (H.R. Trib.)[hereinafter *Deux-Montagnes*], where the tribunal found that the respondent school board failed to protect a teacher against racial harassment by students. See also *Jubran* v. *Board of Trustees, School District No. 44*, [2002] BCHRT 10 (H.R. Trib.), rev'd [2003] 3 W.W.R. 288 (S.C.), aff'd [2005] B.C.J. No. 733 (C.A.), 253 D.L.R. (4th) 294 [hereinafter *Jubran*], the case of a student who, for the five years he attended high school, was taunted with homophobic epithets and assaulted because of his perceived sexual orientation.

52 *Andrews* v. *Law Society of British Columbia*, [1989] 1 S.C.R. 143, 56 D.L.R. (4th) 1 [hereinafter *Andrews*].

53 *Law* v. *Canada*, [1999] 1 S.C.R. 497, 170 D.L.R (4th) 1 [hereinafter *Law* cited to S.C.R.].

54 Ibid., at § 88.

55 The reliance on dignity in *Law* has generated considerable controversy, notably, the extent to which dignity is a *helpful* construct for advancing substantive equality. E. Chadna & C.T. Sheldon, 'Promoting Equality: Economic and Social Rights for Persons with Disabilities under Section 15,' (2004–5) 16 N.J.C.L. 27 at 69, consider that 'there now appears to be some strain among the Bench [of the Supreme Court of Canada]' regarding this controversy.

56 Thus, e.g., in *Gosselin* v. *Quebec (Attorney General)*, [2002] 4 S.C.R. 429, (2002) 221 D.L.R. (4th) 257 [hereinafter *Gosselin* cited to S.C.R.] at § 17, the Supreme Court of Canada summarized the third stage of the *Law* test as follows: 'the law in question has a purpose or effect that is discriminatory in the sense that it denies human dignity or treats people as less worthy on one of the enumerated or analogous grounds.' In *Trociuk* v. *British Columbia (Attorney General)*, [2003] 1 S.C.R. 835, 226 D.L.R. (4th) 1 [hereinafter *Trociuk* cited to S.C.R.], at the heading preceding § 14, Deschamps J refers to the analysis of this stage as 'The Dignity Analysis.'

57 In Canada, more than minimal effort has long been required to satisfy the duty to accommodate, which for many years has meant 'reasonable accommodation,' often defined as extending to the point of 'undue hardship.' See *O'Malley* v. *Simpson Sears Ltd.* (sub nom. *Ontario Human Rights Commission* v. *Simpson Sears Ltd.*), [1985] 2 S.C.R. 536, 23 D.L.R. (4th) 321 [hereinafter *O'Malley*].

58 A preferential program is simply one that explicitly or implicitly makes a distinction, exclusion, or preference based on grounds on which discrimination is prohibited. When such a program contemplates groups that are not considered disadvantaged in a given context, then it should not be considered as affirmative action.

59 [2000] 1 S.C.R. 950, 188 D.L.R. (4th) 193 [hereinafter *Lovelace* cited to S.C.R.] at § 93.

60 *Ross* v. *New Brunswick School District No. 15*, [1996] 1 S.C.R. 825, 133 D.L.R. (4th) 1 [hereinafter *Ross* cited to S.C.R.].

61 Ibid., at § 42.

62 [2002] 4 S.C.R. 710, 221 D.L.R. (4th) 156 [hereinafter *Chamberlain*].

63 W.J. Smith & C. Lusthaus, 'Equal Educational Opportunity for Students with Disabilities in Canada: The Right to Free and Appropriate Education,' (1994) 4 *Exceptionality Education in Canada* 37, at 56.

64 *Concerned Parents for Children with Learning Disabilities Inc.* v. *Saskatchewan (Minister of Education)*, (1998) 170 Sask. R. 200, [1998] S.J. No. 566 (Q.B.) [hereinafter *Concerned Parents*].

65 Ibid., at § 55. The complainants in *Eldridge* were deaf and alleged that the failure to provide sign language interpretation in relation to health care received from doctors or hospitals violated their equality rights under the *Charter*; see *Eldridge*, supra n45, at § 92.

66 *Auton (Guardian ad litem of)* v. *British Columbia (Attorney General)*, [2004] 3 S.C.R. 657, 245 D.L.R. (4th) 1 [hereinafter *Auton* cited to S.C.R.], rev'g (2002), 6 B.C.L.R. (4th) 201, 220 D.L.R. (4th) 411 (B.C.C.A.) [hereinafter *Auton Appeal* cited to B.C.L.R.], aff'g (2000), 78 B.C.L.R. (3d) 55, [2000] 8 W.W.R. 227 (B.C.S.C.) [hereinafter *Auton BCSC* cited to B.C.L.R.].

67 'In order to succeed, the claimants must show ... that they failed to receive a benefit that the law provided, or was [*sic*] saddled with a burden the law did not impose on someone else.' *Auton*, ibid., at § 27. The therapy in question was not included in the services covered by the relevant legislation.

68 Ibid., at § 38.

69 *Hodge* v. *Canada (Minister of Human Resources Development)*, [2004] 3 S.C.R. 357, 244 D.L.R. (4th) 257 [hereinafter *Hodge*]. As stated in *Auton*, supra n66 at § 53: 'The comparator group should mirror the characteristics of the claimant or claimant group relevant to the benefit or advantage sought, except for the personal characteristic related to the enumerated or analogous ground raised as the basis for the discrimination.'

70 *Auton*, supra n66 at § 55.

71 Ibid., at § 62. The Supreme Court did not deal with the second or third stage of the *Law* test nor the s.1 arguments, given its earlier findings but dealt briefly with the complainants' arguments under s.7, which it rejected. The Court of Appeal had moved to the third stage and found that the policy and practice was discriminatory which led to a consideration of the government's defence under s.1.

72 See, e.g., *Arzem* v. *Ontario (Minister of Community and Social Services)*, [2006] O.H.R.T.D. No. 17 [hereinafter *Arzem*] at § 2, which notes that between 12 August 2003 and 15 December 2005, the Ontario Human Rights Commission referred 245 cases involving minors with autism to the Human Rights Tribunal of Ontario.

73 *Wynberg* v. *Ontario*, [2006] O.J. No. 2732 (Ont. C.A.) [hereinafter *Wynberg*], rev'g [2005] O.J. No. 1228 (Ont. Sup. Ct.), 252 D.L.R. (4th) 10; leave to appeal to the SCC denied on 12 April 2007, CanLII 11900 (S.C.C.). We do not attempt to deal with all aspects of this long and complex decision,

merely with its key findings in relation to equality rights for school-age children. The treatment of reasonable limits is dealt with in § 3(c) p. 27ff.

74 *Child and Family Services Act*, R.S.O. 1990, c.11, ss.1(1), 7(1), 7(2), 30.

75 *Wynberg*, supra n73 at § 79.

76 *Education Act*, R.S.O. 1990, c. E.2, s.8(3). This case illustrates the important nexus between equality rights and statutory entitlement, a matter to which we return below.

77 *Wynberg*, supra n73 at § 145.

78 The expression usually found in the codes is bona fide occupational qualification (or requirement), referring to employer rules advanced in defence of a discrimination complaint. These expressions have now acquired a more general meaning, hence our preference for a generic expression, bona fide requirement.

79 This occurs because the primacy clause (see n38) in both these codes allows override.

80 Similarly, this public policy interest lens will be used to assess what constitutes 'reasonable accommodation' and 'undue hardship': see discussion below surrounding n95. See also *Lalji* v. *British Columbia (Human Rights Commission)*, [2004] B.C.J. No. 10 (B.C.S.C.) [hereinafter *Lalji*].

81 This group can be considered 'privileged' because the school system used to be structured with school boards for Catholics and boards for Protestants, without any accommodation for other religious groups; see W.J. Smith & W.F. Foster, 'Religion and Education in Canada: Part I – The Traditional Framework' (2001) 10 *Education & Law Journal* 393 [hereinafter 'Religion and Education Part I'].

82 Regardless of how any given ground is defined, the program in question must meet *Charter* standards as well as any relevant requirement from the human rights code of the jurisdiction.

83 D. Lepofsky, 'A Report Card on the Charter's Guarantee of Equality to Persons with Disabilities after 10 Years – What Progress? What Prospects?' (1997) 7 N.J.C.L. 263, at 331. Such an erroneous approach was overturned in *Battlefords and District Co-operative Ltd.* v. *Gibbs*, [1996] 3 S.C.R. 566, 140 D.L.R. (4th) 1 [hereinafter *Battlefords*], but resurfaced in *Eaton*, supra n41 at § 69.

84 Education statutes or regulations may specify if or under what conditions special schools may be operated.

85 *British Columbia (Public Service Employee Relations Commission)* v. *British Columbia Government Employees' Union (B.C.G.S.E.U.) (Meiorin Grievance)*, [1999] 3 S.C.R. 3, 176 D.L.R. (4th) 1 [hereinafter *Meiorin* cited to S.C.R.]. The complainant was a female firefighter who was dismissed after failing an

aerobics test, which was defended as a bona fide requirement under the British Columbia *Human Rights Code* [hereinafter *British Columbia Code*].

86 Ibid., at § 54.

87 *British Columbia (Superintendent of Motor Vehicles)* v. *British Columbia (Council of Human Rights)*, [1999] 3 S.C.R. 868, 181 D.L.R. (4th) 385 [hereinafter *BC Superintendent of Motor Vehicles*].

88 In other words, the exception in the code is treated as an enabling provision that permits the bona fide requirement or the preferential program, even when established by a private actor, to constitute a limit prescribed by law and therefore nominally allowable under s.1 of the *Charter*.

89 [2001] R.J.Q. 5, 41 C.H.R.R. D/268 (Que. C.A.) [hereinafter *Notre-Dame*] at § 42, rev'g [1994] R.J.Q. 1324 (Que. Sup. Ct.).

90 The relevant provision of the *Quebec Code*, s.20, reads as follows: 'A distinction, exclusion or preference based on the aptitudes or qualifications ... justified by the charitable, philanthropic, religious, political or educational nature of a non-profit institution or of an institution devoted exclusively to the well-being of an ethnic group, is deemed non-discriminatory.'

91 *Notre-Dame*, supra n89 at § 29. The reference to s.10 contemplates the various grounds on which discrimination is prohibited in the *Quebec Code*.

92 The second criterion, namely, that the requirement be adopted in good faith, was ignored, presumably because s.20 of the *Quebec Code* contains no reference to 'good faith.' We contend that the second criterion of the *Meiorin* standard does apply even in the absence of 'good faith' language in a code; see Smith & Foster Part II, supra n7 at 240.

93 *Notre-Dame*, supra n89 at § 38.

94 Ibid., at s.39 (free translation).

95 See, e.g., *Central Alberta Dairy Pool* v. *Alberta (Human Rights Commission)*, [1990] 2 S.C.R. 489, 72 D.L.R. (4th) 417 [hereinafter *Alberta Dairy* cited to S.C.R.] at 521.

96 *Schachter* v. *Canada*, [1992] 2 S.C.R. 679, 93 D.L.R. (4th) 1 [hereinafter *Schachter*].

97 Ibid., at 709. The majority (per Lamer CJC, Sopinka, Gonthier, Cory, and McLachlin JJ concurring) went on to state: 'However, such considerations are clearly relevant once a violation which does not survive s.1 has been established, s.52 is determined to have been engaged and the Court turns its attention to what action should be taken thereunder.'

98 *Nova Scotia (Workers' Compensation Board)* v. *Martin*; *Nova Scotia (Workers' Compensation Board)* v. *Laseur*, [2003] 2 S.C.R. 504, 231 D.L.R. (4th) 385 [hereinafter *Martin* cited to S.C.R.] at § 6.

99 *Newfoundland (Treasury Board)* v. *N.A.P.E.*, [2004] 3 S.C.R. 381, 244 D.L.R. (4th) 294 [hereinafter *NAPE*].

100 As stated in *Symes* v. *Canada*, [1993] 4 S.C.R. 695, 19 C.R.R. (2d) 1 [herein-
    after *Symes* cited to S.C.R.] at 765: 'We must take care to distinguish
    between effects which are wholly caused, or are contributed to, by an
    impugned provision, and those social circumstances which exist in-
    dependently of such a provision.'
101 *Eldridge*, supra n45 at § 85.
102 *Egan* v. *Canada*, [1995] 2 S.C.R. 513, 124 D.L.R. (4th) 609 [hereinafter *Egan*
    cited to S.C.R.] at §§ 97 (per L'Heureux-Dubé) & 104–10 (per Sopinka J).
103 Ibid., at § 216 (per Iacobucci and Cory JJ concurring).
104 *Eldridge*, supra n45 at § 87. The cost was calculated to equal approximate-
    ly 0.0025% of the provincial health care budget at the time.
105 Such a determination might depend on whether the service constituted a
    separate service in lieu of regular education services or as a means by
    which students could benefit from the latter. The line between access and
    services is not always clear-cut, nor what constitutes accommodation in
    particular cases. Drawing the line depends, in part, on the extent to which
    opportunities to attend school must be equalized through positive
    measures. For example, in a case where school transport was provided
    and the issue was the lack of *adapted* transport, the case might turn on a
    defence of reasonable limits (if such a defence were allowed as per steps 3
    and 4). However, if no transportation were provided, the case might turn
    on the answer to the following question: Does the non-provision of such a
    service constitute a denial of equality rights?
106 B.L. Berger, 'Using the *Charter* to Cure Health Care: Panacea or Placebo?'
    (2003) 8(1) *Rev. Const. Stud.* 20, at 39, makes the following comment about
    the place of the *Charter* in securing rights in the health sector: 'Section 15
    is highly effective when invoked to remedy an inequality in the provision
    of extant policies or services ... Yet this is where the section's utility ends
    when applied in the health care context. The legal formalism of the courts
    combined with a firmly negative approach to rights narrows the applica-
    tion of s.15 to only those inequalities that are sourced in the law and do
    not require formal policy formation or interrogation of a government's
    budgetary choices.'
107 *Wynberg*, supra n73 at § 150.
108 For the criteria that courts consider in the *Oakes* test, see n40.
109 *Moore* v. *British Columbia (Ministry of Education)*, [2005] B.C.H.R.T.D.
    No. 580 [hereinafter *Moore*]. In this case, involving services to students
    with learning disabilities, the tribunal also rejected the government's
    arguments that its only obligation was to provide the framework for
    educational services, while school boards were responsible for delivering

services. The tribunal viewed school boards as creatures of legislation exercising delegated authority and held that the minister had the ultimate responsibility for education, stating, at § 715: 'With that responsibility comes accountability for ensuring that the system, as a whole, does not discriminate against the needs of the special education students that it services.'

110 Cruikshank, supra n25 at 68.

111 Ibid., at 70.

112 See text surrounding n67.

113 Thus, in *Gosselin*, supra n56 at § 93, the Supreme Court of Canada opted for an interpretation of s.45 of the *Quebec Code* which provides rights to social assistance 'provided for by law' that foreclosed a court's jurisdiction in assessing the adequacy of such assistance, noting that: 'This interpretation is also consistent with the respective institutional competence of courts and legislatures when it comes to enacting and fine-tuning basic social policy.'

114 For example, public administration in Quebec is governed by a results-based framework: *Public Administration Act*, R.S.Q., c. A-6.01. In keeping with this general approach, the recent reform of education in Quebec is explicitly presented as a shift from the emphasis previously placed on universal *access to* schooling, to *success from* schooling; see Ministère de l'Éducation du Québec, *A New Direction for Success: Policy Statement and Plan of Action* (Québec, 1997) [hereinafter *A New Direction for Success*]. Thus, the mission of public schools stated in the *Education Act*, s.36, R.S.Q., c. I-13.3 [hereinafter Quebec *Education Act*], is as follows: 'In keeping with the principle of equality of opportunity, the mission of a school is to impart knowledge to students, foster their social development and give them qualifications, while enabling them to undertake and achieve success in a course of study.' This approach explicitly includes students with special needs; see Ministère de l'Éducation du Québec, *Adapting Our Schools to the Needs of All Students: Policy on Special Education* (Québec, 1999) [hereinafter *Adapting Our Schools*].

115 The *Quebec Code*, s.40, states: 'Every person has a right, to the extent provided for by law, to free public education.' This 'circular right' entitles everyone only to what education legislation provides as an entitlement.

116 See n39.

117 *Eaton*, supra n41 at § 77.

118 D. Greschner & S. Lewis, '*Auton* and Evidenced-Based Decision-Making: Medicare in the Courts,' (2003) 82 *Canadian Bar Review* 501 at 506–7, state: 'Its core notion is the idea that systematically accumulated scientific

evidence, rather than tradition, hunch, anecdote, or peer pressure, should guide medical practice.'

119 Educational policy and practice is not as amenable to being codified, as evidenced by the consistent failure over time to transfer the concept of medical malpractice to an education setting: see W.F. Foster, 'Educational Malpractice: A Tort for the Untaught,' (1985) 19 *U.B.C. Law Review* 161. However, codes of practice have been in use in the U.K. for several years (e.g., Department for Education and Skills, *Special Education Needs Code of Practice* (London, 2001)) and are used in some jurisdictions in Canada (e.g., Council of the Ontario College of Teachers, *Standards of Practice for the Teaching Profession* (Toronto, 1999)). S. Ben Jaafar, 'Fertile Ground: Instructional Negligence and the Tort of Educational Malpractice,' (2002) 12 *Education & Law Journal* 1, asserts that this matter has not been settled. However, Anderson's recent analysis affirms that a successful educational malpractice action is no more likely now than in the past: S.M. Anderson, 'Liability for Education Malpractice – Coming Soon to a School Near You?' in R. Flynn, ed., *Law and Education: The Practice of Accountability* (Markham: Canadian Association for the Practical Study of Law in Education, 2005) 1, at 50: 'In Canada, the door to educational malpractice claims is ajar but still held by a lock and chain. It remains for a plaintiff to bring a claim in which the facts show egregious conduct, well below the standard of teacher professionalism, which has resulted in measurable, quantifiable damage to a child.'

120 The best interests principle is meant to distinguish the rights of children from parental rights and authority and must be seen in light of the evolving capacity of children and youth to express their own views and ultimately to make decisions that affect their lives.

121 An example of this can be found in the amendments to the Quebec *Education Act*, see supra n114, s.235, dealing with the integration of students with special needs. Rather than crafting a presumption in favour of integration, or adopting a neutral stance, the amended provision states that integration is only permissible if two conditions are met, namely, 'that it has been established on the basis of the evaluation of the student's abilities and needs that such integration would facilitate the student's learning and social integration and would not impose an excessive constraint or significantly undermine the rights of the other students.'

122 T.A. Sussel & M.E. Manley-Casimir, 'The Supreme Court of Canada as a "National School Board,"' in *Courts in the Classroom*, supra n4 at 213 and 219.

123 The expression 'national school board' was taken from a U.S. article, E.S. Corwin, 'The Supreme Court as a National School Board,' (1949) 14 *Law &*

Contemporary Problems 3, which in turn refers to *McCollum* v. *Board of Education*, 333 U.S. 203 (1948) [hereinafter *McCollum*].

124 D.L. Corbett, K. Spector, & J. Strug, 'Section 15 Jurisprudence in the Supreme Court of Canada in 2000,' (2001) 14 *Supreme Court Law Review* (2d) 29 at 39.

125 Ibid., at 38.

126 See A.W. MacKay and J. Burt-Gerrans, 'Inclusion and Diversity in Education: Legal Accomplishments and Prospects for the Future,' (2003) 13 *Education & Law Journal* 77, for an assessment of the importance of the *Meiorin* standard for the continued evolution of equal educational opportunity rights.

127 P. Westen, 'The Empty Idea of Equality,' (1982) 95 *Harvard Law Review* 537.

128 A *normative* perspective asserts what the *Charter* should mean, based on one's values and beliefs, as opposed to an *interpretative* perspective, which states what it does mean, based on an analysis of relevant jurisprudence.

129 The contrast in these two approaches can be summarized thus: from a minimalist perspective, the courts would quash a complaint because no legislative rights have been denied or none denied in a manner that constitutes discrimination; from an expansionist perspective, the courts would uphold a complaint because of the absence of legislative rights which are required in order to provide equal protection and benefit of the law.

130 B. McLachlin, 'Equality: The Most Difficult Right,' (2001) 14 *Supreme Court Law Review* (2d) 17 at 20.

131 Ibid., at 27.

132 A.W. MacKay, 'Human Rights and Education: Problems and Prospects,' (1996–97) 8 *Education & Law Journal* 69, at 70.

133 Thus, A. Giddens, *The Third Way – The Renewal of Social Democracy* (Cambridge: Polity, 1998), at 102, states: 'In a society where work remains central to self-esteem and standard of living, access to work is one main context of opportunity. Education is another,' cited in C. Sheppard, 'Inclusive Equality and New Forms of Social Governance,' (2004) 24 *Supreme Court Law Review* 45 at 63.

134 As observed by J. Jensen & D. Saint-Martin, *Building Blocks for a New Welfare Architecture: Is LEGO™ the Model for an Active Society?* (Montreal: Université de Montréal, 2003), at 1: social policy in many jurisdictions can be characterized by a shift 'from the supposedly 'passive' spending on social *protection* to investments that will generate an 'active society' and an 'active citizenship.'' Retrieved from: http://www.cccg.umontreal.ca/pdf/997%20Jenson%20REV%2003-03-06.pdf. Accessed 3 May 2009. To take an example from Quebec, public policy in general and educational

policy in particular reflects an emphasis on regionalization and private-public partnerships to achieve public policy goals: see Gouvernement du Québec, *Briller parmi les meilleurs: La vision et les priorités d'action du gouvernement du Québec* (Québec, 2004).

135 D. Réaume, 'Discrimination and Dignity,' (2003) 63 *Louisiana Law Review* 645, at 695.

136 *Convention on the Rights of the Child*, GA Res. 44/25, UN GAOR, 44th Sess., Annex, Supp. No. 49, UN Doc. A/44/49 (1989) 167 (entered into force 2 September 1990).

137 A. Stone, 'Human Rights Education and Public Policy in the United States: Mapping the Road Ahead,' (2002) 24 *Human Rights Quarterly* 537.

138 See, e.g., N. Tymochenko, 'Special Education in Ontario – Is It Workable?' (2002) 12 *Education & Law Journal* 213, for a discussion of the limits of legal frameworks for promoting the rights of students with special needs.

139 See *World Declaration on Education*, supra n2.

2 The Lighthouse of Equality: A Guide to 'Inclusive' Schooling

*Professor MacKay acknowledges the research and drafting contributions to the part III disability case study, of Janet Burt-Gerrans, his administrative and research assistant on the New Brunswick Inclusion Review.

1 Part I of the Constitution Act, 1982, being Schedule B to the Canada Act 1982 (U.K.), 1982, c. 11, s.2 [hereinafter *Charter*]

2 W. MacKay, *Connecting Care and Challenge: Tapping Our Human Potential, Inclusive Education: A Review of Programming and Services in New Brunswick*. (Paper submitted to New Brunswick Department of Education, December 2005). Available on-line at the New Brunswick Department of Education Webpage at http://www.gnb.ca/0000/publications/mackay/MACKAY-REPORTFINAL.pdf. Accessed 3 May 2009.

3 W. MacKay, *Inclusion: What Is Inclusion Anyway?* (Booklet submitted to the New Brunswick Department of Education, July 2007) [hereinafter *Inclusion Booklet*]. Available at http://www.gnb.ca/0000/publications/mackay/Inclusion%20Booklet%20LR%20English.pdf. Accessed 3 May 2009.

4 Ibid.

5 [1996] 1 S.C.R. 825 [hereinafter *Ross*].

6 Ibid., at § 42.

7 Manitoba, *Follow-up to the Manitoba Special Education Review: Proposals for a Policy, Accountability and Funding Framework* (Winnipeg: Manitoba Education, Training and Youth, September 2001).

8 *Law* v. *Canada (Minister of Employment & Immigration)* [1999] 1 S.C.R. 497 [hereinafter *Law*] at 549.

9 B. Pentney, 'Equality Values and the Canadian Promise of Community' (Paper prepared for the Canadian Association of Statutory Human Rights Agencies, October 1996) 25 C.H.R.R. No.6 C/6-C15.

10 M. Haddon, *The Curious Incident of the Dog in the Night-time* (Toronto: Anchor, 2004).

11 Ibid., at 43.

12 *Inclusion Booklet, supra* n4 at 10–11.

13 *Eaton* v. *Brant County Board of Education*, [1997] 1 S.C.R. 241 [hereinafter *Eaton*].

14 Ibid., at § 77.

15 W. MacKay & V. Kazmierski, 'And on the Eighth Day, God Gave Us ... Equality in Education: *Eaton* v. *Brant (County) Board of Education and Inclusive Education*,' (1996) 7 N.J.C.L. 2.

16 *Charter* at s.1.

17 *British Columbia Public Service Employee Relations Commission* v. *British Columbia Government and Service Employees' Union (BCCGSEU) (Meiorin Grievance)* [1999] 3 S.C.R. 3 [hereinafter *Meiorin*].

18 *British Columbia (Superintendent of Motor Vehicles)* v. *British Columbia (Council of Human Rights)* [1999] 3 S.C.R. 868 [hereinafter *Grismer*].

19 Ibid., at 869.

20 *Central Okanagan School District No. 23* v. *Renaud*, [1992] 2 S.C.R. 970 [hereinafter *Renaud*] at 974.

21 *Newfoundland (Treasury Board)* v. *Newfoundland and Labrador Association of Public and Private Employees (NAPE)* [2004] 3 S.C.R. 381 [hereinafter *NAPE*].

22 *Eaton*, supra n13 at § 67.

23 *C.N.R.* v. *Canada (Human Rights Commission)* [1987] 1 S.C.R. 1114 [hereinafter *CNR*].

24 R.S. Abella, *Report of the Commission on Equality in Employment* (Ottawa: Minister of Supply and Services Canada, 1984).

25 *CNR*, supra n23 at § 34.

26 [1997] 3 S.C.R. 624 [hereinafter *Eldridge*].

27 S. Day & G. Brodsky, 'The Duty to Accommodate: Who Will Benefit?' (1996) 75 *Canadian Bar Review* 433, as quoted by the Supreme Court of Canada in *Meiorin*, supra n17 at 26.

28 *Grismer, supra* note 18 at 869.

29 (2004) 245 D.L.R. (4th) 1 (SCC) [hereinafter *Auton*].

30 Ibid., at §§ 55-58

31 Ibid., at § 62.

32 See *Cudmore (Human Rights Commission)* v. *New Brunswick (Minister Education) and School District 2*, [2004] Human Rights 3 Member Tribunal LEB File No. HR-003-01 [hereinafter *Cudmore*] and see also *Auton*.

33 See both *Cudmore* and *Auton*, ibid.

34 [2005] O.J. No. 1228 (Ont. S.C.J.) [QL] [hereinafter *Wynberg*].

35 *Wynberg*, ibid., at 20. It should be noted that recent cases such as *Clough* v. *Simcoe County District School Board*, [2005] O.J. No. 2124 (Ont. S.C.J.) [hereinafter *Clough*], have upheld placement-level decisions stating that IBI treatment is more therapeutic than educational and consequently that alternative educational measures are appropriate. The Ontario Superior Court of Justice in *Clough* was faced with an application for judicial review of a placement decision, as opposed to the full course of litigation in *Wynberg*. As such, the Court's ability to make certain crucial findings of fact was extremely limited. This was a factor cited by the Court in *Clough* for the difference in its decision from *Wynberg*.

36 *Wynberg*, ibid., at 440.

37 *Wynberg* v. *Ontario*, [2006] O.J. No. 2732 (Ont. C.A.) [hereinafter *Wynberg Appeal*].

38 See *Dassonville-Trudel (Guardian Ad Litem)* v. *Halifax Regional School Board*, [2004] N.S.C.A. 82; 50 R.F.L. (5th) 311 [hereinafter *Dassonville-Trudel*]; see also *Acheson* v. *New Brunswick (Minister of Education)*, (2000), 228 N.B.R. (2d) 223 (N.B.Q.B.) [hereinafter *Acheson*].

39 MacKay, supra n2.

40 [1998] 1 S.C.R. 493 [hereinafter *Vriend*].

41 R.S.A. 1980, c. I-2, am. S.A. 1985, c. 33, S.A. 1990, c. 23 [hereinafter *IRPA*]. The *IRPA* has since been amended and is now called the *Human Rights, Citizenship and Multiculturalism Act*, R.S.A. 1980, c. H-11.7.

42 [2001] 1 S.C.R. 772 [hereinafter *Trinity Western*].

43 [1997] 41 B.C.L.R. (3d) 158 (B.C.S.C.) [hereinafter *Trinity Western BCSC*].

44 R.S.B.C. 1996, c. 449.

45 [1998] 59 B.C.L.R. (3d) 241 (B.C.C.A.) [hereinafter *Trinity Western Appeal*].

46 [2002] 4 S.C.R. 710 [hereinafter *Chamberlain*].

47 R.S.B.C. 1996, c. 412.

48 *Chamberlain*, supra n46 at §§ 21 & 23.

49 Ibid., at § 65.

50 Ibid., at § 66.

51 Ibid., at § 69.

52 [2006] 1 S.C.R. 256 [hereinafter *Multani*].

53 [2002] J.Q. No. 1131 (Qué. Sup. Ct.) [hereinafter *Multani Trial Judgment*].

54 [2004] Q.J. No. 1904 (Qué. C.A.) [hereinafter *Multani Appeal*].

55 R.S.Q. c. C-12.

56 *Multani*, supra n52 at §§ 76, 78, & 89.

57 [2002] B.C.H.R.T.D. No. 10 [hereinafter *Jubran Tribunal*]. The authors note that the school board sought judicial review on the point that since Azmi Jubran openly identified himself as not being homosexual, that he could not rely on the grounds of sexual orientation for his claim of discrimination. The British Columbia Supreme Court agreed and overturned the entire decision of the Human Rights Tribunal; (2003), 9 B.C.L.R. (4th) 338 (B.C.S.C.) [hereinafter *Jubran Trial Judgment*]. That decision was reversed on appeal to the B.C. Court of Appeal, [2005] B.C.J. No. 733 (B.C.C.A.) [hereinafter *Jubran Appeal*].

58 *Jubran Appeal*, ibid., at § 47.

59 Haddon, supra n10 at 44.

60 *Convention on the Rights of the Child*, GA Res. 44/25, UN GAOR, 44th Sess., Annex, Supp. No. 49, UN Doc. A/44/49 (1989) 167 (entered into force 2 September 1990) [hereinafter *Convention on the Rights of the Child*].

61 News Release, Alanna Palmer (Chair New Brunswick Human Rights Commission) 23 September 2004. Available at http://www.gnb.ca/cnb/news/hrc/2004e1048hr.htm. Accessed 3 May 2009.

62 The Supreme Court of Canada has made strong statements about the duty of educators to proactively address discriminatory attitudes by teachers in schools in *Ross*. Human rights tribunals have also extended these principles to harassing and discriminatory behaviour by students: see *Kafe et Commission des droits de la personne du Quebec c. Commission scolaire Deux-Montagnes* [1993], 19 C.H.R.R. D/1 (Qué. H.R.Trib.) [hereinafter *Kafe*]; see also *Jubran Tribunal*, *supra* n57 (although this Tribunal decision was quashed on judicial review on a separate matter, that decision was restored on appeal to the British Columbia Court of Appeal in *Jubran Appeal*).

63 *Ross* is seen as a seminal case within Canadian Education Law jurisprudence, with the Supreme Court stating that school boards have a duty to 'maintain a positive school environment for all persons.'

3 Special Education and the *Charter*: The Effect of the Equality Provisions and *Charter* Litigation on Educational Policy and Practice in Ontario

1 *Canadian Charter of Rights and Freedoms*, Part I of the *Constitution Act, 1982*, being Schedule B to the *Canada Act 1982* (U.K.), 1982, c. 11 [hereinafter *Charter*].

2 While the focus of our review is Ontario, the experience in Ontario generally mirrors the experience of other provinces from a legal perspective.

3 *Education Amendment Act, 1980*, S.O. 1980, c. 61 [hereinafter *Bill 82*].

4 348 F. Supp 866 (D.C. 1972) [hereinafter *Mills*].

5 20 U.S.C. 1400 [hereinafter *IDEA*]. This legislation was reauthorized and amended pursuant to the *Individuals with Disabilities Education Improvement Act*, Pub. L. No. 108-446, 118 Stat. 2647 (2004).

6 *Human Rights Code*, S.O. 1981, c. 53, proclaimed in force June 15, 1982.

7 However, given the timing of the drafting of the *Charter* by the provinces and federal government, it must also be observed that these same societal imperatives underlay the inclusion of s.15 in the *Charter*.

8 Ontario, *Report of the Royal Commission on Education in Ontario* (Toronto: B. Johnston, 1950) (Chairman: J.A. Hope) [hereinafter Hope Report].

9 Information Program developed for Ontario Special Education Advisory Committee (SEAC) members by the Ontario Ministry of Education [hereinafter SEAC Information Program].

10 Ibid.

11 Ontario, *Living and Learning: Report of the Provincial Committee on Aims and Objectives of Education in the Schools of Ontario* (Toronto: The Committee, 1968) (Co-Chairmen: E.M. Hall & L.A. Dennis) [hereinafter *Hall-Dennis Report*].

12 B.J. Bowlby, C. Peters, & M. Mackinnon, *An Educator's Guide to Special Education Law* (Aurora: Aurora Professional Press, 2001).

13 R.S.O. 1980, c. 129 [hereinafter Act].

14 *Education Act*, R.S.O. 1990, c. 129, s.34 [hereinafter *Education Act, 1990*].

15 Ibid., at s.182.

16 Regulation 297, which became O. Reg. 306/90, subsequently amended by O. Reg. 136/01.

17 O. Reg. 306/90, amended by O. Reg. 136/01.

18 Regulation 554/81 which became O. Reg. 305/90, as rep. by O. Reg. 181/98.

19 Ontario, *Special Education Materials and Resources Handbook* (Toronto: Ministry of Education, 1982) [hereinafter *Handbook, 1982*].

20 Ontario, *Special Education Information Handbook* (Toronto: Ministry of Education, 1984) [hereinafter *Handbook, 1984*].

21 *Handbook, 1982*, supra n19 at 48.

22 K. Weber, *Special Education in Ontario Schools*, 3rd ed. (Thornhill: Highland, 1993).

23 *Education Statute Law Amendment Act* S.O. 1993, c. 11 [hereinafter *Education Statute Law Amendment Act, 1993*].

24 Hansard, Subcommittee report, *Education Statute Law.Amendment Act, 1993, Bill 4* (7 June 1993). Available at no charge when requested by telephone from: Committees Branch, 99 Wellesley St. W., Rm. 1405, Whitney Block, Toronto, ON, M7A 1A2, (416) 325-3525.

25 *Education Quality Improvement Act*, S.O. 1997, c. 31 [hereinafter Bill 160].

26 See O. Reg. 464/1997.

27 O. Reg. 181/98 [hereinafter Exceptional Pupils Regulation].

28 Ibid., at s.9.

29 [1997] 1 S.C.R. 241 [hereinafter *Eaton*].

30 Ibid.

31 It is important to note that s.15 applies not just to the 'law' but also to the application of the law, which must also be consistent with s.15. Therefore, it is not just the legislative and regulatory framework of special education that must meet the requirements of s.15, but the steps taken in implementing special education under the legislative and regulatory framework also must be consistent with s.15.

32 *Andrews* v. *Law Society of British Columbia*, [1989] 1 S.C.R. 143 [hereinafter *Andrews*].

33 *Eaton*, supra n29.

34 See, e.g., *Lewis* v. *York Region Board of Education (No. 5)* (1996), 27 C.H.R.R. D/261 (Ont. Bd. Inq.) [hereinafter *Lewis*].

35 See *Eaton*, supra n29.

36 [1991] 92 Sask. R. 229 [hereinafter *Trofimenkoff*].

37 *Re Emily Eaton*, (24 February 1992), (Brant County I.P.R.C.) [unreported] [hereinafter *Re Emily Eaton*].

38 *Eaton* v. *Brant County Board of Education*, (19 November 1993), (Ont. Spec. Ed. Trib.) [unreported] [hereinafter *Eaton Tribunal*].

39 *Eaton* v. *Brant County Board of Education*, [1994] O.J. No. 203 (Ont. Ct. (Gen. Div.)) [hereinafter *Eaton Ontario Court General Division*].

40 *Eaton* v. *Brant County Board of Education*, (1995) 123 D.L.R. (4th) 43 (Ont. C.A.) [hereinafter *Eaton Appeal*].

41 Ibid., at 65.

42 *Eaton*, supra note 29 at § 67.

43 Ibid. at § 69.

44 Ibid. at § 77.

45 [1997] 3 S.C.R. 624 [hereinafter *Eldridge*].

46 [2004] O.J. No. 2524 (Ont. Sup. Ct.) [hereinafter *Neiberg*].

47 S.O. 1992, c.6 [hereinafter *Class Proceedings Act, 1992*].

48 Ibid., at s.5(1).

49 [1998] S.J. No. 566 (Sask. Q.B.) [hereinafter *Concerned Parents*].

50 [2004] 3 S.C.R. 657, 2004 SCC 78 [hereinafter *Auton* cited to SCC].

51 (30 March 2005) 2005 CanLII 8749 (Ont. Sup. Ct.) [hereinafter *Wynberg*].

52 See *Clough* v. *Simcoe County District School Board*, (15 September 2003) (Ont. Spec. Ed. Trib.) [hereinafter *Clough*]; see also *Walsh* v. *Simcoe County District*

School Board, (27 May 2004) (Ont. Spec. Ed. Trib.) [hereinafter *Walsh*]; and see also *Tobin* v. *Simcoe County District School Board* (28 May 2004) (Ont. Spec. Ed. Trib.) [hereinafter *Tobin*].

53 *Wynberg*, supra n51 at § 702.

54 Ibid., at § 515.

55 *Wynberg et al.* v. *Ontario*, 2007 CanLII 11900 (S.C.C.) [hereinafter *Wynberg SCC*].

56 *Clough (Litigation Guardian of)* v. *Simcoe County District School Board*, [2005] O.J. No. 2124 (Ont. Sup. Ct.) [hereinafter *Clough Judicial Review*].

4 Equity, Equality of Opportunity, Freedom of Religion, Private School Funding, and the *Charter*

1 *Canadian Charter of Rights and Freedoms*, Part I of the *Constitution Act, 1982*, being Schedule B to the *Canada Act 1982* (U.K.), 1982, c.11 [hereinafter *Charter*].

2 J. Paquette, 'Public Funding for "Private" Education: The Equity Challenge of Enhanced Choice' (paper presented at the conference School Choice: Public Education at a Crossroads, University of Calgary, 11 May 2002.)

3 J. Paquette, 'Public Funding for "Private" Education: Enhanced Choice at What Price in Equity?' (2002) 12(2) *Education & Law Journal* 133 [hereinafter 'Enhanced Choice at What Price?'] at 164.

4 Ibid., at 151–9.

5 For details see ibid. Ontario began phasing in an 'Equity in Education Tax Credit' in 2002 but the current government cancelled this tax credit retroactively to the beginning of 2003.

6 W.J. Smith and W.F. Foster, 'Religion and Education in Canada: Part I – The Traditional Framework,' (2001) 3 *Education & Law Journal* 10 [hereinafter Smith & Foster Part I]; W.F. Foster and W.J. Smith, 'Religion and Education in Canada: Part II – An Alternative Framework for the Debate,' (2001) 11 *Education & Law Journal* 1 [hereinafter Foster & Smith Part II].

7 M. Fahmy, 'The Private School Funding Debate: A Second Look through Charter First Principles,' (2004) 3 *Education & Law Journal* 13.

8 (1996), 140 D.L.R. (4th) 385 (S.C.C.) [hereinafter *Adler*].

9 C. Chitty, *Towards a New Education System: The Victory of the New Right?* (London: Falmer, 1989). See J. Paquette, *Social Purpose and Schooling: Alternatives, Agendas, and Issues* (London: Falmer, 1991) [hereinafter *Social Purpose and Schooling*].

10 K. Strike, 'The Ethics of Resource Allocation in Education: Questions of Democracy and Justice,' in D.H. Monk & J. Underwood, eds., *Microlevel School Finance: Issues and Implications for Policy* (Cambridge: Ballinger, 1988) 143.

11 H.M. Levin, 'Educational Vouchers: Effectiveness, Choice, and Costs' (Paper presented at the Annual Meetings of the American Economics Association, New Orleans, 4 January 1996); D.M. Topolnicki, 'Why Private Schools Are Rarely Worth the Money,' (1994) 23 *Money* 89.

12 J.E. Coons, 'Dodging Democracy: The Educator's Flight from the Specter of Choice,' (2005) 111(4) *American Journal of Education* 596.

13 [1999] S.C.J. No. 12, [1999] 1 S.C.R. 497, 170 D.L.R (4th) 1 [hereinafter *Law*].

14 (2002), 59 O.R. (3d.) 481 (Ont. C.A.) [hereinafter *Falkiner*].

15 J. Paquette, 'Democratic Education and School Choice Revisited,' (2005) 111(4) *American Journal of Education* 609 [hereinafter 'Democratic Education'].

16 (1989), 56 D.L.R. (4th) 1 (S.C.C.) [hereinafter *Andrews*].

17 [1995] 2 S.C.R. 513 [hereinafter *Egan*].

18 [1998] 1 S.C.R. 493 [hereinafter *Vriend*].

19 *Law*, supra n13 at 23.

20 Although appealed to the Supreme Court of Canada, the case was eventually discontinued. Notice of discontinuance filed 1 Sept. 2004, (2004) S.C.C. Bulletin at 1330.

21 *Falkiner*, supra n14 at 506.

22 Ibid., at 506–7.

23 Ibid., at 507.

24 (1999), 173 D.L.R. (4th) 1, [1999] 2 S.C.R. 203 [hereinafter *Corbiere*].

25 [2000] 1 S.C.R. 703 [hereinafter *Granovsky*].

26 *Falkiner*, supra n14 at 508.

27 Ibid.

28 Ibid., at 510.

29 Ibid., at 510–13.

30 H.M. Levin, 'The Necessary and Sufficient Conditions for Achieving Educational Equity,' in R. Berne & L. Picus, eds., *Outcome Equity in Education* (Thousand Oaks: Corwin, 1994) 167 [hereinafter 'Achieving Educational Equity'].

31 *Falkiner*, supra n14 at 511–13.

32 Ibid., at 512.

33 The Supreme Court of Canada did rule recently on another welfare benefit reduction case, this time from Quebec (*Gosselin* v. *Quebec (Attorney General)*, [2002] 4 S.C.R. 429). In a 5–4 split decision with considerable dissent on several issues including the question of whether Quebec's 1989 reduction of welfare benefits to under-30 persons coupled with a requirement for participation in education and training programs by such persons as a prerequisite to reinstatement of some or most of their welfare benefits

violated s.15 of the *Charter* by affronting the basic dignity of the plaintiffs. The facts of this class action suit, however, were very different from *Falkiner*, most notably for purposes of this chapter in regard to the majority insistence that under-30 welfare recipients did not constitute a group suffering from pre-existing disadvantage and stigmatism on the basis of age and majority acceptance of the government's rationale for the impugned policy as an attempt to improve employability of affected young persons and thus reduce their future dependence on welfare – a measure designed, the government argued, to enhance not detract from their dignity. As well, this decision reflects ongoing reluctance on the part of the Supreme Court to recognize any s.7 fundamental justice argument to support a positive law obligation on the part of the state to fund social programming.

34 See Chitty, supra n9; see also G. Walford, 'How Dependent Is the Independent Sector?' (1987) 3 *Oxford Review of Education* 13.

35 See Coons, supra n12.

36 J.F. Witte, 'The Milwaukee Voucher Experiment: The Good, the Bad, and the Ugly,' (1999) 1 *Phi Delta Kappan* 81.

37 Coons, supra n12.

38 Fahmy, supra n7.

39 For details, see 'Enhanced Choice at What Price?' supra n3.

40 Commission des états généraux sur l'éducation, *Les États Généraux Sur L'éducation, 1995–1996: Exposé De La Situation* (Quebec: Éducation Québec, 2001). Last retrieved 5 May 2009 from http://www.meq.gouv.qc.ca/ etat%2Dgen/menu/chap8.htm#DEBAT.

41 Coons, supra n12 at 608.

42 Ibid., at 604.

43 Any such scheme, like the Dutch scheme, would presumably also have to make provision for non-religious, secular schools. Interestingly, such schools have historically attracted only about a quarter of overall enrolment in the Netherlands.

44 Smith and Foster Part I, supra n6; Foster & Smith Part II, supra n6.

45 Smith and Foster Part I, ibid., at 446.

46 Section 22 of the *Manitoba Act*, 1879, 33 Vict., c. 3 (Canada), confirmed by the *Constitution Act*, 1871.

47 Section 17 of the *Alberta Act*, 4-5 Edw. VII, c. 3 1905 (Canada).

48 Section 17 of the *Saskatchewan Act*, 4-5 Edw. VII, c. 42 1905 (Canada).

49 Confirmed by the *Newfoundland Act*, 12-13 Geo. VI, c. 22 (U.K.).

50 Fahmy, supra n7, at 429.

51 See E. James, 'Benefits and Costs of Privatized Public Services: Lessons from the Dutch Educational System,' (1984) 4 *Comparative Education Review* 28.

52 Coons, supra n12 at 602, waffles on the admissions issue too by suggesting that 'Charter schools and participating private schools should be required either to randomize some portion of their selections or to set aside 15–20% of spaces for the poor, should so many apply.'

53 Ibid., at 606.

54 Ibid.

55 Fahmy, supra n7 at 430.

56 A. Watkinson, 'To Whom Do We Entrust Public Education?' (2004) 4 Education & Law Journal 191.

57 'Enhanced Choice at What Price?' supra n3.

58 James, supra n51.

59 For what appears to be an extreme exemplar of this type of position, see Watkinson, supra n56.

5 Religion in Canadian Education: Whither Goest Thou?

1 Canadian Charter of Rights and Freedoms, Part I of the Constitution Act, 1982 being Schedule B of the Canada Act, 1982 (U.K.), 1982, c. 11 [hereinafter. Charter]. The Charter was proclaimed 17 April 1982 but was not fully effective until 1985, there having been a three-year delay in the implementation of s.15, Equality Rights.

2 See J.C. Long & R.F. Magsino, 'Legal Issues in Religion and Education,' (1993) 4 Education & Law Journal 189; R.F. Magsino, J.C. Long, & R.G. Theberge, 'Canadian Pluralism, the Charter and Citizenship Education,' in R. Bruno-Jofre & N. Aponiuk, eds., Educating Citizens for a Pluralistic Society (Calgary: Canadian Ethnic Studies, 2001) 115; J.C. Long, 'Encouraging Spirituality: Constraints and Opportunities,' in C.M. Shields, M.M. Edwards, & A. Sayani, eds., Inspiring Practice: Spirituality and Educational Leadership (Lancaster: ProActive Publications, 2005) 17.

3 Long & Magsino, ibid., at 214.

4 Constitution Act, 1867 (U.K.), 30 & 31 Vict., c. 3 (formerly, s.93 of the British North America Act, 1867).

5 See W.F. Foster & W.J. Smith, 'Religion and Education in Canada: Part II – An Alternative Framework for the Debate,' (2001) 11 Education & Law Journal 1.

6 Art. 93(1) of the Constitution Act, 1867.

7 This section did not apply to other provinces.

8 Foster & Smith, supra n5 at 5.

9 Denominational schools have existed in Alberta and Saskatchewan since 1905. The constitutional entitlement to separate schools in these provinces

is provided for in s.17 of the *Alberta Act* (1905) and the *Saskatchewan Act* (1905) together with s.93(2), (3), and (4).

10 See especially T.A. Sussel, *Canada's Legal Revolution: Public Education, the Charter and Human Rights* (Toronto: Emond Montgomery, 1995).

11 R.A. Sedler, 'Constitutional Protection of Individual Rights in Canada: The Impact of the New *Canadian Charter of Rights and Freedoms,*' in A.W. MacKay & I. Grant, eds., *Constitutional Law Materials* (Halifax: Dalhousie University Press, 1984) 20, at 36.

12 We attribute the term 'rights paradigm' (the scheme, structure, and pattern of rights) to Professor A.W. MacKay. See A.W. MacKay, 'The Rights Paradigm in the Age of the *Charter,*' in R. Ghosh & D. Ray, eds., *Social Change and Education in Canada* (Toronto: Harcourt Brace, 1995) 224.

13 *Constitution Act, 1982*, being Schedule B to the *Canada Act 1982* (U.K.), 1982, c. 11.

14 Foster & Smith, supra n5 at 15.

15 [1986] 1 S.C.R. 103 [hereinafter *Oakes*].

16 For a recent and especially clear example of a § 1 analysis, see *Kempling* v. *British Columbia College of Teachers*, [2004] B.C.J. No. 173 (B.C.S.C.) [hereinafter *Kempling*].

17 *R.* v. *Edwards Books & Art Ltd.*, [1986] 35 D.L.R. (4th) 1 (S.C.C.) [hereinafter *Edwards Books*] at 34.

18 Foster & Smith, supra n5 at 25.

19 The American First Amendment provision reads: 'Congress shall make no law respecting the establishment of religion or prohibiting the free exercise thereof.'

20 (1988) 65 O.R. (2d) 641 (Ont. C.A.) [hereinafter *Zylberberg*].

21 R.S.O. 1980, c. 129.

22 *Zylberberg*, supra n20 at 655.

23 374 U.S. 203 (1963) [hereinafter *Abington*].

24 370 U.S. 421 (1962) [hereinafter *Engel*].

25 *Zylberberg*, supra n20 at 659.

26 Ibid., at 656.

27 Ibid., at 657. Section 27 of the *Charter* reads: 'This *Charter* shall be interpreted in a manner consistent with the preservation and enhancement of the multicultural heritage of Canadians.'

28 *Zylberberg*, supra n20 at 663.

29 Ibid.

30 403 U.S. 602 (1971) [hereinafter *Lemon*].

31 (1989), 35 B.C.L.R. (2d) 29 (B.C.S.C.) [hereinafter *Russow*].

32 (1992), 82 Man. R. (2d) 39 (Man. Q.B.) [hereinafter *Manitoba*].

33 This also serves to indicate the promise and utility of interprovincial comparisons, such as are already available with respect to religious exercises, and other issues, in the impressive work of Foster & Smith. See especially Smith & Foster, 'Religion and Education in Canada: Part III – An Analysis of Provincial Legislation,' (2001) 11 *Education & Law Journal* 203.

34 R.S.B.C. 1979, c. 375.

35 Ibid., at s.164.

36 R.S.M. 1987, c. P250.

37 Manitoba, 'Religious Exercises,' in *Administrative Handbook for Schools* (Winnipeg: Ministry of Education, 2000) 2.

38 Ibid.

39 It is interesting that Manitoba's approach to religious exercises has been characterized as both confusing and perhaps deficient constitutionally. Smith & Foster, supra n33 at 247–8, say: 'The situation with respect to religious exercises in Manitoba is somewhat confusing … the right to religious exercises is limited to those students whose parents have so requested to opt in accordance with this provision. The problem with this provision is that the right is vested solely in parents, which may be viewed as an infringement of *Canadian Charter* standards.' See also Foster & Smith, supra n5.

40 (1988), 64 O.R. (2d) 577 (Ont. Div. Ct.) [hereinafter *CCLA*].

41 *Canadian Civil Liberties Assn.* v. *Ontario (Minister of Education)*, (1990), 71 O.R. (2d) 341 (Ont. C.A.) [hereinafter *CCLA Appeal*].

42 Ibid., at 376.

43 Ibid., at 342.

44 [1996] 3 S.C.R. 609 [hereinafter *Adler*].

45 (1997), 34 O.R. (3d) 484 (Ont. C.A.) [hereinafter *Bal*], leave to appeal to S.C.C. refused (1998) 49 C.R.R. (2d) 188. In both *Adler* and *Bal*, the claims were brought by a coalition of Christian and non-Christian groups.

46 (1994), 19 O.R. (3d) 1 (Ont. C.A.) [hereinafter *Adler Appeal*].

47 *Bal*, supra n45 at 715.

48 (1997), 145 D.L.R. (4th) 659 (Ont. Gen. Div.) [hereinafter *Islamic Federation*], leave to appeal refused (29 July 1997), Doc. CA M20514 (Ont. C.A.).

49 (1990), 12 C.H.R.R. D/364 (Ont. Bd. of Inq.) [hereinafter *Pandori*].

50 S.O. 1981, c. 53.

51 *Peel Board of Education* v. *Ontario Human Rights Commission* (1991), 3 O.R. (3d). 531 (Ont. Ct. Gen. Div.) [hereinafter *Pandori Appeal*]; application for leave to appeal dismissed [1991] O.J. No. 3200 (Ont. C.A.).

52 *Multani* v. *Marguerite-Bourgeoys (Commission scolaire)* 2006 SCC 6, [2006] 1 S.C.R. 256 [hereinafter *Multani*].

53 [2004] J. Q. no 1904 (Que. C.A.) [hereinafter *Multani Appeal*].

54 *Multani,* supra n52 at 258–9.

55 Ibid., at 259.

56 Ibid., at 259–60.

57 [2002] S.C.J. No. 87 [hereinafter *Chamberlain*].

58 Ibid., at § 59.

59 R.S.B.C. 1996, c. 412.

60 *Chamberlain,* supra n57 at §§ 208 & 211.

61 Ibid., at § 207.

62 2001 SCC 31 [hereinafter *Trinity Western*].

63 Ibid., at §§ 36–7.

64 (1996), 133 D.L.R. (4th) 1 (S.C.C.) [hereinafter *Ross*].

65 Ibid., at § 41.

66 Ibid., at §§ 42 & 44. Support for this judicial view can be found elsewhere: see, e.g., *Cromer* v. *B.C.T.F.,* (1986), 29 D. L.R. (4th) 641 (B.C.C.A) [hereinafter *Cromer*]; see also *Abbotsford School District 34* v. *Shewan,* (1987), 21 B.C.L.R. (2d) 93 (B.C.C.A.) [hereinafter *Shewan*]. See also The Honourable Mr Justice G.V. La Forest, 'Off-Duty Conduct and the Fiduciary Obligation of Teachers,' (1998) 8 *Education & Law Journal* 120.

67 [2004] B.C. J. No. 173 (B.C.C.A.) [hereinafter *Kempling Appeal*].

68 Ibid., at § 104.

69 Ibid., at § 82.

70 Ibid., at § 110.

71 *Kempling* v. *British Columbia College of Teachers* [2005] S.C.C.A. No. 381.

72 (1984), 19 C.C.C. (3d) 254 (Alta. Q.B.) [hereinafter *Keegstra QB*]; rev'd (1988), 60 Alta. L.R. (2d) 1 (Alta. C.A.) [hereinafter *Keegstra Appeal*]; aff'd [1990] 3 S.C.R. 697 [hereinafter *Keegstra*].

73 R.S.C. 1985, c. C-46. Keegstra was convicted of promoting hatred against an identifiable group.

74 Keegstra appealed the termination of his teaching contract. His appeal was heard and dismissed by Justice McFayden of the Alberta Queen's Bench sitting as a Board of Reference under provisions of the Alberta *School Act*, R.S.A. 1980. See *Keegstra* v. *Board of Education of Lacombe No. 14* (1983), 25 Alta. L.R. (2d) 370.

75 E.L. Hurlbert & M.A. Hurlbert, *School Law under the Charter of Rights and Freedoms* (Calgary: University of Calgary Press, 1992), at 226.

76 (1949) 12 & 13 Geo. VI, c. 22 (U.K.).

77 J. Smallwood quoted in M. Hareema, 'Newfound Religion: Term 17(3) of the Newfoundland Act and Its Challenge to the Current Discourse on

Freedom of Religion in the Public Sphere,' (2005) 14 *Dalhousie Journal of Legal Studies* 111, at 115.

78 (2000), 189 Nfld. & P.E.I.R 183 (Nfld. C.A.) [hereinafter *Hogan*].

79 *Constitution Amendment, 1998 (Newfoundland Act)*, amending the *Newfoundland Act*, 1949, 12 & 13 Geo. VI, c. 22 (U.K.). The 1998 Act dropped the proviso that the province may not pass any legislation prejudicially affecting the denominational schools already existing at the time of Confederation. Instead, it revised Term 17 to give the province the unqualified 'exclusive authority to make laws in relation to education.'

80 The Evangelical Fellowship of Canada, 'Presentation to the Special Joint Committee To Amend Section 93 of the Constitution Act, 1867, Concerning the Quebec School System,' SJQS Minutes of Proceedings, Meeting No. 12, 29 October 1997, at 2115.

81 *Constitutional Amendment, 1999 (Quebec)*, amending the *Constitution Act, 1867*.

82 Section 29 of the *Charter* reads: 'Nothing in this *Charter* abrogates or derogates from any rights or privileges guaranteed by or under the Constitution of Canada in respect of denominational, separate, or dissentient schools.'

83 This paragraph owes much to H.G. Elliott, 'Reflections on Religion in the Schools of Newfoundland and Labrador,' (1998) 26 *Morning Watch* 1. See also J.P. McEvoy, 'Denominational Schools and Minority Rights: *Hogan* v. *Newfoundland (Attorney General)*,' (2000–01) 12 N.J.C.L. 449, and, for extended detail, see M.T. Clemens, *The Catholic Education Council of Newfoundland and Labrador: A Case Study in Interest Articulation* (M.Ed. Thesis, University of Manitoba, 1999).

84 Newfoundland and Labrador, Department of Education, *Our Children, Our Future: The Royal Commission of Inquiry into the Delivery of Programs and Services in Primary, Elementary, Secondary Education* (St John's: Author, 1992).

85 Ibid. See especially the Commission's observations at 215–51.

86 For an extensive discussion of *Hogan*, see Hareema, supra n77 and McEvoy, supra n83.

87 *Newfoundland Act, 1998*, supra n79.

88 Newfoundland and Labrador, Department of Education, 'Religious Education: Interim Edition.' Available at http://www.cdli.ca/depted/rel/toc.htm. Retrieved 5 May 2009.

89 Newfoundland and Labrador, Department of Education, *Religious Education 3101/3106. World Religions. A Curriculum Guide Interim Edition* (St John's: Author, 2004) [hereinafter 'World Religions']. Also available at:

http://www.ed.gov.nl.ca/edu/k12/curriculum/guides/religion/
rel_ed3101_3106.pdf. retrieved 5 May 2009.

90 Discussion in this paragraph owes much to W.J. Smith, W.F. Foster, & H.M.
Donahue, 'The Transformation of Educational Governance in Quebec: A
Reform Whose Time Has Finally Come,' (1999) 34(3) *McGill Journal of
Education* 207. Also, see their 'Systemic Education Reform in Quebec: How
Far Have We Come? Where Are We Headed?' (2000) 14 (2) *EAF Journal* 12.

91 L.A. Bracken, 'School Reform in Quebec, Canada: A Multi-faceted
Approach." (2005) [unpublished paper]. On file with J.C. Long.

92 (1993) 2 S.C.R. 511 [hereinafter *Reference re Quebec Education Act*].

93 S.Q. 1988, c. 84.

94 The increasing secularization of Canadian society and that Quebec leads the
country in the abandonment of religious adherence and practice, especially
since the 1960s, is documented and examined in a number of sources. See,
e.g., L.W. Roberts et al., *Recent Social Trends in Canada, 1960–2000* (Montreal &
Kingston: McGill-Queen's University Press, 2005); R.W. Bibby, *Unknown Gods:
The Ongoing Story of Religion in Canada* (Toronto: Stoddart, 1993), and G. Baum
'Catholicism and Secularization in Quebec,' in D. Lyon & M. Van Die, eds.,
Rethinking Church, State and Modernity: Canada between Europe and America
(Toronto: University of Toronto Press, 2000) 87.

95 *Constitutional Amendment, 1999 (Quebec)*, supra n81. D. Young & L.
Bezeau, 'Moving from Denominational to Linguistic Education in
Quebec,' (2003) 24 *Canadian Journal of Educational Administration and Policy*.
Available at http://www.umanitoba.ca/publications/cjeap/articles/
youngbezeau.html. Retrieved 5 May 2009.

96 Smith, Foster, & Donahue, supra n90 at 3.

97 [2001] S.C.J. No. 14 [hereinafter *OECTA*]. For a case comment, see G.M.
Dickinson, 'Unanimous Supreme Court Refuses to Permit Denominational Rights Claims to Invalidate Ontario's Education Funding Model,'
(2003) 12 *Education & Law Journal* 109. See also Dickinson, 'Looking into
the Foggy Mirror of Denominational School Rights in Ontario,' (1999) 9
Education & Law Journal 115 [hereinafter 'Looking into the Foggy Mirror'].

98 S.O. 1997, c. 31

99 *OECTA*, supra n97 at §49.

100 [2000] 2 S.C.R. 409 [hereinafter *Public School Boards Association*]. Available
at http://www.lexum.umontreal.ca/csc-scc. Retrieved 5 May 2009.

101 (2002), 213 D.L.R. (4th) 308 (Ont. S.C.J.) [hereinafter *Hall*]. Available at
http://www.samesexmarriage.ca/docs/MacKinnon_Hall.pdf (cited to
on-line manuscript). Retrieved 5 May 2009. For extensive comment, see
J.K. Donlevy, 'Re-visiting Denominational Cause and Denominational

Breach in Canada's Constitutionally Protected Catholic Schools,' 15 *Education & Law Journal* 85, and Z. Oxaal, 'Second-Guessing the Bishop: Section 93, the *Charter* and the "Religious Government Actor" in the Gay Prom Date Case,' (2003) 66 *Saskatchewan Law Review* 445.

102 *Hall*, ibid., at 9 [on-line manuscript].

103 Ibid.

104 Ibid.

105 Ibid., at 10.

106 Oxaal, supra n101 at 479.

107 (1979) 89 D.L.R. (3d) 445 (Ont. C.A.) [hereinafter *Porter*].

108 (1984) 5 D.L.R. (4th) 665 (Ont. C.A) [hereinafter *Tremblay-Webster*].

109 (1987) 51 Alta. L.R. (2d) 349 (Alta. Q.B.) [hereinafter *Casagrande*].

110 [1993] N.H.R.B.I.D. No. 1 (Nfld. H.R.T.) [hereinafter *Kearley*].

111 [1997] O. J. No. 5040 (Ont. Ct. Gen. Div) [hereinafter *Daly*]; aff'd [1999] 44 O.R. (3d) 349 (Ont. C.A.); application for leave to appeal denied [1999] S.C.C.A. No. 321.

112 See, e.g., K. Roach, *The Supreme Court on Trial: Judicial Activism or Democratic Dialogue?* (Toronto: Irwin Law, 2001).

113 Smith & Foster, supra n33 at 248. It is interesting at this point to note that religious instruction will have ceased in Quebec public schools as of the year 2008 by virtue of Bill 95, approved by the National Assembly in the summer of 2005.

114 Smith & Foster, ibid., at 60.

115 Ibid.

6 The Teacher in Dissent: Freedom of Expression and the Classroom

1 This chapter was first presented as a paper for the 2005 CAPSLE conference, 'Law as an Agent of Change in Education,' in Regina, Saskatchewan. The author is grateful for the helpful comments and fruitful discussion which arose out of that conference.

2 *R. v. Keegstra*, [1990] 3 S.C.R. 697 [hereinafter *Keegstra*], McLachlin J (dissenting) at § 171. *Keegstra* involved a teacher who perpetuated racist views in the classroom and was prosecuted criminally for hate speech. The Supreme Court of Canada upheld the hate speech laws against a s.2(b) challenge in that case, though the case was not specifically analysed in the education context. McLachlin J did not agree with the majority on the results of the case, but her overall comments about freedom of expression have been generally treated as the Court's most significant statement of principle on the subject.

3 These are summarized in *Keegstra*, ibid., at § 181.

4 *R. v. Sharpe*, [2001] 1 S.C.R. 45 [hereinafter *Sharpe*] at § 25.

5 *Keegstra*, supra n2.

6 *R. v. Mara*, [1997] 2 S.C.R. 630 [hereinafter *Mara*].

7 *Sharpe*, supra n4.

8 *Keegstra*, supra n2 at §§ 35–8.

9 *R. v. Butler*, [1992] 1 S.C.R. 452 [hereinafter *Butler*].

10 *R. v. Guignard*, [2002] 1 S.C.R. 472 [hereinafter *Guignard*].

11 *Little Sisters Book and Art Emporium* v. *Canada (Minister of Justice)*, [2000] 2 S.C.R. 1120 [hereinafter *Little Sisters Book and Art Emporium*].

12 *Irwin Toy Ltd.* v. *Quebec (Attorney General)*, [1989] 1 S.C.R. 927 [hereinafter *Irwin Toy*] at §§ 47–53. This case dealt with Quebec legislation limiting advertisements aimed at children; the Court found that the restrictions violated s.2(b), but that the violation was justified.

13 *Dagenais* v. *Canadian Broadcasting Corp.*, [1994] 3 S.C.R. 835 [hereinafter *Dagenais*].

14 *R.W.D.S.U., Local 558* v. *Pepsi-Cola Canada Beverages (West) Ltd.*, [2002] 1 S.C.R. 156 [hereinafter *R.W.D.S.U.*].

15 After the often-cited decision in *R. v. Oakes*, [1986] 1 S.C.R. 103 [hereinafter *Oakes*], in which the test was developed. The test summarized herein has been refined somewhat since *Oakes*.

16 P. Clarke, 'Canadian Public School Teachers and Free Speech: Part I – An Introduction,' (1998) 8 *Education & Law Journal* 297 [hereinafter Clarke Part I]; P. Clarke, 'Canadian Public School Teachers and Free Speech: Part II – An Employment Law Analysis,' (1999) 9 *Education & Law Journal* 43 [hereinafter Clarke Part II]; P. Clarke, 'Canadian Public School Teachers and Free Speech: Part III – Constitutional Law Analysis,' (1999) 9 *Education & Law Journal* 315 [hereinafter Clarke Part III].

17 [1996] 1 S.C.R. 825 [hereinafter *Ross*].

18 The implications of *Ross* continue to be highly relevant to teachers, and are still controversial. The case of British Columbia teacher Christopher Kempling, who was suspended for publishing anti-homosexual opinions in local media, continues to test the limits of the principles espoused in *Ross*; see *Kempling* v. *British Columbia College of Teachers*, 2004 BCCA 535 [hereinafter *Kempling*].

19 *Morin* v. *Prince Edward Island Regional Administrative Unit No. 3 School Board*, (2002) 213 D.L.R. (4th) 17 (P.E.I.S.C.A.D.) [hereinafter *Morin*].

20 Damages were originally set at $15,000 in a subsequent trial level decision: *Morin* v. *Prince Edward Island Regional Administrative Unit No. 3 School Board*

(2004), 233 Nfld. & P.E.I.R. 271 (P.E.I.S.C.T.D.) [hereinafter *Morin Damages*]. That damage award was increased to $75,000 on appeal: (2005), 254 D.L.R. (4th) 410 (P.E.I.S.C.A.D.) [hereinafter *Morin Damages Appeal*]. The Appeal Court found that the original damage 'did not, in a meaningful way, vindicate the rights and freedoms of the appellant.'

21 *Morin*, supra n19 at § 221.
22 Ibid., at §§ 231–2.
23 Ibid., at § 232.
24 Ibid., at § 242.
25 Ibid., at § 75.
26 Ibid., at § 63. The majority chooses to recognize a line of American cases which stand for this principle; in reality, the American jurisprudence is somewhat divided on the issue.
27 Ibid., at § 96.
28 Ibid., at § 67.
29 *Hamilton-Wentworth District School Board*, [2002] O.L.R.D. No. 2676 (O.L.R.B.) [hereinafter *Hamilton-Wentworth*].
30 Ibid., at § 49.
31 *British Columbia Public School Employers' Assn. and B.C.T.F. (Re)*, (2004), 129 L.A.C. (4th) 245 (Arbitrator Munroe) [hereinafter *B.C. Public School Employers' Association*]; upheld 2005 BCCA 393 (B.C.C.A.) [hereinafter *B.C. Public School Employers' Association Appeal*].
32 *B.C. Public School Employers' Association*, ibid., at 257–66.
33 *B.C. Public School Employers' Association Appeal*, supra n31 at § 19.
34 Ibid., at § 72.
35 Ibid., at § 67.
36 Ibid., at § 72.
37 Ibid., at §§ 83–4.
38 Ibid., at §§ 92 and 101.
39 In *Morin*, that evidence may well have been available had the school board chosen to put on a s.1 case.
40 See, e.g., the debate between the present author and Rod Dolmage and Paul Clarke in a set of articles on this topic: R. Dolmage & P. Clarke, 'Copyright Ownership of Teacher-Prepared Teaching Materials: An Examination of Issues in the Contemporary Context,' (Feb. 2002) 11 *Education & Law Journal* 321; K. Kindred, 'Copyright Ownership of Teacher-Prepared Teaching Materials: A Response to Dolmage and Clarke,' (Nov. 2003) 13 *Education & Law Journal* 299. Each side in this debate recognizes that the degree of control exercised by the teacher

and school board over the classroom is relevant to the determination of this question.

7 School Searches and Student Rights under the *Charter*: Old Wine in New Bottles

1 393 U.S. 503 (1969) [hereinafter *Tinker*].
2 Ibid., at 506.
3 478 U.S. 675 (1986) [hereinafter *Fraser*].
4 484 U.S. 260, 108 S. Ct. 562 (1988) [hereinafter *Hazelwood*].
5 The controversy concerned teen pregnancy, birth control, and divorce.
6 *Fraser*, supra n3 at 682.
7 N. Findlay, 'Students' Rights, Freedom of Expression and Prior Restraint: The *Hazelwood* Decision,' (2000–01) 11 *Education & Law Journal* 343, at 352.
8 See, e.g., A.W. MacKay, *Education Law in Canada* (Toronto: Emond Montgomery, 1984) at 30, and G. Dickinson & A.W. MacKay, eds., *Rights, Freedoms and the Education System in Canada* (Toronto: Emond Montgomery, 1989) at 304, 318.
9 [1971] 4 W.W.R. 161 (Sask. Q.B.) [hereinafter *Ward*].
10 R. Stamp, *The Schools of Ontario, 1876–1976* (Toronto: University of Toronto Press, 1982), at 227. Educational historian Robert Stamp observed that '[as] late as 1967, most Ontario high schools banned miniskirts, beads and long hair, smoking, holding hands, and participation in school-based radical political clubs.'
11 *Ward*, supra n9 at 185.
12 *Re Nicholson and Haldimand-Norfolk Regional Board of Com'rs of Police*, [1979] 1 S.C.R. 311 (S.C.C.) [hereinafter *Nicholson*]. In this landmark case, the Supreme Court of Canada held that it was inappropriate for courts to decline jurisdiction to review actions of statutory decision-makers based on a questionable dichotomy between quasi-judicial and administrative acts. Even so-called purely administrative acts that affect individuals' rights and interests should be subject to judicial review to ensure that the affected parties have been given at least notice and a reasonable opportunity – oral or written – to make their cases.
13 *Ward*, supra n9 at 186.
14 The same cannot be claimed in matters of religion – at least regarding confessional practices and curriculum in public schools. Ontario courts, e.g., have used *Charter* analysis to secularize public schools and legally reverse the educational agenda of Ontario schools – established in the mid-nineteenth century and reinforced in the Hope Commission Report of

1950 – of teaching a 'common Christianity' to students. See G.M. Dickinson & W.R. Dolmage, 'Education, Religion, and the Courts in Ontario,' (1996) 21 *Canadian Journal of Education* 363.

15 A.W. MacKay, 'The Canadian *Charter* of Rights and Freedoms: Implications for Students' [hereinafter 'Implications for Students'], in M. Manley-Casimir & T. Sussel, eds., *Courts in the Classroom: Education and the Charter of Rights and Freedoms* (Calgary: Detselig, 1986) 9 at 10.

16 Ibid., at 10–11 and 13.

17 I develop this point in Dickinson, 'The *Charter of Rights* and Educational Governance: Much Ado about Nothing?' in J. De Groof et al., eds., *Governance of Educational Institutions in South Africa: Into the New Millennium* (Ghent: Mys & Bressch, 2000) 225.

18 West coined the term 'moral panic' in describing public attitudes to media reports of school violence: see W. West, 'Escalating Problem or Moral Panic? A Critical Perspective,' (1993) 24 *Orbit* 6. In his acclaimed history of Ontario education between 1950 and the late 1990s, Gidney concurs that this moral panic helped define the Harris era, although he concludes that the public's concern was not entirely unjustified: see R. Gidney, *From Hope to Harris: The Reshaping of Ontario's Schools* (Toronto: University of Toronto Press, 1999), at 181.

19 Indeed, in commenting on a school search that occurred in Edmonton in the year of the *Charter*'s proclamation, MacKay noted that, despite the school board's backing the principal, the 'possibility of *Charter* violations was ... raised' by parents contemplating court action. See 'Implications for Students,' supra n15 at 10.

20 Available online at http://www.allthingswilliam.com/home.html. Last retrieved 5 May 2009.

21 (1765), 95 E.R. 807 (K.B.) [hereinafter *Entick*].

22 [1984] 2 S.C.R. 145 [hereinafter *Hunter*].

23 389 U.S. 347 (1967) [hereinafter *Katz*].

24 *Hunter*, supra n22 at 159–60.

25 R. Sharpe, K. Swinton, & K. Roach, *The Charter of Rights and Freedoms*, 2nd ed. (Toronto: Irwin Law, 2002).

26 K. Roach, *Criminal Law*, 2nd ed. (Toronto: Irwin Law, 2000). See also D. Stuart, 'The Unfortunate Dilution of Section 8 Protection: Some Teeth Remain,' (1999) 25 *Queen's Law Journal* 65.

27 Sharpe et al., supra n25.

28 William F. Foster is the Sir William Macdonald Professor of Law and Associate Provost (Policies & Procedures), McGill University, Montreal. He has written widely about Education Law in the *Education & Law Journal*

and elsewhere and is a founding member of the Canadian Association for the Practical Study of Law in Education (CAPSLE).

29 Unsurprisingly, by the time the first constitutional challenge of a student search occurred in Canada a number of U.S. cases existed; one at the Supreme Court level provided much of the judicial reasoning underpinning subsequent Canadian jurisprudence on the subject. See *New Jersey* v. *T.L.O.*, 469 U.S. 325 (1985) [hereinafter *T.L.O.*].

30 (1987), 33 D.L.R. (4th) 277, 56 O.R. (2d) 705 (Ont. C.A.) [hereinafter *J.M.G.*].

31 Ibid., at 281.

32 (1998), 166 D.L.R. (4th) 261, [1998] 3 S.C.R. 393 [hereinafter *M.R.M.*].

33 That the actions of school boards and their employees are subject to *Charter* review is no longer seriously contested.

34 *T.L.O.*, supra n29 at 340.

35 Ibid.

36 Ibid., at 347.

37 Ibid., at 341.

38 Ibid., at 342.

39 Ibid., at 343.

40 *J.M.G.*, supra n30 at 281.

41 Ibid., at 283.

42 Ibid., at 282.

43 S. AvRuskin, 'In Defence of Young Offenders: Search and Seizure in Schools –A Scholarly Reduction of Young Persons' Rights,' (Sept. 1987) 8 *Ontario Criminal Lawyers' Association Newsletter* 19, at 20.

44 Ibid.

45 A.W. MacKay, 'Students as Second Class Citizens under the *Charter*,' (1987) 54 *C.R.* (3d) 390 [hereinafter 'Students as Second Class'].

46 Ibid., at 398.

47 Ibid., at 397. His words were portentous as *M.R.M* and other cases proved: see *R.* v. *Samms*, Action 1985 No. C.B. 573 (unreported Nfld. S.C.) [hereinafter *Samms*]; see also *R.* v. *W.(J.J.)*, Action 1988 No. C.B. 196 (Nfld. S.C.) [hereinafter *W.(J.J.)*]; see also *R.* v. *Z.(S.M.)* [1988] M.J. No. 81 (Man. Q.B.) [hereinafter *Z.(S.M.)*]; and see also *R.* v. *H.(M.)* (26 June 1986), (Alta. Q.B.) [unreported – No. 8503-04478-S2] [hereinafter *H.(M.)*].

48 'Students as Second Class,' supra n45 at 394.

49 Ibid., at 395.

50 G.M. Dickinson, 'Principals and Criminal Investigations of Students: Recent Developments,' (1989) 14 *Canadian Journal of Education* 203 [hereinafter 'Recent Developments'] at 216 (emphasis added).

51 Ibid., at 216–17.

52 See S. Colman & A. Otten, *The Intersection of the Safe Schools Act and the YCJA* (Toronto: Ontario Principal's Council, 2005).

53 See, e.g., *Samms*, supra n47; see also *W.(J.J.)*, supra n47; and see also *Z.(S.M.)*, supra n47.

54 See, e.g., *R. v. Johnson* (1997), 48 C.R.R. (2d) 176 (Ont. Ct. Prov. Div.) [hereinafter *Johnson*], where the Court excluded evidence under s.24(2) of the *Charter* because a putative school search had really been a police search, the judge having found that the police had enlisted the principal 'as their agent to do a search that they were not entitled to do.'

The Court distinguished *J.M.G.* regarding the right to counsel on detention: 'the presence of two police officers in the principal's office ... makes it clear that the defendant was under their control as well as the principal's.' Hence, the student had a s.10 right to counsel. Although the presence of the police was a determining fact for this judge, it was not for the Supreme Court of Canada in *M.R.M.* (see discussion below). In a second case, *R. v. J.R.G.*, (25 June 1991), No. 1731 (B.C. Youth Court) [hereinafter *J.R.G.*], the court appeared to pick up on Justice Grange's dicta in *J.M.G.* envisioning a transmogrification of sorts at the point an investigating principal determines that 'heinous misconduct' is involved and 'significant legal consequences' are 'inevitable.' The principal is thereupon transformed from a state agent performing educational duties to an agent of the criminal justice system who has decided (likely with no choice) to hold the student for the police and turn over all evidence to them.

The salient portion of the *J.R.G.* court's unreported reasons on this point are summarized as follows by the British Columbia Civil Liberties Association: 'the court suggested that school officials should treat allegations of wrongdoing in one of two ways: as a matter of internal school discipline in which they have authority to conduct the investigation or as a criminal matter in which they should allow the police to undertake the investigation ... [T]he court was concerned that the school officials in effect misled the student into providing the evidence *while knowing that they intended to treat the incident as a criminal matter* without telling the student' (emphasis added). British Columbia Civil Liberties Association, *BCCLA Position Paper: Civil Liberties in the Schools*, 1997. Available online at: www.bccla.org/positions/children/97schools.html. Last retrieved 5 January 2009.

55 I have commented on both the Court of Appeal and Supreme Court of Canada decisions in this case: see 'Searching for Reason,' (1996–98) 8 *Education & Law Journal* 441 [hereinafter 'Searching for Reason'], and 'Still Searching for Reason,' (2000–01) 10 *Education & Law Journal* 125 [hereinafter 'Still Searching for Reason'].

56 Quoted by Major J. (dissenting) in *M.R.M.*, supra n32 at 292.

57 Utilitarianism wedded to moral and political panic – whether generated intentionally or not by the government or the media – is a dangerous foe of personal liberty and rights. Thomas Berger recounts the examples of the Second World War internment of Japanese Canadians and the abuse of *War Measures Act* powers by the police in places and circumstances having nothing to do with the expressed reason for invoking the *Act* – the FLQ 'crisis' in Quebec. Most disturbing was the apparent 'indifference of the great public' to these serious abridgments of civil liberties and legal rights. See T. Berger, *Fragile Freedoms: Human Rights and Dissent in Canada* (Toronto: Clarke, Irwin, 1981).

58 A.W. MacKay, 'Don't Mind Me, I'm from the R.C.M.P.: *R. v. M.(M.R.)* – Another Brick in the Wall between Students and their Rights,' (1997) 7 C.R. (5th) 24 [hereinafter 'Another Brick'].

59 'Students as Second Class,' supra n45.

60 'Searching for Reason,' supra n55.

61 'Still Searching for Reason,' supra n55 at 127.

62 [1991] 3 S.C.R. 595 [hereinafter *Broyles*].

63 Ibid., at 608.

64 *M.R.M.*, supra n32 at 276.

65 Ibid., at 278. Stuart, supra n26, decries the *Hunter* rule's erosion through the courts' identification, using 'contextual analysis,' of several circumstances and places (including schools) in which a lesser 'reasonable expectation of privacy' is said to exist.

66 *M.R.M.*, ibid., at 279.

67 'Still Searching for Reason', supra n55 at 129–30. See also R. Dolmage, 'One Less Brick in the Wall: The Myths of Youth Violence and Unsafe Schools,' (1995–96) 7 *Education & Law Journal* 185, and 'Lies, Damned Lies, and Statistics: The Media's Treatment of Youth Violence,' (2000–01) 10 *Education & Law Journal* 1 [hereinafter 'Lies, Damned Lies'].

68 *M.R.M.*, supra n32 at 284–5 (emphasis added).

69 'Still Searching for Reason,' supra n55 at 132.

70 *M.R.M.*, supra n32 at 290.

71 For example, the Ontario Ministry of Education's *Ontario Schools Code of Conduct* (Toronto: Ministry of Education, 2000) [hereinafter *Code of Conduct*] and *Provincial Model for a Local Police/School Board Protocol* (Toronto: Ministry of Education, 2003) [hereinafter *Local Protocol*] list several occurrences that must result in police involvement, including drug offences. Most of these are also grounds for mandatory expulsion under the safe schools amendments to the *Education Act*: see *Education Act*, R.S.O. 1990, c. E.2, s.309.

72 'Still Searching for Reason,' supra n55 at 134. Section 56 of the *Young Offenders Act*, R.S.C. 1985, c. Y-1 was applied to a principal in *H.(M.)*, supra n47.

73 See S. Tracey, 'Student's Drug Charge Thrown Out,' *[Kitchener] Record* (5 February 2001) B10. The discussion of the case is taken from this news account.

74 [2004] O.J. No. 2716 (Ont. C.J.) [hereinafter *A.M.*].

75 Ibid., at § 16.

76 As far as I can determine it was not the British Columbia Court of Appeal but the Supreme Court of British Columbia that made this observation in *R. v. G.A.W.* [1996] B.C.J. No. 2329 (B.C.S.C.) [hereinafter *G.A.W.*].

77 *A.M.*, supra n74 at § 25. In a subsequent British Columbia case, *R. v. M.W.S.* [2005] B.C.J. No. 1270 (B.C. Prov. Ct. Youth Div.) [hereinafter *M.W.S.*] at § 63, Seidemann J spoke approvingly of Justice Hornblower's refusal to adulterate *Charter* protections by admitting evidence simply because of the school context: 'To admit the evidence would be to say that the protections from unreasonable search of all the students are really of no worth in a school setting, and that is a wrong message to send' (at § 63).

78 (2006), 79 O.R. (3d) 481 (Ont. C.A.).

79 2008 S.C.C. 19. Two justices ruled that no *Charter* search had taken place, seven justices ruled a *Charter* search had taken place and that it violated section 8. Six justices ruled that the illegally obtained evidence should be excluded under section 24(2) whereas one ruled it should be admitted.

80 I had the good fortune to teach Justice Hornblower more than twenty years ago at the Faculty of Law at the University of Western Ontario; but I do not pretend that this has anything to do with the judicial wisdom he displayed here!

81 *T.L.O.*, supra n29 at 385.

82 'Students as Second Class,' supra n45 at 400.

83 Ibid.

84 Ibid.

85 Quoted in Berger, supra n57 at 217.

86 'Another Brick in the Wall,' supra n58 at 32.

87 *Miranda v. Arizona*, 384 U.S. 436 (1966) [hereinafter *Miranda*] is the celebrated or infamous (depending on one's perspective) U.S. Supreme Court ruling that suspects in police custody are constitutionally entitled, prior to interrogation, to be advised of their right to remain silent; that anything they say may be used against them in court; and, that they

have a right to consult with a lawyer and have the lawyer present during interrogation.

88 See *Local Protocol*, supra n71. A local board protocol shall '[s]pecify that school personnel should not conduct searches of persons.'

8 Corporal Punishment and Education: Oh Canada! Spare Us!

1 *R. v. Peterson*, (1995), 98 C.C.C. (3d) 253 (Ont. C.J. Prov. Div.) [hereinafter *Peterson*].

2 A.M. Watkinson, 'Children Still Unprotected From Violence,' *Saskatoon Star Phoenix* (11 May 1995) A11. See also A.M. Watkinson, 'Prohibiting Corporal Punishment: In the Name of the Charter, the Child and Societal Values' [hereinafter 'Prohibiting Corporal Punishment'] in S. Natale, ed., *The Management of Values: Organizational and Educational Issues* (Boston: University Press of America, 1998). See also Watkinson, 'Suffer the Little Children Who Come into School' [hereinafter 'Suffer the Little Children'], in J. Ross Epp & A.M. Watkinson, eds., *Systemic Violence: How Schools Hurt Children* (London: Falmer, 1996).

3 R.S.C. 1985, c. C-46 [hereinafter *Criminal Code*].

4 Ibid., at s.43.

5 Part I of the *Constitution Act, 1982*, being Schedule B to the *Canada Act 1982* (U.K.), 1982, c.11 [hereinafter *Charter*].

6 The Court Challenges Program was a federal program designed to assist individuals and groups in challenging federal laws and policies that violated their constitutional equality rights. It was a program that gained international praise through the United Nations but was dismantled by the Conservative government in 2006.

7 *Canadian Foundation for Children, Youth and the Law* v. *Canada (Attorney General)*, [2004] 1 S.C.R. 76 [hereinafter *Canadian Foundation*]. Also available at http://www.lexum.umontreal.ca/csc-scc/en/index.html. Last retrieved 5 May 2009.

8 H. Weiner, 'Teachers and Section 43: What Does the High Court's Decision Mean to Teachers?' (2004) 38(11) *Alberta Teachers' Association News* 3 at 3.

9 W. Blackstone, *Commentaries on the Law of England* (Baton Rouge: Claitors, 1915) at 453.

10 A. McGillivray, 'Child Physical Assault: Law, Equality and Intervention,' (2004) 30 *Manitoba Law Journal* 133, at 137–9. See also A. McGillivray, '"He'll Learn It on His Body": Disciplining Childhood in Canadian Law,' (1998) 5 *International Journal of Children's Rights* 193 [hereinafter 'He'll Learn It'];

G. Ryley Scott, *The History of Corporal Punishment: A Survey of Flagellation in Its Historical, Anthropological and Sociological Aspects* (London: Luxor, 1959).

11 'He'll Learn It,' supra n10 at 206–10. At one time, English and Canadian common law allowed for the beating of wives and servants by their husbands and masters, a legal entitlement that ended in the 1860s.

12 M.A Strauss & D.A. Donnelly, 'Corporal Punishment of Adolescents by American Parents,' (1993) 24 *Youth and Society* 419, at 420.

13 J.E. Durrant, R. Ensom, & Coalition on Physical Punishment of Children and Youth, *Joint Statement on Physical Punishment of Children and Youth* (Ottawa: Coalition on Physical Punishment of Children and Youth, 2004).

14 W.K. Mohr, T.A. Petti & B.D. Mohr, 'Adverse Effects Associated with Physical Restraint,' (2003) 48 *Canadian Journal of Psychiatry* 330, at 330.

15 Durrant et al., supra n13 at 2.

16 S.M. Turner, *Something to Cry About: An Argument against Corporal Punishment of Children in Canada* (Waterloo: Wilfrid Laurier University Press, 2002).

17 Ibid., at 16.

18 Ibid.

19 *Canadian Teachers' Federation Handbook, 2003–2004* [hereinafter *CTF Handbook*] at art. 5.4.

20 Canadian Teachers' Federation Factum filed with Supreme Court of Canada, 2004 [hereinafter CTF Factum] at § 18.

21 Sections 34–37 of the *Criminal Code* are defences in cases where one is protecting himself or herself or another from assault, sections 43–45 provide defences for those in authority to carry out their tasks. In addition there are the common law defences of necessity which excuses breaches of law, 'where the harm done by breaking the law is less than the harm that would have been done by obeying the law' (see McGillivray, supra n10 at fn3).

22 CTF Factum, supra n20 at § 59.

23 Ibid., at § 61.

24 The majority decision was written by Chief Justice Beverly McLachlin and was concurred with by Justice Charles Gonthier (since retired), Justice Frank Iacobucci, Justice John Major, Justice Michel Bastarache, and Justice Louis LeBel. The dissenting judges were Justice Louise Arbour, Justice Ian Binnie, and Justice Marie Deschamps. The dissenting judges each wrote their own minority decisions.

25 The Coalition is made up of the following right-wing conservative religious organizations: Focus on the Family (Canada) Association; Canada Family Action Coalition; the Home School Legal Defence Association of Canada; and REAL (Realistic, Equal and Active for Life) Women of Canada.

26 Bill C-15B, enacted 4 June 2002.
27 McGillivray, supra n10 at fn22. See s.446 of the *Criminal Code*. An earlier, anonymous reviewer questioned how the law could be written this way since it would mean that he could not 'tug on his dog's leash without fear of criminal sanctions.' In effect he is correct but the chances of him being prosecuted are minimal if at all. On the other hand, if there is no defence for owners of animals or birds who wilfully cause pain, suffering, or injury – why do we provide one for those who cause pain, suffering, or injury to children?
28 Section 43 came into being in 1892 with the codification of Canada's first *Criminal Code*. The wording has changed little over this time.
29 *R. v. Wetmore*, (1996), 172 N.B.R. (2d) 224 (N.B.Q.B.) [hereinafter *Wetmore*].
30 *R. v. Caouette*, [2002] Q.J. No.1055 (Que. Crim. Ct.) [hereinafter *Caouette*].
31 *R. v. Skidmore*, No. 8414/00, June 27, 2000 (Ont. C.J.) [hereinafter *Skidmore*]. These cases and others were referred to in Justice Arbour's dissenting opinion. See also cases cited in A.M. Watkinson, *Education, Student Rights and the Charter* (Saskatoon: Purich, 1999) [hereinafter *Education, Student Rights and the Charter*] at c. 11.
32 *R. v. Holmes*, (31 August 2000), Campbell's Bay, Que. No. 555-01-0267-998 (Prov. Ct.) [hereinafter *Holmes*]. See Repeal 43 Committee website for more cases at http://www.repeal43.org. Last retrieved 5 May 2009.
33 *Canadian Foundation*, supra n7 at § 1.
34 Ibid., at § 2.
35 M. Carter, 'The Constitutional Validity of the Corporal Punishment Defence in Canada: A Critical Analysis of *Canadian Foundation for Children, Youth and the Law versus Canada (Attorney General)*,' (2005) 12 *International Journal of Victimology* 189, at 201.
36 I applied for funding from the Court Challenges Program to research the constitutionality of s.43 as it relates to the equality rights of children. As a result, I was successful in obtaining $45,000 to challenge this section. However, I could not take the case forward on my own and was required to find an organization that had a history of working with children and youth and experience in equality rights cases. I selected the Canadian Foundation for Children Youth and the Law, an Ontario-based organization, since there was no other organization that I knew of with a history in both areas. In fact, they had tried twice to intervene at the Supreme Court level on cases involving the physical punishment of children so as to challenge the constitutionality of s.43 (*R. v. Halcrow*, [1993] B.C.J. No 1227 (B.C.C.A.) [hereinafter *Halcrow*]; *R. v. K.(M.)* (1993) 16 C.R. 121 (Man. C.A.) [hereinafter *K.(M.)*].

37 The text of s.7 is included in Appendix A.

38 The text of s.12 is included in Appendix A.

39 The text of s.15 is included in Appendix A.

40 *Canadian Foundation*, supra n7 at § 50.

41 Ibid., at § 62.

42 *Education, Student Rights and the Charter*, supra n31 at 143.

43 In *Canadian Foundation*, the Court noted at § 5 that '[i]t is a principle of fundamental justice that accused persons must be accorded adequate procedural safeguards in the criminal process.' In the case of *R. v. Nova Scotia Pharmaceutical Society*, [1992] 1 S.C.R. 606 [hereinafter *Nova Scotia Pharmaceutical*], the Supreme Court affirmed that the principles of fundamental justice are not met when a law is too vague. The Court said at 639: '[a] vague provision does not ... sufficiently eliminate any area of risk, and thus can provide neither fair notice to the citizen nor a limitation of enforcement discretion.'

44 *Canadian Foundation*, supra n7 at § 4.

45 Ibid., at § 6. This was an argument that struck me as odd considering it was the Crown who was leading the challenge to retain s.43.

46 Ibid.

47 *R. v. Malmo-Levine*, [2003] 3 S.C.R. 571 [hereinafter *Malmo-Levine*]. This decision was issued one month prior to the Court's ruling in *Canadian Foundation*. This meant that the new rules were not available when the case was originally argued before the Supreme Court in June 2003.

48 Ibid., cited in *Canadian Foundation*, supra n7 at § 8.

49 *Canadian Foundation*, ibid., at § 9.

50 Ibid., at § 8 citing *Rodriguez* v. *British Columbia (Attorney General)*, (1993) 3 S.C.R. 518 [hereinafter *Rodriguez*] at 590.

51 *Canadian Foundation*, ibid., at § 8.

52 Ibid., at § 10.

53 Ibid.

54 Ibid., at § 8.

55 Ibid., at § 191.

56 Ibid., at § 185.

57 Ibid., at § 196 referring to the Committee on the Rights of the Child, *Report on the Eighth Session*, 209th Mtg., UN Doc. CRC/C/38 (1995) § 218.

58 *Canadian Foundation*, ibid., at § 48.

59 Ibid., at §§ 23-38.

60 Ibid., at § 125. The use of corporal punishment on prisoners and sailors was removed from the *Criminal Code* in 1972 and 2001, respectively.

61 *Andrews* v. *Law Society of British Columbia*, [1989] 1 S.C.R. 143 [hereinafter *Andrews*] at 154.

62 Canadian Foundation for Children Youth and the Law Factum filed with the Supreme Court of Canada, 2003 [hereinafter Foundation Factum] at §§ 64–69. See also, 'Prohibiting Corporal Punishment,' supra n2. This chapter is a revised version of the paper I submitted to the Court Challenges Program as part of the research into the question of whether s.43 of the *Criminal Code* violated the equality rights of children.

63 The *Criminal Code* does not define the term 'child.' However, according to the *Convention on the Rights of the Child*, GA Res.44/25, UN GAOR, 44th Sess., Annex, Supp. No. 49, UN Doc. A/44/49 (1989) 167 (entered into force 2 September 1990), 'a child means every human being below the age of eighteen years unless, under the law applicable to the child, majority is attained earlier.' The age of 18 is used as the age of majority in Canada for purposes of voting. In addition, Saskatchewan legislation establishing the Children's Advocate defines children as being under the age of 18.

64 *McGillivray*, supra n10 at 140.

65 *Canadian Foundation for Children, Youth and the Law* v. *Canada (Attorney General)*, (2000) 188 D.L.R. (4th) 718 (Ont. Sup. Ct.) [hereinafter *Canadian Foundation Ontario Superior Court*] at §§ 130 and 131.

66 *Canadian Foundation for Children, Youth and the Law* v. *Canada (Attorney General)*, (2002), 207 D.L.R. (4th) 632 (Ont. C.A.) [hereinafter *Foundation Appeal*] at § 57. Also available at http://www.ontariocourts.on.ca/coa.en. Last retrieved 5 May 2009. For the text of s. 1 of the *Charter*, see Appendix A.

67 *Canadian Foundation*, supra n7 at § 50.

68 *Law* v. *Canada (Minister of Employment and Immigration)*, [1999] 1 S.C.R. 497 [hereinafter *Law*]. The case, brought forward by Ms. Law, a 30-year-old widow, examined the survivor benefits of the Canada Pension Plan that limited payouts to surviving spouses only if they were disabled, had dependent children, or were over the age of 35. The Court ruled the CPP provisions did not discriminate against Ms. Law on the basis of her age.

69 Ibid., at § 497.

70 B. Ryder, C. Fafia, & E. Lawrence, 'What's Law Good For? An Empirical Overview of Charter Equality Rights Decisions,' (2004) 24 *Supreme Court Law Review* (2d) 103; W. Black & L. Smith, 'The Equality Rights,' in W.A. Tarnopolsky, G.-A. Beaudoin, & E. Mendes, eds., *Canadian Charter of Rights and Freedoms* (Markham: LexisNexis, 2005) 927.

71 Ryder et al, ibid., at 105–6.

72 Ibid. The similarly situated test is another form of 'formal equality.' Aristotle's principle of the formal principle of equality states that 'things that are alike should be treated alike, while things that are unalike should

be treated unalike in proportion to their unalikeness' (Aristotle, *Ethica Nichomacia, Book V3*, trans. W.D. Ross (London: H. Milford, Oxford University Press, 1925)), at 1131a06, cited in Black & Smith, supra n70. The criticism facing this theory is that there are no identifiable variables to be used in determining what is or is not alike.

73 D. Greschner, 'Does Law Advance the Cause of Equality?' (2001) 27 *Queen's Law Journal* 299.

74 [1998] 1 S.C.R. 493 [hereinafter *Vriend*].

75 Greschner, supra n73 at 305.

76 J. Bakan, *Just Words: Constitutional Rights and Social Wrongs* (Toronto: University of Toronto Press, 1997) at 46–7, cited in Greschner, ibid., at 303.

77 Ryder et al., supra n70 at 106.

78 Ibid.

79 Ibid.

80 Greschner, supra n73 at 305.

81 Ryder et al., supra n70 at 107.

82 Carter, supra n35 at 205.

83 *Canadian Foundation*, supra n7 at § 91.

84 Ibid., at § 55. For further discussion of the contextual factors see Black & Smith, supra n70; Ryder et al., supra n70; and Greschner, supra n73.

85 *Canadian Foundation*, supra n7 at § 56.

86 Ibid.

87 See Ryder et al., supra n70 at 104, in which they review the record of the *Law* test and report that the 'correspondence' factor which they say 'restates the similarly situated test ... has functioned as the determinative factor in the Court's equality decisions since *Law*.'

88 *Canadian Foundation*, supra n7 at § 57 citing *Law* at § 70.

89 *Canadian Foundation*, ibid., at § 58.

90 Ibid., at § 51.

91 Ibid.

92 Ibid., at § 68.

93 J. Mosoff & I. Grant, (2005) 'Upholding Corporal Punishment: For Whose Benefit?' 31 *Manitoba Law Journal* 177 at fn17.

94 *Canadian Foundation*, supra n7 at § 51.

95 Ibid., at § 102.

96 Carter, supra n35 at 191.

97 Ibid.

98 *Canadian Foundation*, supra n7 at § 19.

99 Ibid., at § 135.

100 Ibid.

101 Ibid., at § 22.

102 Ibid.

103 Ibid., at § 24.

104 Ibid., at § 25.

105 In *Canadian Foundation*, ibid., at § 39, Chief Justice McLachlin recognized this when she said: 'On occasion judges erroneously applied their own subjective views on what constitutes reasonable disciplining – views as varied as different judges' backgrounds.'

106 The majority's decision, written by Chief Justice McLachlin did not provide any references to support their reliance on 'social consensus and expert evidence.'

107 *Canadian Foundation*, supra n7 at § 30.

108 Ibid., at § 40. Section 2 of Canada's *Criminal Code* refers to the words 'transient' and 'trifling' in the definition of 'bodily harm.' It states: '"bodily harm" means any hurt or injury to a person that interferes with the health or comfort of the person and that is more than merely transient or trifling in nature.'

109 *Covenant on Civil and Political Rights*, 16 December 1966, Can. T.S. 1976 No. 47 (entry into force 23 March 1976; in force for Canada, 19 August 1976).

110 *Canadian Foundation*, supra n7 at § 33.

111 Concluding Observations of the Committee on the Rights of the Child: CANADA (27 October 2003) UN Doc. CRC/C/15/Add.215 at § 33. Available at: http://www.unhcr.ch/html/menu2/6/crc/doc/co/ Canada%20co2.pdf. Last retrieved 5 May 2009.

112 Ibid., at § 45(d).

113 *Canadian Foundation*, supra n7 at §§ 25 & 40.

114 Ibid., at § 25.

115 Ibid.

116 Ibid.

117 Ibid., at §§ 37 & 40.

118 Ibid.

119 Ibid.

120 Ibid. at § 40.

121 Ibid.

122 Ibid., at § 38.

123 Ibid.

124 See CTF Factum, supra n20 for a counter-argument to this point. See also Justice Louise Arbour's dissent on this matter in *Canadian Foundation*, ibid., at § 143.

125 *R. c. G.B.*, [2004] J. Q. no. 4568 (Que. Crim. Ct.) [hereinafter *G.B.*]. This case
    made no distinction on the status of a day care worker as to whether they
    are teachers or acting in the place of a parent. However, in a subsequent
    case the same Quebec Court found that the Director and 'educatrice de
    garderie' of a day care are given the same entitlements as a parent; see
    R. c. Martineau, [2004] R.D.S.D. no 195 (Que. Crim. Ct.) [hereinafter
    Martineau]. For a discussion of both cases see http://www.repeal43.org.
    Last retrieved 5 May 2009.
126 Mohr et al., supra n14 at 331 citing the U.S. General Accounting Office,
    Mental Health: Improper Restraint or Seclusion Use Placed People at Risk, GAO
    publication HEH-99-176 (Washington, DC: USGAO, 1999).
127 Mohr et al., ibid., at 335.
128 Ibid.
129 'Spare the Rod, Spoil the Child,' *Maclean's* (10 March 1997) 50.
130 Bible: Proverbs 23:13–14. There are other quotations from Proverbs that
    are relied on to justify the physical punishment of children. See, e.g.: 'Rod
    and reprimand impart wisdom, but a boy who runs wild brings shame on
    his mother' (Proverbs 29:15); 'Correct your son, and he will be a comfort
    to you and bring you delights of every kind' (Proverbs 29:17).
131 The maxim is not a direct quote from the Bible but comes from what is
    described as a sado/masochistic seventeenth-century satire entitled
    Hudibras by Samuel Butler:
    > If matrimony and hanging go
    > By dest'ny, why not whipping too?
    > What med'cine else can cure the fits
    > Of lovers when they lose their wits?
    > Love is a boy by poets stil'd;
    > Then spare the rod and spoil the child.
    > (Part II Canto I)
132 J.C. Dobson, *The New Dare to Discipline* (Wheaton: Tyndale House, 1992).
133 The following are examples of Dobson's advice, ibid., at 51: 'I am recom-
    mending a simple principle: when you are defiantly challenged, win
    decisively'; ibid., at 64: 'I recommend [for spanking] a neutral object of
    some type ... I suggest a switch or paddle'; ibid., at 72: 'The spanking may
    be too gentle. If it doesn't hurt it isn't worth avoiding the next time. A slap
    with the hand on the bottom of a multi-diapered thirty-month old is not a
    deterrent to anything. While being careful not to go too far, you should
    ensure he feels the message.' These excerpts were cited in the Factum of
    the Ontario Association of Children's Aid Societies, Intervenor in the
    Canadian Foundation Appeal. More recently, on his website Dobson

responded to questions about using the hand to administer punishment. He again recommended a neutral object, such as the switch his own mother used on him, since the hand 'should be seen as an object of love – to hold, hug, pat and caress.' He also supports the use of corporal punishment of younger aged children in school. See http://www.fcs .utah.edu/-herrin/dobson.quotes.rtf. Last retrieved 5 May 2009. These excerpts were also cited in McGillivray, supra n10 at fn8.

134 E. Reilly, 'School Staff Facing Assault Charges,' *Toronto Star* (16 February 2008). Retrieved March 23, 2008 from http://www.thestar.com/News/GT.

135 *Universal Declaration of Human Rights*,10 December 1948, GA Res.217(III), UN GAOR, 3d Sess., Supp. No. 13, UN Doc. A/810 (1948) 71 at art. 26.

136 *International Covenant on Economic, Social and Cultural Rights*,16 December 1966, GA Res.2200A (XXI), UN Doc. A/6316 (1966), 993 U.N.T.S. 3 (entered into force on January 3, 1976) at art. 13.

137 *Convention on the Rights of the Child,* supra n63 at art. 29.

138 *Convention on the Elimination of all Forms of Discrimination Against Women,* 1 March 1980, Can. T.S. 1982 No. 31, 19 I.L.M. 33 at art. 10.

139 *Convention on the Elimination of all Forms of Racial Discrimination*, 21 December 1965, G.A. Res.2106 (XX), 660 U.N.T.S. 212 (signed by Canada 24 August 1966, entered into force 4 January 1969, ratified by Canada 14 October 1970) at art. 7.

140 See Durrant et al., supra n13; see also E. Gershoff, 'Corporal Punishment by Parents and Associated Child Behaviours and Experiences: A Meta-analytic and Theoretical Review,' (2002) 128 *Psychological Bulletin* 539; see also A. Grogan-Kaylor, 'The Effect of Corporal Punishment on Antisocial Behavior in Children,' (2004) 28 *Social Work Research* 153; see also N. Trocmé, *Canadian Incidence Study of Reported Child Abuse and Neglect: Final Report* (Ottawa: Health Canada, 2001).

141 Statistics Canada, 'National Longitudinal Survey of Children and Youth: Home Environment, Income and Child Behaviour,' *The Daily* (21 February 2005). Available at http://www.statscan.gc.ca/daily-quotidien/050221/dq050221b-eng.htm. Last retrieved 5 May 2009. The study involved 4,129 children aged 2–5 during the first collection of data in 1994–95, who were 10–13 during the collection period (2002–03) reported upon in this report. In the study at 3, Child Aggressive behaviour was measured by asking 'how often a child behaved or reacted in aggressive ways, such as whether they got into fights, or how often they bullied or were mean to others.'

142 Statistics Canada, 'Parenting Style and Children's Aggressive Behaviour,' *The Daily* (25 October 2004) [hereinafter 'Parenting Style']. Available at http://www.statscan.gc.ca/ daily-quotidien /041025/dq041025b-eng .htm. Last retrieved 5 May 2009.

143 C.P. Cohen, 'Beating Children Is as American as Apple Pie,' (Spring 1978) *Human Rights* 24, at 26.

144 See, e.g., V.I. Cherian, 'Corporal Punishment and Academic Achievement of Xhosa Children from Polygamous and Monogamous Families,' (1994) 134 *Journal of Social Psychology* 387.

145 See, e.g., J.E. Durrant & L. Rose-Krasnor, *Corporal Punishment: Research Review and Policy Recommendations* (Winnipeg: University of Manitoba Press, 1995).

146 See, e.g., Cohen, supra n143; H.A. Turner, 'Corporal Punishment as a Stressor among Youth,' (1996) 58 *Journal of Marriage and the Family* 155; H.L. MacMillan, 'Slapping and Spanking in Childhood and Its Association with Lifetime Prevalence of Psychiatric Disorders in a General Population Sample,' (1999) 161 *Canadian Medical Association Journal* 805.

9 Children's *Charter* Rights: A Slogan Still in Need of Judicial Definition

1 *Baker* v. *Canada (Minister of Citizenship and Immigration)*, [1999] 2 S.C.R. 817 [hereinafter *Baker*] at § 67.

2 *R.* v. *Sharpe*, [2001] 1 S.C.R. 45 [hereinafter *Sharpe*] at § 170.

3 Part I of the *Constitution Act, 1982*, being Schedule B of the *Canada Act, 1982* (U.K.), 1982, c. 11 [hereinafter *Charter*].

4 *Convention on the Rights of the Child*, GA Res. 44/25, UN GAOR, 44th Sess., Annex, Supp. No. 49, UN Doc. A/44/49 (1989) 167 (entered into force 2 September 1990) [hereinafter *Convention on the Rights of the Child*].

5 H. Rodham, 'Children under the Law,' (1973) 4 *Harvard Education Review* 487.

6 *Young* v. *Young*, [1993] 4 S.C.R. 3 [hereinafter *Young*]; *P.(D.)* v. *S.(C.)*, [1993] 4 S.C.R. 141 [hereinafter *P.(D.)*].

7 *D.B.S.* v. *S.R.G.; L.J.W.* v. *T.A.R.; Henry* v. *Henry; Hiemstra* v. *Hiemstra*, [2006] SCC 37 [hereinafter *D.B.S.*].

8 R.S.C. 1985, c. I-2.

9 The children in this case sought standing at two levels of court, but each time were denied, with costs being ordered against them at the Federal Court of Appeal.

10 [1998] 3 S.C.R. 393 [hereinafter *M.(M.R.)*] at 401–2.

11 [2008] S.C.C. 19 [hereinafter *A.M.*].

12 [2003] 1 S.C.R. 835 [hereinafter *Trociuk*].

13 Ibid., at § 31.

14 [2005] 3 S.C.R. 99 [hereinafter *R.C.*].

15 S.C. 2002, c. 1.

16 *R.C.*, supra n14 at § 41.

17 [2008] S.C.C. 25 [hereinafter *D.B.*].

18 [1997] 1 S.C.R. 241 [hereinafter *Eaton*].
19 A. Watkinson, *Education, Student Rights and the Charter* (Saskatoon: Purich, 1999), at 117.
20 [2004] 1 S.C.R. 76 [hereinafter *Canadian Foundation*].
21 Ibid., at § 53.
22 [1989] 1 S.C.R. 143 [hereinafter *Andrews*].
23 Ibid., at 164.
24 *Canadian Foundation*, supra n20 at § 68. This conclusion is drawn from the majority's reasoning with respect to the s.15 argument.
25 *McKinney* v. *University of Guelph*, [1990] 3 S.C.R. 229 [hereinafter *McKinney*], further established that there were important differences between age discrimination and the other grounds of discrimination found in s.15 of the *Charter*.
26 C. Smith, 'Children's Rights: Judicial Ambivalence and Social Resistance,' (1997) 11 *International Journal of Law, Policy & the Family* 103, at 109–10.
27 M. Carter, 'The Constitutional Validity of the Corporal Punishment Defence in Canada: A Critical Analysis of *Canadian Foundation for Children, Youth and the Law versus Canada (Attorney General)*,' (2005) 12 *International Review of Victimology* 189, at 199.
28 [2002] A.J. No. 1544 (Alta. Q.B.) [hereinafter *Fitzgerald*]; aff'd [2004] A.J. No. 570 (Alta. C.A.) [hereinafter *Fitzgerald Appeal*]; leave to appeal refused [2004] S.C.C.A. No. 349.
29 [2002] 3 S.C.R. 519 [hereinafter *Sauvé*]. This case held that denying federal prisoners the right to vote was unconstitutional.
30 *Fitzgerald*, supra n28 at §§ 61–2.
31 *Sauvé*, supra n29 at § 37.
32 Ibid., at § 14.
33 For example, Cory J for the majority of the Court in *M.(M.R.)*, supra n10, held that the compelled attendance of a student at a principal's office or some other form of restraint by a school authority is not to be considered detention for the purposes of s.10(b) of the *Charter*. Evidence obtained in the context was admissible against the student in a criminal prosecution.
34 *Youth Criminal Justice Act*, supra n15.
35 In *R.C.*, supra n14, the Court held that the *Youth Criminal Justice Act* requires greater privacy protections for young people than for adults in respect of DNA collection.
36 *D.B.*, supra n17 at § 62.
37 See *L.E.G.* v. *A.G.*, [2002] B.C.J. No. 2319 (B.C.S.C.) [hereinafter *L.E.G.*]; see also *C.U.* v. *McGonigle*, [2003] A.J. No. 238 (Alta. C.A.) [hereinafter *McGonigle*].
38 M. Freeman, *The Moral Status of Children: Essays on the Rights of the Child* (The Hague: Martinus Nijhoff, 1997), at 37.

39 See *R.* v. *Jones*, [1986] 2 S.C.R. 284 [hereinafter *Jones*].

40 See *B.(R.)* v. *Children's Aid Society of Metropolitan Toronto*, [1995] 1 S.C.R. 315 [hereinafter *B.(R.)*]; see also *Blencoe* v. *British Columbia (Human Rights Commission)*, [2000] 2 S.C.R. 307 [hereinafter *Blencoe*].

41 *A.C. et al* v. *Director of Child and Family Services [Manitoba]*, heard 20 May 2008, on reserve [hereinafter *A.C.*].

42 See *B.(R.)*, supra n40 at 433; see also *Young*, supra n6; and see also *P.(D.)*, supra n6.

43 K. Hunt Federle, 'Children's Rights and the Need for Protection,' (2000) 34 *Family Law Quarterly* 421, at 427; A.B. Smith, 'Interpreting and Supporting Participation Rights: Contributions form Sociocultural Theory,' (2002) 10 *International Journal of Children's Rights* 73, at 74 and 85.

44 *Eaton*, supra n18.

45 [2004] 1 S.C.R. 336 [hereinafter *McGonigle Supreme Court*].

46 *McGonigle*, supra n37.

47 *A.C.*, supra n41.

48 Smith, supra n26 at 120. It is worth noting that the Court took a similar approach to vulnerable adults in *Rodriguez* v. *British Columbia (Attorney General)*, [1993] 3 S.C.R. 519 [hereinafter *Rodriguez*], finding that the state paternalism inherent in a criminal prohibition against assisted suicide did not infringe the s.7 *Charter* rights of dying adults.

49 [2006] S.C.J. No. 6 [hereinafter *Multani*].

50 *B.(R.)*, supra n40.

51 Ibid., at § 86.

52 Ibid., at § 88.

53 See O. O'Neill, 'Children's Rights and Children's Lives,' (1988) 98 *Ethics* 445, reprinted in R.E. Ladd, ed., *Children's Rights Re-visioned* (Belmont: Wadsworth, 1996); see also L. Purdy, *In Their Best Interest? The Case against Equal Rights for Children* (Ithaca: Cornell University Press, 1992).

54 O'Neill, ibid., at 39.

55 *B.(R.)*, supra n40 at § 211.

56 Ibid., at § 215.

57 [1984] 2 S.C.R. 173 [hereinafter *Ogg-Moss*] at 183.

58 S. Turner, *Something to Cry About: An Argument against the Corporal Punishment of Children in Canada* (Waterloo: Wilfrid Laurier Press, 2002), at 179.

59 See *New Brunswick (Minister of Health and Community Services)* v. *G.(J.)*, [1999] 3 S.C.R. 46 [hereinafter *G.(J.)*]; see also *Rodriguez*, supra n48.

60 Ibid.; *Winnipeg Child and Family Services* v. *K.L.W.*, [2000] 2 S.C.R. 519 [hereinafter *K.L.W.*].

61 *K.L.W.*, ibid., at § 13.

62 (2002), 61 O.R. (3d) 449 [hereinafter *Louie*].

63 *Baker*, supra n1 at § 74.

64 See *Hawthorne* v. *Canada (Minister of Citizenship and Immigration)*, [2003] 2 F.C. 555 (F.C.A.) [hereinafter *Hawthorne*].

65 *Canadian Foundation*, supra n20 at § 10.

66 (2003), 10 C.R. (6th) 281 (Q.C.A.), [2003] Q.J. No. 2850 [hereinafter *Québec*]. This was noted by S. Anand, in 'Reasonable Chastisement: A Critique of the Supreme Court's Decision in the "Spanking' Case,"' (2004) 41 *Alberta Law Review* 871, at 874. This argument was also rejected by the Ontario Court of Appeal in *R.* v. *B.(D.)*, (2006), 79 O.R. (3d) 698 [hereinafter *D.B. Appeal*], a decision that the Supreme Court of Canada upheld in *D.B.*, based on the reasoning in the *Canadian Foundation* case.

67 J. Wilson, *Wilson on Children and the Law* (Toronto: Butterworths, 1994) at § 1.20.

68 For example, in *Auton (Guardian ad litem of)* v. *British Columbia (Attorney General)*, [2004] 3 S.C.R. 657 [hereinafter *Auton*], the court focused solely on the issue of disability and failed even to bring into the contextual analysis of the s.15 and s.7 arguments the fact that the claimants were children.

69 M. Minow, 'Rights for the Next Generation: A Feminist Approach to Children's Rights,' (1986) 9 *Harvard Women's Law Journal* 1, at 5.

70 Susan Turner took this position in a panel discussion at the annual meeting of the Canadian Law and Society Association at the University of Manitoba, Winnipeg, on 4 June 2004.

71 For this type of analysis, see N. Kim & T. Piper, '*Gosselin* v. *Quebec*: Back to the Poorhouse…' (2003) 48 *McGill Law Journal* 474; see also D. Majury, 'The Charter, Equality Rights and Women: Equivocation and Celebration,' (2002) 40 *Osgoode Hall Law Journal* 297 at § 74; and see also J. Keene, 'The *Law* Decision – A Misstep in the Quest to Define Discrimination,' in D. McAllister & A. Dodek, eds., *The Charter at Twenty: Law and Practice* (Toronto: Ontario Bar Association, 2002) 417.

10 The Judicial Contours of Minority Language Educational Rights under the *Charter*

1 [1985] 1 S.C.R. 721 [hereinafter *Manitoba Language Reference*].

2 Ibid., at 744.

3 Part I of the *Constitution Act, 1982*, being Schedule B to the *Canada Act 1982* (U.K.), 1982, c. 11 [hereinafter *Charter*].

4 For example, s.16 of the *Charter* states: '(1) English and French are the official languages of Canada and have equality of status and equal rights and privileges as to their use in all institutions of the Parliament and government

of Canada. (2) English and French are the official languages of New Brunswick and have equality of status and equal rights and privileges as to their use in all institutions of the legislature and government of New Brunswick. (3) Nothing in this *Charter* limits the authority of Parliament or a legislature to advance the equality of status or use of English and French.'

5 [1990] 1 S.C.R. 342 [hereinafter *Mahe*].

6 Ibid., at 369–70.

7 *Positive* rights can be contrasted with traditional *negative* rights contained in the *Charter* such as the constitutional guarantee to freedom of religion set out in s.2(a) of the *Charter*. This section states: 'Everyone has the right to freedom of religion. Freedom of religion requires the state to refrain from imposing, on its citizens, orthodox views about the good life, including belief in things religious and non-religious, through the apparatus of government. Rather, the state must respect the personal dignity and autonomy of its citizens and not interfere with individual freedom absent some compelling justification such as the prevention of harm to others.

8 [1988] 2 S.C.R. 712 [hereinafter *Ford*].

9 Ibid., at 751.

10 Not surprisingly, governments cannot rely on the notwithstanding clause in s.33 of the *Charter* to avoid their constitutional obligations vis-a-vis s.23. Section 33 only applies to s.2 and sections 7 through 15. As the section states: '(1) Parliament or the legislature of a province may expressly declare in an Act of Parliament or of the legislature, as the case may be that the Act or a provision thereof shall operate notwithstanding a provision included in section 2 or sections 7 to 15 of this *Charter*. (2) An Act or a provision of an Act in respect of which a declaration made under this section is in effect shall have such operation as it would have but for the provision of this *Charter* referred to in the declaration.'

11 In contradistinction, other sections of the *Charter*, such as s.2, protect only individual rights. The fundamental freedoms enshrined in s.2 are premised on the political philosophy of liberalism which places a strong emphasis on the need for the state to treat each person with equal respect and concern. For example, s.2(b) of the *Charter* states: 'Everyone is entitled to ... freedom of expression. Consequently, in the context of s.2(b), a Chinese Canadian has no greater (or lesser) claim to freedom of expression under s.2(b) than a Francophone or Anglophone Canadian. In this sense, as individuals, they are both on a level playing field as far as the law is concerned.'

12 [2005] S.C.J. No. 14 [hereinafter *Solski*].

13 Ibid., at §§ 22–3.

14 [1984] 2 S.C.R. 66 [hereinafter *Quebec (Attorney General)*].

15 Ibid., at 75.

16 [1986] 1 S.C.R. 549 [hereinafter *Société des Acadiens*].

17 Ibid., at 578.

18 [1998] 2 S.C.R. 217 [hereinafter *Quebec Secession Reference*].

19 Ibid., at §§ 79–80.

20 *Société des Acadiens*, supra n16 at 559.

21 *Mahe*, supra n5 at 362. With respect to the vital link between language and culture, the Court noted at 362: '[A]ny broad guarantee of language rights, especially in the context of education, cannot be separated from a concern for the culture associated with the language. Language is more than a mere means of communication, it is part and parcel of the identity and culture of the people speaking it. It is the means by which individuals understand themselves and the world around them.'

22 *Solski*, supra n12 at § 21.

23 [2003] 3 S.C.R. 3 [hereinafter *Doucet-Boudreau*].

24 Ibid., at 23.

25 Ibid., at 25.

26 *Solski*, supra n12 at § 5.

27 Ibid.

28 *Mahe*, supra n5.

29 *Constitution Act, 1982*, enacted as Schedule B to the *Canada Act, 1982*, (U.K.) 1982 c. 11.

30 *Quebec (Attorney General)*, supra n14 at 82.

31 Ibid., at 87.

32 The procedure for such amendments is prescribed in ss.38–49 of the *Constitution Act, 1982*.

33 Section 15(1) of the *Charter* states: 'Every individual is equal before and under the law and has the right to the equal protection and equal benefit of the law without discrimination and, in particular, without discrimination based on race, national or ethnic origin, colour, religion, sex, age or mental or physical disability. '

34 Section 27 of the *Charter* states: 'This *Charter* shall be interpreted in a manner consistent with the preservation and enhancement of the multicultural heritage of Canadians.'

35 *Mahe*, supra n5 at 369.

36 [2005] S.C.J. No. 15. [hereinafter *Gosselin*].

37 Ibid., at § 2.

38 Ibid., at § 22.

39 (1987), 16 B.C.L.R. (2d) 255 (B.C.S.C.) [hereinafter *Whittington*].

40 Ibid., at 262.

41 (1999), 42 O.R. (3d) 481 (Ont. C.A.) [hereinafter *Abbey*].

42 *Solski*, supra n12.

43 Ibid., at § 25.

44 Ibid., at § 28.

45 Ibid., at § 48.

46 Ibid., at § 35.

47 R.S.Q. c. 28.

48 Most recently, Quebec's Court of Appeal has ruled on the constitutionality of these amendments to the *Charter of the French Language* (known as Bill 104). *H.N.* c. *Québec (Ministre de l'Éducation)*, [2007] J.Q. no 9410 [hereinafter *H.N.*]. See *An Act to amend the Charter of the French Language*, S.Q. 2002, c. 28, which came into force on 1 October 2002. These amendments read: 'However, instruction in English received in Québec in a private educational institution not accredited for the purposes of subsidies by the child for whom the request is made, or by a brother or sister of the child, shall be disregarded. The same applies to instruction in English received in Québec in such an institution after 1 October 2002 by the father or mother of the child.'

Instruction in English received pursuant to a special authorization under section 81, 85, or 85.1 shall also be disregarded. The effect of the amendment was to require that instruction in English received by children of Canadian citizens in an unsubsidized private school in Quebec be disregarded as 'instruction in English' for the purposes of determining their admissibility to public schools in which the language of instruction is English. In 2007, a majority of Quebec's Court of Appeal ruled that this attempt to disqualify this type of prior instruction amounted to a violation of s.23 of the *Charter.*

49 *Mahe*, supra n5.

50 Ibid., at 365.

51 The Chief Justice contrasted the sliding scale approach with the view that s.23 encompassed two distinct rights – one for instruction and one for facilities: 'On this interpretation of s.23, which could be called the "separate rights" approach, a specified number of s.23 students would trigger a particular level of instruction, while a greater, specified number of students would require, in addition, a particular level of minority language educational facilities. Where the number of students fell between the two threshold numbers, only the lower level of instruction would be required' (ibid., at 366).

He ultimately rejected the separate rights approach for the following reasons: 'The sliding scale approach is preferable to the separate rights approach, not only because it accords with the text of s.23, but also because it is consistent with the purpose of s.23. The sliding scale approach ensures that the minority group receives the full amount of protection that its numbers warrant. Under the separate rights approach, if it were accepted, for example, that "X" number of students ensured a right to full management and control, then presumably "X – 1" students would not bring about any rights to management and control or even to a school building' (ibid., at 366–7).

52 Ibid., at 366.
53 Ibid., at 375.
54 Ibid., at 376.
55 Ibid., at 377.
56 Ibid., at 378–80.
57 The ill-fated FLU (French language unit) system in Ontario provides the reasons. In this regard, see the *Status Report: Minority Language Educational Rights* (Ottawa: Official Languages Support Programs Branch, Government of Canada, 1996). Available for purchase on-line at http://www.pch.gc.ca/pgm/lo-ol/cntct/frm/103-eng.cfm. Last accessed 5 May 2009.
58 *Mahe*, supra n5.
59 Ibid., at 385.
60 Ibid., at 384.
61 Ibid.
62 Ibid.
63 Ibid., at 385.
64 Ibid., at 367.
65 See M. Power & P. Foucher, 'Language Rights and Education,' in M. Bastarache, ed., *Language Rights in Canada*, 2d ed. (Montreal: Yvon Blais, 2004). The authors take issue with the SCC's opinion in *Mahé* that when 'too few students' exist, governments are relieved of their constitutional obligations under s.23. They maintain, at 424, that: 'With respect, this cannot be so. All entitled parents have the right to have their children instructed in the minority language. Only the way in which instruction is provided (i.e., within the context of a choice between the opening of a class in a majority school, the opening of a minority school, transportation to another facility, etc.) should be a function of what the numbers warrant. We find support for this position in the remedial purpose of section 23. This is consistent with the individual and collective character of section 23. In any event, it is the legal situation in certain jurisdictions. It should be recognized that the fact that only a single child of an entitled parent resides in a jurisdiction does not render that child's instruction in the minority

language an impossibility. The provision of bus transportation or room and board come to mind. Also, new technology allows for minority language instruction to be provided on an individual basis and at a reasonable cost anywhere in Canada. Numbers must be considered in the implementation of the right for administrative and practical reasons, but not for the purpose of determining whether the right exists. This in fact is no more difficult to accept than the right to instruct a child at home.'

66 [2000] 1 S.C.R. 3 [hereinafter *Arsenault-Cameron*].

67 Ibid., at 30.

68 Ibid., at 31–2.

69 [2004] N.J. No. 174 (Nfld. S.C.T.D.) [hereinafter *Chubbs*].

70 Ibid., at § 55.

71 *Arsenault-Cameron*, supra n66 at 37.

72 Ibid at 40.

73 [1986] 1 S.C.R. 103 [hereinafter *Oakes*].

74 In *Oakes*, ibid., at 139, the SCC ruled that there are three important components of the proportionality test: 'First, the measures adopted must be carefully designed to achieve the objective in question. They must not be arbitrary, unfair or based on irrational considerations. In short, they must be rationally connected to the objective. Second, the means, even if rationally connected to the objective in this first sense, should impair "as little as possible" the right or freedom in question: ... Third, there must be a proportionality between the effects of the measures which are responsible for limiting the *Charter* right or freedom, and the objective which has been identified as of "sufficient importance."'

75 *Mahe*, supra n5 at 380.

76 Ibid., at 394.

77 Ibid.

78 Ibid.

79 Power & Foucher, supra n65 at 426–7.

80 The province of Alberta is governed by a slightly different constitutional provision. When Alberta became a province in 1905, it adopted s.93 of the *British North America Act, 1867* (later renamed the *Constitution Act, 1867*), but with an amendment to s.93(1). The amendment is set out in s.17 of the *Alberta Act* which states: 'Section 93 of the Constitution Act, 1867, shall apply to the said province, with the substitution for paragraph (1) of the said section 93, of the following paragraph: Nothing in any such law shall prejudicially affect any right or privilege with respect to separate schools which any class of persons have at the date of the passing of this Act,

under the terms of chapters 29 and 30 of the Ordinances of the North-west Territories, passed in the year 1901, or with respect to religious instruction in any public or separate school as provided for in the said ordinances.'

81 *Mahe*, supra n5 at 382.

82 Ibid., at 365.

83 The five districts are: Kingston/Greenwood, Chéticamp, Île Madame-Arichat (Petit-de-Grat), Argyle, and Clare.

84 The minority board's name is *le Conseil scolaire acadien provincial*.

85 The majority judges included: McLachlin CJ and Gonthier, Iacobucci, Bastarache, and Arbour JJ; Iacobucci and Arbour JJ wrote the majority opinion.

86 By the time the case reached the SCC, the schools in question had been constructed. Consequently, the appeal was moot. Nonetheless, the Court decided to hear the case because it raised considerations deserving of a hearing.

87 *Doucet-Boudreau*, supra n23 at 30.

88 Ibid. at 26.

89 Ibid., at 33.

90 Ibid., at 37–8.

91 Ibid., at 40.

92 Ibid., at 37–8.

93 Ibid., at 38.

94 See Statement of Claim, Conseil Scolaire Fransaskois, Paulette Gaudet et Andre Tetreault c. Le Gouvernement de la Saskatchewan, 2004 [hereinafter CSF Statement of Claim].

95 Translated as: 'equality of results in education.'

96 CSF Statement of Claim, supra n94 at § 16.

97 *Mahe*, supra n5 at 378.

98 Ibid.

99 *Arsenault-Cameron*, supra n66 at 27–8.

100 J.E. Magnet, *Modern Constitutionalism: Identity, Equality and Democracy* (Markham: LexisNexis, 2004) at 234.

101 In the Canadian context, Magnet, ibid., notes that the Constitution protects four minority nations: certain denominational communities' English and French linguistic minorities, Aboriginal peoples, and the national minority of Quebec.

102 Ibid., at 235.

103 Ibid., at 236.

104 Only Nunavut has still to grant full school governance to its francophone minority. See *Annual Report: Special Edition, 35th Anniversary* (Ottawa:

Office of the Commissioner of Official Languages, 2005) [hereinafter Office of Commissioner of Official Languages] at 15. For a good discussion of government policy initiatives with respect to s.23, and outside Quebec, see Troy Riddell's article, 'The Impact of Section 23 of the Charter of Rights on Official Minority Language Education Policy Outside Quebec since 1982,' (2002) 21 *Windsor Yearbook of Access to Justice* 277.

105 Canada's official minority language educational communities present great diversity and special challenges. In Quebec, e.g., there were nine Anglophone school boards in 2003 operating 360 English language schools that served some 105,000 students. In the rest of Canada, there are now 30 francophone school boards in minority communities managing some 675 French language schools serving about 146,000 students. The francophone minority's school enrolments have, however, decreased by about 25% since 1971. In Quebec, almost all young anglophones (92%) attend English language schools. Outside Quebec, by contrast, the francophone school system recruits only half of the students entitled to its services (Office of the Commissioner of Official Languages, supra n104 at 67–9.) In Saskatchewan, where approximately 1,068 s.23 students are dispersed throughout 12 different communities, only 12% of eligible francophone minority students attend French schools. This makes the province's Fransaskois community prone to the highest assimilation rates in Canada. See CSF Statement of Claim, supra n94 at §§ 8–9.

106 *Arsenault-Cameron*, supra n66 at 27.

107 *Solski*, supra n12 at § 3.

108 *Ford*, supra n8 at 748–9.

11 The Courts and the School: The Judicial Construction of the School

1 T.A. Sussel & M.E. Manley-Casimir, 'The Supreme Court of Canada as a "National School Board": The Charter and Educational Change,' in M.E. Manley-Casimir & T.A. Sussel, eds., *Courts in the Classroom* (Calgary: Detselig, 1986) 213, at 228.

2 Part I of the *Constitution Act, 1982*, being Schedule B to the *Canada Act 1982* (U.K.), 1982, c. 11 [hereinafter *Charter*]

3 C. Oliverio & M. Manley-Casimir, 'The Judicial Construction of the Role of the Teacher,' (2005) 40(3) *McGill Journal of Education* 405.

4 R.S.O. 1990, c. E-2 [hereinafter Ontario *Education Act*].

5 'School' means: 'a body of students that is organized as a unit for the educational purposes under the supervision of a principal, vice principal or director of instruction,(a) the teachers and other staff members associated

with the unit, and (b) the facilities associated with the unit, and includes a Provincial resource program and a distance education school' (*School Act*, R.S.B.C. 1996, c. 412 [hereinafter B.C. *School Act*]).

6 'School' means the body of school students that is organized as a unit for the purpose of education and includes the teachers and other staff members associated with the unit and the lands and premises used in connection with the unit (*Schools Act*, S.N.L. 1997, c. S-12.2 [hereinafter Newfoundland *School Act*]).

7 'School' means a building or a part of a building which is designated as a school (*School Act*, R.S.P.E.I. 1988, c. S-2.1 [hereinafter P.E.I. *School Act*]).

8 'School' means a structured learning environment through which public education is provided to a pupil (*Education Act*, R.S.N.B. 1997 c. E-1.12 [hereinafter New Brunswick *Education Act*]).

9 *Education Act*, R.S.Q., c. I-13.3 [hereinafter Quebec *Education Act*].

10 (1986), 29 D.L.R. (4th) 596 (Ont. H.C.J.) [hereinafter *Marchand*].

11 Ibid., at 616.

12 (1987), 51 Alta. L.R. (2d) 349 (Alta. Q.B.) [hereinafter *Casagrande*].

13 (1984), 15 D.L.R. (4d) 1 (S.C.C.) [hereinafter *Caldwell*].

14 *Casagrande*, supra n12 at 356.

15 Ibid.

16 (2002), 59 O.R. (3d) 423 (Ont. Sup. Ct.) [hereinafter *Hall*].

17 Ibid., at 430.

18 Ibid., at 432.

19 P. Pound & I. Benson, 'The Court Claims to Extend Its Jurisdiction to Church Matters: Hall (*Litigation guardian of*) v. *Powers*,' (2003) *Lex View*, no. 52.

20 Ibid.

21 [2001] J.Q. No. 3881 (Que. C.A.) [hereinafter *Commission scolaire*].

22 Ibid., at § 97, quoted from J.J. Quillen, 'Problems and Prospects,' in G.D. Spindler, ed., *Education and Culture, Anthropological Approaches* (New York: Holt, Rinehart & Winston, 1963) 50.

23 Ibid.

24 (2001), 150 B.C.A.C. 228 (B.C.C.A.) [hereinafter *Young*].

25 [1996] 1 S.C.R. 825 [hereinafter *Ross*].

26 Ibid., at 856–7.

27 *Young*, supra n24 at 240.

28 *Ross*, supra n25 at 837.

29 Ibid., at 853.

30 Ibid., at 861.

31 347 U.S. 483 (1954) (U.S.S.C.) [hereinafter *Brown*].

32 *Ross*, supra n25 at 873.

33 [1997] 1 S.C.R. 487 [hereinafter *Toronto Board of Education*].
34 Ibid., at 513.
35 [2001] 1 S.C.R. 772 [hereinafter *T.W.U.*].
36 Ibid., at 801.
37 Ibid., at 820.
38 [2002] 4 S.C.R. 710 [hereinafter *Chamberlain*].
39 Ibid., at 728.
40 Ibid., at 729.
41 Ibid., at 730.
42 Ibid., at 731.
43 Ibid., at 738.
44 Ibid., at 788.
45 Ibid., at 802.
46 *Ross*, supra n25 at 856–7.
47 Ibid.

References

Cases Cited

Abbey v. *Essex County Board of Education*, (1999) 42 O.R. (3d) 481 (Ont. C.A.).

Abbotsford School District 34 v. *Shewan*, (1987) 21 B.C.L.R. (2d) 93 (B.C.C.A.).

A.C. et al. v. *Director of Child and Family Services* [Manitoba], heard 20 May 2008, on reserve.

Acheson v. *New Brunswick (Minister of Education)*, (2000) 228 N.B.R. (2d) 223 (N.B.Q.B.).

Adler v. *Ontario*, (1994) 19 O.R. (3d) 1 (Ont. C.A.).

Adler v. *Ontario*, [1996] 3 S.C.R. 609.

Andrews v. *Law Society of British Columbia*, [1989] 1 S.C.R. 143, 56 D.L.R (4th) 1.

Arsenault-Cameron v. *Prince Edward Island*, [2000] 1 S.C.R. 3.

Arzem v. *Ontario (Minister of Community and Social Services)*, [2006] O.H.R.T.D. No. 17.

Auton (Guardian ad litem) v. *British Columbia (A.G.)*, [2000] B.C.J. No. 1547 (B.C.S.C.).

Auton (Guardian ad litem) v. *British Columbia (A.G.)*, [2002] B.C.J. No. 2258 (B.C.C.A.).

Auton (Guardian ad litem of) v. *British Columbia (Attorney General)*, [2004] 3 S.C.R. 657.

Bal v. *Ontario (Attorney General)*, (1997) 34 O.R. (3d) 484 (Ont. C.A.).

Baker v. *Canada (Minister of Citizenship and Immigration)*, [1999] 2 S.C.R. 817.

Battlefords and District Cooperative Ltd. v. *Gibbs*, [1996] 3 S.C.R. 566.

Blencoe v. *British Columbia (Human Rights Commission)*, [2000] 2 S.C.R. 307.

Bouchard v. *School Commissioners of Saint-Mathieu-de-Dixville*, [1950] S.C.R. 479.

B.(R.) v. *Children's Aid Society of Metropolitan Toronto*, [1995] 1 S.C.R. 315.

British Columbia Public School Employers' Assn. and B.C.T.F. (Re), (2004) 129
L.A.C. (4th) 245 (Arbitrator Munroe).
British Columbia Public School Employers' Assn. and B.C.T.F. (Re), [2005] BCCA
393 (B.C.C.A.).
British Columbia (Public Service Employee Relations Commission) v. *British
Columbia Government and Service Employees' Union (B.C.G.S.E.U.)(Meiorin
Grievance)*, [1999] 3 S.C.R. 3.
British Columbia (Superintendent of Motor Vehicles) v. *British Columbia (Council of
Human Rights)*, [1999] 3 S.C.R. 868.
Brown v. *Board of Education of Topeka*, 347 U.S. 483 (1954).
Caldwell et al. v. *Stuart et al.*, (1984) 15 D.L.R. (4d) 1 (S.C.C.).
Canadian Civil Liberties Association v. *Ontario (Minister of Education)*, (1988) 64
O.R. (2d) 577 (Ont. Div. Ct.).
Canadian Civil Liberties Association et al. v. *Ontario (Minister of Education)*, (1990)
71 O.R. (2d) 341 (Ont. C.A.).
Canadian Foundation for Children, Youth and the Law v. *Canada (Attorney General)*,
(2000) 188 D.L.R. (4th) 718 (Ont. Sup. Ct.).
Canadian Foundation for Children, Youth and the Law v. *Canada (Attorney General)*,
(2002) 207 D.L.R. (4th) 632 (Ont. C.A.).
Canadian Foundation for Children, Youth and the Law v. *Canada (Attorney General)*,
[2004] 1 S.C.R. 76.
Carrière v. *County of Lamont*, (1978) Edmonton 107/134 (Alta. S.C.T.D.)
[unreported].
Casagrande v. *Hinton Roman Catholic Separate School District No. 155*, (1987) 51
Alta. L.R. (2d) 349 (Alta. Q.B.).
Central Alberta Dairy Pool v. *Alberta (Human Rights Commission)*, [1990] 2 S.C.R.
489.
Central Okanagan School District #23 v. *Renaud*, [1992] 2 S.C.R. 970.
Chamberlain v. *Surrey School District No. 36*, [2002] 4 S.C.R. 710, S.C.J. No. 87.
Chubbs v. *Newfoundland and Labrador*, [2004] N.J. No. 174 (Nfld. S.C.T.D.).
Clough v. *Simcoe County District School Board*, (15 Sept. 2003) decision of the
(Ontario Spec. Education Trib.).
Clough (Litigation Guardian of) v. *Simcoe County District School Board*, [2005] O.J.
No. 2124 (Ont. Sup. Ct.).
C.N.R. v. *Canada (Human Rights Commission)*, [1987] 1 S.C.R. 1114.
Commission scolaire crie c. *Canada (Procureur General)*, [2001] J.Q. No. 3881 (Que.
C.A.).
Concerned Parents for Children with Learning Disabilities Inc. v. *Saskatchewan
(Minister of Education)*, [1998] S.J. No. 566 (Sask. Q.B.).
Corbiere v. *Canada (Minister of Indian and Northern Affairs)*, [1999] 2 S.C.R. 203.

Cromer v. *B.C.T.F.*, (1986) 29 D. L.R. (4th) 641 (B.C.C.A).

C.U. v. *McGonigle*, [2003] A.J. No. 238 (Alta. C.A.).

C.U. v. *McGonigle*, [2004] 1 S.C.R. 336.

Cudmore (Human Rights Commission) v. *New Brunswick (Minister Education) and School District 2*, [2004] Human Rights 3 Member Tribunal LEB File No. HR-003-01.

Dagenais v. *Canadian Broadcasting Corp.*, [1994] 3 S.C.R. 835.

Daly v. *Ontario (Attorney General)*, [1997] O. J. No. 5040 (Ont. Ct. Gen. Div).

Dassonville-Trudel (Guardian ad litem of) v. *Halifax Regional School Board*, [2004] N.S.J. No. 241 (N.S.C.A.).

D.B.S. v. *S.R.G.; L.J.W.* v. *T.A.R.; Henry* v. *Henry; Hiemstra* v. *Hiemstra*, [2006] S.C.C. 37.

Doucet-Boudreau v. *Nova Scotia (Minister of Education)*, [2003] 3 S.C.R. 3.

Eaton v. *Brant County Board of Education*, (19 Nov. 1993) (Ont. Spec. Ed. Trib.) [unreported].

Eaton v. *Brant County Board of Education*, [1994] O.J. No. 203 (Ont. Ct. Gen. Div.).

Eaton v. *Brant County Board of Education*, (1995) 123 D.L.R. (4th) 43 (Ont. C.A.).

Eaton v. *Brant County Board of Education*, [1997] 1 S.C.R. 241.

Egan v. *Canada*, [1995] 2 S.C.R. 513.

Eldridge v. *British Columbia (Attorney General)*, [1997] 3 S.C.R. 624.

Engel v. *Vitale*, 370 U.S. 421 (1962).

Entick v. *Carrington*, (1765) 95 E.R. 807 (K.B.).

Falkiner v. *Ontario (Ministry of Community and Social Services)*, (2002) 59 O.R. (3d.) 481 (Ont. C.A.).

Fitzgerald (Next friend of) v. *Alberta*, [2002] A.J. No. 1544 (Alta. Q.B.).

Fitzgerald (Next friend of) v. *Alberta*, [2004] A.J. No. 570 (Alta. C.A.).

Ford v. *A.G. Quebec*, [1988] 2 S.C.R. 712.

Gosselin v. *Quebec (Attorney General)*, [2002] 4 S.C.R. 429.

Gosselin (Tutor of) v. *Quebec (Attorney General)*, [2005] 1 S.C.R. 238.

Granovsky v. *Canada (Minister of Employment and Immigration)*, [2000] 1 S.C.R. 703.

H.N. c. *Québec (Ministre de l'Éducation)*, [2007] J.Q. No. 9410.

Hall (Litigation Guardian of) v. *Powers*, (2002) 213 D.L.R. (4th) 308 (Ont. Sup. Ct.).

Hamilton-Wentworth District School Board, [2002] O.L.R.D. No. 2676 (O.L.R.B.).

Hawthorne v. *Canada (Minister of Citizenship and Immigration)*, [2003] 2 F.C. 555 (F.C.A.).

Hazelwood School District v. *Kuhlmeier*, 484 U.S. 260 (1988).

Hodge v. *Canada (Minister of Human Resources Development)*, [2004] 3 S.C.R. 357.

Hogan v. *Newfoundland (Attorney General)*, (2000) 189 Nfld. & P.E.I.R 183 (Nfld. C.A.).

Hunter v. *Southam*, [1984] 2 S.C.R. 145.

Irwin Toy Ltd. v. *Quebec (Attorney General)*, [1989] 1 S.C.R. 927.

Islamic Schools Federation of Ontario v. *Ottawa Board of Education*, (1997) 145 D.L.R. (4th) 659 (Ont. Ct. Gen. Div.).

Jubran v. *North Vancouver School Dist. No. 44*, [2002] B.C.H.R.T.D. No. 10 (B.C.H.R.T.).

Jubran v. *North Vancouver School Dist. No. 44*, (2003) 9 B.C.L.R. (4th) 338 (B.C.S.C.).

Jubran v. *North Vancouver School Dist. No. 44*, [2005] B.C.J. No. 733 (B.C.C.A.).

Kafe et Commission des droits de la personne du Quebec c. *Commission scolaire Deux-Montagnes*, [1993] 19 C.H.R.R. D/1 (Qué. H.R.Trib.).

Katz v. *United States*, 389 U.S. 347 (1967).

Kearley v. *Pentecostal Assemblies Board of Education*, [1993] N.H.R.B.I.D. No. 1 (Nfld. H.R.T.).

Keegstra v. *Board of Education of Lacombe No. 14*, (1983) 25 Alta. L.R. (2d) 370 (Alta. Q.B.).

Kempling v. *British Columbia College of Teachers*, [2004] B.C.J. No. 173 (B.C.S.C.).

Kempling v. *British Columbia College of Teachers*, [2004] BCCA 535.

Kempling v. *British Columbia College of Teachers*, [2005] S.C.C.A. No. 381.

Lalji v. *British Columbia (Human Rights Commission)*, [2004] B.C.J. No. 10 (B.C.S.C.).

Law v. *Canada (Minister of Employment and Immigration)*, [1999] 1 S.C.R. 497.

L.E.G. v. *A.G.*, [2002] B.C.J. No. 2319 (B.C.S.C.).

Lemon v. *Kurtzman*, 403 U. S. 602 (1971).

Lewis v. *York Region Board of Education (No. 5)*, (1996) 27 C.H.R.R. D/261 (Ont. Bd. Inq.).

Little Sisters Book and Art Emporium v. *Canada (Minister of Justice)*, [2000] 2 S.C.R. 1120.

Louie v. Lastman, (2002) 61 O.R. (3d) 449 (Ont. C.A.).

Lovelace v. *Ontario*, [2000] 1 S.C.R. 950.

Mahe v. *Alberta*, [1990] 1 S.C.R. 342.

Manitoba Association for Rights and Liberties Inc. v. *Manitoba (Minister of Education)* (1992), 94 D.L.R. (4th) 678, 82 Man. R. (2d) 39 (Man. Q.B.).

Marchand v. *Simcoe County Board of Education et al.*, (1986) 29 D.L.R. (4th) 596 (Ont. H.C.J.).

McCollum v. *Board of Education*, 333 U.S. 203 (1948).

McKinney v. *University of Guelph*, [1990] 3 S.C.R. 229.

Mills v. *Board of Education of the District of Columbia*, 3483 F. Supp 866 (D.C. 1972).

Miranda v. *Arizona*, 384 U.S. 436 (1966).

Moore v. *British Columbia (Ministry of Education)*, [2005] B.C.H.R.T.D. No. 580 (B.C.H.R.T.).

Morin v. *Prince Edward Island Regional Administrative Unit No. 3 School Board*, (2004) 233 Nfld. & P.E.I.R. 271 (P.E.I.S.C.T.D.).

Morin v. *Prince Edward Island Regional Administrative Unit No. 3 School Board*, (2005) 254 D.L.R. (4th) 410 (P.E.I.S.C.A.D.).

Morin v. *Prince Edward Island Regional Administrative Unit No. 3 School Board*, (2002) 213 D.L.R. (4th) 17 (P.E.I.S.C.A.D.).

Multani (tuteur de) c. *Commission scolaire Marguerite-Bourgeoys*, [2002] J.Q. No. 1131 (Qué. Sup. Ct.).

Multani (tuteur de) c. *Commission scolaire Marguerite-Bourgeoys*, [2004] J. Q. No. 1904 (Que. C.A.).

Multani c. *Commission scolaire Marguerite-Bourgeoys*, 2006 SCC 6, [2006] 1 S.C.R. 256.

Neiberg (Litigation guardian of) v. *Simcoe County District School Board*, [2004] O.J. No. 2524 (Ont. Sup. Ct.).

New Brunswick (Minister of Health and Community Services) v. *G.(J.)*, [1999] 3 S.C.R. 46.

New Jersey v. *T.L.O.*, 469 U.S. 325 (1985).

Newfoundland (Treasury Board) v. *N.A.P.E.*, [2004] 3 S.C.R. 381.

Nova Scotia (Workers' Compensation Board) v. *Martin; Nova Scotia (Workers' Compensation Board)* v. *Laseur*, [2003] 2 S.C.R. 504.

O'Malley v. *Simpson Sears Ltd.*, [1985] 2 S.C.R. 536.

Ontario English Catholic Teachers' Association v. *Ontario (Attorney General)*, [2001] 1 S.C.R. 470.

P.(D.) v. *S.(C.)*, [1993] 4 S.C.R. 141.

Pandori v. *Peel Board of Education*, (1990), 12 C.H.R.R. D/364 (Ont. Bd. Inq.).

Peel Board of Education v. *Ontario Human Rights Commission*, (1991), 3 O.R. (3d) 531 (Ont. Ct. Gen. Div.).

Picard v. *Commission scolaire Prince-Daveluy*, [1991] R.J.Q. 167 (Que. Sup. Ct)

Picard v. *Commission scolaire Prince-Daveluy*, [1992] R.J.Q. 2369 (Que. C.A.).

Plessy v. *Ferguson*, 163 U.S. 537 (1896).

Public School Boards' Assn. (Alberta) v. *Alberta (Attorney General)*, [2000] 2 S.C.R. 409.

Québec (Attorney General) v. *Québec Assn. of Protestant School Boards*, [1984] 2 S.C.R. 66.

Québec (Commission des droits de la personne) c. *Commission scolaire Deux-Montagnes*, [1993] R.J.Q. 1297 (Que. H.R. Trib.).

Québec (Commission des droits de la personne et des droits de la jeunesse) v. *Collège Notre-Dame du Sacré-coeur (Corp.)*, [2001] R.J.Q. 5 (Que. C.A.).

Québec (Minister of Justice) v. *Canada (Minister of Justice)*, (2003) 175 C.C.C. (3d) 321 (Que. C.A.).

R. v. *A.M.*, [2004] O.J. No. 2716 (Ont. Ct. J. – Yth. Ct.).

R. v. A.M., (2006) 79 O.R. (3d) 481 (Ont. C.A.).

R. v. A.M., [2008] S.C.C. 19.

R. v. B.(D.), (2006) 79 O.R. (3d) 698 (Ont. C.A.).

R. v. B.(D.), [2008] S.C.C. 25.

R. v. Broyles, [1991] 3 S.C.R. 595.

R. v. Butler, [1992] 1 S.C.R. 452.

R. v. Caouette, [2002] Q.J. No. 1055 (Que. Crim. Ct.).

R. v. Edwards Books & Art Ltd., [1986] 35 D.L.R. (4th) 1 (S.C.C.).

R. v. G.A.W., [1996] B.C.J. No. 2329 (B.C.S.C.).

R. c. G.B., [2004] J. Q. No. 4568 (Que. Crim. Ct.).

R. v. G.(J.M.), (1987) 56 O.R. (2d) 705 (Ont. C.A.).

R. v. Guignard, [2002] 1 S.C.R. 472.

R. v. H.(M.), (26 June 1986), (Alta. Q.B.) [No. 8503-04478-S2] [unreported].

R. v. Halcrow, [1993] B.C.J. No 1227 (B.C.C.A.).

R. v. Holmes, (31 Aug. 2000), Campbell's Bay, Que. No. 555-01-0267-998 (Que. Prov. Ct).

R. v. J.R.G., (25 June 1991), No. 1731 (B.C. Youth Court).

R. v. Johnson, (1997) 48 C.R.R. (2d) 176 (Ont. Ct. Prov. Div.).

R. v. Jones, [1986] 2 S.C.R. 284.

R. v. K.(M.), (1993) 16 C.R. 121 (Man. C.A.).

R. v. Keegstra, (1984) 19 C.C.C. (3d) 254 (Alta. Q.B.).

R. v. Keegstra, (1988) 60 Alta. L.R. (2d) 1 (Alta. C.A.).

R. v. Keegstra, [1990] 3 S.C.R. 697.

R. c. Martineau, [2004] R.D.S.D. No. 195 (Qué. Crim. Ct.).

R. v. Malmo-Levine, [2003] 3 S.C.R. 571.

R. v. Mara, [1997] 2 S.C.R. 630.

R. v. M.R.M., [1998] 3 S.C.R. 393.

R. v. M.W.S., [2005] B.C.J. No. 1270 (B.C. Prov. Ct. – Youth Div.).

R. v. Nova Scotia Pharmaceutical Society, [1992] 1 S.C.R. 606.

R. v. Oakes, [1986] 1 S.C.R. 103.

R. v. Ogg-Moss, [1984] 2 S.C.R. 173.

R. v. Peterson, (1995) 98 C.C.C. (3d) 253 (Ont. C.J. Prov. Div.).

R. v. R.C., [2005] 3 S.C.R. 99.

R. v. Samms, Action 1985 No. C.B. 573 (Nfld. S.C.) [unreported].

R. v. Sharpe, [2001] 1 S.C.R. 45.

R. v. Skidmore, No. 8414/00, (27 June 2000) (Ont. C.J.)

R. v. W.(J.J.), Action 1988 No. C.B. 196 (Nfld. S.C.).

R. v. Wetmore, (1996), 172 N.B.R. (2d) 224 (N.B.Q.B.).

R. v. Z.(S.M.), [1988] M.J. No. 81 (Man. Q.B.).

R.W.D.S.U., Local 558 v. *Pepsi-Cola Canada Beverages (West) Ltd.*, [2002] 1 S.C.R. 156.

Re Emily Eaton, (24 Feb. 1992) (Brant County I.P.R.C.) [unreported].

Re Essex County Roman Catholic Separate School Board and Tremblay-Webster, et. al., (1984) 5 D.L.R. (4th) 665 (Ont. C.A).

Re Essex Roman Catholic Separate School Board and Porter, et al., (1979) 89 D.L.R. (3d) 445 (Ont. C.A.).

Re Nicholson and Haldimand-Norfolk Regional Board of Com'rs of Police, [1979] 1 S.C.R. 311.

Re s. 24 of BNA Act; Edwards v. *A.G. Can.*, [1930] 1 D.L.R. 98 (P.C.).

Reference re Education Act (Quebec), (1993) 2 S.C.R. 511.

Reference re Manitoba Language Rights, [1985] 1 S.C.R. 721.

Reference re Secession of Quebec, [1998] 2 S.C.R. 217.

Rodriguez v. *British Columbia (Attorney General)*, [1993] 3 S.C.R. 519.

Ross v. *New Brunswick School District No. 15*, [1996] 1 S.C.R. 825, 133 D.L.R. (4th) 1.

Russow v. *British Columbia (Attorney General)*, (1989) 35 B.C.L.R. (2d) 29 (B.C.S.C.).

Sauvé v. *Canada (Chief Electoral Officer)*, [2002] 3 S.C.R. 519.

Schachter v. *Canada*, [1992] 2 S.C.R. 679.

School District No. 403 v. *Fraser*, 478 U.S. 675 (1986).

School District of Abington Township v. *Schempp*, 374 U.S. 203 (1963).

Société des Acadiens du Nouveau-Brunswick Inc. v. *Association of Parents for Fairness in Education*, [1986] 1 S.C.R. 549.

Solski (Tutor of) v. *Quebec (Attorney General)*, [2005] 1 S.C.R. 201, S.C.J. No. 14.

Stoffman v. *Vancouver General Hospital*, [1990] 3 S.C.R. 483.

Symes v. *Canada*, [1993] 4 S.C.R. 695.

Tinker v. *Des Moines*, 393 U.S. 503 (U.S.C.A. 1969).

Tobin v. *Simcoe County District School Board*, (28 May 2004) (decision of the Ont. Spec.Ed.Trib.).

Toronto Board of Education v. *Ontario Secondary School Teachers' Federation, District 15*, [1997] 1 S.C.R. 487.

Trinity Western University v. *British Columbia College of Teachers*, [1997] 41 B.C.L.R. (3d) 158 (B.C.S.C.), 5 2001 SCC 31.

Trinity Western University v. *British Columbia College of Teachers*, [1998] 59 B.C.L.R. (3d) 241 (B.C.C.A.).

Trinity Western University v. *British Columbia College of Teachers*, [2001] 1 S.C.R. 772.

Trociuk v. *British Columbia (Attorney General)*, [2003] 1 S.C.R. 835.

Trofimenkoff et al. v. *Saskatchewan (Minister of Education)*, [1991] 92 Sask. R. 229 (Sask. Q.B.).

University of British Columbia v. *Berg*, [1993] 2 S.C.R. 353.

Vriend v. *Alberta*, [1998] 1 S.C.R. 493.

Walsh v. *Simcoe County District School Board*, (27 May 2004) (decision of the Ont.Spec.Ed.Trib.).

Ward v. *Board of Trustees of Blaine Lake*, [1971] 4 W.W.R. 161 (Sask. Q.B.).

Whittington v. *Saanich School District No. 63*, (1987) 16 B.C.L.R. (2d) 255. (B.C.S.C.).

Winnipeg Child and Family Services v. *K.L.W.*, [2000] 2 S.C.R. 519.

Wynberg and Deskin v. *Her Majesty the Queen in the Right of Ontario*, (judgment dated 30 March 2005), 2005 CanLII 8749 (Ont. Sup. Ct.).

Wynberg v. *Ontario*, [2005] O.J. No. 1228 (Ont. S.C.J.).

Wynberg v. *Ontario*, [2006] O.J. No. 2732 (Ont. C.A.).

Wynberg et al. v. *Ontario*, (2007) CanLII 11900 (S.C.C.).

Young v. *British Columbia College of Teachers*, (2001) 150 B.C.A.C. 228 (B.C.C.A.).

Young v. *Young*, [1993] 4 S.C.R. 3.

Zylberberg v. *Sudbury Board of Education*, (1988) 65 O.R. (2d) 641 (Ont. C.A.).

Secondary Sources

Abella, R.S. (1984). *Report of the Commission on Equality in Employment*. Ottawa: Minister of Supply and Services Canada.

Anand, S. (2004). 'Reasonable Chastisement: A Critique of the Supreme Court's Decision in the "Spanking" Case.' 41 *Alberta Law Review* 871.

Anderson, S.M. (2005). 'Liability for Education Malpractice – Coming Soon to a School Near You?' in R. Flynn, ed., *Law and Education: The Practice of Accountability*. Markham: Canadian Association for the Practical Study of Law in Education, 1.

Aristotle. (1925). *Ethica Nichomacia, Book V3*, trans. W.D. Ross. London: H. Milford, Oxford University Press.

AvRuskin, S. (1987). 'In Defence of Young Offenders: Search and Seizure in Schools – A Scholarly Reduction of Young Persons' Rights.' 8 (Sept.) *Ontario Criminal Lawyers' Association Newsletter* 19.

Bakan, J. (1997). *Just Words: Constitutional Rights and Social Wrongs*. Toronto: University of Toronto Press.

Baum, G. (2000). 'Catholicism and Secularization in Quebec,' in D. Lyon & M. Van Die, eds., *Rethinking Church, State and Modernity: Canada between Europe and America*. Toronto: University of Toronto Press, 87.

Bayefsky, A.F. (1985). 'Defining Equality Rights,' in A.F. Bayefsky & M. Eberts, eds., *Equality Rights and the Canadian Charter of Rights and Freedoms*. Toronto: Carswell, 1.

Ben Jaafar, S. (2002). 'Fertile Ground: Instructional Negligence and the Tort of Educational Malpractice.' 12 *Education & Law Journal* 1.

Berger, B.L. (2003). 'Using the Charter to Cure Health Care: Panacea or Placebo?' 8(1) *Review of Constitutional Studies* 20.

Berger, T. (1981). *Fragile Freedoms: Human Rights and Dissent in Canada.* Toronto: Clarke, Irwin.

Bibby, R.W. (1993). *Unknown Gods: The Ongoing Story of Religion in Canada.* Toronto: Stoddart.

Black, W., & L. Smith. (2005). 'Equality Rights,' in W.A. Tarnopolsky, G.-A. Beaudoin, & E. Mendes, eds., *Canadian Charter of Rights and Freedoms*, 4th ed. Markham: LexisNexis, 925.

Blackstone, W. (1915). *Commentaries on the Laws of England.* Baton Rouge: Claitors.

Bowlby, B.J., C. Peters, & M. Mackinnon. (2001). *An Educator's Guide to Special Education Law.* Aurora: Aurora Professional Press.

Bracken, L.A. (2005). 'School Reform in Quebec, Canada: A Multi-faceted Approach.' (unpublished paper). In collection of J.C. Long.

British Columbia Civil Liberties Association. (1997). *BCCLA Position Paper: Civil Liberties in the Schools.* Vancouver: Author.

Canada. (1996). *Status Report: Minority Language Educational Rights.* Ottawa: Official Languages Support Programs Branch, Government of Canada.

Canadian Teachers' Federation. (2003–04). *Canadian Teachers' Federation Handbook.* Ottawa: Canadian Teachers' Federation.

Carter, M. (2005). 'The Constitutional Validity of the Corporal Punishment Defence in Canada: A Critical Analysis of *Canadian Foundation for Children, Youth and the Law versus Canada (Attorney General).*' 12 *International Review of Victimology* 189.

Chadna, E., & C.T. Sheldon. (2004–05). 'Promoting Equality: Economic and Social Rights for Persons with Disabilities under Section 15.' 16 *National Journal of Constitutional Law* 27.

Cherian, V.I. (1994). 'Corporal Punishment and Academic Achievement of Xhosa Children from Polygamous and Monogamous Families.' 134 *Journal of Social Psychology* 387.

Chitty, C. (1989). *Towards a New Education System: The Victory of the New Right?* London: Falmer.

Clarke, P. (1998). 'Canadian Public School Teachers and Free Speech: Part I – An Introduction.' 8 *Education & Law Journal* 297.

Clarke, P. (1999). 'Canadian Public School Teachers and Free Speech: Part II – An Employment Law Analysis.' 9 *Education & Law Journal* 43.

Clarke, P. (1999). 'Canadian Public School Teachers and Free Speech: Part III – Constitutional Law Analysis.' 9 *Education & Law Journal* 315.

Clemens, M.T. (1999). *The Catholic Education Council of Newfoundland and Labrador: A Case Study in Interest Articulation.* M.Ed. Thesis, University of Manitoba.

Cohen, C.P. (1978). 'Beating Children Is as American as Apple Pie.' (Spring) *Human Rights* 24.

Coleman, J.S. (1968). 'The Concept of Equality of Educational Opportunity.' 38 *Harvard Education Review* 7.

Colman, S., & A. Otten. (2005). *The Intersection of the Safe Schools Act and the YCJA*. Toronto: Ontario Principal's Council.

Commission des états généraux sur l'éducation. (2001). *Les États Généraux Sur L'éducation, 1995–1996: Exposé De La Situation*. Quebec: Éducation Québec. Last retrieved 5 May 2009 from http://www.meq.gouv.qc.ca/etat%2Dgen/menu/chap8.htm#DEBAT.

Committee on the Rights of the Child. (1995). *Report on the Eighth Session*, 209th Mtg., UN Doc. CRC/C/38.

Committee on the Rights of the Child. (2003). Concluding Observations of the Committee on the Rights of the Child. 27 October. CANADA UN Doc. CRC/C/15/Add.215 § 33. Available at: http://www.unhcr.ch/html/menu2/6/crc/doc/co/canada%20c02.pdf. Last retrieved 5 May 2009.

Coons, J.E. (2005). 'Dodging Democracy: The Educator's Flight from the Specter of Choice.' 111(4) *American Journal of Education* 596.

Corbett, D.L., K. Spector, & J. Strug. (2001). 'Section 15 Jurisprudence in the Supreme Court of Canada in 2000.' 14 S.C.L.R. (2d) 29.

Corwin, E.S. (1949). 'The Supreme Court as a National School Board.' 14 *Law & Contemporary Problems* 3.

Council of the Ontario College of Teachers. (1999). *Standards of Practice for the Teaching Profession*. Toronto: Author.

Cruickshank, D. (1986). 'Charter Equality Rights: The Challenge to Education Law and Policy,' in M.E. Manley-Casimir & T.A. Sussel, eds., *Courts in the Classroom: Education and the Charter of Rights and Freedoms*. Calgary: Detselig.

Day, S., & G. Brodsky. (1996). 'The Duty to Accommodate: Who Will Benefit?' 75 *Canadian Bar Review* 433.

Department for Education and Skills. (2001). *Special Education Needs Code of Practice*. London: Author.

Dickinson, G.M. (1989). 'Principals and Criminal Investigations of Students: Recent Developments.' 14 *Canadian Journal of Education* 203.

Dickinson, G.M. (1996–98). 'Searching for Reason.' 8 *Education & Law Journal* 441.

Dickinson, G.M. (1999). 'Looking into the Foggy Mirror of Denominational School Rights in Ontario.' 9 *Education & Law Journal* 115.

Dickinson, G.M. (2000). 'The Charter of Rights and Educational Governance: Much Ado about Nothing?' in J. De Groof, J. Heystek, R. Malherbe, & J. Squelch, eds., *Governance of Educational Institutions in South Africa: Into the New Millennium*. Ghent: Mys & Bressch, 225.

Dickinson, G.M. (2000–01). 'Still Searching for Reason.' 10 *Education & Law Journal* 125.

Dickinson, G.M. (2003). 'Unanimous Supreme Court Refuses to Permit Denominational Rights Claims to Invalidate Ontario's Education Funding Model.' 12 *Education & Law Journal* 109.

Dickinson, G.M., & W.R. Dolmage. (1996). 'Education, Religion, and the Courts in Ontario.' 21 *Canadian Journal of Education* 363.

Dickinson, G.M., & A.W. MacKay, eds. (1989). *Rights, Freedoms and the Education System in Canada*. Toronto: Emond Montgomery.

Dobson, J.C. (1992). *The New Dare to Discipline*. Wheaton: Tyndale House.

Dolmage, R. (1995–96). 'One Less Brick in the Wall: The Myths of Youth Violence and Unsafe Schools.' 7 *Education & Law Journal* 185.

Dolmage, R. (2000–01). 'Lies, Damned Lies, and Statistics: The Media's Treatment of Youth Violence.' 10 *Education & Law Journal* 1.

Dolmage, R., & P. Clarke. (2002). 'Copyright Ownership of Teacher-Prepared Teaching Materials: An Examination of Issues in the Contemporary Context.' 11 *Education & Law Journal* 321.

Donlevy, J.K. (2005). 'Re-visiting Denominational Cause and Denominational Breach in Canada's Constitutionally Protected Catholic Schools.' 15 *Education & Law Journal* 85.

Durrant, J.E., R. Ensom, & Coalition on Physical Punishment of Children and Youth. (2004). *Joint Statement on Physical Punishment of Children and Youth*. Ottawa: Coalition on Physical Punishment of Children and Youth.

Durrant , J.E., & L. Rose-Krasnor. (1995). *Corporal Punishment: Research Review and Policy Recommendations*. Winnipeg: University of Manitoba Press.

Elliott, H.G. (1998). 'Reflections on Religion in the Schools of Newfoundland and Labrador.' 26 *Morning Watch* 1.

Fahmy, M. (2004). 'The Private School Funding Debate: A Second Look through Charter First Principles.' 3 *Education & Law Journal* 13.

Findlay, N. (2000–01). 'Students' Rights, Freedom of Expression and Prior Restraint: The *Hazelwood* Decision.' 11 *Education & Law Journal* 343.

Foster, W.F. (1985). 'Educational Malpractice: A Tort for the Untaught.' 19 *U.B.C. Law Review* 161.

Foster, W.F., & W.J. Smith. (2001). 'Religion and Education in Canada: Part II – An Alternative Framework for the Debate.' 11 *Education & Law Journal* 1.

Foster, W.F., & W.J. Smith. (2003). 'Equal Opportunity and the School House: Part II – Access to and Benefit from Education for All.' 13 *Education & Law Journal* 173.

Freeman, M. (1997). *The Moral Status of Children: Essays on the Rights of the Child*. The Hague: Martinus Nijhoff.

Gershoff, E. 'Corporal Punishment by Parents and Associated Child Behaviours and Experiences: A Meta-analytic and Theoretical review.' (2002) 128 *Psychological Bulletin* 539.

Giddens, A. (1998). *The Third Way – The Renewal of Social Democracy.* Cambridge: Polity.

Gidney, R. (1999). *From Hope to Harris: The Reshaping of Ontario's Schools.* Toronto: University of Toronto Press.

Gouvernement du Québec. (2004). *Briller parmi les meilleurs: La vision et les priorités d'action du gouvernement du Québec.* Quebec: Author.

Greschner, D. (2001). 'Does *Law* Advance the Cause of Equality?' 27 *Queen's Law Journal* 299.

Greschner, D., & S. Lewis. (2003). '*Auton* and Evidenced-Based Decision-Making: Medicare in the Courts.' 82 *Canadian Bar Review* 501.

Grogan-Kaylor, A. (2004). 'The Effect of Corporal Punishment on Antisocial Behavior in Children.' 28 *Social Work Research* 153.

Haddon, M. (2004). *The Curious Incident of the Dog in the Night-time.* Toronto: Anchor.

Hansard, Subcommittee Report. (1993). *Education Statute Law Amendment Act, 1993, Bill 4.* Available at no charge when requested by telephone from: Committees Branch, 99 Wellesley St. W., Room 1405, Whitney Block, Toronto, ON, M7A 1A2, (416) 325-3525.

Hareema, M. (2005). 'Newfound Religion: Term 17(3) of the Newfoundland Act and Its Challenge to the Current Discourse on Freedom of Religion in the Public Sphere.' 14 *Dalhousie Journal of Legal Studies* 111.

Hogg, P. (1997–2005). *Constitutional Law of Canada,* 4th ed. Loose-leaf with supplements. Toronto: Carswell.

Howe, K.R. (1997). *Understanding Equal Educational Opportunity: Social Justice, Democracy, and Schooling.* New York: Teachers College Press.

Hunt Federle, K. (2000). 'Children's Rights and the Need for Protection.' 34 *Family Law Quarterly* 421.

Hurlbert, E.L., & M.A. Hurlbert. (1992). *School Law under the Charter of Rights and Freedoms.* Calgary: University of Calgary Press.

Ignatieff, M. (2000). *The Rights Revolution.* Toronto: Anansi.

James, E. (1984). 'Benefits and Costs of Privatized Public Services: Lessons from the Dutch Educational System.' 4 *Comparative Education Review* 28.

Jenson, J., & D. Saint-Martin. (2003). *Building Blocks for a New Welfare Architecture: Is LEGO™ the Model for an Active Society?* Montreal: Université de Montréal. Also available at: http://www.cccg.umontreal.ca/pdf/997%20Jenson%20REV%2003-03-06.pdf. Last retrieved 3 May 2009.

Keene, J. (2002). 'The *Law* Decision – A Misstep in the Quest to Define Discrimination,' in D. McAllister & A. Dodek, eds., *The Charter at Twenty: Law and Practice.* Toronto: Ontario Bar Association, 417.

Kim, N., & T. Piper. (2003). '*Gosselin* v. *Quebec*: Back to the Poorhouse…' 48 *McGill Law Journal* 474.

Kindred, K. (2003). 'Copyright Ownership of Teacher-Prepared Teaching Materials: A Response to Dolmage and Clarke.' 13 *Education & Law Journal* 299.

La Forest, G.V. The Honourable Mr Justice. (1998). 'Off-Duty Conduct and the Fiduciary Obligation of Teachers.' 8 *Education & Law Journal* 120.

Lepofsky, D. (1997). 'A Report Card on the Charter's Guarantee of Equality to Persons with Disabilities after 10 Years – What Progress? What Prospects?' 7 *National Journal of Constitutional Law* 263.

Levin, H.M. (1994). 'The Necessary and Sufficient Conditions for Achieving Educational Equity,' in R. Berne & L. Picus, eds., *Outcome Equity in Education*. Thousand Oaks: Corwin, 167.

Levin, H.M. (1996). 'Educational Vouchers: Effectiveness, Choice, and Costs.' Paper presented at the Annual Meetings of the American Economics Association, New Orleans, 4 January.

Llewellyn, K.N., & E.A. Hoebel. (1941). *The Cheyenne Way*. Norman: University of Oklahoma Press, 28–9.

Long, J.C. (2005). 'Encouraging Spirituality: Constraints and Opportunities,' in C.M. Shields, M.M. Edwards, & A. Sayani, eds., *Inspiring Practice: Spirituality and Educational Leadership*. Lancaster: ProActive, 17.

Long, J.C., & R.F. Magsino. (1993). 'Legal Issues in Religion and Education.' 4 *Education & Law Journal* 189.

MacKay, A.W. (1984). *Education Law in Canada*. Toronto: Emond Montgomery.

MacKay, A.W. (1986). 'The Canadian Charter of Rights and Freedoms: Implications for Students,' in M. Manley-Casimir & T. Sussel, eds., *Courts in the Classroom: Education and the Charter of Rights and Freedoms*. Calgary: Detselig, 9.

MacKay, A.W. (1987). 'Students as Second Class Citizens under the Charter.' 54 C.R. (3d) 390.

MacKay, A.W. (1995). 'The Rights Paradigm in the Age of the Charter,' in R. Ghosh & D. Ray, eds., *Social Change and Education in Canada*. Toronto: Harcourt Brace, 224.

MacKay, A.W. (1997). 'Don't Mind Me, I'm from the R.C.M.P.: *R.* v. *M.(M.R.)* – Another Brick in the Wall between Students and Their Rights.' 7 C.R. (5th) 24.

MacKay, A.W. (1996–97). 'Human Rights and Education: Problems and Prospects.' 8 *Education & Law Journal* 69.

MacKay, A.W. (2005). *Connecting Care and Challenge: Tapping Our Human Potential, Inclusive Education: A Review of Programming and Services in New Brunswick*. Paper submitted to New Brunswick Department of Education,

December. Available on-line at http://www.gnb.ca/0000/publications/mackay/MACKAYREPORTFINAL.pdf . Last retrieved 3 May 2009.

MacKay, A.W. (2007). *Inclusion: What Is Inclusion Anyway?* Booklet submitted to the New Brunswick Department of Education, July. Available on-line at http://www.gnb.ca/0000/publications/mackay/Inclusion%20Booklet%20LR%20English.pdf . Last retrieved 3 May 2009.

MacKay, A.W., & J. Burt-Gerrans. (2003). 'Inclusion and Diversity in Education: Legal Accomplishments and Prospects for the Future.' 13 *Education & Law Journal* 77.

Mackay, A.W., & V.C. Kazmierski. (1996). 'And on the Eighth Day, God Gave Us … Equality in Education: *Eaton* v. *Brant (County) Board of Education* and Inclusive Education.' 7 *National Journal of Constitutional Law* 2.

MacMillan, H.L. (1999). 'Slapping and Spanking in Childhood and Its Association with Lifetime Prevalence of Psychiatric Disorders in a General Population Sample.' 161 *Canadian Medical Association Journal* 805.

Magnet, J.E. (2004). *Modern Constitutionalism: Identity, Equality and Democracy.* Markham: LexisNexis.

Magsino, R.F., J.C. Long, & R.G. Theberge. (2001). 'Canadian Pluralism, the Charter and Citizenship Education,' in R. Bruno-Jofre & N. Aponiuk, eds., *Educating Citizens for a Pluralistic Society.* Calgary: Canadian Ethnic Studies, 115.

Majury, D. (2002). 'The Charter, Equality Rights and Women: Equivocation and Celebration.' 40 *Osgoode Hall Law Journal* 297.

Manitoba. (2000). *Administrative Handbook for Schools.* Winnipeg: Ministry of Education.

Manitoba. (2001). *Follow-up to the Manitoba Special Education Review: Proposals for a Policy, Accountability and Funding Framework.* Winnipeg: Manitoba Education, Training and Youth.

Manley-Casimir , M.E., & T.A. Sussel, eds. (1986). *Courts in the Classroom: Education and the Charter of Rights and Freedoms.* Calgary: Detselig.

Manley-Casimir, M.E., & T.A. Sussel. (1986). 'The Equality Provisions of the Canadian Charter of Rights and Educational Policy: Preparations for Implementation.' 17(3) *Interchange* 1.

McEvoy, J.P. (2000–01). 'Denominational Schools and Minority Rights: *Hogan* v. *Newfoundland (Attorney General).*' 12 *National Journal of Constitutional Law* 449.

McGillivray, A. (1998). '"He'll Learn It on His Body": Disciplining Childhood in Canadian Law.' 5 *International Journal of Children's Rights* 193.

McGillivray, A. (2004). 'Child Physical Assault: Law, Equality and Intervention.' 30 *Manitoba Law Journal* 133.

McLachlin, B. (2001). 'Equality: The Most Difficult Right.' 14 S.C.L.R. (2d) 17.

Ministère de l'Éducation du Québec. (1997). *A New Direction for Success: Policy Statement and Plan of Action.* Quebec: Author.

Ministère de l'Éducation du Québec. (1999). *Adapting Our Schools to the Needs of All Students: Policy on Special Education.* Quebec: Author.

Minow, M. (1986). 'Rights for the Next Generation: A Feminist Approach to Children's Rights.' 9 *Harvard Women's Law Journal* 1.

Mohr, W.K., T.A. Petti, & B.D. Mohr. (2003). 'Adverse Effects Associated with Physical Restraint.' 48 *Canadian Journal of Psychiatry* 330.

Mosoff, J., & I. Grant. (2005).'Upholding Corporal Punishment: For Whose Benefit?' 31 *Manitoba Law Journal* 177.

Newfoundland and Labrador, Department of Education. *Religious Education: Interim Edition.* Available at http://www.cdli.ca/depted/rel/toc.htm. Last retrieved 5 May 2009.

Newfoundland and Labrador, Department of Education. (1992). *Our Children, Our Future: The Royal Commission of Inquiry into the Delivery of Programs and Services in Primary, Elementary, Secondary Education.* St John's: Author.

Newfoundland and Labrador, Department of Education. (2004). *Religious Education 3101/3106. World Religions. A Curriculum Guide Interim Edition.* St John's: Author. Also available at: http://www.ed.gov.nl.ca/edu/k12/ curriculum/guides/religion/rel_ed3101_3106.pdf. Last retrieved 5 May 2009.

O'Neill, O. (1988). 'Children's Rights and Children's Lives.' 98 *Ethics* 445. Reprinted in R.E. Ladd, ed., *Children's Rights Re-visioned* (Belmont: Wadsworth, 1996).

Office of the Commissioner of Official Languages. (2005). *Annual Report: Special Edition, 35th Anniversary.* Ottawa: Author.

Oliverio, C., & M. Manley-Casimir. (2005). 'The Judicial Construction of the Role of the Teacher.' 40(3) *McGill Journal of Education* 405.

Ontario. (1950. *Report of the Royal Commission on Education in Ontario.* (Chairman: J.A. Hope). Toronto: Baptist Johnston.

Ontario. (1968). *Living and Learning: Report of the Provincial Committee on Aims and Objectives of Education in the Schools of Ontario.* (Co-Chairmen: E.M. Hall & L.A. Dennis). Toronto: The Committee.

Ontario. (1982). *Special Education Materials and Resources Handbook.* Toronto: Ministry of Education.

Ontario. (1984). *Special Education Information Handbook.* Toronto: Ministry of Education.

Ontario. (2000). *Ontario Schools – Code of Conduct.* Toronto: Ministry of Education.

Ontario. (2003). *Provincial Model for a Local Police/School Board Protocol.* Toronto: Ministry of Education.

Oxaal, Z. (2003). 'Second-Guessing the Bishop: Section 93, the Charter and the "Religious Government Actor" in the Gay Prom Date Case.' 66 *Saskatchewan Law Review* 445.

Palmer, Alanna, Chair New Brunswick Human Rights Commission. (2004). News Release. 23 September. Available at http://www.gnb.ca/cnb/news/hrc/2004e1048hr/htm. Last retrieved 3 May 2009.

Paquette, J. (1991). *Social Purpose and Schooling: Alternatives, Agendas, and Issues.* London: Falmer.

Paquette, J. (2002). 'Public Funding for "Private" Education: Enhanced Choice at What Price in Equity?' 12(2) *Education & Law Journal* 133.

Paquette, J. (2002). 'Public Funding for "Private" Education: The Equity Challenge of Enhanced Choice.' Paper presented at the conference School Choice: Public Education at a Crossroads, University of Calgary, 11 May.

Paquette, J. (2005). 'Democratic Education and School Choice Revisited.' 111(4) *American Journal of Education* 609.

Pentney, B. (1996). 'Equality Values and the Canadian Promise of Community.' 25(6) C.H.R.R. C/6-C15.

Pentney, W.F. (1994–2005). *Discrimination and the Law Including Equality Rights under the Charter.* Loose-leaf with supplements. Toronto: Carswell.

Pound, P., & I. Benson. (2003). 'The Court Claims to Extend Its Jurisdiction to Church Matters: *Hall (Litigation guardian of)* v. *Powers.*' *Lex View*, no. 52.

Power, M., & P. Foucher. (2004). 'Language Rights and Education,' in M. Bastarache, ed., *Language Rights in Canada*, 2d ed. Montreal: Yvon Blais.

Purdy, L. (1992). *In Their Best Interest? The Case against Equal Rights for Children.* Ithaca: Cornell University Press.

Quillen, J.J. (1963). 'Problems and Prospects,' in G.D. Spindler, ed., *Education and Culture: Anthropological Approaches.* New York: Holt, Rinehart & Winston, 50.

Réaume, D. (2003). 'Discrimination and Dignity.' 63 *Louisiana Law Review* 645.

Reilly, E. (16 February 2008). 'School Staff Facing Assault Charges.' *Toronto Star.*

Riddell, T. (2002). 'The Impact of Section 23 of the Charter of Rights on Official Minority-Language Education Policy Outside Quebec since 1982.' 21 *Windsor Yearbook of Access to Justice* 277.

Roach, K. (2000). *Criminal Law*, 2nd ed. Toronto: Irwin Law.

Roach, K. (2001). *The Supreme Court on Trial: Judicial Activism or Democratic Dialogue?* Toronto: Irwin Law.

Roberts, L.W., R.A. Clifton, B. Ferguson, K. Kampen, & S. Langlois. (2005). *Recent Social Trends in Canada, 1960–2000.* Montreal: McGill-Queen's University Press.

Rodham, H. 'Children under the Law.' (1973). 4 *Harvard Education Review* 487.

Royal Commission on Aboriginal Peoples. (1996). *Report of the Royal Commission on Aboriginal Peoples,* vol. 4, *Perspectives and Realities.* Ottawa: Canada Communication Group.

Ryder, B., C. Fafia, & E. Lawrence. (2004). 'What's Law Good For? An Empirical Overview of Charter Equality Rights Decisions.' 24 S.C.L.R. (2d) 103.

Ryley Scott, G. (1959). *The History of Corporal Punishment: A Survey of Flagellation in Its Historical, Anthropological and Sociological Aspects.* London: Luxor.

Sedler, R.A. (1984). 'Constitutional Protection of Individual Rights in Canada: The Impact of the New Canadian Charter of Rights and Freedoms,' in A.W. MacKay & I. Grant, eds., *Constitutional Law Materials.* Halifax: Dalhousie University Press, 20.

Sharpe, R., K. Swinton, & K. Roach. (2002). *The Charter of Rights and Freedoms,* 2nd ed. Toronto: Irwin Law.

Sheppard, C. (2004). 'Inclusive Equality and New Forms of Social Governance.' 24 S.C.L.R. 45.

Smith, A.B. (2002). 'Interpreting and Supporting Participation Rights: Contributions form Sociocultural Theory.' 10 *International Journal of Children's Rights* 73.

Smith, C. (1997). 'Children's Rights: Judicial Ambivalence and Social Resistance.' 11 *International Journal of Law Policy & Family* 103.

Smith, W.J. (1992–93). 'Rights and Freedoms in Education: The Application of the Charter to Public Schools.' 4 *Education & Law Journal* 107.

Smith, W.J., & W.F. Foster. (2001). 'Religion and Education in Canada: Part I – The Traditional Framework.' 3 *Education & Law Journal* 10.

Smith, W.J., & W.F. Foster. (2001). 'Religion and Education in Canada: Part III – An Analysis of Provincial Legislation.' 11 *Education & Law Journal* 203.

Smith, W.J., & W.F. Foster. (2003). 'Equal Opportunity and the School House: Part I – Exploring the Contours of Equality Rights.' 13 *Education & Law Journal* 1.

Smith, W.J., W.F. Foster, & H.M. Donahue. (1999). 'The Transformation of Educational Governance in Quebec: A Reform Whose Time Has Finally Come.' 34(3) *McGill Journal of Education* 207.

Smith, W.J., W.F. Foster, & H.M. Donahue. (2000). 'Systemic Education Reform in Quebec: How Far Have We Come? Where Are We Headed?' 14(2) *EAF Journal* 12.

Smith, W.J., & C. Lusthaus. (1994). 'Equal Educational Opportunity for Students with Disabilities in Canada: The Right to Free and Appropriate Education.' 4 *Exceptionality Education in Canada* 37.

'Spare the Rod, Spoil the Child.' (10 March 1997). 110(10) *Maclean's,* 50.

Stamp, R. (1982). *The Schools of Ontario, 1876–1976.* Toronto: University of Toronto Press.

Statistics Canada. (25 October 2004). 'Parenting Style and Children's Aggressive Behaviour.' *The Daily.* Available at http://www.statscan.gc.ca/daily-quotidien/041025/dq041025b-eng.htm. Last retrieved 5 May 2009.

Statistics Canada. (21 February 2005). 'National Longitudinal Survey of Children and Youth: Home Environment, Income and Child Behaviour.' *The Daily.* Available at http://www.statscan.gc.ca/daily-quotidien/050221/dq050221b-eng.htm. Last retrieved 5 May 2009.

Stone, A. (2002). 'Human Rights Education and Public Policy in the United States: Mapping the Road Ahead.' 24 *Human Rights Quarterly* 537.

Strauss, M.A., & D.A. Donnelly. (1993). 'Corporal Punishment of Adolescents by American Parents.' 24 *Youth and Society* 419.

Strike, K. (1988). 'The Ethics of Resource Allocation in Education: Questions of Democracy and Justice,' in D.H. Monk & J. Underwood, eds., *Microlevel School Finance: Issues and Implications for Policy.* Cambridge: Ballinger, 143.

Stuart, D. (1999). 'The Unfortunate Dilution of Section 8 Protection: Some Teeth Remain.' 25 *Queen's Law Journal* 65.

Sussel, T.A. (1995). *Canada's Legal Revolution: Public Education, the Charter and Human Rights.* Toronto: Emond Montgomery.

Sussel, T.A., & M.E. Manley-Casimir. (1986). 'The Supreme Court of Canada as a "National School Board": The Charter and Educational Change,' in M.E. Manley-Casimir & T.A. Sussel, eds., *Courts in the Classroom.* Calgary: Detselig, 213.

Topolnicki, D.M. (1994). 'Why Private Schools Are Rarely Worth the Money.' 23 *Money* 89.

Tracey, S. (5 February 2001). 'Student's Drug Charge Thrown Out.' *[Kitchener] Record,* B10.

Trocmé, N. (2001). *Canadian Incidence Study of Reported Child Abuse and Neglect: Final Report.* Ottawa: Health Canada.

Turner, H.A. (1996). 'Corporal Punishment as a Stressor Among Youth.' 58 *Journal of Marriage and the Family* 155.

Turner, S.M. (2002). *Something to Cry About: An Argument against the Corporal Punishment of Children in Canada.* Waterloo: Wilfrid Laurier University Press.

Tymochenko, N. (2002). 'Special Education in Ontario – Is It Workable?' 12 *Education & Law Journal* 213.

U.S. General Accounting Office. (1999). *Mental Health: Improper Restraint or Seclusion Use Placed People at Risk.* GAO publication HEH-99-176. Washington: Author.

Walford, G. (1987). 'How Dependent Is the Independent Sector?' 3 *Oxford Review of Education* 13.

Watkinson, A.M. (11 May 1995). 'Children Still Unprotected from Violence.' *Saskatoon Star Phoenix* , A11.

Watkinson, A.M. (1996). 'Suffer the Little Children Who Come into School,' in J. Ross Epp & A.M. Watkinson, eds., *Systemic Violence: How Schools Hurt Children.* London: Falmer.

Watkinson, A.M. (1998). 'Prohibiting Corporal Punishment: In the Name of the Charter, the Child and Societal Values,' in S. Natale, ed., *The Management of Values: Organizational and Educational Issues.* Boston: University Press of America.

Watkinson, A.M. (1999). *Education, Student Rights and the Charter.* Saskatoon: Purich.

Watkinson, A.M. (2004). 'To Whom Do We Entrust Public Education?' 14 *Education & Law Journal* 191.

Weber, K. (1993). *Special Education in Ontario Schools*, 3rd ed. Thornhill: Highland.

Weiner, H. (2004). 'Teachers and Section 43: What Does the High Court's Decision Mean to Teachers?' 38(11) *Alberta Teachers' Association News* 3.

West, W. (1993). 'Escalating Problem or Moral Panic? A Critical Perspective.' 24 *Orbit* 6.

Westen, P. (1982). 'The Empty Idea of Equality.' 95 *Harvard Law Review* 537.

Wilson, J. (1994). *Wilson on Children and the Law.* Toronto: Butterworths.

Witte, J.F. (1999). 'The Milwaukee Voucher Experiment: The Good, the Bad, and the Ugly.' 1 *Phi Delta Kappan* 81.

Young, D., & L. Bezeau. (2003). 'Moving from Denominational to Linguistic Education in Quebec.' 24 *Canadian Journal of Educational Administration and Policy.* Available at http://www.umanitoba.ca/publications/cjeap/articles/youngbezeau.html. Last retrieved 5 May 2009.

Contributors

Rachel Arbour is an associate in the law firm of Hicks Morley, LLP, where she has assisted Brenda Bowlby in a number of matters related to special education law, including representing a school board at a special education tribunal hearing and human rights and civil litigation matters related to the educational needs of students with autism. She developed her interest in special education through her mother, who works in special education. Rachel has an Honours BA from the University of Toronto, where she also worked briefly in the area of student affairs and student services, and an LLB from the University of Windsor. More recently, she has expanded her areas of legal practice to focus on matters related to pensions and benefits.

Brenda Bowlby is a partner in the law firm of Hicks Morley LLP and has been practising education, human rights, and employment law since she joined the firm in 1981. She acts for a number of school boards and was counsel for the school board in *Eaton* v. *Brant County Board of Education* from the Special Education Tribunal up to the Supreme Court of Canada. She is a frequent speaker at conferences and has written a number of articles on human rights and special education issues. She is currently working on new editions of *An Educator's Guide to Human Rights* and *An Educator's Guide to Special Education Law*.

Paul T. Clarke is an associate professor teaching in the Faculty of Education at the University of Regina. He holds a BA and BEd from Acadia University, an MA from Dalhousie, an LLB from the University of Western Ontario, and a PhD in Education from the University of Saskatchewan. He is currently completing an LLM at the University of Saskatchewan. He teaches in the area of educational administration and works with students at both the undergraduate and graduate levels. His research focuses on school law, and he has a particular interest in human rights claims in the context of Canada's public school system.

Gregory M. Dickinson, BA (Hons.), LLB, EdD, of the Bar of Ontario is a professor in the Faculty of Education at the University of Western Ontario, where he has taught education law and social foundations of education since 1983. He has also been a member of the Faculty of Law at Western, where he was director of the Clinical Legal Education Program and the London Legal Clinic. Co-author and co-editor of several books on education and the law, including *Understanding the Law* (1989, 1996), *Rights, Freedoms, and the Education System in Canada* (1989), and *Beyond the 'Careful Parent': Tort Liability in Education* (1998), he is also the founding and continuing editor in chief of the *Education & Law Journal*. He is currently director of publications for Althouse Press.

William F. Foster, LLM, is Sir William Macdonald Professor of Law and Associate Provost (Policies & Procedures) at McGill University. He specializes in Canadian education law and with William Smith has conducted research and published on a range of education law issues. He is a founding (and the first honorary) member of the Canadian Association for the Practical Study of Law in Education. Educated in New Zealand and Canada, he has been with the McGill Faculty of Law since 1968.

Kevin A. Kindred was formerly an associate with the Labour and Employment Law group of Cox Hanson O'Reilly Matheson, practising out of the firm's Halifax office. His research and analysis draws from his experience representing the Nova Scotia Teachers' Union, and he would like to thank the staff of the NSTU and his colleagues at Cox Hanson O'Reilly Matheson for their insights into this topic. Kevin now practises as in-house counsel with one of Atlantic Canada's largest employers.

John C. Long, PhD, is professor of educational administration at the University of Manitoba. His research interests in educational policy, politics, and law have focused recently on the impact of *Charter*-inspired litigation on Canadian school systems. His most recent published work is 'Encouraging Spirituality: Constraints and Opportunities,' in *Inspiring Practice: Spirituality and Educational Leadership* (2005) and 'Canadian

Pluralism, the Charter, and Citizenship Education,' in *Educating Citizens for a Pluralistic Society* (2001).

Wayne Mackay, CM, BA, MA, MEd, LLB, a graduate of Mount Allison University, recently completed a three-year term serving as that university's twelfth president and vice-chancellor. He has returned to teach at Dalhousie Law School, where he was the founding director of the law school's Indigenous, Black and Mi'kmaq Program (one of the first such programs in the country). He was director of the Nova Scotia Human Rights Commission from 1995 to 1998. As a lawyer and a legal consultant, he has an impressive background in research and writing, including five books on education law and some seventy-five academic articles, primarily in the fields of constitutional law and human rights. He is nationally renowned as a legal scholar and specialist in human rights. Widely sought as a conference speaker, Professor MacKay has delivered more than one hundred conference presentations. Among his numerous teaching awards are the 1995 Association of Atlantic Universities Distinguished Teacher Award and the 1999 W.P.M. Kennedy Memorial Award as the top law professor in Canada. He was also named co-recipient of the 2001 Alumni Award of Excellence for Teaching by Dalhousie University for enthusiasm and interest in student needs. He holds the International Commission of Jurists' Walter S. Tarnopolsky Human Rights Award for his extensive contribution to the field of human rights. He was recently awarded the Order of Canada.

Romulo F. Magsino, PhD, is professor and dean emeritus in the Faculty of Education at the University of Manitoba. Former president of the Canadian Philosophy of Education Society, he has co-authored/co-edited several books and has published monographs and numerous articles dealing with multiculturalism and multicultural education, the law and rights in education, the role of religion in education, and citizenship education.

Kirsten Manley-Casimir is currently a PhD student in the Faculty of Law at the University of British Columbia. Prior to engaging doctoral studies, she completed her BA in Honours English at York University and subsequently, her LLB and LLM at Osgoode Hall Law School. She was admitted to the Ontario bar in 2004 and is focusing her academic work on issues of aboriginal law.

Michael Manley-Casimir is professor of education and director of the Tecumseh Centre for Aboriginal Research and Education at Brock University. He received his BA from the University of Exeter (UK), his MEd) from the University of British Columbia, and his PhD from the University of Chicago. Prior to his appointment as Dean of Education at Brock in 1998, Dr Manley-Casimir spent 24 years in the Faculty of Education at Simon Fraser University in a variety of academic and administrative roles. In May 2004, he completed an LLM through the Faculty of Law at the University of British Columbia and wrote a thesis on the meaning of 'freedom of conscience' in the *Canadian Charter of Rights and Freedoms*.

Cheryl Milne is the executive director of the David Asper Centre for Constitutional Rights at the Faculty of Law, University of Toronto. She was called to the Ontario Bar in 1987 and completed her MSW at the University of Toronto in 1991. Until 2008 she was a lawyer with the Justice for Children and Youth legal aid clinic in Toronto, where she had practised since 1991, appearing at all levels of court and various administrative tribunals on behalf of young people under the age of 18 years and the clinic itself in interventions and applications such as the section 43 constitutional challenge. She is the chair of the Ontario Bar Association, Constitutional, Civil Liberties and Human Rights section, and has been vice-chair of the Canadian Coalition for the Rights of Children. She teaches Social Work and the Law in the School of Social Work at Ryerson University.

Cesare Oliverio holds a BA and a BEd from Brock University, an LLB from Osgoode Hall Law School, and has recently completed an MEd at Brock University. He has practised law for a number of years and is a member in good standing of the Law Society of Upper Canada. He also has many years of teaching experience both in the elementary and secondary panel. At present he is employed by the Niagara Catholic District School Board.

Jerry Paquette earned a PhD in educational administration from the University of Toronto in 1986 and is currently a professor in the Faculty of Education of the University of Western Ontario, where he has taught, conducted research, and engaged in consulting since 1987. His work focuses on education finance and minority education policy, with particular attention to aboriginal education. His publications also focus on broader critiques of educational policy including issues related to choice and equity. Dr Paquette has served on the UWO Research Ethics Board for Non-Medical Research on Human Subjects since 1996, and has chaired it since 2004.

William J. Smith, PhD, is the head of Talleyrand Professional Services, a private consulting firm specializing in public policy and administration. In 1993, after spending more than twenty years in the Quebec education system as a teacher, administrator, and consultant, he returned to university to complete his doctorate. Subsequently he became director of the Office of Research on Educational Policy (OREP) and then the co-director of its successor, Ed-Lex, the Research Network on Education Law and Policy, Faculty of Law, McGill University. Equal educational opportunity, the theme of his chapter, reflects a long series of publications for both researchers and practitioners, including (with William Foster) 'Equal Educational Opportunity for Students with Disabilities in Canada: A Moral or Legal Right?' (2000), and (with Jerry Paquette) 'The Cost of Inclusion in the Community: Funding Special Needs in First Nations Community Schools in Québec' (2004).

Ailsa M. Watkinson is a professor with the Faculty of Social Work, University of Regina. Her graduate studies were in the area of educational administration. Her master's thesis, for which she received the Canadian Association for the Study of Educational Administration's award for the best master's thesis at a Canadian university, focused on the rights of students. She received her PhD in educational administration from the University of Saskatchewan. Her research was on the courts' interpretation of the *Canadian Charter of Rights and Freedoms* and its implications for administrators. In 1995 Professor Watkinson began the legal process challenging the use of corporal punishment on children. She argued that s.43 of the *Criminal Code*, which allows for the use of force to correct a child's behaviour, was a violation of rights under the *Charter of Rights and Freedoms*. The case was eventually heard by the Supreme Court of Canada in 2004. The Court ruled that s.43 did not violate the rights of children but imposed substantial limits on its use. Co-editor of *Contesting Fundamentalisms* (2004), she is also the author of *Education, Student Rights and the Charter* and co-editor of two books on systemic violence in schools. She has published a number of articles on such topics as women's and children's equality rights, employment equity, religion in public spaces, sexual harassment, the *Charter* as policy advocate, corporal punishment, and the administration of equality rights.

Index

366   Index